THE LIFE OF GIROLAMO SAVONAROLA

HIERONYMI·FERRARIENSIS·A·DEO·
~·MISSI·PROPHETÆ·EFFIGIES·

Girolamo Savonarola

Portrait by Fra Bartolomeo
Museo di San Marco, Florence.

THE LIFE OF GIROLAMO SAVONAROLA

by
ROBERTO RIDOLFI

Translated from the Italian by
CECIL GRAYSON

Alfred A. Knopf New York
1959

Printed in Great Britain by Wyman & Sons Limited
London, Fakenham, and Reading

Translator's Note

In making this translation I have adhered strictly to Marchese Ridolfi's Italian text. The few essential additions made by me in the text and footnotes are enclosed in square brackets.

C. G.

Publisher's Note

In this first English translation of *The Life of Girolamo Savonarola*, the extensive documentation of the original has been omitted. Scholars wishing to pursue their studies in the field are referred to the Italian edition, published by Angelo Belardetti in Rome, *Vita di Girolamo Savonarola.*

CONTENTS

CONTENTS

PREFACE

I F a martyr's true day of birth is the day on which he is martyred, then the place in which he died is his native land. I would say, therefore, that Florence is Savonarola's true fatherland.

Yet the two greatest biographers of the Prophet of San Marco today are Villari, a Neapolitan, and Schnitzer, a German; and German too are Rudelbach and Meier. The very mediocre Perrens was French. Among the biographies of some importance written shortly after the Friar's death, one is by the younger Pico, a Mirandolan; while we know nothing of the authorship of another that goes incorrectly under the name of a certain Burlamacchi of Lucca. The good Serafino Razzi was no more than an honest and devoted apologist, and his work, which is in any case unpublished, has no value for the historian. Of the rest we need not speak.

Therefore, it seems to me, as a Florentine of ancient family, that I am paying only part of an immense debt in publishing, for the fifth centenary of his other birthday, a life of Savonarola in that land where he gathered his harvest of love and hatred, where he rose to greatness, and where he suffered martyrdom. And may this Florentine ancestry of mine avail me in the task, no less than my long study and my great affection and my twenty years' work on the writings and the history of the Friar.

Quite apart from the repayment of that sacred debt, it must be admitted that a biography of the Friar is needed today. Because of its age, few pages of Villari's monumental work can still stand. Schnitzer's work is, and will remain for a long time, *ære perennius*, a most learned and valuable collection of information gathered with

German diligence, but not well digested, nor always sifted with critical acumen, and never enlivened with artistic virtues.

Even Schnitzer's final edition, the Italian one of 1931, was able to take advantage only of a small part of my earliest researches. Two courageous attempts were made to bring the biography up to date with the help of my discoveries, by Del Fante (1933) and Berzero (1942), but there is nothing in their labours which can be praised beyond the excellence of their intentions.

Therefore I set myself to harvest all that I have sown and cultivated for so great a part of my life. And, so as not to duplicate much that is already in Schnitzer's vast work, I have tried to write simply a biography, relying for the study of the Friar's works on those who have done and could do it better than me. In these pages his life will speak openly of his doctrine—his life, which among his many books is undoubtedly his best one.

Now that for good or ill my labours are ended, I am glad to be able to thank those kind friends who for long encouraged me to undertake them—though most of those friends are now among the dead. But my thanks go also to a great living scholar, Giovanni Papini. Sometimes with flatteries (which come hard to him), and more often with mocking sallies, playfully delivered as from one Florentine to another, he finally provoked me to the task.

It may seem a strange trick of fate that such a work should have fallen to my lot, descended as I am in direct line, *ex filia,* from Lorenzo de' Medici, and at the same time also from that Giovambattista Ridolfi who was, together with Valori and Soderini, practically the leader and standard-bearer of the Friar's faction. I know only too well that this will not confer any special distinction on my work; but, between jest and earnest, I should like to hope that from such opposed hereditary forces my book might gain that balance of judgment which should be the means and the end of those who write history.

La Baronta
   21 Sept., 1951   R. R.

Chapter I

FAMILY BACKGROUND; STUDIES; RELIGIOUS VOCATION; EARLY CONVENT YEARS

◇◇◇◇◇◇◇◇◇◇◇◇◇◇◇◇◇◇◇◇◇◇◇◇◇◇◇◇◇◇◇◇◇◇◇◇◇◇

GIROLAMO SAVONAROLA was born in Ferrara on St. Matthew's Day, the 21st of September, 1452, half an hour before sunset. At his christening on the 4th of October his godfather was Ser Francesco da Libanori, chancellor of Borso d'Este, Duke of Ferrara. Girolamo, who was also given the names Maria, Francesco, and Matteo, was the third son of Niccolò di Michele dalla Savonarola and of Elena Bonacossi, a descendant of the celebrated family of the Bonacolsi, lords of Mantua. Niccolò's other children were Ognibene and Bartolomeo, both older than Girolamo, and Marco, Alberto, Beatrice, and Chiara, who were younger. We know nothing of the first two, except that Ognibene became a soldier. Marco was in minor orders until he received the Dominican habit at the hands of Girolamo, when he took the name of Fra Maurelio. Alberto became a well-known and respected doctor.

The Savonarolas were a proud family who in their present status as merchants had not forgotten the military renown of their ancestors. They came originally from Padua, where one of the gates of the ancient walls still bears their name, in memory either of their reputation or of their residence there. One branch of the family had migrated to Ferrara in 1440, when Michele, grandfather of Girolamo, a famous doctor in his day, author of medical works often reprinted in the fifteenth and sixteenth centuries, and a teacher in the University of Padua, was engaged by Marchese Niccolo III d'Este as chief physician to himself and his court.

Maestro Michele was a man of exemplary piety and ascetic habits, simple and ingenuous of nature, a severe moralist, a courtier hating court life, 'which', he wrote, 'he who would serve God must flee'. He was a reader no less of the Bible and St. Thomas than of Galen, and certain of the minor writings of his old age, which have the air of being written by some learned anchorite rather than by a doctor at the court of Este, are full of moralizing and doctrinal subtleties. Girolamo as a child was in the care of this aged and scholarly man who belonged entirely to the fourteenth century, not only by birth (he was born in 1385) but also by education and outlook—to that fourteenth century which was as remote from Humanism as it was steeped in Scholasticism. It is, therefore, not to be wondered at if his grandson's mind and spirit in those years were modelled like soft clay on some of the qualities that we have described in Michele, whose authority and power were great in the city, and in the family of which he was head, were supreme.

The child, who early gave promise of possessing a brilliant mind, was instructed by Maestro Michele in Latin, or, as it was then called, Grammar. 'This art he quickly mastered, and he also taught himself something of the art of drawing,' we are told by a professional artist who lived with him for many years, the miniaturist Fra Benedetto. We may assume that, following the educational rules he had himself laid down, the aged Michele must have begun teaching his grandchild at the age of five. The boy soon showed the utmost diligence in his studies as well as great intelligence and enthusiasm, so much so that 'in order not to fall ill [through overwork], he learned to play various musical instruments', and in particular the lute.

The death of his grandfather in 1468 was undoubtedly a great loss to Girolamo, who was not only his pupil and grandchild, but also his spiritual heir. However, he was now in his sixteenth year, and his character and intellect had already been formed by the old scholar at the most impressionable age. Even if Michele had the satisfaction at his death of seeing his work completed, he could never have dreamed that from the small seed he had sown would grow so great a plant.

He left to his favourite grandson a dual inheritance: on the one hand, religious zeal, a strict and devout view of life, and among his own writings a plan for preparing oneself for a great mission; on the other, his own scholastic inflexibility, and a character no less inflexible. He also left him a love of the Scriptures and a fund of pious maxims, from which Girolamo was later to quote: 'That which God has ordained, the Popes and their Vicars cannot order otherwise. This I say for the many who take as their excuse certain wider dispensations which please them, whereas stricter ones do not.'

Shortly after his grandfather's death, Girolamo abandoned his humanistic studies, which he may have followed in the school of Battista Guarino, son of the great humanist, who continued the teaching work of his father. Later he writes that he had frequented the schools of the poets and had submitted to their discipline before the love of God caused him to leave the unfruitful woods of metrical form for the sweet fruits of the orchards of the Church. For the time being, however, he studied the liberal arts. It was his father's wish that after these studies he should take up medicine and attain fame and riches, as his grandfather had done. Messer Niccolò hoped for these future earnings with all the anxiety of the head of a family who sees his house in decline and its fortunes diminished. He himself was in business as a banker, but had suffered losses, apparently in standing surety for others, and his share of his father's large fortune had decreased considerably.

Girolamo proved equally successful in his new studies. He applied himself with diligence and profit to philosophy, to which his subtle and speculative intelligence was especially well adapted. Here he soon left Plato for Aristotle, and Aristotle for St. Thomas. In maturity he said of St. Thomas: 'I always loved him and revered him until I left worldly things.' He has rightly been called Aristotelian in so far as he was a Thomist, but he had a complete knowledge of the works of Aristotle even if his interpretation of them was derived largely from St. Thomas.

When he had obtained the degree of Master of Arts and begun the study of medicine, other authors must have come into his hands, but to little effect. His mind was already turned to the search for supreme Truth, a search which his philosophical studies had intensified, not satisfied, and it was certain that his spirit could not find rest or fulfilment in Galen or Mesue.

He then abandoned science for that which he regarded as the

highest science, theology, in which St. Thomas was again his guide amid the works of ancient doctors and modern scholars. However, to all books he preferred the Book, the Bible, whose treasures had been revealed to him by his grandfather, and which in a short time, we find, he had learned entirely by heart.

He was now in his eighteenth year, and in his ardent spirit there began to ferment the moral leaven of his grandfather's teachings. The decadence of morals which had troubled Michele's heart became an ever-increasing torment to Girolamo in his first experience of public life in the easy and liberal atmosphere of Ferrara. He had been taken once to the court, and was so displeased by what he saw that he would never set foot there again. But what most amazed and anguished him, as he said later, was the lukewarmness of the clergy, and the little Grace conferred on them by a long familiarity with the Sacraments. This was incomprehensible to his own piety, and even more so to the iron logic that always governed his thoughts and actions.

Anyone who reflects upon the characteristics and progress of this spiritual ferment in the young Savonarola will be forced to accord less importance and less credence to the tale of his love for Laudomia, a natural child of one of the Ferrara Strozzis—an episode more childish even than youthful, which, like many other things in his life, must have been, if not distorted in order to find in it 'important meaning and great mystery', certainly magnified by the biographer who related it on the authority of Fra Maurelio before it was later exaggerated by the Romantics and the romancers of history.

According to this story, Girolamo is supposed to have asked the Strozzi girl to marry him when both were leaning out of windows in their respective homes separated only by a narrow alleyway (surely an odd proposal of marriage!). Laudomia having arrogantly rejected this proposal on the grounds that the great house of Strozzi would hardly think of allying themselves with the Savonarolas, Girolamo is said to have replied that it was even less likely that the Savonarolas would think of marrying one of their legitimate sons to a Strozzi bastard. Legends usually grow from a grain of truth, and I would not care to deny entirely the veracity of the retort, which possesses the authentic Savonarolan ferocity; but I am inclined to think that it concluded an exchange of words and insults rather than a love affair. At that age Girolamo was already in love, but his love was not of this world. He himself tells us elsewhere that when he lived in the world he 'never desired any woman'.

Rarely if ever does one find in the adolescence of a great man, not merely the germs of his future actions and life, but also their whole and perfect image; but we do so in Girolamo Savanorola. In spite of the consistency and unbroken continuity of his character, one is yet astonished to find so early, in his youthful *canzone, De ruina mundi,* composed in his twentieth year, the same sentiments and almost the same words that he was to utter in his most terrible later sermons and write down on the eve of his martyrdom. At twenty, when his contemporaries were pilfering from Petrarch rhymes and images for their own more or less sincere love verses, he was borrowing from Petrarch the metres of this angry satire on the vices of Italy and the Church:

> *Quivi se estima chi è de Dio nemico*
> *Catone va mendico;*
> *Ne le man di pirata è gionto il scetro:*
> *A terra va San Pietro;*
> *Quivi lussuria et ogne preda abunda*
> *Che non so come il ciel non si confunda.*
> . . . .
> *La terra è sì oppressa da ogne vizio,*
> *Che mai da se non levarà la soma:*
> *A terra se ne va il suo capo, Roma,*
> *Per mai più non tornar al grande offizio.*
> . . . .
> *Canzon, fa' che sia accorta.*
> *Che a purpureo color tu non te appoggie:*
> *Fuggi palazzi e loggie,*
> *E fa' che toa ragion a pochi dica:*
> *Chè a tutto el mondo tu serai nemica.*[1]

[1] 'Here the enemies of God are held in high esteem, Cato goes begging; power has fallen into the hands of pirates; St. Peter is overthrown. Here lust and greed abound. How then is Heaven not enraged?

'Earth is so weighed down by every vice that it may never throw off the burden by itself. Its leader, Rome, goes down to destruction, and will never return to her great estate.

'Beware, my song, beware the great, beware their palaces and halls; let few hear your message, for you will be unwelcome everywhere.'

5

And three years later in another *canzone*, *De ruina ecclesiæ*, even more Petrarchan in form and Savonarolan in substance:

> Così dissi io alla pia Madre antica,
> Per gran desio ch'io ho di pianger sempre:
> E lei, che par che gli occhi mai non tempre,
> Col viso chino e l'anima pudica,
> La man mi prese, et alla soa mendica
> Spelonca mi condusse lacrimando;
> E quivi disse: Quando
> Io vidi a Roma intrar quella superba,
> Che va tra' fiori e l'erba
> Securamente, mi ristrinsi alquanto
> Ove io conduco la mia vita in pianto.
> . . . .
>
> Dopoi Madonna, dissi: Se 'l ve piace,
> Di pianger con voi l'alma si contenta.
> Qual forza ve ha così del regno spenta?
> Qual 'arrogante rompe vostra pace?
> Rispose sospirando: Una fallace
> Superba meretrice, Babilona.
> Et io: Deh, per Dio, Dona,
> Se romper se portria quelle grande ale!
> E lei: Lingua mortale
> Non po', nè lice, non che mover l'arme.
> Tu, piangi e taci: e questo meglio parme.[1]

This revolt against the decadence of morals and religion, planted in his mind by his grandfather, had in the meantime grown until it preoccupied him entirely. For some time past, as he wrote to his father,

[1] 'When out of the constant sorrow of my heart I had thus spoken to ancient Mother Church, She, who never changes, with eyes modestly downcast took me by the hand and led me weeping to her beggarly cave. Then she said: When I saw that proud woman enter Rome, who now walks there unhindered mid pomp and show, then did I withdraw to live here, weeping.

'Then, Lady, I said: If it please you, my soul gladly joins in your sorrow. What power drove you from your kingdom? What proud creature has destroyed your peace? She answered, sighing: A false proud harlot, Babylon. Then I: Ah, Lady, if we could but break those great wings. To which she replied: Mortal tongue can do nothing, nor may you take up arms. Weep and be silent: this seems best to me.'

he had found it impossible to 'suffer the blind wickedness of the peoples of Italy'.

He did not yet realize that in that disquiet lay the seeds of his vocation; he did not know how to translate it into work, into life, into action. He was not yet thinking of taking orders; indeed, at this time he used to say that he would never be a monk. Painfully exercised by such thoughts and anxieties, he 'constantly uttered this prayer, saying devoutly: *Notam fac mihi viam in qua ambulem, quia ad te levavi animam meam*' (Psalm cxliii, 8). And God in the end answered him, showing him that way.

On the 1st May, 1474, Girolamo had gone for pleasure to Faenza, and with him went his constant anxiety. Entering by chance the church of Santo Agostino, in which a friar of that Order was preaching, he was suddenly struck by a word, not of the preacher, but of God, a word from Genesis: '*Egredere de terra tua!*' ['Get thee out of thy country, and from they kindred, and from thy father's house.']. This call now gave him no rest; he heard it everywhere; it cast a shadow over family affections; it woke him from his sleep. The conflict within him raged fiercely, but only for a short time. Before a year had passed, the young man, his mind finally made up by a dream, set out to follow that call.

He told no one of his decision. He loved those nearest to him with all the strength of his passionate nature, and he was unwilling to face his mother's entreaties, his father's displeasure, and the agonies of parting. As the feast of St. George, patron saint of the city, fell on the 24th of April, he decided to leave home while the family was absorbed in the festivities and religious ceremonies of that day. However, the night before, turning in sadness to his lute, he drew from it sounds that so clearly echoed the sorrows of his heart that his mother realized intuitively what was to come, and said: 'My son, what you are playing today is the sign of parting.' At these words, though his heart was heavy, he smiled and said that she should not be afraid. In the morning, having gone out early as though for a stroll or to church, he set out on foot toward Bologna, and there, following the footsteps of his beloved St. Thomas, he knocked at the door of the convent of San Domenico. When he abandoned the home that had been his for so many years, he left no letter of farewell or explanation, but only a few meditations in Latin, in which, after the usual expressions of contempt for the world, he alluded to his resolve in a note to a passage from Exodus.

The day after, the 25th of April, he wrote a long letter to his father, comforting him and giving the reasons for his departure. It is evident that this is no ordinary letter from a young man leaving home to enter a convent: in this letter there is already all the future reformer:

In primis, the reason which moves me to take orders is this . . . the great wretchedness of the world, the sins of men, lecheries, adulteries, theft, pride, idolatry, cruel blasphemies; for the world is come to this, that no one can be found to do well; many times a day I used to sing this line, weeping: *Heu fuge crudeles terras, fuge litus avarum* [Alas! fly from this cruel land, fly from this shore of avarice.]. This was because I could not suffer the blind wickedness of the peoples of Italy, and the more so when I saw virtue cast down and vice exalted. This was the greatest suffering that could come upon me in this world. . . . Would it not have been base ingratitude on my part, had I prayed God to show me the straight path on which I must walk, and when he had stooped to show it me, I had not taken it? Alas, Lord Jesus, rather may I suffer a thousand deaths than that I should ever show Thee such ingratitude. And so, *dulcissime pater,* rather than weep, you must thank Lord Jesus. He has given you a son, has preserved him to you until his twenty-second year, and, further, has deigned to make him one of His champions. Alas, do you not hold it a privilege to have a son who is a soldier of Christ? . . . Do you not believe that it is a great sorrow for me to leave you? Believe me that never since I was born have I suffered greater pain or affliction of mind than in leaving my own flesh and blood and going among strangers to sacrifice my body to Christ, and delivering my own free will into the hands of those of whom I know nothing; but then, thinking that it is God who calls me, and that He was not too proud to come down and serve miserable creatures like ourselves, I could not dare to disobey His gentle and loving voice: *Venite ad me omnes qui laboratis et onerati estis et ego reficiam vos: tollite iugum meum super vos* [Come unto me, all ye that labour and are heavy laden, and I will give you rest. Take my yoke upon you]. But because I know that you blame me for going away secretly, and almost fleeing from you, know that my pain was such that, had I shown the suffering I felt in my heart at leaving you, I truly believe that before I could have gone, my heart would have broken, and my resolution would have been destroyed. . . . I therefore pray you, my dear father, to make an end of weeping, and to spare me pain and sadness more than I suffer already: not for regret at what I have done, for I would not undo it were I thereby to rival Caesar's glory, but because I too am flesh and blood, and our senses quarrel with our reason. I have a hard fight to prevent the Devil leaping on my shoulders, and all the more when I feel for you. Soon these days in which our grief is fresh will pass, and then I hope that you and I will have consolation in this world through grace, and in the next through salvation. Nothing remains but for me to beg you to be manful and comfort my mother. I pray both of you to give me your blessing. . . .

It seems that the family was not soothed by this letter, and Girolamo, who in the meantime, on the 26th of April, had received the habit from Fra Giovanni da Vercelli, Prior of the convent, took offence at their attitude and reproved his parents with bitter words. This is expressed in a short letter which has come down to us without any address or signature, but which may be accepted as his. It begins: 'For what do you weep, blind fools, why do you lament, why do you murmur, you who lie in darkness?' Here, after again commending his own action, burning with pious zeal, he breaks out: 'What can I say of you if you grieve at this, if not that you are my chief enemies, and even the enemies of virtue? If this is so, I can say to you only, *Discedite a me* . . . [Begone].' He ends by exhorting the family to rejoice that God should have made him a doctor of souls rather than of bodies.

We know little of Savonarola in these obscure beginnings, and very little (nor could it be otherwise) of the first years of his cloistered life. As I have already said elsewhere, the silence that surrounds him for seven whole years seems the symbol of that silence in which the young man entered the cloister, intent on building his new life in humility and contemplation. In entering religion he would have preferred not to become a priest, but to cultivate the garden, sew the brothers' clothes, and give himself to humble labours in holy peace, rather than devote himself to vain disputations, exchanging the Aristotelianism of the world for that of the monastery. He wished to free himself of all his philosophy, not to go on with studies that he regarded as utterly useless to the attainment of his final purpose. But his superiors, having examined him according to custom, were unwilling to waste an intelligence and fund of learning which seemed likely to be an ornament to the Order; so they decided otherwise about his future. Girolamo at once prepared to obey.

The monastery of San Domenico in Bologna had the reputation of being a model of strict observance, exemplary even in its own Congregation of Lombardy, which was regarded as a stronghold of the Dominican rule. To the novice this observance appeared mere hypocrisy; and to bring it back to the strict rule intended by the founder soon became one of his greatest preoccupations, even before he dared to contemplate still greater things. In the meantime, not being able to do more, he strictly observed that primitive Rule and moved others to follow his example: assiduous in abstinence, in fasting, and in prayer, admirable in obedience and humility. As he was dispensed from Latin lessons because of his previous education, he was able in the year of his novitiate—perhaps the happiest of his life—to cultivate spiritual perfection, prayer, and contemplation in absolute peace.

Even in the days of glory and triumph Girolamo always recalled with words of longing, as for a lost good, those first happy times of his taking refuge in the harbour of religion, 'where', he said, 'I found freedom, where I did everything that I wanted, for I desired nothing but to do everything that I was told or commanded'. And not only his superiors but, as we are told by one who knew him at that time, the least of the lay brothers could make him come and go at their pleasure.

As it was the will of his superiors that he should prepare himself for the pulpit, when the year of his novitiate ended and he took his vows (perhaps at the beginning of May 1476) he was obliged again to immerse himself in study. Every Dominican house was a school, according to the rule of the Order, and the house in learned Bologna, raised to the rank of *Studium generale,* enjoyed a great reputation and was adorned by the most eminent teachers. In the course of his theological studies Fra Girolamo had as *magister regens* and *lector principalis* in 1476 and 1477 Pietro da Bergamo, and in 1478 and 1479 Domenico da Perpignano. The first of these was himself a great theologian, author of the famous *Tabula aurea,* and from his school issued learned and famous men; but the greatest of his pupils was Savonarola. The bachelors—that is, assistants of the *lector principalis*—were in 1476 Antonio da Trento, in 1477 and 1478 Tommaso da Bergamo, and in 1479 Bartolomeo da Bologna. Vincenzo Bandelli, a fiery orator and renowned theologian, later General of the Order, was wrongly included by Schnitzer in the list of Savonarola's teachers in the Studio of San Domenico in Bologna. Finally, among the *magistri studentium* of those years was Niccolò da Pisa (1478), a learned preacher and author of various works of an ascetic character. Having already taken a degree before joining the Order, and being therefore very strong in philosophy, Fra Girolamo was able to devote himself largely and with greater profit to theological studies. The eyes of the masters and superiors were now on the new recruit from Ferrara as one of the future hopes of the Order. Soon he was to return as a very young teacher to one of those high desks at the foot of which he now sat as a student. In 1479 he was sent to Ferrara: according to Schnitzer, to complete his training. And so, after being away four years, he was again to see his native town and family.

Perhaps it was during this stay in Ferrara, and more precisely at the end of 1479 or in 1480, that Savonarola made the acquaintance of Count Giovanni Pico della Mirandola, who was then sixteen; almost certainly he could have heard the disputation that this boy prodigy sustained with Leonardo Nogarola. However, the basis of the strange friendship between these two outstanding men, with so much to unite and so much to divide them, was laid in 1482 during the Chapter of the Congregation of Lombardy celebrated in Reggio on the 28th of April. Having gone there to sustain, in his turn, a disputation that was to have great influence on his life, Savonarola was heard by that young prince. Pico had probably come from Padua, where he studied, to hear the disputations of some famous theologians who took part, notably that Pietro da Bergamo whom we recently found among Savonarola's masters. Instead, he fell in love with the rough but impressive eloquence of the obscure brother from Ferrara. Pico was not alone in appreciating his learning, for Savonarola was, at this same Chapter, elected to the office of lecturer in the Convent of San Marco in Florence.

The impending war between Venice and Ferrara may have had some influence in this election (without, however, having been its cause, as some have suggested). Perhaps, as the storm gathered, the superiors of the Congregation may have wished to transfer to a safe place some part of the monks of the Ferrara convent, selecting, as was often done in such circumstances, the young men who gave most promise for the future of the Order. Thus Savonarola, as he had been commanded, set out on foot on the road to Florence, carrying all he possessed: a Bible and a breviary.

Chapter 2

FIRST STAY IN FLORENCE AND FIRST DIVINE REVELATION

<><><><><><><><><><><><><><><><><><><><><><><><><><><><><><><><><>

I T was in May, therefore, the month when Florence is at her most beautiful, that Fra Girolamo first saw the city of his destiny, the Florence that one day was to become the object of all his labours, and later, in another month of May, was to reward him with shame and death.

Florence may have been richer and greater in former days, but never was she more like that ideal picture of happiness and beauty she represents in men's minds, than at the time Savonarola first knew her. Rich and powerful in commerce, splendid in her buildings, exquisitely corrupt as the capital of a civilization can be when it reaches its peak, possessing more great artists than the whole of the rest of Italy, adorned with outstanding men in every branch of knowledge, her people subtle and clever, she was now peacefully governed by the poet of fleeting youth.

It is most fitting that history in Lorenzo's case alone should have changed the style of *Magnifico,* otherwise one of mere courtesy, into a title of praise; for he was magnificent beyond all others, a great patron of artists and himself an artist, likeable and highly intelligent, witty of speech, urbane rather than lordly in manner, and exceedingly generous. In every other characteristic Lorenzo was remarkably like the portrait of a tyrant drawn by Savonarola in his later sermons and books— perhaps because the portrait was drawn from life. He appears proud, cruel, vengeful, ambitious, the corruptor of morals, embezzler of public moneys, spoiler of widows and orphans, and 'wonderfully involved in amorous affairs'. To a city such as this with such a ruler, there came the man who from his childhood had felt acutely the world's burden of cruelty, avarice, and lechery, a man with great and daring ambitions for reform and the renewal of virtue.

Perhaps the events we are about to recount arose inevitably from the collision between these two opposites; perhaps Savonarola's great work was inspired by the favourable circumstances and conditions obtaining in this 'heart of Italy', as he often called Florence. At any rate, if this stay in Florence had no power to alter his mind, character, and feelings, if it had no influence on his philosophy, I am nevertheless certain that the greater Savonarola arose from this contact with the then universal city.

He was not quite thirty. An unknown world opened before him; for even before seeing the streets, the buildings, the many beauties of this superb city, he found himself in the new convent with its soaring cloisters by Michelozzo, in summer full of flowers, and with its beautiful pictures.

Some modern writers speak of Savonarola as he first arrived in Florence as though he were a barbarian. There may be a greatly exaggerated grain of truth in this, for which his education, rather than his country of origin, is responsible. However, the rough Ferrarese monk appeared on the banks of the Arno to be conquered as well as to conquer. His dialect, his pronunciation, his manners became more civilized, and his intellect more subtle. On the other hand, he dominated the Florentines, enervated, indifferent, and sceptical, with his own faith, ardour, and strength.

First he won the affection of his fellow-monks and the esteem of his superiors, particularly that of the Prior Vincenzo Bandelli, later to be General of the Order, who had already had an opportunity of knowing him in Bologna or in Ferrara, and who must have been responsible to a great extent for bringing him to Florence. As the chronicler of the convent tells us, with Savonarola there came into San Marco a new spirit of true poverty, a new feeling of brotherly love. So much so that the most beautiful of the precepts of the Divine Master—'*Hoc est præceptum meum: ut diligatis invicem*' ['I give you this rule: that you love one another']—which had found only lukewarm

observance for many centuries, was revived in that house by the exhortations and teachings of the new lecturer.

His task consisted primarily in explaining the Scriptures, and these
he knew and understood better than any other scholar of his day, so it
is no wonder if from the beginning he gave his pupils the greatest
satisfaction. To his scholarship was added a vigorous spiritual life, excessively strict in his observance of the rule, humble, gentle, assiduous
in fasting and prayer. Thus, adding example to precept, he greatly
edified his hearers. One of these, years later, told how most times Fra
Girolamo would come to the lesson with eyes full of tears, having
evidently been lost in some divine meditation rather than preparing
the lesson, 'but because he was so learned, he always satisfied his hearers
exceedingly'. Another of his pupils, although he later denounced
Savonarola, described his teaching of Scripture as something almost
divinely inspired. To the monks and novices of San Marco the lectures
of the new master appeared to come from a higher being, and not to
be ordinary human rhetoric vainly satisfying the senses.

'His teachings . . . raised men's hearts above all human things and
made them burn with love for God.' His hearers were unanimous in
believing 'that from the time of the early Christian Fathers no one
equalled him in the teaching of the sacred books'.

Schnitzer justly observes that his *lectio ordinaria* was a sermon as
well. His chair as *lector principalis* was already a kind of pulpit—even
if sometimes this 'chair' was not the solemn setting that constitution
and custom assigned to his office, but instead a delightful meadow, of
which some tiny flower would often lend him illustration for his mystical expositions. His were not arid lessons full of doctrine and erudition; he wished to make saints, not scholars. The teaching of the
canonical books gave him occasion for constant moral example and
exhortation. The Old Testament, especially, which was his favourite
text, became on his lips and to the ears of his astonished and absorbed
audience a real thing, no longer the relic of a remote past, but the
mirror of the present day and the key to the future.

Since, therefore, he had so successfully turned his reader's chair
into a pulpit, and as he was a born preacher before he became an
orator, Savonarola could not in fairness to his own vocation and the
reputation of the Order long delay his first attempts at sermons. These,
surprising though it may seem, were a good deal less successful than

his work as a lecturer. He preached 'like the apostles, without divisions in his sermons', an old chronicler tells us, and his speech was still strongly reminiscent of Ferrara. He used to say *mi* and *ti,* and was laughed at for it by everyone, including his fellow-monks.

His first attempt at a sermon was in the church of the Benedictine nuns called the Murate (the 'walled-in') because of their strict enclosure. Here he preached for Advent in 1482 and for Lent in the following year. At the same time he preached in the church of Orsanmichele, an unusual double task that he may have undertaken to strengthen his voice, which in those early days was rather weak. These were small beginnings in small churches, where success or the lack of it can have been of little significance. However, in spite of what the old biographers say, these early attempts cannot have been complete failures, for in Lent the following year, 1484, he was given the pulpit of one of the main churches in the city, the cathedral of San Lorenzo, which was also the parish church of the city's ruling family.

Here things went worse with him. In Brunelleschi's great and elegant building, his voice, still hoarse and uncertain, his foreign pronunciation, his rough gestures displeased the congregation. These were in number and quality quite different from those at the church of the Murate, and were used to a very different and more civilized method of preaching. They liked subtle arguments, quotations from the poets, something unusual, whereas this foreign monk only gave them verses from the Bible. 'Talk to us about the things we like,' the courtiers of the Magnifico would later say to him, but he went on attacking those who sang the impious verses of Pulci, Lorenzo's favourite.

If we are to believe Fra Placido Cinozzi, who heard all his sermons for that Lent, Savonarola gained so little favour with the public that at the end there remained of his audience only about twenty-five men, women, and children. I agree with Schnitzer (as I have had occasion to write elsewhere) that the contemporary biographers and apologists have greatly exaggerated the lack of success of these first beginnings. They did so to throw into greater relief the popularity and huge audiences that the Prophet of San Marco was to enjoy a few years later, and to endow this change with a supernatural aura. However, there was some truth in this, and we should believe Savonarola himself, who referred several times to this initial weakness, and especially in one of his last Lenten sermons. 'All those who know me . . .

are aware that I had neither voice, vigour, nor talent for preaching; indeed, my sermons bored everyone.' And again, elsewhere: 'When I began to preach, few came to listen: only a few simple men on one side, and on the other some poor women; they were like two flocks or herds of goats, one of men and the other of women.' In such circumstances it is perfectly possible, even if it may not be true, that in some moment of depression he proposed giving up preaching altogether, as Cinozzi says he heard from his own lips, and as in consequence has been repeated since then by all the chorus of biographers.

I myself feel, however, that Savonarola's lack of success at this time was due less to his barbarous speech and pronunciation, than to the fact that he had not yet developed a manner of his own, or those powerful arguments to move the spirit of the masses, of which he later had abundance. Averse from the elegant and empty humanistic sermon that the Florentines loved so much, he may perhaps have overdone his scriptural commentaries, while yet lacking that prophetic style that was to make his reputation. In fact, if he had, as we have said, made his lecturer's chair into a pulpit, I believe that at first he made the pulpit serve as a lecturer's chair. In the meantime, his hour of fame drew nearer.

When he was still a child, or barely an adolescent, Savonarola's preoccupation and sorrow had been 'the blind wickedness of the peoples of Italy', and the vices of the clergy and decay of the Church, and this feeling had not changed or weakened. On the contrary, as his knowledge of such wickedness grew, so did his revolt from it. And to mature this knowledge and revolt there came the events of the year 1484.

On the 12th of August, Sixtus IV died. He had been one of the worst of Popes, and for reasons of greed and family intrigues had kept Italy at war for thirteen years. As he had received the day before his death the treaties made with Venice, it was rumoured that he died at the very sound of the word 'peace'. At once divisions and quarrels arose among the cardinals, the sequel of those which the dead Pope had aroused in his lifetime. Some feared a schism in the Church. However, these divisions were soon mended, not by religious zeal, but by money. And for money—the intermediary in the deal being that depraved cardinal Rodrigo Borgia, who was to become even more depraved as Alexander VI—Innocent VIII was elected to the papacy, a better man certainly than his predecessor, but not much better as a Pope.

One can imagine how much these events affected the sensitive and fervent spirit of Savonarola. It was then that he wrote, in the same vein as his youthful *canzoni*, *De ruina mundi* and *De ruina ecclesiæ*, his *Oratio pro ecclesia*, which begins:

> *Iesù, dolce conforto e sommo bene*
> *d'ogni affannato core.*
> *risguarda Roma cum perfetto amore.*
>
> *De! mira cum pietade in che procella*
> *si trova la tua sposa,*
> *e quanto sangue, oimè!, tra nui s'aspetta,*
> *se la tua man pietosa,*
> *che di perdonar sempre se diletta,*
> *non la riduce a quella*
> *pace, che fu quand'era poverella.*
> *Risguarda la bontà che già ti mosse*
> *a prender carne umana,*
> *e per noi farti come un verme in terra:*
> *soccurri a la Romana*
> *tua Santa Chiesa, che 'l demonio atterra.*[1]

Another *laude, O anima cecata,* belongs, I believe, to this same period, in which we find his poetic vein reviving. Although the autograph of this poem is known, it is to be found in some old editions, in which similar misattributions are frequent, under the name of Feo Belcari. In these verses Savonarola passes from the usual laments over the vices and evils of the times to threats of punishment and scourges:

> *Tu senti mille segni*
> *a Prato e a Bibbona*
> *e perchè tu non degni*
> *di credere a persona*
> *la mente tua è prona*

---

[1] 'Jesu, sweet comfort and highest good of every suffering heart, look upon Rome with perfect love. Alas! see with pity in what a tempest Thy bride is tossed, and how much blood, alas! must be shed if Thy merciful hand, delighting ever in forgiveness, does not return her to that peace she knew when young and poor. Remember the love that once led Thee to take on human flesh and to make Thyself for our sakes like a vile creature on this earth. Save Thy Holy Roman Church, which the devil is destroying.'

a ogni vizio:
ecco el supplizio
che presto viene a te.
   Omè omè omè!
   timor de Dio non c'è.

   Vidi l'Italia in guerra
e la carestia grande;
la peste Iddio disserra
e suo iudicio espande:
queste son le vivande
de la tua vita,
cieca e smarrita
per la tua poca fè.
   Omè omè omè!
   timor di Dio non c'è.

   Astrologi e profeti,
omini dotti e santi,
predicator discreti,
t'han preditti i tuo' pianti;
tu cerchi suoni e canti,
perchè sei stolta;
nei vizi involta,
in te virtù non è.
   Omè omè omè!
   timor di Dio non c'è.[1]

The cup was full, or, to use his own expression, the wicked priests had filled the sack to overflowing. While he was composing these

[1] 'A thousand signs you see at Prato and Bibbona, and because you are unwilling to believe anyone, your mind is prone to every vice; behold the punishment that soon will come upon you. Alas, alas, alas! all fear of God is lost.

'I saw Italy at war, with famine everywhere; God lets loose the plague, and His judgment falls upon us; these are the fruits of your way of life, blind and helpless from your little faith. Alas, alas, alas! all fear of God is lost.

'Astrologers and prophets, learned and holy men, worthy preachers, all have foretold your tears; in your folly you seek delights of song and music; but, sunk in vice, you have no virtue in you. Alas, alas, alas! all fear of God is lost.'

[In recent years miracles had been performed by images of the Virgin in Prato and Bibbona.]

poems with his thoughts turned disdainfully upon the evil example set by Rome, how often must there have come to his lips, as happens to all poets with their own work or that of others, that line of his which to posterity seems to express completely the spirit and achievement of Savonarola:

se romper si potria quelle grande ale!

If in the past he had always replied to this proud cry of revolt and struggle with the same humble counsel which at that time he gave to himself—

lingua mortale
non po' nè lice, non che muover l'arme:
tu piangi e taci, e questo meglio parme

—things had now come to such a pass that he seemed to have lamented in silence long enough. 'To take up arms', he now awaited but the sign; and that sign came.

In that same year, 1484, a sudden vision determined finally the direction his life was to take. He tells us of it in the evidence given at his trial—in a document, that is, written when, according to his own despairing words, the spirit of prophecy had quite gone out of him and he was therefore inclined, in his discouragement and yielding to the anger of his enemies, to understate rather than to exaggerate the revelations he received.

He tells us that one day he had accompanied to the monastery of San Giorgio a certain Fra Tommaso Strada, who was visiting his sister, a nun; and while he was alone in the churchyard he thought of composing a sermon. Suddenly there appeared to him 'many reasons (they were at least seven) showing that some scourge of the Church was at hand'. Although he here chose words that the torturers would not feel obliged to make him retract (as they had done with many of his earlier statements), it is quite clear that he is speaking, not of a process of reasoning, but of sudden revelation. 'And from that moment I fell to thinking much on these things,' his account continues. Nor was he able to rid himself of such ideas, however much he tried in response to the reproval and persuasion of others.

The peace that had surrounded him when he entered the monastery was now no more than a distant and longed-for treasure. In this state of anxiety he probably turned again to that 'small prayer' of his youth, 'saying unto God with great devotion: "Show me the way in which I may walk"'. Once more his prayer was answered, and this time it showed him the high road that leads great spirits to great thoughts and great actions.

Chapter 3

FROM THE SERMONS AT SAN GIMIGNANO TO THE SECOND PERIOD IN FLORENCE

◇◇

IT might be tempting, as there is no record of any sermon by Savonarola in Advent 1484, to imagine him struck dumb by the revelation he had received, meditating in silence the mystery of the reform of the Church. But the truth is often very different from the imaginative conjectures of historians. In this case he may quite simply have gone to preach in some other town within Florentine territory, or even in the church of San Marco itself; and it is perhaps for this or some other reason that there is no trace of the collections for his sermons in the appropriate register, which has provided us with information on previous occasions. It was in Lent 1485, when he was sent to San Gimignano, that his prophetic sermons began, 'expressing the following conclusion: that the Church must be castigated and reformed with the greatest speed'. We know nothing, apart from what he tells of these beginnings at his trial, about the success or approval of these sermons.

News of the death of his father, Niccolò, in Ferrara on the 9th of March, 1485, reached him in that little walled town of San Gimignano while midway through Lent he was absorbed in spreading the new word. It must certainly have been sorrowful news, but we know Girolamo too well to suppose that affection for his earthly father might have distracted him for one moment from his love for his Heavenly Father,

22

which alone could move him now. This is confirmed by what he wrote to his mother, answering the letter in which she sent the sad news to that son now doubly distant from her since he had become 'Christ's knight-at-arms'. This reply, the contents of which we know only through a reference in a later letter, told her that, since he had chosen his Order as his family, and Christ as his Father, she should from now on regard him as dead to her. This was all the consolation he had to offer his unhappy mother.

But when on the 23rd of October of that same year the unfortunate woman was again bereaved, this time of her brother Borso—her only support, as Niccolò had left behind him little but debts—her tears did finally touch her son's heart. On the 5th of December he sent her a long and affectionate letter, written over a period of several days—a letter that was also in a sense a sermon.

In it he said, among other things, that he thanked God for the adversities of his family, as He was preparing for their ultimate salvation by striking at their worldly possessions and thus warning them to direct their minds to heavenly things. He exhorted his mother to free herself from such earthly concerns, encouraging her not to worry about his sisters Beatrice and Chiara, if poverty had prevented them from marrying, and adding these words: 'I would wish you to be so much in love with Jesus that you care not for your children except in so far as you are not able to do otherwise; I would wish your faith to be such that you could see them die and even martyred, like that saintly Jewish woman who saw her seven sons tortured and slain, without ever weeping; nay, rather did she comfort them to die'.

Saintly words of a saintly man, yet so far removed from our ordinary human feelings that they appear inhuman. We must believe that that unhappy courageous woman did in the end understand them and receive them into her heart, as she did that dreadfully bitter medicine which, as Fra Benedetto tells us, she one day by sheer strength of mind managed to take and hold down, though her enfeebled constitution rejected it.

On the subject of the Advent of 1485 we must repeat what was said about the preceding year, and we shall have to repeat it again for the following year: either Fra Girolamo did not preach at all, or he preached out of Florence. But Lent 1486 is now at hand, and we do know that Savonarola again went to preach at San Gimignano—

an indication that he had probably found favour there the previous year.

On Quinquagesima Sunday, the 5th of February, he cries out a joyful greeting to the congregation with these words: 'Behold, I am returned among my children. I thought of you like a flock without its shepherd. . . . Like the owner of the vineyard in the parable, I return to ask you for the fruits of my earlier sermons . . .; and so I greet you, again I greet you, and beg you rejoice with me. Today we are again united. . . .' These words come from the rough draft in Latin of these sermons in Savonarola's own hand, the earliest and most valuable evidence we possess of his prophetic preaching.

But what is most important in these drafts, or rather plans, is the first references to the castigation and renovation of the Church, which we find in greater numbers in the sermons of the two days following Ash Wednesday. In the first of these he developed the argument that the words of Luke, 'And now also the axe is laid unto the root of the trees', would come to pass in their own day: 'We expect at any moment a scourge, or Antichrist, or war or plague or famine. If you ask me with Amos if I am a prophet, I answer with him: "I am not a prophet".' The following day he repeated the same things, and insisted: 'Know that I do not tell you this as a prophet, but that I infer from the Scriptures that the Church awaits a great scourge.' Thus he hid his inspiration by turning to the evidence of the Scriptures, as he will always do from now until 1495, but with particular insistence down to 1492.

If those 'reasons' for the imminent scourge which had been revealed to him in the church of San Giorgio were 'seven in number', he gave eight reasons at San Gimignano, and it will be helpful to compare them with those he gave later: First, the wickedness of men, become so great that the measure was now full; and he reminded his listeners of murders, lechery (in particular, sodomy: literally 'postribulum puerorum', the prostitution of boys), idolatry and incantations, particularly through astrology ('astrologia domina vera est'), simony, etc. Second, because God gave to the Church wicked 'shepherds'. Third, because He sent prophecy among men. Fourth, the good had lost strength in every condition of men. Fifth, the decline of faith in human hearts. Sixth, the extreme rottenness of the Church. Seventh, contempt of the Saints. Eighth, the decay of religious observance.

According to Schnitzer, who however did not know their contents, these sermons at San Gimignano aroused a great deal of excitement in Florence on account of their novelty, boldness, and vehemence. But this is pure supposition. There is no trace of any such reaction in the histories or in the diaries and memoirs (in which Florentine history of the time is so extremely rich), or even in public or private letters. This should be sufficient proof that Florence showed neither excitement nor even the slightest whisper of interest in these sermons. An additional proof lies in the continued obscurity surrounding Savonarola's life and actions at that time. For a whole year after his return from San Gimignano nothing whatever is known of him, and nowhere is he even mentioned. This does not seem natural for anyone who might recently have made himself an object of special interest.

He was a preacher, and we must therefore again wait until Lent 1487 to find a mention of him preaching in the church of the monastery of Santa Verdiana. It seems impossible, but Schnitzer regarded this as proof that after the 'scandal' aroused by his sermons at San Gimignano, he was not allowed to preach in any other pulpit in Florence. There is worse to come! As Savonarola did not finish his series of sermons but suddenly left Santa Verdiana and Florence, Schnitzer would have us believe that this was the doing of Lorenzo de' Medici, whose suspicions and fears had been aroused by the famous sermons.

The truth is (as I have proved elsewhere with fresh documentary evidence) that Savonarola had been appointed 'maestro degli studi' for that year, 1487, in the Studium generale, or University, of San Domenico in Bologna—an appointment that besides establishing the true reason for his movements, is clear evidence of the reputation for learning and virtue which the young monk had acquired. Returning as a teacher to that Studio in which not many years before he had been a pupil, he took the place of Fra Paolo da Soncino, a great ornament of the Dominican Order. His canzone to the Blessed Caterina de' Vigri—which he sent, in the unfinished state in which we still know it, to the sisters of the convent of Santa Chiara, among whom the Saint had lived—probably dates from this period rather than from that in which he was a student in Bologna.

When he had completed his year of teaching in the Studio of Bologna, he was sent by his superiors to Ferrara, probably before Lent 1488; and so at last he saw his mother and his birthplace again. He remained there for some two years in the convent of Santa Maria degli Angeli, preaching also in a number of other places, 'travelling in many cities' ,as he writes in a letter to his mother during one of his tours. Seeing all his comings and goings, his compatriots in Ferrara, where he could not (as the Bible says) be regarded as a prophet, used to say jestingly that the friars of his Order must be very short of men.

In these sermons he kept up the prophetic manner first heard in San Gimignano. 'In this way,' he will later say at his trial, 'I preached in Brescia and in many other places in Lombardy, sometimes on these same subjects, remaining there for nearly four years.' He should have said three, counting the year spent in Bologna but not the early months of 1487, when he was in Florence, or the early months of 1490, spent in Genoa. However, Savonarola evidently counted the years on his fingers without worrying whether some of them were represented only by a few months. Which these Lombard towns were— apart from Brescia, of which we have evidence—it is impossible to guess, especially as for Savonarola the geographical extent of Lombardy was even broader and less precise than was normally understood at the time. We know from a passing reference by a biographer who had been his fellow-monk that Girolamo went to Modena and Piacenza. Another old biographer tells us that he was once in Mantua, and that as he travelled down the Po from Ferrara to Mantua in a boat with eighteen rough soldiers, all of whom were blaspheming and cursing, he straightway converted eleven of them.

He seems to have gone to Brescia more than once, or to have stayed there longer than in other places, probably preaching there for Lent in 1489. At any rate, among much that is obscure and uncertain, we know that he went there in the last half of November of that year to preach for Advent, and that he gave a series of notable sermons in his new style. The most memorable of all was the sermon for St. Andrew's Day (November 30th) on the four-and-twenty elders of the Apocalypse, in which Savonarola apparently prophesied in a most striking way a great scourge that was about to descend on the city, 'saying that fathers would see their children slain and shamefully mangled in the streets'. Many citizens of Brescia remembered these words in 1512 when the French sacked the city and put it to the sword with the utmost cruelty. There is no reason to doubt this prophecy, for we have even the name of the trustworthy person who, having heard it from the lips of the preacher, later gave evidence of it. However, we should rightly be suspicious of the amplifications of this story by the biographers—not only the oldest ones, in whom it would be understandable, but certain modern ones too. These, as usual, speak of a great scandal supposed to have been aroused by the sermons at Brescia, of a great outcry throughout all Italy making notorious the name of this obscure Ferrarese preacher. And yet in Brescia itself chroniclers careful to write down the smallest events of the life of the city are silent on the subject. Still, a pious legend recounts that at the time of his stay in Brescia Savonarola spent five hours motionless in prayer at matins on Christmas night, and that when all lights had been extinguished, the face of this great servant of God was seen to glow with ecstasy.

However, not even in Brescia did Savonarola remain for long. If his reputation was not already known throughout Italy, with the superiors of his Order it was now very great indeed. And as soon as he had finished these sermons, he was sent to Genoa to preach for Lent. And to make that journey on foot from Brescia, as he did, was a good long walk.

He set out, therefore, the great distance to be covered making it urgent that he should not delay. When he reached Pavia on the 25th of January, 1490, he wrote to his mother as he had intended on leaving Brescia whence there were very seldom posts for Ferrara. This poor woman had again complained, in a message brought after Christmas by a monk from the Convento degli Angeli at Ferrara, of her son's prolonged silence. In his letter, 'written in haste', he dutifully excuses himself on account of the irregular mails and press of work, especially during the recent Church festivities, and then attempts to persuade his mother, once more sorrowing for her favourite son who was again travelling far away from her, of the necessity for his perpetual wanderings:

You should not be sorrowful if I am far away and travelling in many cities, because all this I do for the good of many souls, preaching, exhorting, hearing confession, reading and giving counsel, and this is the only reason why I go from place to place, and why my superiors send me; and you should therefore take comfort from the fact that one of your children has been chosen by God for such work. If I were continually in Ferrara, you may be sure that I would not do as much good work as I do out of it. Hardly ever does a religious man work fruitfully in his own country, and for that reason we are constantly told in the Scriptures to go out of our own country, for a native is never given the same confidence as a stranger for his sermons and counsel; therefore our Saviour says that a prophet has no honour in his own country, for even He was not accepted in his own country. Therefore, since God has deigned to elect me from my sinful state to so high an office, you should be content that I labour in Christ's vineyard far from my own country. . . . In Ferrara I have often been told by those who observed my travels from city to city that my Order must be lacking for men, as though to say: 'If they use you, who are worthless, for so many duties, they must indeed lack for men.' But outside my own country such things have not been said to me; nay, when it is time for me to leave, men and women weep and set great store by my words. I do not write thus because I seek the praise of men, nor because I delight in worldly esteem, but to make you understand my purpose in staying away from my own country, and so that you should know that I am glad to be away, knowing that my work is more pleasing to God and more profitable to myself and to the souls of my fellow men. . . .

These dialogues of Girolamo with his mother are all the same; and not only during her lifetime but even after her death we find him addressing similar words to her in one of his sermons. Comparing this letter, however, with the one of five years before, I feel that there is here, beneath his pious resolution, a certain current of tenderness not to be found in the earlier letter.

We ought at this point to discuss the sermons preached in Genoa, but no echo of them has reached us, no witness or record remains. We cannot, therefore, say whether the desire expressed in Girolamo's letter—'to be of great profit to that people'—was in fact achieved. Two or three references to Genoese matters in his sermons, one of them being a commendation of the women of that city for their modesty, are too little evidence from which to deduce, as Schitzner does, that he must have been pleased with the result of his work there.

Easter fell that year (1490) on the 11th of April. About the middle of the month, we may surmise, he set off again for Brescia or for Ferrara or for some other town. Where he went, it is certain that he did not stay there long.

As long before as the 29th of April of the preceding year, Lorenzo de' Medici had written, as we find recorded in one of his memorials, 'to the General of the Preaching Brothers, requesting him to send here Fra Jeronimo da Ferrara'. There is good reason to believe that he did this to please Giovanni Pico. The latter, who moved to Florence at the end of 1483 and remained there until July 1485, had had ample time and opportunity to confirm himself in the admiration he had conceived for the Friar at the Chapter of Reggio in 1482. Very little is known of the friendship between these two great intellects in the early years, or of the contacts between them; yet I believe that the influence of Savonarola, if it was not the only cause nor even the principal cause of the profound transformation that overtook Pico in 1486, was already at work on him. Thus, in 1488, when Pico, after being reprimanded in Rome and imprisoned in France, had returned to settle again on the happy banks of the Arno and had found that the one man who he was certain could bring peace to his troubled soul was no longer there, he had set to work to have him recalled to Florence.

Lorenzo willingly agreed to his friend's request, thinking that it was but a small matter; instead, it was to be of the greatest importance for himself and his family. 'So that you may be assured that I desire to serve you sincerely and faithfully,' Lorenzo told Pico, according to the early biographer, 'Your Lordship shall write the letter in whatever form you please, and my chancellor will write it out and seal it with your seal.'

It may seem surprising that Pico's wishes, with such powerful support from Lorenzo, should have had to wait more than a year to be fulfilled. But the General could only pass on the recommendation to the Vicar of the Lombard Congregation, who in turn, in addition to the ordinary delays of letters and replies, must have had to consider the present duties of Savonarola. We may also suppose that the proposal, involving as it did the appointment of a 'lecturer', had to be referred to the Chapter of the Order (this receives confirmation from the biography falsely attributed to Burlamacchi), and as such meetings normally took place on the third Sunday after Easter, the transfer of Savonarola may well have been discussed on the 2nd of May.

The return of Savonarola to Florence must, then, have taken place in June 1490, or perhaps at the end of May (May, as we have seen before, seems to have been his fateful month). And again on foot he set out on that long and arduous journey. On reaching Pianoro, ten miles this side of Bologna, worn out with walking, exhausted by the heat, his strength and appetite gone, he was fed and restored by an unknown traveller, who then came with him as far as Florence, and at the gate of San Gallo said to him: 'Do what you have been sent by God to do in Florence'; and Savonarola never set eyes on him again. This perfectly ordinary episode, which Savonarola told to Fra Bartolomeo da Faenza, was later given a supernatural and miraculous interpretation by his followers as they built up the Savonarolan legend.

Chapter 4

THE RETURN TO FLORENCE AND THE CONQUEST OF THE FLORENTINES

✦✦

'*CON altra voce omai, con altro vello*' ['with other voice and fleece of other grain'], as Dante had hoped to, Savonarola returned to Florence. More mature of intellect and spirit, strengthened by the many sermons delivered to a great variety of people in recent years, confirmed by meditation and prayer, having entered 'with all the strength and industry of his mind' into those revelations experienced in the church of San Giorgio and become more sure of them, he was no longer afraid of the magnitude of his task, but had faith in the aid of Providence.

According to Savonarola's followers, it had been prophesied to him in Brescia and to others in Florence that his ministry here would bear wonderful fruit. I do not wish either to believe or to disbelieve such reports, nor to go into them here at any length, though I feel it my duty as a biographer to mention them. One may easily imagine that, after the event, vague and general predictions were given more specific meaning and significance. However, I prefer to leave legend on one side and return to the facts of history.

In San Marco, therefore, Fra Girolamo again took up his former post as lecturer. Modern biographers, misinterpreting a perfectly clear statement by Savonarola himself in his *Compendio di rivelazioni*, and in the face of all contemporary evidence, state that he began to read the

31

Apocalypse to the monks immediately on his return. We have first-hand evidence that at the very beginning of this period he taught logic. It seems that on Sundays after vespers it was his custom to explain passages from the Scriptures—not, however, the Apocalypse—beneath a damask rose-bush in the garden of San Marco. The beauty of the setting, of the hour, and of the season, joined with the spiritual attraction of the subject and the wonderful gifts of the speaker, fascinated all who listened to him, and the fame of these lessons soon spread beyond the walls of San Marco. First the devouter citizens and benefactors of the convent began to come, among them a few learned men and people of importance in the city. Eventually, as the crowd of secular hearers grew, and the place became unsuitable for so large an audience, the monks begged their teacher to continue his feast-day lessons in church. He put off his decision until the following Sunday, probably as much to choose the text as to prepare his usual scheme for his sermon. When Sunday came, the date being the 25th of July, Fra Girolamo announced joyfully to those who stood round to hear his reply: 'Next Sunday we shall read in church; it shall be a reading and a sermon.' According to one old biographer, he is supposed to have added: 'I shall preach for more than eight years.' In fact he preached for something less than eight years; but, although to me they seem rather suspect, I have thought it my duty to mention these supposed words of Savonarola.

And so on the 1st of August, in the church of San Marco, Savonarola began his sermons (for such in fact they were, although in his notes he continued to call them '*lezioni*') on the text of the Apocalypse. He himself liked to recall in later years the devastating effect of these sermons, and particularly liked to quote these words, which characterize them very well: 'I am the hailstorm that shall break the heads of those who do not take shelter.' The choice of the text itself gives us an insight into the temperament of the preacher, and helps us to imagine the content of his sermons much better than the short dry summaries that survive or the vague comments of contemporary biographers.

Yet these summaries indicate that right from his exordium Savonarola began his battle for the reform of the Church. As the whole of Italy was at peace, enjoying a seemingly new Augustan age, he said that this calm filled him with suspicion, and that he saw new scourges at hand, not on account of visions and prophecies current among the masses, but for reasons founded on Scripture; and those he gave were entirely similar to the reasons expounded at San Gimignano, which were first revealed to him in the church of San Giorgio. There is little more to be gathered from these meagre, shapeless notes.

One of the biographers, Cinozzi, tells us that Fra Girolamo propounded four universal truths: the truth of the Christian faith, the truth of the virtuous Christian life, the reform of the Church, the conversion of the heathen. According to the pseudo-Burlamacchi, however, which reproduces almost word for word an autobiographical passage from the *Compendio di rivelazioni,* Savonarola in these sermons put forward for the first time in Florence the famous three propositions: reform, castigation of the Church, and the imminence of these things. He strove to prove these propositions 'with reasons, with images or parable, with the authority of the Scriptures; and he based his argument on what was evident in the Church, not claiming to have these matters from any other source than the reasons he gave, since he still felt that the people were not disposed to believe them'.

Not that his arguments convinced everyone; indeed, divisions soon sprang up among the citizens. But there is no doubt that this time, and at the first assault, Savonarola had won the day. Straightway he won to his side the more pious Florentines, who could not approve the depravity of the Church and of morals. The poorest were for him, and so too the malcontents, those who felt oppressed by the arbitrary taxation and confiscations of the Medici; not for nothing was he known from the first as 'the preacher of the despairing'. And hence his reply from the pulpit to the partisans of the Medici, who called him this, that it was they who should despair.

This was not the only daring rebuke directed at those who ruled Florence and at their flattering preachers. Savonarola tells how, when he had answered without realizing it some criticism of himself, Count Giovanni Pico told him: 'You will come to no good end, jousting in this way.' It was true that he was jousting, not only against lukewarm priests but against the Medici government; and all those who were opposed to the government, as well as some not yet openly opposed, gladly went to listen to the unusually bold things this friar was daring to say to the faces of the ruling faction.

If we are looking for all the causes of his popularity, we must also consider the peculiar character of the Florentines themselves, always eager for novelty, who listened readily to this original manner of preaching and the unusual ideas developed by the new preacher. The Florentines were reputed to become bored by everything very rapidly, and Guicciardini remarks that, however good the preacher, interest in him seldom lasted more than one or two Lenten preachings. So, as the tedious artificial style of humanist eloquence had been in favour for many years, even in sermons, it is not surprising that its popularity suddenly vanished and went instead to the spontaneous and vigorous style of Savonarola.

Although enjoying great popular favour, he encountered from the first the opposition of rich and powerful citizens, of all those who found profit and pleasure under the Medici rule. Then some said that the new preacher was a good man but simple; others that he was learned but cunning and astute; others that he pursued false and foolish visions. As was said of Christ, 'Some said He is a good man: others said Nay, but he deceiveth the people'.

Even among his followers there was no lack of fearful and timid men who disliked the vehemence of his denunciation and castigation of the rottenness among priests and princes—which is authentic evidence of the violence of those first sermons. These said to him: 'Father, you go too far, your attack goes too deep.' Others—and this is an excellent example of Florentine subtlety and curiosity—not satisfied with the simple truths he preached, complained: 'Father, you never give us a good argument.' Savonarola, who relates this, continues: 'And I used to turn to God, saying "Oh Lord, is it possible that they will ever give up this desire for disquisition, and seek only the light and the true explanation of Scripture?".

Still others, among those who came to his sermons—'attracted by the truth and usefulness of his teaching', writes the poet Girolamo Benivieni, who was one of them—condemned the roughness of his speech and gestures. Domenico Benivieni, brother of the poet, called 'lo Scotino' on account of his subtlety, one day said to Savonarola's face: 'Father, your manner of preaching, your pronunciation, your graceless gestures deprive you of much favour, as your audience can make comparison with Fra Mariano.' The latter was preaching that year from the pulpit of Santo Spirito and was at the time the Florentines' favourite preacher. He was an exponent of the humanistic style who decorated his sermons with quotations from the ancients, with excerpts from the poets; an orator with an exquisitely modulated voice and gestures resembling an actor's rather than a preacher's. Savonarola replied:

'That is true, but you will see that all this elegance and facility of Fra Mariano will lose much favour, and the simplicity of my own style will be exalted.'

Others disliked his constant attacks on those whom Florence most honoured: philosophers, poets, and men of letters—attacks not only on the living but on the ancients, who were revered almost as gods even by those who barely knew their names. They disliked his placing the Bible before anything else, and his contempt for the grammarians who presumed to criticize its style. There is a letter probably written to him at this time or a little later by Garzoni, who had once been his teacher of rhetoric in Bologna, accusing him of having declared war on Priscian.

The series of sermons on the Apocalypse continued through Advent until after Epiphany 1491, probably until the 9th of January, as the surviving manuscript notes and drafts show. But during that Advent he also preached on the First Epistle of St. John. This may seem odd, the more so as these sermons also were given in the church of San Marco and on the very same feast days. Possibly, however, they were delivered in the morning, as was then the custom, while those on the Apocalypse, which Savonarola continued to call '*lezioni*,' were given in the evenings after vespers.

The sermons on the First Epistle of St. John were printed in 1536, in a Latin version of somewhat dubious authenticity. It is impossible to be sure of this text, as the autograph from which I assume this edition derives, either directly or indirectly, is not at present to be found. Only this autograph, which in the last century was still in the possession of Lord Holland, could tell us whether the original was complete, or merely the usual draft, later cleverly written out and expanded by the sixteenth-century editor, as happened with other works of Savonarola. Although I have no absolute proof, I incline to think that this was the case; and I suspect this not only on account of the many parallel instances, but also because of the brevity of the text and the fact that it is in Latin, which would hardly be justified in the case of sermons delivered in the vulgar tongue, while we know for a fact that Savonarola prepared the notes and drafts for his sermons in Latin. The most we might suppose is that the text which has come down to us is a slightly enlarged version of his notes, made by Savonarola himself for his own satisfaction and that of his fellow-monks.

I have lingered somewhat over this point, not because I feel some nostalgia for my earlier studies, but to explain why these sermons in the state in which we know them—despite one or two fine passages here and there, such as that of the Three Kings so much praised by Villari—represent, not a step forward, but rather a step back in the development of Savonarola's prophetic style of preaching. As they are mere outlines, if a little elaborated, their apparently retrogressive quality is easily explained; it is well known that Savonarola used to rough out in these Latin drafts little more than the exegetical skeleton of his sermons with very occasional and brief indications of the invectives, digressions, and moral illustrations, which he mostly improvised in the pulpit with spontaneous eloquence.

It is true that, if there are here also a few tirades against the vices of the Court of Rome and the clergy, against the depravity of the age, and so forth, such invectives occur more rarely in this text than in other draft sermons of Savonarola. Conjecture is likely to be unreliable, but it is relevant to remember that, as he was preaching at the same time and to the same audience in the same church on the text of the Apocalypse, he may have wished to vary the treatment of the different series, giving the one on the Epistle of St. John a more mystical and less polemical character. This is no more than a hypothesis, and must be regarded as such.

Easter fell very early in 1491, and Savonarola hardly had time to rest after the labour of his double series of sermons before again mounting the pulpit on Ash Wednesday, the 16th of February, to preach for Lent. This time it was the pulpit of Santa Maria del Fiore, 'the principal church of the city'. If any doubt remained of the great and immediate popularity achieved by Savonarola in these first two series of sermons after his return to Florence, this should suffice to dispel them entirely.

Beneath the great vault of the Florentine cathedral there echoed for the first time in that Lent of 1491 the powerful voice of the Friar. And just as his voice was necessarily louder to fill the huge building and reach the vast crowd of his hearers, so also did the contents of his sermons increase in vigour and daring; and his popularity and his audience grew accordingly. Whatever the biographers say, it was from the time of this Lenten preaching, and not before, that Savonarola began to become master, if not of Florence, at least of the Florentine people.

Chapter 5

'THE PREACHER OF THE DESPAIRING' AND THE 'JOUST' WITH GENAZZANO

LORENCE, however, already had a clever and vigilant master who was extremely jealous of his own authority. Master in fact, if not by right or in name and appearance, Lorenzo more than any other prince was obliged to watch, and did in fact watch, over every smallest detail in the state. He could not, therefore, view without suspicion the great following that this Friar had suddenly acquired among the populace. Nor, having a son who was a cardinal and a close friendship with the Pope, could he tolerate the excessively bitter things Savonarola was saying about the Church and the clergy, or his threatening prophecies. Even had he tolerated these things, he certainly could not tolerate that the Friar should so boldly criticize the state and its justice, and the abuses of his government. His suspicions were aroused by the very name of 'Preacher of the Despairing', which his own supporters gave to Savonarola, and he felt that these continual threats of future convulsions and of punishments awaiting wicked rulers must revive the hopes of the malcontents. For these reasons, and perhaps from the time when Savonarola was preaching on the Apocalypse, Lorenzo warned him through Agnolo Niccolini, Pierfilippo Pandolfini, and others 'that he should speak little of future events'. But the Friar was not deterred, and went on in his usual way.

As Savonarola himself tells us, he received a great number of admonitions of this kind 'from almost every class of person', and he may not always have realized, when one of the ruling class gave him

37

such advice, whether the man spoke for himself or had been sent by Lorenzo. But he must have realized whence the warning came when five of the principal citizens gave him a similar warning, still speaking as though on their own account. He replied (as he recalled this incident some years later while four of those involved were still alive, and in the presence and with the approval of two of them): 'You say that no one sent you here, and I say someone did. Go and tell Lorenzo de' Medici to do penance for his sins, for God intends to punish him and his creatures.'

Although threats and warnings from Lorenzo did not intimidate him, at length these continual protests 'from almost every class of person' and even from his fellow-monks, did discourage him to the point where he proposed several times to preach on some other theme. 'And I could not do it,' he later writes in the *Compendio di rivelazioni*, 'because anything else which I read or studied bored me, and when I tried to preach anything else, I disliked it so much that I even bored myself.'

Torn by these inward and outward contradictions, he came to the eve of the second Sunday in Lent. For the day's sermon he had already prepared the usual draft or summary in Latin (which is fortunately preserved, together with all the others of this memorable Lenten series of 1491, which we might entitle *On the Lamentations of Jeremiah and the Gospels Proper*). But, again seized with doubt and discouragement, he decided not to use what he had already prepared, and never again to preach on such themes. Thus he spent the whole of Saturday and that night without being able to find anything else to preach on, and finally on Sunday morning, the 27th of April, being very tired after his long vigil, as he tells us in the *Compendio,* he heard a voice saying: 'O foolish one, do you not see that it is the will of God that you should preach in this manner?' And so he entered the pulpit and preached a 'terrifying sermon'. These are his own words, and we must believe him, for, however many formidable sermons he preached later, he never again described them with that epithet.

In this '*terrifica prædicatio*' (of which we get a clear idea from the summary, though as usual it contains not a thousandth part of what he actually said from the pulpit), besides giving a horrifying picture of the corrupt morals of the Florentines, he did not forbear from covert attacks on Lorenzo, criticizing him for his taxes and arbitrary levies;

38

and there were immediate reactions to his sermon. It appears that Lorenzo considered banishing him from Florence, just as barely three years before he had banished Fra Bernardino da Feltre; he certainly had him threatened with banishment.

Other citizens went to Savonarola and warned him that unless he gave up his attacks he would be banished; to which he replied: 'Be you afraid of exile who have wives and children. I have no fear, for if I did not remain here, your city is but as a grain of sand in comparison with the rest of the earth. I am not alarmed; let him do as he pleases. But let him know this: though I am here a stranger and he the highest citizen, yet I shall remain and he shall depart: I shall remain and not he.' With these words he prophesied Lorenzo's death, and to those nearest to him he even predicted its very date.

Lorenzo, to whom probably no one dared repeat that dreadful prophecy, neither banished him from the city nor even forbade him to preach, remembering perhaps that the exile of Fra Bernardino had made him unpopular with the masses, and perhaps also, as Guicciardini says, 'having some respect for Fra Girolamo, whom he believed to be a man of great piety'. Although no contemporary writer says so, what contributed more than anything else to saving Savonarola from banishment was the ever-increasing devotion of Count Giovanni Pico, who was the favourite of Lorenzo among the many great intellects who adorned his house and the city of Florence.

We find the echo of all the matters we have touched on here in a letter that Fra Girolamo wrote on the 10th of March, 1491, to his friend Fra Domenico Buonvicini da Pescia, who was preaching for Lent in Pisa:

Our affairs prosper through God's great mercy, although we have suffered much opposition from the great. All this I will tell you when you return, as it is not advisable to put it in a letter. Many have feared and still do fear that it will go with me as it did with Fra Bernardino. Certainly, as far as that goes, I have been in some danger, but I have always put my hope in God, knowing, as Scripture says, that the heart of the ruler is in His hands, and will be turned as He wills. I trust in the Lord, who will gain great profit from our ministry. He comforts me daily, and when I lose courage He speaks to me with the voices of His spirits, which often say to me: 'Fear not; say confidently what God inspires you to say, for He is with you; the scribes and Pharisees fight against you, but they shall not be victorious.' I often preach the renovation of the Church and the tribulations to come, not arbitrarily, but basing myself always on the Scripture, so that no one can criticize me except those who do not wish to live an upright life. The Count continues in the way of the Lord, and often comes to our sermons. . . .

The allusions in this letter to the opposition met with, and to the danger that he might be banished by Lorenzo, could not be clearer. The fervent spirit of Fra Domenico must have trembled with longing for the battles to come. But not so Fra Silvestro Maruffi, who one day was to share martyrdom with him and Savonarola. Maruffi was at that time preaching at San Gimignano, where echoes of Savonarola's sermons reached him; and when men criticized Savonarola for his innovations, he defended him with words, though not from the heart. On his return to Florence after Easter, though he had formerly been his pupil, he condemned Savonarola bitterly, even calling him a madman. He received the mild reply that if Silvestro prayed to God, He would inspire him to believe the truth. Silvestro did pray, and dreamed (as he recounts at his trial) that he was reproved for his incredulity. He was given to sleep-walking, and was very much inclined by nature to pursue, even when awake, his dreams and visions; and from then on he offered no further opposition to Savonarola.

In any case, no one, from Lorenzo downwards, let alone Fra Silvestro, could now have stopped Savonarola in his chosen course. Following ancient custom, on Easter Wednesday, the 6th of April, Savonarola preached in the Palace itself in the presence of the Signoria. We do not know if Lorenzo was present, but it was another terrifying sermon, as one can see even from the Latin draft he left.

He began by saying that in that place he felt as though he were on the Sea of Tiberias, and that he did not there feel himself to be master as he did in church, for, like Christ in the house of the Pharisee, he must speak with greater caution. He said that in a city all good and all evil come from the head, and if the head walked in righteousness, the city would become the city of God. If the contrary were true, his sin would indeed be great, though it be only a sin of omission. He went on to say, in substance, that here the tyrants of the community were incorrigible and sunk in darkness because they were proud and listened to flattery, they did not restore that which had been taken unjustly, they levied arbitrary taxes, exploited the peasants, oppressed the poor, bribed voters, farmed out taxes, chose evil officials, and debased the currency, to the infinite distress of the poor. All this sounds more like a later condemnation of Lorenzo by a hostile historian than a sermon delivered while Lorenzo lived and ruled, in the very Palace of the Signori, who, in spite of their apparent authority, had by now become officials of the Medicean tyranny. The boldness with which Savonarola put his finger on the most painful open wounds of such a tyranny appears even today unbelievably reckless, though he always expressed himself in general terms and without naming anyone.

There was a good deal here for Lorenzo to reflect on and make him repent of having, in spite of all his foresight, himself procured the return to Florence of the untameable Friar. In the days of his youth he might have acted more ruthlessly, for he had in the past often shown pitiless firmness. But now in his declining years he chose to proceed by cunning. In a move worthy of his grandfather, he decided that for combating a friar nothing could be better than another friar. His chosen instrument was Fra Mariano da Genazzano of the Augustinians, an old protégé of his house for whom he had lately built that fine convent outside the gate of San Gallo, from which the architect who designed it took his name.[1]

The great reputation of Fra Mariano in Florence is well known. He was considered to be the finest preacher the city had heard for thirty years. It is enough to read the judgment of Politian, who, in a letter written a few months before Savonarola's return to Florence, gives special praise to Fra Mariano's accomplished eloquence. The choice seemed particularly apposite because, in addition to being entirely Lorenzo's creature on account of favours received, and besides being a preacher of great renown, Fra Mariano was also full of jealousy and animosity towards Savonarola, who with his new style of preaching had usurped a good many of Fra Mariano's followers and much of his fame.

Thus, on Ascension Day, the 12th of May, Genazzano preached after vespers in his church of San Gallo, where, owing to the reputation

[1] [Antonio da Sangallo.]

41

of the speaker and rumours of this affair which had leaked out, a great crowd had gathered to hear him. Not only were two great preachers now to be compared, one the rising star, the other at its apogee, but also two very different styles of eloquence; and this was enough to excite Florentine curiosity. There came Lorenzo himself, Pico, Politian, Benivieni, and, among the lesser beings, Placido Cinozzi, who left us a faithful account of the contest.

The sermon took as its theme these words from the Acts of the Apostles: 'It is not for us to know the time nor the moment.' The title alone is sufficient to tell us that this was from beginning to end just what Lorenzo wanted, a philippic against the Savonarolan prophecies. But Fra Mariano, who showed on other occasions that he was by nature inclined to exaggerate, allowed himself to be carried away by his feelings and made obvious his own personal rancour in a way that displeased everyone. When after the sermon there was a general discussion, condemnation of it was almost universal; and not a few of those who, while attending Fra Girolamo's sermons and supporting his cause, had continued to admire the oratory of Fra Mariano, from then on rejected him entirely—as, for example, Pico and Benivieni. Not a few worthy men who until then had despised Savonarola did the same.

Striking while the iron was hot, Savonarola preached on the following Sunday, the 15th of May, taking exactly the same text. After declaring the true meaning of the passage and refuting with ease the arguments of his rival, he turned at the end of his sermon to address Fra Mariano directly. 'With the gentlest manner' he reminded him that not many days before Fra Mariano had been to visit him at San Marco, and had then praised his sermons and predicted that they would have great influence for good. 'Who put it into your head to attack me? For what reasons did you change your mind so soon?' he concluded, thereby letting it be quite clearly understood who had induced Fra Mariano to preach against him. Thus, Lorenzo achieved the exact opposite of what he had intended, and Fra Mariano incurred even more disfavour among the people.

In this way a remark of Fra Girolamo's came true; when first he was told that Fra Mariano was preaching against him, he replied, apparently unmoved: '*Me oportet crescere, illum autem minui*' ('I shall wax, and he shall wane'). As this remark is rather similar to the one made by Savonarola to Domenico Benivieni already referred to above, we might suspect that contemporaries made one such reply into two; but the reports of the time are exact and worthy of belief, and relate to different occasions and different persons. Present when the above remark was made, were Fra Roberto Ubaldini, the future chronicler of San Marco, and that good and saintly Fra Tommaso da Strada who accompanied Savonarola to the convent of San Giorgio on the day of the famous illumination. The latter, though he greatly esteemed Savonarola, was shocked by his reply, and, speaking like the upright man he was, he reproved Savonarola for his apparent pride. But Fra Girolamo replied that he had spoken, not out of vainglory, but because he knew that was the will of God. At this, Fra Tommaso said no more; and throughout his life, he remained faithful to Savonarola.

As for Fra Mariano, we find that some worthy men interceded to reconcile him with Savonarola, and public demonstrations of this reconciliation were made. How sincere these were on the part of the Augustinian became apparent in time, for in fact he never forgave the Dominican the defeat he had suffered. Retiring to Rome, he wasted no opportunity of conspiring for Savonarola's ruin, emerging as the leader of his enemies in Florence and elsewhere. But meanwhile Savonarola, having won that 'joust' concerning which Pico had at first felt some misgivings, remained master of the field.

Chapter 6

THE FRIAR AND THE MAGNIFICO;
THE SERMONS ON GENESIS

‹♦♦›

F RA GIROLAMO SAVONAROLA was elected Prior of San
Marco in July 1491 and set, as an early biographer ingenuously
puts it, 'like a lamp upon its candelabrum'. His success was due
not so much to his recent notoriety and newly-developed eloquence as
to his well-tried virtues. He was spoken of as a saint, assiduous in prayer
and fasting, strictly observing the vow of poverty; in him were recognized and praised purity, charity, humility, and gentleness. The fame
of such virtues now began to pass from the mouths of the friars to
those of the citizens of Florence.

Up to this time the convent of San Marco, which had been rebuilt
by Cosimo de' Medici, Lorenzo's grandfather, and constantly furnished
with alms and every other necessity by the Medici family, had been
entirely under their influence. It cannot, therefore, be said, as we find
in the early biography, that it was a 'foolish abuse' for former Priors
to have established the custom of calling on Lorenzo after their election. Fra Girolamo refused to do so, and retired instead to pray. When
some older monks went to remind him of this duty, he replied: 'Who
elected me Prior, God or Lorenzo?' They answered: 'God.' 'Therefore it is the Lord God I thank,' said Savonarola. In this way he sent
them about their business.

This might appear, and was perhaps, a surly, ill-mannered retort.
But it shows the character of the man very clearly: his proud independence, his dislike of courtesies and flatteries directed at 'great

masters', as he called them. Yet he could show great humility towards
the humble. The omission certainly displeased Lorenzo, particularly in
conjunction with all the things the monk had said publicly and privately
against him; and he is said to have complained to some of his intimates
that 'a foreign monk has come to live in my house, and has not con-
descended to come and see me'.

Similarly, when Lorenzo sometimes came to hear Mass in San
Marco and afterwards remained to walk in the garden or cloisters, the
proud Friar never consented to go and greet him and walk with him
as his predecessors had done, and as some of the older monks still did.
When some of these came running to tell him, all out of breath:
'Prior, Prior, Lorenzo is in the garden,' he replied: 'Is he asking for
me?' And when told he was not, he added: 'Then let him walk as he
pleases.'

The Magnifico also tried bestowing great gifts on the convent.
In return, Savonarola said from the pulpit that the true preacher was
like a good watchdog, which, when a thief comes along and throws
him a bone or a piece of meat, puts it one one side and goes on barking.
'When Lorenzo heard this,' says the biographer, 'he understood that
this was stony ground.'

Lorenzo was skilled in the art of winning men's favour. Having
tried without success various ways of capturing this one, he finally
tried to tempt him, knowing the proverbial avarice of priests. Piero
da Bibbiena, Lorenzo's chancellor, was ordered to place secretly in
the alms chest of San Marco a quantity of gold coins (the biographer,
who probably exaggerates, says there were 300 florins). But when the
Prior opened the box and found this unusual harvest of offerings, he
handed over to the Bursar the silver and copper coins for the needs of
the convent, and bade him take the gold coins to the Brotherhood of
St. Martin for the relief of the deserving poor. Bibbiena later came to
ask if they had found rich alms, and when he heard to what use they
had been put and confirmed this with the Brotherhood, he returned to
report to Lorenzo, saying: 'This is a wily old fox.' Lorenzo acknowledged himself beaten, and attempted nothing further against Savonarola.

On the other hand, if the Magnifico had some respect for the
Friar's good works and exemplary life (according to Guicciardini's
opinion cited above), a respect that may have increased after his fruitless

attempts to corrupt him, he must, as a great patron of letters and talented men, have taken some account of the reputation that Fra Girolamo was acquiring among the learned. They must have given a good account of him to Lorenzo, who was always appreciative of this kind of report.

This Friar was no longer simply the preacher of the despairing, but the confidant of that prodigy of the age Giovanni Pico, who delighted in 'piously philosophizing' with him. And the poet Girolamo Benivieni, who had at first been sceptical about Savonarola, after long observation now followed him as a friend and became every day more devoted to him. The poet Ugolino Verino dedicated to him, in that same year of 1491, his *Carmen de christiana religione ac vitæ monasticæ fœlicitate,* sending it to him with a Latin epistle in which he discusses the good and the evil deriving from the poetic art. In return Savonarola sent him his *Apologeticus de ratione poeticæ artis,* in four books, which was at once published. Savonarola in the same year was preparing for publication his *Compendium logicæ,* which came out in the following year. In this work he collected and summarized the lectures he had given to his monks, which (if we can believe a contemporary source usually reliable in everything but chronology) were evidently continued after his election as Prior.

Though he wished to appear learned among the learned, not out of pride but to lend greater renown and influence to his work, his greatest success was among the simpler people. For them he wrote some simple and easy contemplative works. The first to appear was a *Trattato della vita viduale* (*Treatise on Widowhood*), published in 1491, which seems to have been the first of his works to be printed.

Yet the pulpit was still the favourite battlefield of this good soldier of Christ. After Advent 1491, of which we know only that he probably preached in San Marco and began then the series on Genesis which he continued until Advent 1494, I would put a visit by Savonarola to Lucca, where he gave twelve sermons in various churches with great success, and then to Pisa, where a novice, Stefano da Codiponte, who was tempted to renounce his calling, was moved by Savonarola's words to reaffirm his earlier enthusiasm and intention.

After these two preaching tours (which were known to earlier biographers, though they were unable to place them chronologically) Savonarola returned to Florence and there preached for Lent, this time from the pulpit of San Lorenzo. One might be tempted to think that this was due to the Magnifico, who wished to exclude him from the pulpit of the cathedral, but we should not give substance to shadows; for such unfounded conjectures are indeed nothing but shadows in history. On the other hand, we are well aware that the basilica of San Lorenzo, which had been newly rebuilt by Cosimo, was, more especially than any other, the parish church of the Medici family; and it is satisfying to see in this series of sermons in San Lorenzo a splendid *revanche* for those unsuccessful ones given in 1484.

The audience was not, as on that former occasion, a mere handful of listeners, but a huge crowd packed beneath the fine Brunelleschi vault to listen to the powerful voice of the Ferrarese Friar. During that Lent, virtually the whole population of Florence was divided among three churches. The greater part was shared between San Lorenzo and Santa Maria del Fiore, where the Franciscan Fra Domenico da Ponzo was preaching. Later, out of jealousy, avarice, and a desire to please those in power, he became Savonarola's bitter enemy, but at this period he spoke well of him and called on the Florentines to believe in him, speaking from the same pulpit that a year before had set the seal on Savonarola's success. The preacher at Santa Maria Novella also enjoyed a certain popularity. In Santa Croce, where there was a certain Fra Francesco d'Aragona specially brought in by Lorenzo (who had very little luck with his preachers), 'hardly ten men were present'.

Some of the usual Latin drafts for this Lenten series survive—and, as it happens, they are autograph—but only those up to the Saturday after the second Sunday in Lent. While their extreme brevity tells us little of the content of the sermons, they are sufficient to indicate that this series had a more marked prophetic theme than the previous one. The reform of the Church, the conversion of the infidel, the imminence of the scourge have now become recurrent themes, and Savonarola has here begun to introduce the description of some of his visions. The limitations of this book preclude me from giving lengthy quotations, but I cannot resist citing the comparison he makes between these and his earlier sermons: 'Once I said that I was nearly sure [of the things foretold], then that I was sure of them, and now I say that I am more than sure . . . and I shall no longer, as last year, relate things that are past, but shall tell of things to be, just as one would speak of things that have already happened.'

A true and really astonishing prophecy is to be found in the third sermon, given on the first Friday of Lent. After describing the great prelates of the Church with the image of Leviathan (and for 'the great prelates' we may here read 'the Court of Rome'), he says that in these men the words of the Scripture regarding the whale are come true: 'There is no power as great as his.' For power they have both the spiritual arm, exercised through excommunications and interdicts, and the temporal arm. For cunning they have secular and ecclesiastical learning—that is to say, the devices of both sacred and profane matters. And after commenting on other qualities of theirs, such as malice, obstinacy, and hypocrisy, he continues thus: 'Think, therefore, how great and of what kind this persecution will be when the true preacher falls into their hands. Who will believe him when he has been excommunicated? When he has been seized, when the masses have been seduced with cunning and false doctrine, when the great of the Church hypocritically make show of holiness to the people?'. In the margin Savonarola here noted: '*Polluerunt templum sanctum tuum*' ['They have profaned Thy holy temple']. To me this seems one of the most extraordinary prophecies of Savonarola.

From these Latin notes of the Lenten sermons we may briefly quote a few other points. For instance, these remarks, which the hearers must have believed to be directed at Lorenzo and his supporters: 'I ought to begin with the princes and the great, but two considerations prevent me: the first is that rarely, if ever, do they go to hear sermons; the second is that when they do go, they ask to hear things that do not displease them.' And elsewhere: 'These powerful men call the citizens to take part in the government of the state and in its offices, to force them to vote as they wish.' Further on he attacks the poets and men of learning who flatter princes—another obvious allusion to those who surrounded Lorenzo. Or again: 'These great men, as though they did not know they were men like others, want to be honoured and blessed by all. Yet the true preacher cannot flatter them; rather will he attack their vices; hence, because he does not behave to them like others, they cannot suffer him. He must therefore expect of them war and tribulations, either openly or by insidious guile.'

Such were the things Fra Girolamo was saying on the 17th of March, the Saturday after the second Sunday in Lent. This is the last day for which we have the Latin summaries, but it did not mark the end of Savonarola's sermon's. To judge by the little information that has come down to us, he became even more heated and emphatic in his pronouncements, as though, like a good sailor, he sensed the approach of the storm. A portent of the storm seemed to come when the lantern of the cupola of Santa Maria del Fiore was struck by lightning during the night of the 5th of April, causing great damage to the marbles and the vaulting.

That night Savonarola had been unable to sleep, and had sat late over the preparation of his sermon for the next day, endeavouring without success to develop it on the Gospel story of Lazarus. Suddenly there burst from his lips the famous words: '*Ecce gladius Domini super terram, cito et velociter*' ['Behold the sword of the Lord, swift and sure, over the peoples of the earth'], which the next morning he elaborated and explained in a sermon that was the more terrifying for its hearers in that they were already aghast at the disaster which had occurred during the night, especially as the rumour was already current that 'this was something more than a thunderbolt'. That same morning Ponzo, preaching in the cathedral, increased the terror of the populace by asserting that this rumour was true. In fact, he declared himself ready to dispute with anyone that it had not been a thunderbolt, and added that Savonarola had repeatedly foretold the scourge that was to fall upon them, and they had never been willing to believe him, but they ought to do so because he was a holy man. Such were the opinions then of a man who a few years later was to become one of Savonarola's bitterest enemies.

Meanwhile, in that hour grave with threats and terror, Lorenzo lay dying in his villa at Careggi. The gout which had tortured him for years had grown worse that winter, and after a brief but slight improvement during the latter half of February and March, it had attacked him again with such violence that on the 5th of April he was already *in extremis*. On the 6th, according to a diarist, when he was told of the incident of the thunderbolt, he said: 'Ah well, I shall die; it fell on the side nearest my house.' And he did indeed die, with great serenity, 'extraordinary in death as he had been in life', on the 8th of April, with demonstrations of fervent piety, and having first asked and obtained the blessing of Savonarola. Fra Girolamo, who always had pity for the sinner while being pitiless towards sin, then made, probably at Lorenzo's request, that visit to him as a dying man which he had refused to pay him as master of Florence. Thus came true the words (unknown to all the biographers) of his sermon of barely two weeks before, on the 24th of March: 'God fulfils the prayers of the humble, and finds strange ways by which the great also, almost in spite of themselves, come to honour Him; either because they are compelled to it by illness, or because the humble are exalted by God.'

The early writers of Savonarola's faction, and first among them Cinozzi, from whom the others derive much information, gave currency to the legend that Savonarola refused absolution and the sacraments to Lorenzo. According to this legend, when Lorenzo asked Fra Girolamo to hear his confession, he said that three sins above all caused him remorse: the sack of Volterra, his thefts from the Monte delle Doti, and his cruelty after the conspiracy of the Pazzi. Fra Girolamo is said to have replied that God was willing to have mercy on him provided he would agree to do three things: first, to have faith in Him— and Lorenzo answered that he had great faith; secondly, to make restitution of what had been unjustly taken—to which Lorenzo agreed; thirdly, to give back to Florence her liberty. At this last requirement the sick man is reputed to have turned his back, and, the Friar having departed, Lorenzo is said to have died soon afterwards without any other confession.

But this legend appears to have had its origin in some tale of Fra Silvestro Maruffi, a man who often regarded as true the innumerable things that appeared to him in dreams; and it must have flourished and spread in the anti-Medicean conventicles in the republican convent of San Marco at the time of the restoration of the Medicis and in the last years of the Republic. The legend was also encouraged by the pseudo-Burlamacchi and by Pico (though, strangely enough, only in the later version of his *Life*), and continued to flourish in the favourable climate of the Romantic and Neo-Guelph Risorgimento down to Aquarone and Villari, who was especially partial to it. If it fits in fairly well with the republican and Jacobin portrait of the Friar which many have painted and like to imagine, it does not really resemble the likely words or behaviour in such circumstances of the great servant of God that Savonarola truly was.

Doubtful in its origins, suspect in its lateness, this legend needs only the letters of Politian and Carlo del Benino to destroy it. They both describe the last hours of Lorenzo and bear witness that Savonarola, when asked, gave him his blessing. Benino's account, which is particularly reliable on account of its personal and private nature, also adds (and there is no reason why he should say so if it were not true) that Lorenzo was greatly consoled by the Friar's visit. To these testimonies we may add the fact that the relations between Savonarola and Piero de' Medici were, despite what some people have unjustifiably imagined to the contrary, excellent throughout the latter's short rule in Florence. Piero would not have been on such terms with him if Savonarola had treated his dying father in the manner described in the legend.

After the death of Lorenzo, Savonarola went on with his Lenten sermons without any change of tone, as we know from a letter written by Niccolò Guicciardini on the 13th of April: 'Fra Girolamo each morning returns to the subject that all men shall feel the scourge of God . . . and this morning I hear he said that God had passed judgment, and that nothing can now save us.' These terrible prophecies must be the same as the ones Fra Girolamo himself describes in more detail in his famous sermon on the reform of the Church, given on the 13th of January, 1495, when all his predictions had been fulfilled: 'Remember what I told you three years ago: that a great wind would come like that described by Elias, and that the wind would strike the mountains. . . .'

Savonarola also tells us how in his sermon for Good Friday (20th April) he expounded another famous vision of his, that of the two crosses and the reprobation of Rome. He also touched on other visions he had experienced. Of others, for fear of being ridiculed by the incredulous, he told only the actual words he had heard, allowing his hearers to believe they were taken from the Scriptures, whereas they were 'newly descended from heaven', or at least Savonarola believed them to be.

It is not, therefore, surprising that these Lenten sermons caused a tremendous stir, greater than the preceding ones, and that for some time they gave people plenty to talk about. 'Here everyone is busy pondering on the prophecies of Fra Girolamo,' wrote Bernardo Vettori on the 7th of May, when the sermons had come to an end some time before and Fra Girolamo was in Venice, where he had been obliged to go for the Chapter General of the Lombard Congregation. From Venice on the 16th of May Savonarola wrote to Fra Battista da Firenze, his Vicar, a letter containing allusions (for us now obscure) to the favourable disposition of the administrative body of the Order towards the requests of the friars of San Marco; these requests probably concerned a reform of the convent to a more rigorous observance of the rule, and received 'a favourable answer with great joyfulness'.

In the same letter Savonarola wrote: 'I believe we shall return on the kalends of June, not before.' In fact he did return earlier, for on the 22nd of May, perhaps having travelled by some more rapid means, he was already in Florence, whence he wrote a fine letter in Latin to that Fra Stefano da Codiponte who we saw above had been confirmed in his vocation by hearing one of Savonarola's sermons. He was a young man of warm and impulsive temperament, and had in fact become so enthusiastic that he had gone to the other extreme and was much troubled at the failings and lukewarmness of his companions. Savonarola wrote to him, attempting among other things to moderate his excessive zeal:

> If you wished to separate yourself completely from evil men, you would have to leave this world altogether. It is true that you have left the world, and you therefore expected to enter at once into Paradise; while in fact you are now only in the forecourt of Paradise, and not yet in Paradise itself. In the world you lived among the wicked; in the convent you have to live among the perfect, among those who are progressing towards perfection, and among the imperfect, but not among the wicked. Even if some false monk is to be found there, you should not be surprised; rather should you be surprised if there were none. In the house of Abraham, in the house of Isaac, in the house of Jacob, in the house of Moses, in the house of David, in the house of our Lord Jesus Christ, and of the apostles and all the saints, there have been some who were impious and wicked and persecutors of the good; how can you then believe that in this world you will find a house without evil men? You are wrong, you are wrong, brother. These ideas of yours are a great temptation, subtly engineered by the devil. Seek peace and pursue it; walk in the sight of the Lord, and humble yourself beneath his great hand. Pick the roses among the thorns, and think everyone better than yourself. If you see something you disapprove of, think that the intention was good; many are better within than they appear outwardly. Therefore, calm yourself, calm yourself, brother. . . .

Again the good seed scattered by the good sower found in the spirit of Codiponte a fertile soil. We shall see him soon among the most faithful followers of the Savonarolan reforms; and after the Master's death, having lost none of his original impulsiveness, he preached in Lucca on the theme '*Jerusalem, Jerusalem quæ occidis prophetas*'. This sermon aroused such strong papal indignation, as the General of his Order wrote, that if Stefano had not died shortly afterward, there was a very strong likelihood 'that he would have been the fourth to go the stake'.

The letter to Codiponte is a most important document for the understanding of the mind of Savonarola. His scorn and severity, albeit most saintly, are known to everyone, while the wonderful spiritual structure he had created within himself and constantly laboured to create in others, both priests and laymen, by example, by preaching, and by writing, remains virtually unknown. Of this same period is a whole group of his brief ascetic treatises, among them the one *On the Love of Jesus,* which he sent to the printers before leaving for Venice, and the one *On Humility,* which came out a little more than a month after his return.

On the subject of this journey to Venice, we know neither what he expected of it, nor what results it had for his plans. But the exemplary reforms prepared for San Marco were nearing readiness, and meanwhile the number of novices increased and the zeal for charity grew in the cloisters of Michelozzo. That which before had seemed sufficient will now no longer appear so. Events themselves seemed to be developing favourably for these reforms. If the death of Lorenzo had been propitious, other things too, which at first might have seemed stumbling-blocks, will turn out to be favourable or at least to precipitate these changes. On the 25th of July, Innocent VIII died, and we find that Savonarola had privately predicted his death to various people, and even given its date. On the 11th of August there occurred perhaps the most important event in Savonarola's life since he had entered into religion and since his first vision in the church of San Giorgio: Cardinal Rodrigo Borgia, by committing simony, occupied the throne of St. Peter, and took the name of Alexander VI.

Chapter 7

THE SEPARATION FROM THE
LOMBARD CONGREGATION

✧✧✦✦✦✦✦✦✦✦✦✦✦✦✦✦✦✦✦✦✦✦✦✦✦✦✦✦✦✦✦✦✦✧✧

'MOST wicked customs, without sincerity, without shame, without truth, without faith, without religion; insatiable avarice, immoderate ambition, cruelty more than barbarous'—these are but a fraction of the vices and hateful qualities that a contemporary historian and dispassionate seeker after truth, Francesco Guicciardini, recognized in the new Pope. To these were added a consuming passion for aggrandizing in whatever way he could his numerous children, who were no less abominable than their father.

Borgia had these children by a variety of women. One was the famous Vannozza, whose mother he had loved earlier, as he is said later to have loved their common daughter Lucrezia. There were to be others during his papacy, which from beginning to end is a story of foulness, abominations, and crimes which would dishonour a chapter of Suetonius, the difference being only that the latter was describing, often with exaggerations, the shameful deeds of the pagan Caesars, while Alexander called himself a Christian and Vicar of Christ. Even if not all the horrors attributed to Alexander are true, as not all the barbarous acts recounted by Suetonius are true, Gino Capponi has wisely said that the crimes falsely attributed to the Borgias are the just punishment for those they really did commit.

Such stories as these, and worse, about Alexander were then on everyone's lips. The bargaining for votes by which he bought himself the papacy was quite open for all to see. Some (and one of them was his

54

successor on the throne of St. Peter) even declared him to be a *marrono* —a Jew falsely converted to Christianity. It is more likely that he was an atheist or an unbeliever; certainly he was impious. If the good King Ferdinand of Aragon, who had borne his own children's death without a tear, could not refrain from weeping at the infamous election of this infamous Pope, one may well imagine what the feelings of Savonarola must have been. But for him the time of weeping in silence was over; he must break those great and evil wings now or never.

Some time later, referring in one of his sermons to this election, Savonarola said: 'From the beginning, when I told you that the Church would be renewed . . . there occurred in Rome something which caused many to say to me: "Now you will see how your prediction will come true, and how well the Church will be reformed!" And I then said: "This is it, this is the way." Then there began evil doings in Rome, and I said: "This is the seed from which the regeneration shall spring." You do not know the ways of God; I tell you that if St. Peter himself came on earth now and wished to reform the Church, he could not do so; nay, he would be put to death.'

As if to convince him further that the time had come, while he went on during that Advent of 1492 with his sermons on Genesis, he experienced on the night preceding the last sermon one of his most famous visions. Contemporary artists commemorated it in medallions and intaglios, for it became, as Villari rightly says, almost a symbol of Savonarola and his doctrine. He saw in the heavens an arm, holding in its hand a sword bearing the prophetic words 'Gladius Domini super terram cito et velociter'. And a great voice was heard saying: 'Hear, all ye dwellers on the earth. The Lord saith unto you: "I am the Lord, and speak unto you with holy love. Lo, the time is near when I shall bare my sword above you. Turn, therefore, your hearts to me before my wrath shall be accomplished, for when the time of tribulation is come, you will seek peace and find it nowhere."' After these words had been uttered, clouds of angels dressed in white, bearing red crosses, came down upon the earth and offered to every mortal a white robe and a cross. Some accepted the robe and put it on, others neither accepted it themselves nor allowed others to do so, and these were the half-hearted and wicked priests. Then that heavenly hand turned the sword towards the earth, and straightway the air was darkened, and swords and hail rained down, and fire and lightning and terrible peals of thunder struck the earth, which was at once assailed by plague, war, famine, and dreadful tribulation. After other divine comforts to the virtuous, and threats to the wicked if they would not be converted, the vision disappeared, and Savonarola heard another voice saying: 'My son, if sinners had eyes to see, they would know how terrible is this plague and how keen this blade.' 'By this terrible plague and keen blade he meant the rule of wicked priests ... who neither enter the Kingdom of Heaven nor permit others to do so; and he wished thereby to show that the Church was so diseased that the warring of these priests was more grievous to her than all the bodily tribulations that can befall her.'

Going into the pulpit the following morning still absorbed in this vision, he decided not to tell it to the congregation, fearing the mockery of the incredulous; but, without saying anything of the dream itself, he put into his sermon many of the words he had heard or seen written that night; and among them one sentence seemed especially directed at the new Pope: '*Iniquitas sanctuarii mei clamat ad me de terra*' ['The wickedness of my sanctuary cries out to me from the earth'].

It seems that that very same morning he first uttered the famous prophecy of One who should come 'from beyond the mountains like Cyrus, and God shall be his guide and leader, and no one will be able to resist him, and he will take cities and fortresses with great ease'; he should be like Cyrus in *Isaiah*: '*Et aperiam coram eius ianuas et portæ non claudentur*' ['And I shall open before him their gates and their doors shall not be shut']. Unfortunately, we have not even the Latin draft for this sermon or for any others of that Advent, nor have we any information other than what Savonarola himself tells us in the *Compendio di rivelazioni*; and to some of this information, including the prophecy of the new Cyrus, it is impossible to ascribe an exact date.

Savonarola's remark that the election of Alexander VI, however dreadful in the eyes of every Christian, would turn to the advantage of the Church might in a sense be applied to Savonarola's own labours. These had been favoured by the death of Lorenzo, and since then there had been maturing within the walls of San Marco certain ideas of reform which from humble beginnings and appearances would open the way for greater things: the separation of the convent of San Marco from the Congregation of Lombardy. It may seem, and in fact was, a small thing in itself, but it implied greater independence for Savonarola and the certainty of his staying on in Florence without the risk of having to break off his work at any moment; it gave him, too, greater authority to introduce very strict reforms that should be an example to the city, to the Order, and to the whole of Christendom.

The convents of San Marco in Florence and San Domenico in Fiesole, which once belonged to the Roman-Tuscan Congregation, had separated from it after the plague of 1448 had so reduced the numbers of the monks, that in 1456 there were in San Marco only two novices. Not even the inducement of a relaxation of the rule, obtained by Sant'Antonino, had succeeded in repopulating the deserted cloisters. In that same year, therefore, the two convents had been permitted to join the flourishing Congregation of Lombardy, only to leave it again in 1469 together with the convents of Ferrara and Modena; but they had rejoined it for the second time in 1474.

From the time when Savonarola had begun to teach new things in a new way at San Marco, and especially since he had become Prior, its friars had multiplied in an unheard-of manner, and now numbered about a hundred. The alms collected by the convent had formerly been barely sufficient to maintain the few monks there; now, because of the renewed devotion in the city and the veneration that had come to surround the convent, they were more than enough for the large numbers of newly recruited monks. Therefore, as the conditions that had given rise to the affiliation with the Lombard Congregation no longer obtained, it was quite natural that the connection should now be broken. Furthermore, because all the hundred monks were unanimous in wishing to live a more perfect life in the strict observation of the rules of the Order, it was neither reasonable nor charitable that they should be compelled against their will to remain in a Congregation in which those rules were not so observed.

It has not been at all clear up to the present at what precise moment the first thoughts of this separation arose. Schnitzer is totally mistaken when he states that Savonarola had discussed this matter at the Chapter of Venice in 1492, where we know that he urged upon the Elders certain matters of the utmost importance to himself and his brethren. Admitting that this was the place most suitable for dealing with such a matter, I cannot believe that the Lombards, who within a short while we will find defending with tooth and claw their possession of this, one of their finest and most flourishing convents, could at that moment have greeted the demand for separation 'with great joyfulness' and kind promises.

Furthermore (and it is strange to see how even the best historians sometimes nod), Savonarola himself, recalling the whole story in a letter to the Abbess of San Domenico in Pisa after the separation, gives a fairly exact chronology of these events, if only we study it closely enough. We can establish that, though it had taken shape in the minds of Savonarola and others of his brethren unbeknown the one to the other, in the spring of 1492 (i.e. shortly before or soon after Fra Girolamo's return from Venice), this idea of separation was not discussed in any way for several months. Eventually Savonarola decided to broach the matter to the older and more revered friars, and consultations were held among them. Then, after the middle of October, having communicated the matter to all the other friars and found them in agreement, he gave orders that they should pray continuously to God that He might bring about that which was of most benefit to the salvation of their souls.

There has been preserved a full autograph summary of a sermon preached by Savonarola to his friars, to which I find no difficulty in assigning the date of the 21st of October, 1492, the feast of the Purity of the Virgin Mary. In this sermon he takes as his starting-point the psalm 'In Domino confido'. Saying that he has begun to build a new city of the spirit, he calls on them in the words of the apostle, 'Orate omni tempore in spiritu', and explains the need for continuous prayer that the work begun might be brought to successful conclusion. The date and the subject-matter of this sermon correspond very well with what I have written above, and amply confirm my statements about the chronology of the distant and obscure beginnings of these moves for separation. I now take up the thread of my narrative at the point where I broke off to develop this subject—at the end of Advent 1492.

Immediately after Advent, Savonarola was obliged to go again to Venice, where on the 2nd of February, 1493, he wrote to his Vicar at San Marco, Fra Battista da Firenze. The reason for this journey is obscure; but he knew when he went that he was due to preach in Bologna for Lent, because in this letter he promises to send to his monks, if he can find time to write them, 'some exhortation in lieu of a sermon'. He kept his promise. Shortly afterwards, between the 10th and the 15th of February, having already reached Bologna, he sent 'to his beloved sons in Christ Jesus, joined together in the convent of San Marco in Florence', a long letter that was printed before the end of the century.

Reading this letter, one is moved by the expression of his love for his brethren and his longing for the spiritual joys of San Marco. Fra Basilio, who had accompanied him, shared that homesickness and that affection. 'This love,' wrote Savonarola, 'has grown in him the more, because he finds no such sweet companionship in these places; and so we are very lonely, like two turtle-doves waiting for spring, when they may return to a warm country where we are used to living among the flowers and joys of the Holy Spirit. And although we have found here many good souls, nevertheless they have not our accustomed simplicity.'

When Savonarola wrote this letter (as he himself tells us) he had not yet spoken before the people. His sermons must have begun on Quinquagesima Sunday (15th February), and we may assume that they went on as usual at least until Easter Monday (8th April) if nothing occurred to interrupt them. We do not know the subject of his sermons. As for his popularity with his audience, if we may believe the pseudo-Burlamacchi, who in these matters is not too reliable, 'the first few days there was no great concourse of people', as usual because 'he did not preach out-of-the-way things such as please the men of learning, but matters useful and pious and fruitful for the soul'. However, later on, according to the same biographer, something occurred which caused 'so great a concourse of people that the building would no longer hold them all'.

He tells how the wife of Giovanni Bentivoglio, ruler of the city, regularly attended the sermons of Savonarola, and always entered the church after the sermon had begun with a great following of noble ladies and courtiers. What with the disturbance she made with her suite and that made by the congregation rising to do her honour, the Friar was obliged to stop, and 'he lost the force and persuasion of his oratory'. Eventually one morning he quietly asked all the congregation to be punctual at the beginning of the sermon; but she went on in the same way, or worse, and another morning he addressed her personally, politely begging her not to disturb him and his hearers in this way. Finally, the third time, seeing her enter the church one day with much pomp in the middle of the sermon, he shouted out in a terrible voice: 'Here is the devil, here is the devil, come to disturb the word of God!' At this insult, the proud noblewoman is said to have ordered two of her guards to slay him in his pulpit. Then, as these two did not dare to commit such sacrilege, she sent two more to the convent; but these, when they came into the presence of this servant of God, merely offered him the help and good graces of their lady.

This tale, as it is, seems scarcely credible, but it was believed by Villari without qualification. On the other hand, Schnitzer rejected it completely. For my part, I think they were both wrong. The early biographers among Savonarola's followers were men of holy life and, I believe, incapable of inventing absolute falsehoods, but they probably did enlarge on the smallest events and give them an air of the miraculous. I imagined that in this case, as in many other episodes of the Savonarolan legend, a fact of small importance grew and grew as it circulated among the posthumous followers of the Friar; but I would never go so far as to deny that that small foundation in truth ever existed. It is very likely that Bentivoglio's wife really did come in late to the sermons, and that Savonarola, at first speaking politely and generally, as was his custom, did say something against this bad habit; and perhaps later on, seeing that the disturbance continued, he may, with the same courage he had shown in facing Lorenzo de' Medici, have made some stronger comment, though still indirectly. It is also within the bounds of possibility that Bentivoglio's wife, who had a reputation for piety, may afterwards have sent two messengers to offer him her good graces, to show that she had taken the affair in good part. Around this kernel of truth there later grew the flesh of the legend.

Now we must discuss some charges brought against Savonarola in Bologna, of which we have certain information but no exact details. He was accused of having spoken ill of the Pope; it was all a silly business, however, and soon came to nothing. Although we do not know the date of this accusation, one is tempted to relate it to this sermon and his courageous reproof of the wife of the ruler of the city. Furthermore, in attempting to establish the chronology of the Friar's biography, I can find no better moment for these charges. He could not reprove the vices of the Pope in such a way as to incur such charges otherwise than in a sermon, and certainly not while busy with his studies, as some would have it; and it is not improbable that Bentivoglio himself, or some zealous minister, may have sought revenge against this too daring preacher. These are conjectures, and I offer them as such: the historian cannot always abstain from them as he would wish, but must simply select among them those which have the greatest verisimilitude.

At the end of this Lent in Bologna, on the 3rd of April, Ash Wednesday, Savonarola wrote to a pious woman, Bartolomea Gianfigliazzi, asking her to pray that God should give him guidance as to whether he should return to Florence before the Chapter of the Congregation, as he wished, or after it. As we know, this usually met on the third Sunday after Easter, and in that year it would be on the 28th of April. We do not know how God did inspire him, but this letter finally disposes of that other legend of a Savonarola proscribed by Piero de' Medici. This is an entirely modern legend created by Villari as a necessary consequence of, and support for, the old one of the refusal of absolution to Lorenzo. But a man who has been proscribed does not pray to God for inspiration as to when he should go back home.

Some mystery, therefore, still surrounds these sermons given outside Florence by the Prior of San Marco. Later on he says that he had to go and preach in Bologna. I may be wrong, but I believe (if I may be permitted a conjecture) that Savonarola himself wished to go there to have more time and opportunity for persuading the Lombard Fathers to look favourably on the separation desired by San Marco. With our present lack of information, we are groping in the dark; yet we are now coming to a crucial moment, and Savonarola returned to Florence on the eve of the decisive battle.

The superiors of the Congregation, backed by Lodovico Sforza— 'il Moro', as he was called—opposed with all their might the request of San Marco. At the Court of Rome it was vigorously supported by the rulers of Florence, by Piero de' Medici together with his brother Cardinal Giovanni de' Medici. Piero was impelled to do so by civic pride; perhaps too by certain political motives, and the pleasure of irritating or merely of contradicting Lodovico il Moro, with whom, by acting against his father's advice and upsetting that political equilibrium he had so ingeniously achieved, he was already on terms of mistrust and ill-feeling. In any case, the warm support given by Piero to the Friar on this occasion and the affectionate terms on which the documents show them to have been, are another blow to the legend of the absolution refused to Lorenzo, and to all the distortions of fact Villari necessarily had recourse to in order to support it.

As, in the end, everything depended on the General of the Order, the feeble Gioacchino Torriani, and even more on the Cardinal Protector, Oliviero Caraffa, a Neapolitan, two friars from San Marco went to Rome to plead the case for the separation: Alessandro Rinuccini and Domenico da Pescia; and when the former fell ill, they were joined by Fra Roberto Ubaldini. The case appeared hopeless, for, although Cardinal Caraffa showed himself favourable, he was opposed by Cardinal Ascanio Sforza, powerful at Court as the brother of '*Il Moro*' and the principal architect of the shameful election of Alexander VI. The friendship which existed at that time among the Sforzas, the Venetians, and the Pope, reinforced the Lombards and weakened the Florentines; while the latter had on their side the King of Naples, who was very useful in influencing Cardinal Caraffa, his subject. Indeed, this case, from being merely a dispute between monks, had grown into an affair of state through the rivalries and alliances that enter into any matter involving the prestige of princes and relations between them. However, it was perhaps not quite such an important affair as the old partisan biographers have tried to make out with their usual exaggerations.

The envoys from San Marco left on the 9th or 10th of May—that is, shortly after the return of Savonarola from Bologna, taking with them letters of warm recommendation from the Signoria, from Piero, and from the Cardinal de' Medici to Cardinal Caraffa, and, in a document drawn up by a lawyer, the expression of the unanimous desire of the monks for separation. In their negotiations they had the help of the Florentine ambassador, Filippo Valori, to whom out of gratitude Savonarola dedicated his fourfold Latin exposition of the '*Pater noster*', translated into Italian and printed that same year. But they were all of them equally lost at the Roman Court when faced with adversaries more astute and more versed in dealing with matters of this kind.

For the Lombards there came, besides Fra Tommaso da Brescia, their Vice-Vicar General, and the Priors of Venice and Cremona, that Francesco Mei, Prior of the convent of San Gimignano, who at first seemed neutral and later became Savonarola's bitter and mortal enemy. With so much opposition, even the unshakeable faith of Fra Domenico seemed at one moment to waver; but, encouraged by letters from Savonarola, he one day, in an excess of zeal, ingenuously suggested throwing himself at the feet of the Pope and offering to resuscitate a dead man to prove that the separation was the will of God. The poor man did not know that at the Court of Rome miracles of quite a different kind were needed, and that it was not the dead who needed reviving, but the living who were more dead than the dead.

In the end Cardinal Caraffa, a man of more practical experience, accomplished a miracle of the sort that really work in courts. One day he remained alone with the Pope after the Consistory and, finding him well disposed, began to jest with him, flattering his mood. Then, taking from his bosom the Brief of separation already prepared, which would annul the union, relieve the Prior and monks of San Marco from obedience to the Lombards, and place them directly under the General of the Order and the Cardinal Protector, he asked the Pope to give it his seal. Alexander lazily refused, saying that he was not going to sign any Briefs that day or discuss any more business. The Cardinal, still jesting, insisted, and playfully slipping the piscatorial ring from the Pope's finger, sealed the Brief with it while the Pope weakly and laughingly protested. Then taking his leave, the Cardinal at once gave the longed-for document to Fra Domenico, who was waiting in the antechamber. He had not left the papal palace before the Lombard friars entered with an urgent letter from Sforza to persuade the Pope not on any account to permit the separation. The answer they received from him was highly characteristic: 'If you had come earlier, your request would have been granted.' This was the 22nd of May, 1493.

The old biographers add the following anecdote. The Vicar of the Lombards, to make sure of Fra Girolamo and take revenge on him, had written not many days before, commanding him in holy obedience to come at once, intending to remove him permanently from San Marco. To have the order presented in the proper way, he had sent the letter to the Prior of Fiesole; but, as the Prior was away, it was left on his desk. On his return the Prior did not notice the letter immediately, and in fact did not see it for several days. He then took it straightway to San Marco and gave it to Savonarola, who replied with a smile: 'Reverend Prior, if you had brought it to me yesterday, I should have carried out what it says. But last evening we received a Brief from Rome saying that we are now separated from Lombardy.' The old biographer then adds, with malicious pleasure, that the Prior of Fiesole went back to his convent a disappointed man.

It is easy to imagine, and in any case we have documents to prove it, that the Brief of May 22nd, so slyly extracted by Caraffa, aroused bitter resentment. It is not easy to appreciate the purpose of a compromise arrived at shortly afterwards, on the 26th of May, between the monks of San Marco and the Lombards, by which the Brief was to be deposited, for a certain space of time and under certain conditions, in the hands of Piero. The Lombards had nothing more to lose by the compromise, and it is not surprising that they should have agreed. Perrens was surprised that Savonarola should have agreed to it, and Villari foolishly imagined that this was a manœuvre of Piero's, belatedly regretting this separation for which he had done so much. It is tempting to think that Piero may have wished to keep a hold on a dangerous friar by means of this pledge. But he was not far-sighted, and he was to show quite soon that he had no regrets about the separation, by giving his whole-hearted support to the separation of other Tuscan convents from Lombardy, and to the increased prosperity of San Marco. And as for the relations between Savonarola and the new ruler of Florence, a letter written by Savonarola to Piero on the subject of the deposition of the Brief (which was never carried out, and was perhaps a mere expedient to silence opposition) shows them to be still on excellent terms. And this in spite of the biographers with preconceived theories.

The complete undoing of the Lombards came from the General of the Order, from now on extremely favourable toward San Marco and Savonarola, whose independence he guaranteed and strengthened in a series of letters. On the 18th of June, he ordered the monks of the Lombard Congregation not to molest those of San Marco, and followed this with another order on the 16th of November, threatening them with excommunication. On the 27th of June, Savonarola and Fra Domenico da Pescia, formerly sons of other convents, were affiliated with the convent of San Marco. On the 15th of November came a letter conferring on the Prior of San Marco *pro tempore* (i.e. on Savonarola) the powers of a Provincial.

Things did not stop here. Once his independence was assured, Savonarola turned to the execution of another broader plan: the removal of other convents from the Lombard Congregation, and first of all the convents of San Domenico in Fiesole and of Santa Caterina in Pisa, with the idea of joining them to San Marco and thus creating a new Congregation. Such a plan could not lack the support of Piero, whose regional ambitions it aroused, especially if the astute Friar allowed him to envisage a future enlarging of the Congregation (which was in fact attempted later) by the addition of other convents outside the Florentine domain.

As far as we know, negotiations for the separation of the convent at Fiesole and its union with San Marco began with a letter from the Signoria to the Cardinal Protector on the 28th of November; those for the separation of the convents of Pisa and San Gimignano with two letters sent by the Signoria on the 17th of December, one to its secretary in Rome, Antonio da Colle, and the other to the Cardinal Protector.

Among all those who had been and still were concerned in these matters of the convents, only Savonarola knew their full significance. As they were not yet aware of the plans and the stature of the Friar, neither the Pope nor the superiors of the Order, nor Piero de' Medici appreciated that significance—not even the monks of San Marco, who had longed for the separation merely that they might attain the spiritual perfection of which their Prior had afforded them a glimpse. But in the great mind and powerful imagination of Savonarola this was the beginning of the reform of the city, and perhaps later of the whole Church.

Chapter 8

THE REFORM OF SAN MARCO

<><><><><><><><><><><><><><><><><><><><><><><><><><><><><><><><>

HE convent of San Marco could not reform others if it did not
begin by reforming itself. This was Savonarola's first concern,
to which he devoted himself with joyful zeal, bringing into
force again the ancient constitutions of the Order, whose disuse he had
always regretted. He was fond of recounting how some years previously in Bologna, while the brothers of the convent of San Domenico
were going in procession, as they did every Sunday, to the shrine of
their founder Saint, singing their usual '*Imple, pater*', they heard a
great voice crying: 'I am not your Father, nor are you my children.'

In 1455 Sant'Antonino, with the full support of the General of the
Order, had without difficulty obtained permission from Pope Callix-
tus III for the convent of San Marco to own property and enjoy a fixed
income, as it had been greatly reduced by the plague of 1448 and was
no longer able to exist on the alms of the citizens. This permission was
later extended by Sixtus IV to the whole Order by the Bull '*Consider-
antes*' of July 1st, 1475, in direct contradiction to the will of the founder.
As soon as the separation had been achieved, Savonarola's first thought
was to sell all the properties of the convent. Even this was not enough
for a man who loved poverty so much that he was unwilling to possess
even a breviary of his own. At the very beginning he frightened his
monks by telling them of a vision in which it had been revealed to him
that out of twenty-eight brethren of San Marco who had died in the
last few years, twenty-five were eternally damned for excessive love
of their superfluity. Without hesitation the monks brought him all their

66

private possessions—books, images, and so forth. The sale of these raised 300 florins, which were at once distributed among the poor.

Also, Savonarola wished the clothes of his brethren to display that holy poverty proper to a mendicant Order. They were to be of coarse, rough cloth, and cut without fullness, using as little material as possible, with short, close-fitting capes. Even when old and patched they were not to be discarded, but they must always be kept very clean. Likewise, he wished their food to be as coarse and common and meagre as possible, both to mortify the flesh and to further the observance of poverty. It is true that, having reduced their diet too stringently (judging the needs of others by his own, which were exceedingly frugal) and made their fasts too severe, he was obliged after a while to relax his severity on account of the many monks who fell ill.

If Sant'Antonino had asked and obtained for the monks of San Marco permission to have property and income because alms had diminished, the truth was also that they had diminished because the citizens could see that the brethren no longer lived as mendicant friars and men of religion should. When Savonarola broke this vicious circle and the Florentines were edified by the new odour of poverty and sanctity emanating from San Marco, alms began to abound, so that there was an excess for distribution to the poor. Fra Girolamo also wished the serving-brothers to contribute to the support of the community, and he began to choose them among men of ability. They practised arts such as painting, sculpture, illuminating, and copying, and with their earnings supported the other monks who were engaged in study and preaching, who thus could preach freely without respect to anyone or anything. He used often to say that he did not wish his preachers to be dependent on charity for their living, because truth engenders hatred ('*veritas odium parit*') and they might in consequence become, in the words of the prophet '*canes muti non valentes latrare*' [dumb dogs, that cannot bark'].

Amid all this fervour of renewal and reform, a project was now revived which Savonarola had outlined to his monks at the beginning of his priorate, and had himself considered down to the smallest details. In San Marco, where everything at all times reminded him of the liberality and magnificence of the Medici, he did not feel free and poor as he would have liked. He planned to build a new convent in a remote and lonely place, which should express throughout the spirit of poverty

THE REFORM OF SAN MARCO

and simplicity. He wished it to be low-built, with small cells divided by partitions of boards or plastered wattle screens, with door frames, thresholds, and latches made of wood; there were to be no iron bolts or keys. The cloisters and the church would have columns of brick, not stone, without any pretence to decoration. The biographer who has left us some account of this plan recalls having heard Savonarola say, while explaining it: 'When the building of this convent is finished, and men come to the door and ask to speak to this or that friar or father, the porter will answer: "Are you simple people? If you are simple, enter; if not, depart, for none enter here but the simple."'

These were not mere empty, if devout, imaginings. The land for the new convent, with a fine grove of chestnuts near by, had already been given by a rich citizen, and there was a benefactor ready to give the money for the building. But in San Marco, and outside its walls among the relatives of the monks, opposition and disagreement arose, protesting that such a hermitage would be 'a slaughter-house of friars'. These disagreements, however, did not, in all probability, contribute as much to preventing this plan (as the early biographer would have us believe) as did the events that now followed in rapid succession, and in a certain sense, outstripped it. The building of the new convent was certainly still under consideration after the separation of San Marco, and while the negotiations were in progress for the separation of San Domenico at Fiesole, for Fra Roberto Ubaldini wrote in a letter to Savonarola on the 1st of May, 1494, that he had obtained the Pope's permission *vivæ vocis oraculo*.

There is no doubt that this new convent, whether in some remote place or within the city, would soon have been needed to accommodate the continual increase of brethren, who were seeking entry in ever larger numbers, attracted by the piety and simplicity emanating from San Marco. To those who, after the separation, objected that so small a community could not stand by itself, Savonarola always replied in the words of Isaiah which were particularly appropriate: '*Angustus est mihi locus; fac mihi spatium ut habitem*' ['The place is too strait for me; give place to me that I may dwell']. He added that men of great intellect and learning would enter San Marco; and this prediction was also soon to come true.

Advent came while negotiations were going on in Rome for the separation of San Domenico at Fiesole and, soon after, the separation

of the convents of San Gimignano and Santa Caterina at Pisa. According to the frontispiece of a late edition of certain of his sermons,
Savonarola preached that Advent in the cathedral. We know for certain
what he preached on, because he tells us himself in the *Compendio* that
he continued his exposition of Genesis, more particularly considering
'the work of the building of Noah's Ark'. His progress with this
exposition was remarkably slow. From the text of the sermons of the
following Lent it appears that in the whole of Advent he expounded
only the first eight verses of Chapter VI. I have dwelt on this point because later on Savonarola will see the hand of God in this dilatoriness
of his.

There is an edition printed in 1528 of certain sermons (not among
the least famous of Savonarola's) on the psalm '*Quam bonus*'; and in the
frontispiece of this edition we read that they were delivered in Santa
Maria del Fiore during Advent 1493. If we may credit the indication
of the place where Savonarola preached that Advent, as being information more likely to stick in the editor's memory than the content of the
sermons, it is difficult to know how far to believe what the rest of the
frontispiece says about the subject of his preaching. Nor would it be
enough in this case to conjecture that Savonarola must have given two
sets of sermons (as he had done in Advent 1490): one on Genesis, as he
himself tells us, and one on the psalm '*Quam bonus*', as the editor of this
edition asserts. I say this because it is obvious that these sermons on
the psalm, if the printed text reflects what was in fact preached, were
not given in Advent at all; and not because, as Schnitzer observed, they
contain no reference to that season (which would be a weak argument),
but because it appears quite clearly that they were, or are presented as
having been, preached on consecutive days, which excludes the possibility that they were given (as Schnitzer maintains) on feasts *infra
annum*. Also, I am unable to understand why Schnitzer assigns them to
1492. It is just possible that they may have been Lenten sermons or,
more likely, a series of lectures given to his monks; but, though I once
favoured this latter hypothesis, I am no longer convinced by it. Let
us see if a better one can be found.

The text printed in 1528 is simply a much enlarged translation of
a Latin text, of which we possess the autograph. This is not one of the
usual rough schemes, but quite a full text, even if here and there some
passages seem mere sketches. Turning therefore directly to this original

version, pruned of the amplifications that the translator confesses he has made, we find that many of the rhetorical effects which occur in the translation, and which are suitable to a public sermon, are in fact interpolations. Further, in the last sermon the work is referred to as a treatise. As if this were not enough, in an old catalogue of the works of Savonarola compiled before the sermons on the psalm 'Quam bonus' were either published or translated, this Latin text is entered with the title 'Quam bonus Israel Deus' per modum sermonum. It would appear, according to this evidence, that these are not the usual summaries for sermons, but an exposition of a psalm, a short treatise drawn up in the form of a cycle of sermons or lectures. This is not the only such example among the exegetical works of Savonarola. We may suppose, if we do not wish to dismiss all the assertions of the translator and editor as pure inventions, that Savonarola really delivered these sermons on the psalm 'Quam bonus', and that after preaching them, moved by the 'pious prayers' of his brethren (as the translator said; and it seemed just another of the usual legends!), he rewrote them, using summaries that are no longer extant. This seems all the more likely, as the autograph is evidently not a first draft but a copy made from an original that has come down to us.

Obviously we are in the field of conjecture, however likely or plausible. Only one thing is certain: that Savonarola preached in Advent 1493 on the verses of Genesis referred to above. As for the sermons on the 'Quam bonus', if they were ever delivered, there is no real evidence of when or where, which after all is what most concerns the biographer. And he, after having discussed the matter at length and perhaps tediously, can neither accept nor reject the assertions of time and place made by the edition of 1528, which at first, owing to various incongruities, seemed totally unacceptable.

This general uncertainty, not only about the time but about the very identity of the sermons, dispenses us from dwelling even briefly on the contents of these 'sermons'. Suffice it to say that if they were really preached in the form in which they have come down to us, they would be quite unlike all the others delivered by Savonarola in the period we have now reached. They contain a few of the usual outbursts against wicked priests and the Court of Rome, but no reference to visions, and none (which is stranger) to the affairs of the city, which, if I am not mistaken, is not even mentioned; and they have none of the characteristic oratorical figures of Savonarola. Rather than sermons, they seem, from their form, style, and content, to be quiet meditations or discussions, now ascetic, now apologetic, now exegetic, on the end of Man, Divine Providence, the love of God, the Christian life, and so on: fine, eloquent discussions, though we must be careful to separate, in the vernacular text that is the only one so far published, the eloquence of Savonarola from that of the translator, who has added a good deal of his own.

We are now at the beginning of the fatal year 1494. The harmony and balance of power between the Italian states had already broken down, as suspicion increased among the various ruling princes. The King of France, his greed for power stimulated by the nefarious Sforza, was already planning his expedition to seize the Kingdom of Naples, to which he laid claim through the Angevins. At the beginning of that year, old King Ferdinand of Aragon died in Naples, and the loss of his wisdom and authority, and the arrogance and imprudence of his son Alfonso seemed to increase the danger to the peace of Italy.

While Lodovico Sforza openly urged Charles VIII to cross the Alps, and while the Venetians stood neutral, the Pope, after an initial coolness, came to side more and more with the Aragonese, with whom Piero de' Medici also strongly allied himself. The fine political edifice so cleverly built by Lorenzo was falling apart like a house of cards. Nor was Lorenzo's son the least cause of this collapse, just as he was the cause of the Medici's decline in favour with the Florentines—a favour won for the family by the wisdom of Cosimo, the brilliance and liberality of Lorenzo, and the civil behaviour of both. The sophisticated and intolerant Florentines, who suspected and resented every form of overlordship, even the most intelligent, could not accept the mediocrity and arrogance and more openly tyrannical behaviour of Piero, who more resembled the feudal Orsini on his mother's side than the civic-minded Medici. Politian's teaching had not sufficed to fortify the mind of this immensely powerful man, who was reputed one of the best in Italy at games of strength.

With the affairs of Italy and of Florence at this pass, Savonarola, seeing here the beginning of those scourges he had continually predicted in recent years, began to preach for Lent in the church of San Lorenzo on Ash Wednesday, February the 12th. The situation was a gift for the preacher of tribulation and renovation—a gift for the man who had so often cried '*Gladius Domini super terram*', now that so mighty a sword hung over the peace of Italy. Even the text of that book of Genesis, on which he had been preaching for two years, now came to his aid, and it will continue to do so in such a way that in the end he will believe the whole affair 'had been guided throughout by the hidden inspiration of God'.

This text, as he took it up again at the beginning of Lent where he had left off the previous Advent, presented him with the mystery of the Ark built by Noah as a refuge from the imminent Flood. He now devoted himself, too, to building day by day in his sermons a mystical Ark where the Florentine people might take refuge from the threatening flood of foreign invaders. In each sermon he cleverly built up ten symbolical planks of this ark, 'with remarkable explanations, declaring that soon the deluge would come—that is, soldiers and princes who would take the cities and fortresses by merely presenting themselves before the walls'. He had foretold something like this as early as Advent 1492, but it is clear that in this Lent of 1494 he was even more explicit when he repeated the prophecy of a king who would come from beyond the mountains in the likeness of Cyrus, and all the gates would open wide for him, and he would take the cities and fortresses with the greatest ease.

Certainly, if what Savonarola predicted in 1492 seems rather to be attributed to supernatural revelation, the things he said while beyond the Alps so many warlike preparations were being made, might easily have been foreseen by merely human insight. All the same, there were in Italy many who did not believe that the King was coming, and particularly the intelligent but ever sceptical Florentines, whom the Friar was to go on mocking for several years, scornfully recalling their 'He's coming! He's not coming'. And—as he was later to remind those with short memories—when they said: 'He will not come; he has no horses, and it is winter,' the Friar cried from the pulpit that God would cross the Alps and take the King by the bridle and lead him into Italy in spite of what everyone believed. At the same time he made a further prophecy which was later to appear no less true: that the Florentines, or rather their ruler—that is, Piero de' Medici—'would do the opposite of what he ought to do'. While this flood menaced Italy, Savonarola again raised against Rome his cry: '*O clerica, propter te orta est hæc tempestas!*' ['O Church, because of Thee this storm has arisen!'].

We have all this information about the Lent sermons of 1494 from the chroniclers and apologists, and from Savonarola himself in his *Compendio* and in other sermons, and not from what remains of the text of the Lent sermons themselves, which consist merely of the usual Latin schemes. These were published in 1536, probably from the autograph, which has since disappeared, but not without some touching up or additions made by the editor, perhaps that same '*instructus*' *prædicator* who supplied the last three sermons missing from the original. In these summaries there is little worth noting apart perhaps from the usual gloomy descriptions of vice, the frequent denunciations of astrology, the invectives against wicked prelates, and a note of a '*cito, cito, cito!*' to be shouted at the congregation in a terrible voice.

Whether the eloquence of the Friar reached new heights, or whether the quality of the times disposed his hearers to listen with greater favour, these sermons increased his following and his reputation, which now passed beyond the boundaries of the Florentine domain. At Lucca, where the devoted Fra Domenico was preaching, the populace became so enthusiastic about the new teaching and new manner of preaching that, having heard the disciple, they greatly desired to hear the master. The Elders, who some time before had sought Savonarola's advice on the subject of tolerating Jewish usurers, wrote to him on the 14th of March, in a tone of almost feverish exitement, reminding him of his brief mission to their city in 1492 and inviting him to preach the following Lent in the cathedral at Lucca. He replied to their letter very kindly, promising to fulfil this request, provided that events did not arise to prevent it; which considering the unsettled times, might easily prove to be the case. To have foreseen such possible obstacles in March 1494 required a greater spirit of prophecy than would have been needed in the following year. Eminent scholars fell into the error of assigning these letters to 1495, and all the biographers of Savonarola have up to now followed that dating.

Lent 1494 and Savonarola's sermons in San Lorenzo came to an end, but the negotiations for the separation of the convents of Fiesole and Pisa from the Lombard Congregation and their union with San Marco were still going on. The Signoria and Piero de' Medici still threw all the weight of their authority into influencing the wavering Cardinal Caraffa. Immediately after Easter, on the 7th of April, the Florentine chancellery wrote again to Ser Antonio da Colle in Rome, telling him to press the matter with the Cardinal, and informing him that this separation was the greatest favour he could do the Republic.

For the community of San Marco the case was presented in Rome by Fra Francesco Salviati and Fra Giovanni Sinibaldi; but they had little influence and were strongly opposed by the Lombard friars, who again had behind them the power and intrigue of Lodovico il Moro. At one point, however, Salviati and his companion were reinforced by Agnolo Niccolini and Pierfilippo Pandolfini, who had gone as ambassadors of the Republic to Rome and Naples. Cardinal Caraffa, under pressure from the letters of the Signoria and Piero, and from the urging of the ambassadors, finally gave them firm assurances of success. The Lombards, however, getting wind of this, managed to obtain from the King of Naples influential letters to Cardinal Caraffa, and he, thinking of his relatives who were the King's subjects, hastily changed sides. At this point, while the Signoria was remonstrating with the cardinal for this *volte-face* and was again urging Ser Antonio da Colle to further efforts, Savonarola wrote the ambassadors three letters in two days, the 20th and 21st of April, to inspire them with fresh enthusiasm and show them the course they should follow. In these letters two things are worthy of note: first, the astuteness of Savonarola in the management of worldly affairs, shown here too by a touch of flattery, which, though used in a good cause, may yet displease those who have a preconceived idea of an austere and unbending Savonarola; and, second, the apparent ease with which he was able to command the favour of the Signoria and Piero in these matters.

Things dragged on slowly, but something was still being achieved, thanks not so much to Salviati as to the Florentine ambassadors, who, when Caraffa had put his terms in writing, succeeded in getting them revised in a sense more favourable to San Marco. But it cannot have been so difficult to obtain, as Savonarola suggested to Niccolini, other letters to Caraffa from the King of Naples to undo the harm done by the first ones; for the King was as favourably disposed to Piero as Lodovico Sforza was hostile. In addition, the Signoria wrote yet again to the cardinal on the 15th of May and the 2nd of June. Caraffa finally gave way to this vigorous pressure, and once again he found the Pope well disposed. Fra Domenico is reputed to have proposed ingenuously that the trick so successful on the previous occasion should be tried again. The Brief was dispatched on the 13th of August. Savonarola was now in possession of the field. It is true that he had to give up the convent of San Gimignano owing to the opposition of the monks led by his implacable adversary Mei, but those of Fiesole and Pisa, separated from the Lombards, were now joined to San Marco.

There was an attempt at this time to join the convent of Santo Spirito in Siena to San Marco. It is a story that deserves to be gone into fully, as the version given by modern historians is not without errors and lacunae. One might be tempted to suppose that Piero de' Medici had some hand in this too, for he would not be sorry to make his influence felt in that neighbouring rival republic. It was, however, the Sienese themselves who, disturbed by the way of life of the monks of Santo Spirito, repeatedly asked the General of the Order to reform their convent. Torriani, who knew no one better than Fra Girolamo to carry out such a reform, ordered him to do so, and advised the Signoria of Siena accordingly in a letter of June the 10th, so that Savonarola might fulfil his orders without impediment.

Taking with him twenty of his own monks as the basis for the reform, Savonarola went to Siena on June the 21st, in obedience to the orders he had received. Having convened the Chapter and read aloud the General's letter, he took possession of the church and convent; when all was over and night fell, everything appeared settled. But the Sienese were madly jealous of the Florentines, and, perhaps exasperated by monks who had been expelled from the convent, their jealousy broke out on the following day. A great riot was organized against Savonarola and his monks, and the very Signoria responsible for seeking the reform had a hand in it. We should hear the account 'of the behaviour of these brutes of Sienese' given by Ser Alessandro Bracci, who was present at the time: 'They got that poor monk Fra Girolamo to come here with about twenty of his brethren from San Marco; and he has been treated, one might say, like a Christian among the Jews, despised, rejected, and threatened by the whole populace, and I really believe that if he had not left when he did, they would have stoned him. Then they started a great rumour that, as the convent of Santo Spirito is on the walls of Siena, we had sent these monks from Florence to take Siena from them. Yesterday, as Fra Girolamo was on his way to speak with the Captain of the People, three of the Signori went up to him uttering the most violent threats, and many citizens followed suit; and even the women attacked him and shouted all manner of insults.'

Finally the Signoria sent its mace-bearers to the convent to expel Savonarola and his monks, though to justify themselves they hypocritically wrote to the General that Fra Girolamo had been persuaded to leave by certain prudent citizens. In the circumstances Savonarola had no alternative but to go; and when he reached the frontier of the republic, following the precept of the Gospel, he shook off the dust of his feet against the city of Siena.

Things went better at Pisa, as long as the city remained under Florentine rule. Savonarola again went in person to take possession of the convent of Santa Caterina. Recording the fact on August the 20th, the chronicler of Santa Caterina refers to him as '*omni laude dignus, iam orbi toti notus*' ['worthy of all praise, and known throughout the world']. Having removed all the monks who objected to a rigorous observance of the rule, and kept only four—among them the faithful Stefano da Codiponte—he admitted in their place twenty-two of his own brethren with the right to a voice in the Chapter.

Thus arose a new Congregation, at first called the Congregation of Tuscany and connected with that of Rome, but later called the Congregation of San Marco. In this new Congregation, later joined by the convents of Santa Maria del Sasso and of Prato, Savonarola strove as the new Vicar General—the words are those of a contemporary chronicler—'to introduce into their studies and way of life an almost divine order'.

Chapter 9

THE ARK AND THE FLOOD;
THE 'NEW CYRUS'

◇✕✕✕✕✕✕✕✕✕✕✕✕✕✕✕✕✕✕✕✕✕✕✕✕✕✕✕✕✕✕✕✕✕✕✕✕✕✕◇

WHILE he was building up this new Congregation, which was to be a kind of Ark which would ensure his own safety and that of his work against future adversity, Savonarola did not forget that other symbolical Ark which he had begun to build during Lent as a refuge for the Florentine people. During the summer he had already started to draft the sermons he was to give on this subject in the coming Advent. These summaries were preserved, and were published for the first time in 1536. Although some parts were never used, others (as I have recently been able to prove) were used in another set of sermons. Altogether they presented until a short time ago an insoluble problem for the student of Savonarola.

Events in the meantime were again outdistancing the plans and opinions of men. Charles VIII, who not long before had given up his project because of lack of funds and popular discontent at home, was again roused to action by the fugitive Cardinal della Rovere, 'that fatal instrument of the ills of Italy', and was preparing to cross the Alps. Gathering his troops together in the Dauphine, he was in Lyons by the 20th of August; then, crossing the Alps by the pass of Montgenevre, he reached Susa on the 3rd of September and Asti on the 9th, there to be met by his ally and instigator Lodovico Sforza.

In Florence perhaps more than in any other part of Italy, excitement and fear were intense. The city was by tradition friendly to France, but she now found herself, against her will, and at the worst

77

possible moment, included among the enemies of the French. And this was all due to the foolish policy, not of her legitimate government, but of a private citizen who had usurped its power. So, as the French King's vast army drew nearer, fear of his coming daily increased, and with it hatred for Piero, who had already fallen into disfavour with the Florentines because of his tyrannical behaviour.

In the face of this danger, the Florentines turned instead to Savonarola, who had foretold precisely all these events. Those who had been deceived by their own cleverness, who had thought it all out, weighed the probabilities and even reckoned up the money in the French King's treasury, were all the more terrified now, at the easy progress of an expedition that seemed to be conducted with truly French levity, and against all the dictates of human reason. Here, then, was the 'new Cyrus' prophesied by the Friar: God had really gone across the Alps, as the humble monk had said, and led him in by the bridle. Here was the man who was to brandish the prophetic sword over the blind peoples of Italy. '*Ecce gladius Domini super terram, cito et velociter.*' Here, for the Florence that would not believe the words of her prophet, the builder of the mystical Ark, here was the Flood!

This was the state of feeling in the city when on the 21st of September, the feast of St. Matthew the Apostle and his own birthday, Savonarola decided to preach again from the pulpit of the cathedral. He did not even look at the notes he had prepared beforehand. Since in the previous Lent he had lingered inexplicably long over the construction of the Ark, 'the hidden inspiration of God' had kept for this occasion a most appropriate and terrible exordium. The very next verse that the book of Genesis offered him on the eve of such a deluge of armies was the one which reads: *Ecce ego adducam aquas diluvii super terram.*'

That very morning a report had reached the city that the King had entered Genoa. This information, which later turned out not to be true, increased the dismay of the Florentines, so that a greater and more terror-stricken crowd pressed into the vast church to listen with a new faith to the words of their prophet. And finally, as the congregation waited in silence, there thundered out, re-echoing from the high vault of the cathedral, the terrible voice of the Friar: 'Lo, I shall loose over the earth the waters of the Flood.' Like a great breath of terror it swept over his hearers, and not only the hearts of women and children and simple people were shaken by it. Giovanni Pico della Mirandola, who

78

was regarded as the greatest intellect of his time, admitted afterwards that he had shuddered and felt his hair stand on end at those words. Weeping, cries, and invocations rose in the church: 'everyone walked in awe-struck silence about the city, as though only half alive.'

Michelangelo was overcome by that breath of terror. The mind of that great artist offered the fearful preacher the most remarkable and most noble material to mould to his design which any man of his kind could wish for, and he left upon it the mark of his terrible hand. The young sculptor of the Medici gardens had assiduously followed the sermons of Savonarola, and had heard him preach of the time that was daily drawing nearer and of the mounting scourge that was to come. Now that the tribulation had truly come and the sword was brandished in the air, he could hold out no longer: he left the house of the man who, as that same preacher had foretold, would in the hour of need do the opposite of everything he should. Michelangelo fled from Florence.

But that voice was to follow him everywhere, and to the last years of his solitary old age he would say that he still heard it. It was to follow him in flight and in exile; he was to hear it in his constant thoughts of death and while he was painting the terrors of his Last Judgment. And if he could have made his terrible figure of Christ speak, threatening a flood of wrath from above the great writhing mass of humanity, he would have put into his mouth the same cry he heard from the lips of Girolamo Savonarola on the morning of the 21st of September, 1494.

While Charles was held up at Asti, where he had fallen ill, he sent another ambassador to Florence to ask for a free passage; but Piero made some stupid pretexts—as, for example, that the matter could not be discussed because the principal citizens were away at their country houses. As a result, the Frenchman went away highly displeased. This seemed 'to everyone a dangerous folly', and popular resentment against Piero increased, while news was spread abroad that the King had sworn to sack the city. Charles, having recovered from his illness, moved in the meantime to Pavia and thence to Piacenza. Then, entering Florentine territory by the Pontremoli road, he took Fivizzano by force on the 29th of October and put it to the sack.

Meanwhile, Piero de' Medici, seeking to amass a great provision of money for the defence of the city, found everyone unco-operative, even his most faithful friends. Then, remembering how his father, with a bold but happy inspiration, had gone to place himself in the hands of the victorious King Ferdinand, Piero tried to emulate him. He left Florence and went to Charles's camp beneath the rock fortress of Serzanello. There, without the knowledge of the Signoria or of any other citizens, he thoughtlessly conceded to the King everything he asked: first of all, the very fortress that the French army was then besieging with slender hope of success, and in addition those of Sarzana and Pietrasanta, which were like the keys of the Florentine dominion, and furthermore the forts of Pisa and Leghorn, which were among the chief cities of the state. In this way the French army had the road opened before it.

Once more the situation was a gift for Savonarola, who, not wishing to leave the people without the consolation of his words in such dire straits, had begun in the cathedral his cycle of sermons which was later called *On Haggai* (though they were intended to continue his exposition of Genesis). On November 1st, he said, among other things: 'You know that some years ago, before there was any hint or rumour of these wars which have now come from beyond the mountains, great tribulations were foretold to you. You know too that less than two years ago I said to you: "*Ecce gladius Domini super terram cito et velociter.*" Not I, but God gave you this prediction, and now it has come. It is now approaching.' My repeated quotations from the actual words spoken will not, I hope, be objected to, for, as Gino Capponi wisely said, words are history too.

The Friar also said:

Vox dicentis clama. A voice cries out saying: O Italy, *propter peccata tua venient tibi adversa.* All you cities of Italy, now is the time for all your sins to be punished. O Italy, for your lust, your avarice, your pride, your ambition, your thieving and extortion, there will come upon you many adversities and many scourges. *Vox dicentis clama.* A voice cries out saying: O *Florentia, propter peccata tua venient tibi adversa.* O Florence, O Florence, O Florence, for your sins, for your brutality, your avarice, your lust, your ambition, there will befall you many trials and many tribulations. *Vox dicentis clama.* On whom do you call? O Clergy, Clergy, Clergy, *propter te orta est hæc tempestas*—O clergy, who are the principal cause of so many evils, through your evildoing comes this storm; by your sins have been prepared so many tribulations; woe, woe, I say unto those that bear the tonsure! *Vox dicentis clama,* a voice still calls. On whom further should I call? *Clama, ne cesses, annuntia populo huic scelera eorum,* cry out without ceasing, declare unto the people their wickedness. It calls and says, keep on: *annuntia populo huic scelera eorum. . . .* I have said it so many times, I have cried out so often, I have wept for you so many times, Florence, that it should suffice. *Orate,* pray for me to the Lord, *ut Deus consoletur me.* O Florence, I have wished to speak this morning to you and each and every one openly and sincerely, for I could do no other. And still the voice cries out: *vox dicentis clama,* the voice of One speaks forth and calls. And whom else should I call? I have called each one to repentance. *Clama ad Dominum Deum tuum,* call and cry out to the Lord, thy God. I turn to Thee, O Lord, Who died for love of us, and for our sins. *Parce, Domine, populo tuo.* Forgive, forgive, Lord, this Thy people; forgive, Lord, the people of Florence, who desire to be Thy people!

The next day, which was a Sunday, and again on the day after, as disquieting news came from the French King's camp, the Friar preached again; for as the danger increased and drew nearer, so the need for his words became all the more urgent. His great voice grew all the more powerful, and, like the gigantic force that emanated from it, that voice seemed all the more superhuman issuing from the small and slender body. He put off as long as possible the closing of the Ark prepared for the people of Florence, to give time for all to enter. And he threatened, he implored, he begged them to placate the wrath of God with prayers and repentance, as the day of great trial drew near. In those three days he shouted so much from the pulpit that, as he himself said, his pectoral vein nearly burst, and he became physically so weak that he was on the point of falling seriously ill.

The King's quartermasters were already in Florence marking with chalk the houses they thought most suitable for billets for the troops. They went in everywhere, inspected the fine rooms decorated with splendid artistry, and said: this will be for such and such a lord, and that for such and such a baron. An order had been promulgated that 'nothing should be touched, or removed from the houses': this way the stay of the French would be the more delightful, and their booty the richer. Only the young girls were sent into convents for safety.

Even greater than their fear of the French was the Florentine's anger at the base and cowardly actions of Piero, and especially for his having disposed, at his own whim, of so many important strongholds of their dominion without consulting the government of the city—something his father and grandfather had never dared to do. He was already being spoken ill of in public, and the citizens were already inciting one another to revolt and regain their freedom, so that when on November the 4th the Council of Seventy was convened by the Signoria, free and courageous voices were raised there for the first time in many years. The frankest words were spoken by Piero Capponi, who said 'that it was now time to cease being governed by children': he proposed that they should send ambassadors to the King, among whom the first should be Fra Girolamo, 'a man of holy life . . . worthy, courageous, able, and highly esteemed'. And this they did.

The day after, they elected a solemn embassy of four citizens, among them Capponi, to be led by Savonarola. He did not accept the nomination straightway, but discussed the matter first in Chapter with his brethren. They no less than the citizens begged him to accept, and, after exhorting them not to boast of the honour thus done to their convent, he set out the same evening on foot with three companions. They took the road to Empoli, for it was not yet known if the King would receive the embassy in Lucca, where he still was, or in Pisa, whither he was about to go. The Signoria, which could not allow one of its ambassadors to proceed in such a simple fashion, sent after him richly caparisoned mules such as were used by prelates at that time.

The other ambassadors set off on horseback the next day and joined Savonarola at Librafatta on the border between Florence and Lucca, where he had stopped to wait for them and rest awhile in the house of the *podestà* or mayor, Carlo Pitti, one of his devoted followers. Here the anonymous biographer takes the opportunity to narrate a miraculous fishing in the Serchio by a servant of the *podestà*, who cast his nets under Savonarola's instructions. When the other ambassadors urged him to set out for Lucca, the Friar told them that they could go if they wished, but they would not have audience of the King in that city. And this turned out to be true.

At Lucca, however, Piero de' Medici, who had already had bad reports of the temper of the Florentines, now saw approaching, without any regard for him, this embassy of citizens to the King, none of whom were well disposed towards him; and he realized that the state was slipping from his grasp. Then, piling folly on folly, instead of re-entering Florence with the arms of the King, whose favour he had bought at the expense of the Florentines, he immediately returned alone. It was an insane decision, and one that lost him his power and gave back to the Florentines their liberty. And so came true the prophecy of Savonarola during the previous Lent, when he had said that at the approach of the 'new Cyrus' the ruler would do the opposite of what he should, like a man drunk and out of his senses.

Reaching Florence on the evening of the 8th, Piero had sweetmeats and wine distributed to the people to ingratiate himself and make pretence of joyfulness and good tidings. He contrived to look more cheerful than he can have felt. The following evening he tried to enter the Palazzo del Comune, taking with him a large armed escort, but he was told that he must enter by the small door, alone and without arms. Then he realized that he had lost the state. As he turned in a rage to leave, the crowd began to bait him and children ran after him with stones. Surrounded by his own men with swords drawn, he returned home; but shortly afterwards he was seized by a strange terror that is difficult to understand in a man so courageous and dedicated to arms. With the help of a small nucleus of troops within the walls, and a small army without, holding the gate of San Gallo for him, he hastily fled from the city that had been ruled for sixty years by the wisdom of his forebears; and he did so almost without being expelled, and in a manner completely base and blameworthy.

Only a few weeks had passed since the Friar had shouted his terrifying '*Ecce adducam aquas diluvii*'. And now for more than three years, with moments of silence and bitter opposition, Florence was to have no other master than that terrible voice.

Chapter 10

FRA GIROLAMO AND CHARLES VIII; THE FRIAR FOUNDER OF THE POPULAR STATE

◇◇

THE same day that Florence regained her liberty by ejecting Piero, Pisa too regained hers, with the consent of Charles VIII, by ejecting her Florentine governors. Savonarola may have been present at this political change. As he had foreseen, the Florentine embassy had not been able to have audience with the King at Lucca, and consequently they had been obliged to follow him to Pisa. There on the very day of the uprising they were finally received by Charles, before whom the Friar pronounced a set speech in Latin which makes one sigh for the spontaneous oratorical vigour of his sermons before the people.

He told the King, calling to witness all the Florentine people, how the humble monk who stood before him had been foretelling his coming for several years, destined by God for the scourge of Italy and the reform of the Church: 'At last you have come, O King! You have come as minister of God, you have come as minister of justice. Welcome! We receive you with joyful hearts and happy faces.' But, having thus saluted him, Savonarola added, not without a vaguely threatening note, that the same humble monk, still inspired by God, warned him to be careful of Florence and to forgive any offence she had offered him, if he wished his enterprise to be victorious. After which he explained the mission with which the Republic had entrusted him.

84

The King had already heard of the reputation and prophecies of the Friar and was himself greatly inclined to such matters, as were some of his ministers. He listened with great care and sympathy to Savonarola's words, and after the public audience was over, he dismissed the other ambassadors and kept the Friar with him for some time. Savonarola probably left Pisa the following day in the King's train together with those Florentines for whom the future boded ill if they remained in Pisa. The King halted at Signa, so that things in Florence might have time to settle down and the magnificent reception for his entrance might be prepared. But the Friar returned directly to the city and, contrary to his usual custom, went into the pulpit on an ordinary week-day, perhaps November 11th, to give his first sermon after the liberation. This sermon, in which no one hitherto has noted the remarkable resemblance of the exordium to that of the speech before the King, is the fourth of those under the title of *Sopra Aggeo* (*On Haggai*).

The text of these sermons, as I have shown elsewhere, must be regarded as a posthumous translation, in a somewhat expanded form, of the usual Latin drafts, which Savonarola may have filled out a little himself after they were delivered. There are other examples of a similar kind. If we wish to give entire credence to the text as we have it, we may imagine that, in view of the nature of the times and the importance of the things said in the sermons, the preacher himself may have rewritten them from his drafts and notes, in Latin of course, like the sermons on the psalm '*Quam bonus*'. In which case, Codiponte or someone else did the rest and translated it. But, quite apart from the results of my philological research, the very brevity of some of the sermons indicates their limitations. The biographer, therefore, cannot hope to gather from them all the information he would wish for, and far less to find in them all that Savonarola must have said to the Florentine people in days so full of strong feelings and significant historical events.

In the little that remains to us of this sermon given after his return from Pisa, there is nothing about his embassy to the King, of which he must have given some account to the people, as he always did after being charged with some mission by the Republic. There is no word, either, of the newly regained liberty as the beginning of a political and spiritual renovation. There is only a meagre reference to the truly miraculous ease and felicity with which this change had been accomplished: 'Be assured that it was not without cause that God cried out to you so often, and made you do so many fasts and penances, through which the ills that were to befall you have been greatly lessened. Believe me, Florence, that much blood was to have been shed in this revolution, but God tempered His hand, and gave you this first salad and let you eat it pleasantly, with mustard.' He went on to ask the Florentines to show towards the friends of the former Medici rule the same clemency that God had shown to them in this revolution; he begged that mercy should temper justice, if they wished the Lord to do likewise to them, on the eve of the entry of the French army.

In the meantime the Signoria was preparing solemn ceremonies of welcome in the city, and also munitions and defences, against the coming of the King. Fra Girolamo was laying up armaments too, but of penance and prayer. In the midst of this turmoil and apprehension, it was again decided to send him at the head of an embassy, with Bernardo Rucellai and three other citizens, 'to learn from His Majesty if it were his desire that the Pisans should act thus against the Florentines'. The credentials are dated November the 13th, but it is likely that the ambassadors did not have audience until the following day, Charles in the meantime having moved to Legnaia, where he lodged in a villa belonging to Piero Capponi. This small detail, which seems to have escaped other historians, may have had some slight influence on the final outcome of the differences with the King.

It is certainly curious that neither the anonymous writer generally referred to by me as the pseudo-Burlamacchi, who always gives the fullest possible account of everything redounding to his hero's credit, nor any other Piagnoni[1] biographer, nor Savonarola himself, tells us anything about this second embassy. It is not, therefore, surprising that some acute and learned scholars have confused it with the first one. From this I do not wish to infer that Savonarola may have refused at the last moment to go; perhaps the mission turned out to be of little importance and Charles did nothing more than give general assurances and repeat, as he frequently did during those days, his refrain: that everything would be settled 'within the great city'.

The solemn entry took place on the 17th of November. The day before, a Sunday, Savonarola again preached to the people, and we have

[1] [The 'weepers'—the name given to Savonarola's followers.]

this sermon in a rather insipid abbreviated form. After excusing himself for not being able to meditate upon it very long on account of his pre-occupation with embassies assigned to him by the Republic, he sought to furnish, as the city was doing, symbolical provisions for his mystical Ark. For this purpose his text provided him with an appropriate verse: 'tolle ex omnibus escis quæ mandi possunt' ['And take thou unto thee of all food that is eaten'] (Gen. VI, 21). Having done this, he now prepared to close the Ark. The time had come.

By entering Florence lance on hip as a sign of conquest, Charles VIII, rather than simply showing a symbol, meant to display a firm intention and, it seems, to put it into effect. This was made clear by his immediate behaviour. When the negotiations were begun which he had refused to hear of before his entry, he made demands that were immoderate and quite unacceptable to the city. He wanted to put Piero back in Florence, and, more than that, to exercise great powers in the city himself, if not that complete and absolute dominion to which he asserted he had gained the right, according to the military law of France, by entering the city as he had done. The difficulties and bitter-ness of the negotiations were such that on November the 20th and 21st it seemed there must be an open break. The rumour then spread that the King had decided to take possession of the city and put it to the sack. This may have been spread purposely by the French ministers and officers to weaken the obstinate resistance of the Florentines.

In this dangerous situation the Signoria again turned to Savon-arola, charging him to go directly to the King and tell him that the city was ready to take arms against him rather than accept such exorbitant terms; they hoped that such a resolute threat, accompanied by the prophetic warnings of the Friar, might have some effect. That day, Friday the 21st, Fra Girolamo was at table with his brethren eating bread and water, and bread and tears too, when the envoys of the Signoria came with their request. Telling the brothers to pray, he rose at once and, taking as his companion Fra Tommaso Busini, went to the Medici Palace, where Charles had his lodging. At the door he was told by the soldiers that he could not have audience, and that the sack of the city was now decided on. In spite of this, he did finally gain admission (by a miracle, according to the early biographer) to Charles's presence. Taking from his bosom a brass crucifix, he said to him (according to the pseudo-Burlamacchi): 'Most Christian King, do not honour me, but honour Him [on this cross] who is King of Kings and Lord of Lords, who grants victory to princes according to his will and justice, but who punishes unjust kings, and will ruin you and your army if you do not desist from your cruel intent regarding this city that is full of many thousands of virgins, orphans, and innocents. Their prayers will be turned against you if, in your pride, you seek that which is not yours. Let it suffice for you to have their affections, and temper your anger against this people which is faithful to you.'

These, or similar darkly menacing words, spoken by Savonarola while all the time holding the crucifix before the King's eyes, and accompanied by that mysterious fascination which emanated from him, especially when he was prophesying, had their effect. The weak and superstitious Charles answered him kindly, saying that he had come to pacify the city and not to despoil it. As for Piero, it did not seem scandalous to the King that he should return to live in Florence as a good citizen, but if they did not want him back, then nothing more should be said about his return. Charles and Savonarola reviewed together the articles that had been debated with the representatives of the Republic, and altered them in a manner more favourable to the city. Savonarola, fearing that the ministers of the King would afterwards alter the articles (as probably they did), had them, as he tells us in one of his sermons, 'repeated three times—that is, in Latin and in our own vernacular and twice more, half in Italian and half in French, by those who did not know our language well'. Thus having made sure of everything, the Friar left the King, and all arms were, for the time being, laid down.

The historians say nothing of these articles agreed on by Savonarola and the King, which certainly did not commit the city, or the King either (who, in any case, did not even feel himself bound by a solemn oath sworn some days later on the high altar of the cathedral). Yet, besides Savonarola's own testimony and the fuller, if less credible, account of an early biographer, we have other evidence of their existence. Whether Charles and his ministers altered something in the articles, despite Savonarola's precautions, or whether Savonarola had felt that, once the King had abandoned his proposal to bring back Piero de' Medici and take possession of the city himself, some royal jurisdiction was permissible, which then turned out to be unacceptable to the Republic, the fact is that differences and disagreement flared up again; and on the 22nd people were saying in the city: 'He is refusing to sign the agreement; this bodes ill.' A worse portent still was the fact that the King's men were getting the city more and more into their power, and went about confiscating any arms they could find; they even became enraged if they saw people carrying stones or pebbles, almost as though they could already imagine them raining down on their heads.

The riot that took place in Borgo Ognissanti on the 24th frightened the French and increased the effectiveness of the bold gesture of Piero Capponi, who on the 25th tore up the agreements in front of the King and threatened him with the fearful sound of the tocsin. There is no hope of ever knowing whether those agreements were the same ones Savonarola had had revised and repeated so many times on the 21st. If I am not greatly mistaken, however, the preamble contains many of the Friar's words, especially where it says that princes, being vicars and ministers of God, must use towards nations the same mercy that He uses towards men; wherefore, the King should forgive the offences done to him by his Florentine people. These are almost the very words of Savonarola's discourse as reported in the *Compendio*! At any rate, it is now evident that in the negotiations on the treaty and in the reaching of an agreement, the part played by Savonarola, if less obvious, was probably no less important than that of Piero Capponi, and that Florence owed her safety and her freedom to Savonarola no less than to him.

However, the King, having signed the articles on the 25th and given a solemn oath in Santa Maria del Fiore *sub verbo et fide regia* showed no signs of departing on the following day. Suspicion and complaint began to be voiced again in Florence. Then Fra Girolamo 'went again . . . and told him that he was not doing God's will, and that the ills which should befall others would be turned upon him. And this was believed to be the cause of his departing sooner'.

Finally, on the 28th the King left Florence and set off with his company on the road to Siena. Now that the danger from without had ended and the Florentines remained alone with themselves, other and perhaps greater dangers threatened them within: private quarrels and civil discord. Oppressors and oppressed, friends and enemies of the Medici rule, those who had expelled Piero and those who had defended him (such as Bernardo del Nero and Niccolò Ridolfi, who, after his expulsion, had ridden into the main square with a company of armed men shouting hypocritically: '*Popolo e Libertà*')—all now faced one another in a city that sixty years of tyranny and sudden liberation had left without a government and almost without a constitution. It had been easy, through the folly of Piero and the disgust of even his own followers, to overthrow the old régime, but what was being built upon the ruins was already threatening to collapse.

On the 2nd of December the bells rang for a general parliament, and the people gathered in the main square. By the normal procedure, the Medici magistrates were deposed—that is, the Council of Eight (Otto di Pratica) and the Council of Seventy—and twenty Accoppiatori were elected. Their task would be to prepare within the year for the election of the Signoria, to be drawn by lot. In the meantime they were themselves to elect the Signoria by nomination (*a mano,* as they used to say), and all the government was to be in their hands, so much so that someone called them the twenty tyrants. The worst part was that they, being men of different tendencies and some of them of equal authority, could not agree. When they came to nominating the first Signoria, it was not possible to get more than three votes for any one candidate. These differences and obstacles in the management of affairs leaked out to the people and increased their discontent.

The old suspicions between the noble and popular factions were again revived. Some wished to get rid of the leaders of the Bigi[1]—such men as Bernardo del Nero, Niccolò Ridolfi, Jacopo Salviati, Pierfilippo Pandolfini. Some, including Piero Capponi and Filippo Valori, though they had been responsible for the expulsion of Piero, were afraid to remain at the mercy of those who had suffered when the Medici came to power in 1434. There were others, the lowest of the populace, who yesterday had been eager to enjoy the games, festivities, and liberality of the Medici, and to shout '*Palle*' (the Medici arms) under the windows of the Palace in Via Larga, and today were ready to pillage the homes of the relatives and friends of the Medici, as they had already done with Piero's. And just as readily, with the sudden impulsive cruelty of a mob, they would have shed the blood of the Medici partisans. It was probably that very same element which had slaughtered the Pazzi, who had conspired against the Medici. According to the unanimous opinion of the most observant contempor-

[1] [The supporters of the Medici.]

aries, it seemed almost impossible that blood would not be shed. Then Girolamo Savonarola rose up between the rival factions and private enmities.

In the sermons given on the 30th of November, the first Sunday of Advent, immediately following the King's departure, and on the 7th and 8th (or perhaps 8th and 9th) of December, he merely gave, and asked all to give, thanks to God for the danger the city had escaped. He ordered that extraordinary alms be gathered for the poor, asking that even the gold and silver of the churches should be used, if necessary, for, he said, charity is above all canons and beyond all laws. Finally, he recommended that shops should be reopened and trade revived so that no one should be without work.

In his sermon on the 13th of December he bitterly rebuked the Florentines for having shed the blood of Antonio di Bernardo, who had been executed the day before to satisfy popular hatred; he was indeed universally hated, but was guilty of nothing more than having been the tool of the Medici. Savonarola had hardly ever preached on other than holy days, but from this time on, as the need became greater, he preached every day. His sermons were attended by immense crowds of thirteen or fourteen thousand people, such as had never before been seen in Florence.

Every day, in that stormy atmosphere, the powerful voice of the Friar hammered away at the Florentines to pacify them and persuade them, above all, of the need for two things: universal peace which would reconcile friends and enemies of the Medici rule, and a wise reform of the state which would remove all suspicions between noble and popular factions, command the respect and confidence of all, and be the foundation of a new city to be built in Florence, the city of God. 'O Florence,' he cried, 'I cannot tell you all that is in my heart, for you are not yet ready to bear it. Oh, if I could only tell you all! You would see that I am like a new jar of full new wine and tightly closed, so that it boils everywhere within and cannot escape.' From this seething vessel, whence in the past had come prophecies of foreboding—'for he will not always be the prophet of evil'—there came that morning the great promise: 'Hear, O Florence, what I say to you; hear that God has inspired me . . . : from you will issue the reform of all Italy.'

As for the form of government, which was to be the foundation of his republic ordered in the best civic and Christian manner, he himself proposed from the pulpit that they should copy the Venetians. To achieve this, he suggested that each of the sixteen *gonfalonieri* (magistrates) should propose a form of government; then the four best of these should be chosen, and the Signoria should have the final choice among the four. While completely absorbed with this idea, he began to expound in his sermons, beginning with the fourteenth in this series, the Book of Haggai. Nothing could have seemed more opportune and fuller of symbols, for Haggai was the prophet who spoke to the chosen people just after they had been freed from the Babylonian captivity, the man who was sent by God that they might begin to rebuild the Temple that had been destroyed. 'So I say unto you, O Florence, now it is time to rebuild the house of God and to renovate His city. . . . God said unto Haggai: "Do you want my house to lie waste?" So now God wishes Church and city to be rebuilt, the city whence shall go forth the light of reform.'

He continued to emphasize the need for harmony among citizens, and mercy to be shown to the friends of the Medici. He knew that there were plans to deal with Ser Giovanni delle Riformagioni, Piero's right-hand man, in the same way as Antonio di Bernardo; and the words of the Friar, well aware that he was thereby making himself unpopular, succeeded in staying the hand of the executioner. 'Peace, I say, peace, Florence,' he cried. 'You who reject peace do so only because of hatred conceived in the past and because you were of this or that party. If you make peace, you will be the friends of God, who wants only peace, and so God will watch over your city . . .; and if you will not make this peace, then remember what I say to you: it will mean your ultimate destruction. And so I say to you, peace, peace.'

Day by day the miracle was achieved. One by one, all the things ordered or suggested by the Friar from the pulpit were put into effect, down to preserving the life of Ser Giovanni, who was confined in the fortress of Volterra, though many continued to resent this mercy forced on them by Savonarola. 'On the 19th many drafts for a government were brought to the Palace; each *gonfaloniere* came with one, as the Friar had said.' These drafts were whittled down to four, which were then put into better form respectively by the councils of Twelve, Twenty, Ten, and Eight. When it was decided that the best of these was that prepared by the Ten, so great was the authority of Savonarola that they did not wish to make the final selection without his approval. So the Friar came to the Palace, and the constitution was read over to him, and he approved it with words of wisdom, saying that any defects in it would become apparent and could be corrected in the course of time. And so this proposal was approved. Briefly, there was to be a Great Council, by which all the officials of the city would be elected; this Council was to elect a smaller one with eighty members, none of them to be less than forty years of age. This smaller council was to consider and approve all the acts of the Signoria before they were given final approval in the larger Council.

In this wise law, which imitated the form of the Venetian government as closely as a popular government can resemble an aristocratic one, Savonarola had probably a greater part than appears from the histories and even from the pages of this book—through his words uttered from the pulpit, as well as those spoken privately within the walls of the Palace. Some have thought to minimize the credit due to him by hinting that the Venetian pattern was suggested to him by Paolantonio Soderini, out of hatred for Piero Capponi and other nobles who wanted a government restricted within their own hands. But this is nonsense, for we give the Friar credit, not for inventing this form, but for its selection and adoption by the city. Neither Soderini nor any other citizen would at that time have had sufficient authority to impose such a choice upon the councils. For this, praise is due to Savonarola; and historians and major political writers have given him that praise in good measure.

These provisions were approved on December the 24th and constituted the main but not the only reform of the state, which was to be perfected in the following year. On the same day a law against murder was promulgated, to restrain the pursuit of private feuds; another against sodomy ('for which Florence is infamous throughout all Italy'), which Savonarola had vehemently called for in his sermon of December the 14th ; and still others, 'all at the Friar's demand'. They sought to obey him even in the promptness of their action and in the choice of the day. He had said in his sermon of December the 21st, while urging such provisions: 'At least let it be before Christmas Eve.' The road of reform was long, and the goal still far off; passions had been quieted but not extinguished. Differences over the form of the new state, and the cursed Florentine suspiciousness had not been swept away, but merely silenced for a time before the immense authority and meritorious deeds of the great Friar. And yet the change that had come about seemed none the less miraculous.

On Christmas Day it was as though an entirely new atmosphere had come over Florence. Savonarola expressed from the pulpit his satisfaction with the laws passed on the previous day. Taking up his text again at the verse '*In die vigesimo quarto*' ['On the twenty-fourth day'] (which again could hardly have been more appropriate), he was able to tell the people that, just as the rebuilding of the temple was accomplished according to the will of God, and 'on the 24th of the month they began to build . . . so you, O Florence, have begun on that date to lay the foundations of your new government, and you have changed your shape, for you are no longer the same Florence as before. All this you may know is the work of God, and you have done well to make this beginning and this foundation, as I exhorted you to do in my previous sermons, at least before this solemn festival we are now celebrating. You may know by many signs that all this comes from God. . . . And you see how every day the Scripture more and more conforms to all that happens and to your own work.'

How could the Florentines fail now to give their faith to this man whose prophecies of misfortune, which before they had not believed, had all come true? Should they not believe him now when he uttered far more welcome prophecies? It was difficult to disbelieve such things, far too difficult for those who saw them come true bit by bit under their very eyes, saw the city flourish miraculously as if to fulfil the promise of its own name. Reverence for Savonarola, which was already great when the King of France came and even greater when he departed, now surpassed what was due to any mortal man. The Ferrarese ambassador wrote to the Duke: 'He is revered and worshipped like a saint.'

Broken and almost worn out in body, but quiet and contented in mind, Savonarola was able to take leave of his people for a few days of much needed rest. This he did in his sermon on the 27th, announcing that for the next few days another would come to preach in his stead. But first he who had cried out so much in recent days against the government of one man, though he recognized with St. Thomas that this was excellent in theory, wished to give one monarch, one ruler, to Florence: Jesus. 'I have told you before, it is not better for every city or country to have a single head to govern it. . . . Now, Florence, God wants to give you a head and a king for your government. And he is Christ.' With this election Savonarola concluded his first efforts to reform the state of Florence.

He set a seal on his leave-taking with the following words: 'Now our ship . . . moves towards the port—that is, towards the peace that Florence will enjoy after her tribulations. New and old officials, work all together for this universal peace, and see that good laws are made to establish and consolidate your government. And the first must be this: no one shall call himself *Bianco* or *Bigio,* but all shall be united in one party. . . . Let there be punishment for those who again use these terms *Bianchi* and *Bigi.* Do this, for it is a matter of great moment! . . . If you do this that I tell you, Florence will really be at peace.' To give the city that quiet and fruitful harmony, Fra Girolamo again went to the Palace on St. Sylvester's Day to discuss this 'universal peace' among the citizens. He could not have concluded the memorable year 1494 in a manner more worthy or more in accord with all his words and deeds.

'Now our ship . . . moves towards the port—that is, towards the peace that Florence will enjoy after her tribulations.' Hardly a week earlier the diarist Landucci, a good man of the people and a faithful mirror of their spirit, recalling the fears expressed in preceding days, had made this note for December the 21st: 'We were all still much afraid, for the citizens could not agree. Some wanted one thing, and some another; and if it had not been for the Friar, it would have come to bloodshed.' Parenti says the same in other words, and so do all the other contemporary chroniclers and historians. Guicciardini writes, too, with his greater political acumen: 'He alone stopped these movements and impulses.'

In so short a space of time, therefore, Girolamo Savonarola had done Florence this other incomparable service.

Chapter 11

THE DEATH OF SAVONAROLA'S
MOTHER AND OF PICO

⤬⤬⤬⤬⤬⤬⤬⤬⤬⤬⤬⤬⤬⤬⤬⤬⤬⤬⤬⤬⤬⤬⤬⤬⤬⤬⤬⤬⤬⤬⤬

Now that Savonarola is alone in his cell for the days of his brief rest, alone with himself and with the burden of his triumph, with his past and his future, we would like to be able to pass through those walls and into his heart. For, if the thoughts of this servant of God seem open and manifest to all in his actions, in his writings, and especially in his sermons, into which he poured the fullness of his heart, the secret feelings of the man were, and still are, jealously hidden from us.

Occasionally in moments of abandon, when he hears boiling about him the waves of opposition and persecution, we shall hear him remembering the day when, at the sound of that Biblical voice '*Egredere de terra tua et de cognatione tua*', he left his home and his family; we shall hear him recalling with nostalgia his early convent years, when, heeding another call, he passed from that great peace into this turbulent sea. Nothing more. Once he has recovered from these rare moments of sentimental weakness, which make us love him even better than certain of his courageous impulses, it is impossible to penetrate further into the secrets of this fervent soul.

We would like him to be more human, to share in human weakness and human passion, although we realize that the fault is in ourselves. At least we would like him to be more clearly sensitive to family affections. No one would dare to say that he was insensitive to them simply because, as the 'militant knight of Jesus Christ' and a good soldier, he subordinated such feelings to the discipline and fired them with the spirit of that service, stripping them of their human and carnal form and transfiguring them in God.

Girolamo has already appeared to us in this guise in certain harsh expressions of his letters to his mother. But under the rough exterior it is not difficult to find a restrained but tender affection, consonant with his sensitive and passionate nature. He must have loved her very dearly, and he resembled her in many ways; both strong and sensitive, she had shown so well that she understood him, had been the first to perceive his mystical vocation on the eve of his departure, and had shed so many tears for him. It must have been a severe blow when news reached him of her death on the 15th or 16th of November, 1494.

The news must have come to him shortly after the entry of the King of France, when Florence was full of French soldiers, and of fear and uncertainty—when, according to the early biographer, 'he fed on bread and tears'. It must have been another sorrow to bear, even if the wound was healed with the comforts of faith, or perhaps ignored amid the intense emotions, the anguish, and the preoccupations of the hour. No word has come down to us in his writings of this silent sorrow. Many months later, preaching before the people and telling how he left his father's house, he said with his usual pious frankness: 'My mother wept for many years. I let her weep. It is enough that she must know now that she was wrong.' This was his public funeral oration on his mother's tomb.

Almost at the same time that he heard of the loss of his mother, Savonarola was deprived of his dearest friend, Giovanni Pico della Mirandola, who died in Florence on the 17th of November, the day of the entry of the King of France. The loss of this universal genius, 'the phoenix among intellects', who enjoyed a tremendous reputation that time has somewhat lessened, would in other circumstances have moved the Florentines deeply. But few noticed, and few cared amid such agitation —just as we have neglected him momentarily in these pages, despite our intention to be as strict as possible in following the proper chronology of events.

The friendship between the young prince and the great Friar, which we have seen kindled at Reggio during the Dominican Chapter of 1482 (if not, in fact, in Ferrara in 1479) and stimulated in Florence in 1484 and 1486, and then becoming the fateful instrument of Savonarola's return to this city, had continued to burn ever brighter, especially after 1491, after the triumphs of the Friar as an orator. Savonarola's powerful fascination and forceful personality had great influence on the noble nature of the Count; and if it is perhaps not true that they persuaded him to renounce his ideas and led him back to perfect orthodoxy, it is certain that they exalted his mystical tendencies and increased his religious fervour in his last years.

On his side, Fra Girolamo was conquered by Pico's gentle nature and by certain spiritual affinities they shared, as well as by his immense learning, of which the Friar once said that 'in mind alone, he was greater than St. Augustine'. But he esteemed Pico above all, in connection with his plan for a centre of the study of Oriental languages, to be set up in San Marco in the service of the great work of converting the infidels. Pico used to go often to the Greek library in San Marco to dispute with Savonarola, and there would be, among others, Politian, Girolamo Benivieni, and that Pietro Crinito who has left us in his *De honesta disciplina* some record of these meetings, which were given the name of *Academia Marciana*.

In these disputations Pico may sometimes have smiled at the uncompromising rigour with which the Friar condemned Plato and Aristotle, but there must have been evident between them a common contempt for the paganism of the humanists, and certain common scholastic tendencies, though different in form and intensity; just as also they had in common the ardour of faith and even, one might say, a similar way of showing it; for it is said of Pico that 'with fiery countenance and flashing eyes . . . filled with heavenly passion, and fired by divine inspiration, he did not dispute, but spoke prophetically'.

Considering the genius and pious disposition of Pico, he seemed to Savonarola the most miraculous catch he could ever make with his mystical nets, and one that might increase enormously the reputation of his labours if he could succeed in drawing Pico into the Dominican Order and get him to take the habit in San Marco. Finding him much inclined to this course, at least in words, he unceasingly urged and incited him, and even threatened him with divine punishment if he resisted that vocation. But Pico, as Domenico Benivieni tells us in a Savonarolan apology of his, more than once 'came halfway to taking orders, and then drew back'.

A hitherto unknown note by a famous companion of Savonarola,

Fra Giovanni Sinibaldi—who, in this and other notes that increase the historical value of a copy of Benivieni's apology, shows himself to be well informed on the secrets of San Marco—states that the Count behaved in this matter with some dissimulation (but perhaps it was only timidity or weakness, which led him to promise more than he intended or was able to carry out), and that, especially after his stay in Ferrara in the spring and summer of 1492, he had drawn back from his religious commitments. From the same note we learn also (and it is a very strange and unexpected thing, considering the marvels of the 'saintly life' he is supposed to have been leading at the time) that he had a concubine. Which was perhaps not the least of the reasons for his resistance to the pressing invitations of the Friar. According to Sinibaldi, Savonarola confided this matter to Fra Roberto Ubaldini.

In any case, nothing interrupted or disturbed in the following years the habitual companionship of Pico and Savonarola; there are good reasons for believing that between the end of 1493 and the early part of 1494 Savonarola helped his friend ('*consilio et iudicio*', we are told by Giovanni Nesi) during the compilation of his *Disputationes in Astrologiam*. It is certain, at least, as I have recently shown, that about this time Pico was reading or passing on to the Friar the first books of this work, which had not yet been circulated among Florentine scholars. In fact, in the drafts of sermons for Advent 1494, prepared by Savonarola the summer before, there is a textual quotation from Pico's book.

On the 16th of November Savonarola was with Fra Roberto Ubaldini at the bedside of his dying friend. After having witnessed a codicil in which Pico declared his last will, Savonarola at last received his vows, and at last had the joy of giving him with his own hands the Dominican habit. On that day houses and palaces were already gay with blue hangings embroidered with the golden lilies of France; and when, on the next day, the sick man rendered up his noble spirit, the standards of the King were entering the city. And so was accomplished a prediction of Camilla Rucellai, who had said in 1492 that, with the encouragement of the Friar, Pico would take the habit 'at the time of the lilies'; and this had been taken at the time to mean the spring.

A few days after Pico's death, on the 23rd of November, when Charles was still in Florence, Fra Girolamo had given his Sunday sermon, and after it he turned suddenly to the congregation saying that he had a secret to reveal. He then gave a brief funeral oration on his friend, 'who had he lived longer, would have outshone with his writings all other men of the past eight centuries'; and he went on to speak of the Count's vocation and of his obstinate resistance to it. He also told how he had threatened Pico and prayed God to punish him a little, but not as much as He had done, depriving him of the great glory he would have known had he lived. Finally he said that it had been revealed to him that, by virtue of the alms the Count had given and the prayers of the brethren, his soul had not been condemned to the eternal fires of hell, but was expiating his sins in purgatory. All who had known him, and especially those who had been benefited by him, should therefore assist him with their prayers. This also was a strange funeral oration, but strange, I would say, rather for the words spoken than for those manifestly left unspoken, which now seem less obscure in the light of Sinibaldi's note.

If Savonarola dwelt a good deal during those days of meditation on the two losses he had suffered, both affecting him deeply if in different ways, other equally painful thoughts must also have troubled him, ones that were perhaps more pressing, such as the thought of the great struggle just begun which would flare up again after the brief truce. These are not merely a biographer's inventions or fancies, for we find such thoughts, with the doubts and hesitations that accompanied them, already present in germ in the sermons preached immediately before his period of rest, and they return with greater force and anxiety in the sermons he preaches immediately after.

We found similar thoughts and doubts in him at the beginning of his prophetic preaching, when, having embarked on so perilous a course, we saw him more than once on the point of turning back to the shore. Now that he had embarked on another no less stormy sea, he felt exactly the same. Like all the traits that bring us closer to this great and extraordinarily severe man, this human reaction of dismay in him is good to see; it arose not from cowardice, but from a clear vision of the bitter struggle on which he was entering, and of the mortal risks that it implied. His courageous actions yet to come would be all the greater for it.

The Friar had too keen a mind not to understand what it meant to involve himself in political affairs with the Florentines, '*ingenia magis acria quam matura*' ['more intelligent than wise'], as the Florentine

Petrarch knew them, and as the Florentine Guicciardini recognized them to be, suspicious and intolerant, factious and changeable. The dangers were especially great for him, a friar, and in times seething with strong passions on account of the recent changes. In his last sermon he had deplored the factions of the *Bianchi* and *Bigi,* the former partisans of liberty, and the latter supporters of the old Medici rule; these, who had taken up again with a touch of Florentine humour the names of the ancient parties of *Bianchi* and *Neri,* were the two great divisions into which the city was now split. For, though probably already at that time the most enthusiastic followers of the Friar had begun to be called *Frateschi* (Friar's Men), his good works were too great and too recent for even the Florentines to forget or weary of them, or become ungrateful. All in those days, whether Bianchi or Bigi, were more or less Frateschi.

But a people that on the eve of the age of princes continued to give its own councillors office for only two months at a time, so that they might not fall into disfavour and suspicion, could not, unanimously, have tolerated much longer the domination of a foreign friar. Some would resent his very interference in the matters of the Republic, others object to his severe moral reforms, others to his clemency towards the Bigi, others to his championing of the popular state and the humble folk, others to his enormous following, still others to the very benefits he had conferred on them. Then the city would be split into two great divisions: the Frateschi, who later, as contempt and bitterness increased between the parties, would be called the *Piagnoni,* and against them those who on account of their rabid factiousness would be most appropriately called the *Arrabbiati* [Enraged]. Outside these two great sects, the Bigi, forgetting that they owed their safety to the Friar, to whom at first they were favourable, little by little drew away from him and finally opposed him.

With such divisions already in existence though as yet hardly visible, Savonarola must have considered how on his account civil discord must increase, though he had done so much to cure it; and, considering this, he could not fail to grieve and waver in his purpose. But he must have thought, too, that this purpose of his of instituting a good republic was an excellent one, and that there was no other way he could achieve, for the glory of God and the benefit of mankind, the planned reform of Florence, of Italy, and of the Church. What it all amounted to, then, was the division of the city into two great, two everlasting parties of the good and the bad; and the Lord had shown him the way, saying: '*Non veni pacem mittere, sed gladium.*'

There was the fact, too, that he was risking his own way of life and, above all, that peace he had sought in the cloister, his meditations and contemplation, his studies and prayers. It would have been better for him to leave Florence, which he had twice saved, after he had given her a wise form of government and halted the first upsurge of civic hatred. It would have been splendid to depart just as he had come— he, the founder of the popular Florentine state, leaving on foot with his tattered cape and nothing else but a stick and a breviary.

A good opportunity was offered him just then of withdrawing from the fray. He had recently been ordered to go to Lucca to preach for the coming Lent. He had now no superiors who could order him to preach in this or that convent of the same Congregation, as had been the case when he was subject to the Lombards; yet this strange order had come from Rome, and, even more unusual, direct from the Pope. The Florentine Signoria, in fact, wrote to the Pope on December the 28th, in alarm at the idea that the city might lose her prophet. There has been a good deal of conjecture about this papal order. Some early biographers and, more especially, modern writers have seen in it the work of the Arrabbiati; but even to them it must have seemed odd that anyone in Florence should have been conspiring to get rid of him in the early days of December, when his influence in affairs of state was not yet so direct or decisive, and when there was general gratitude for his recent services, and all had need of him in some way or another. The truth of the matter, which has become clear to me only after correctly establishing the dates of certain documents hitherto wrongly interpreted by archivists and biographers, is that this time, at least, the Arrabbiati have been wrongly accused. It was all the doing of the elders of Lucca, who, ardently desiring to have Savonarola preach in their city, and not satisfied with the promises he had made them, had had the idea of having him ordered to come by nothing less than an Apostolic Brief, which was probably obtained through Felino Sandei, a papal 'auditor' who was a Ferrarese by birth but of Lucchese origin.

Whatever the underlying cause, this was a propitious occasion for withdrawing from the battle, and a few days later Savonarola tells us that he did consider it. Indeed, he probably thought of it more than once, but he always rejected the easy temptation that would assure his own safety but spell certain ruin for all his work. Though it would have been splendid to go off in the way I have said, at the height of his glory, and accompanied by the blessings, hymns of praise, and deep regrets of a whole people, it was even finer to affront the hatred, the curses, and the contempt, and fight, and if necessary die, for the work he had undertaken.

A few days before, in his sermon for December the 21st, with these thoughts already in his mind, he had told the parable of a young man who had left his home and gone to the sea, and there at a port had begun to fish; and as his skill and liking for the task increased, he was given a boat to go out to sea and take bigger fish; and he went out so far that he found himself, still fishing, on the high seas; and there, because he could no longer see the coast, he began to complain to the master of the boat who had brought him out so far. Savonarola then said:

O Florence, the young man who went out on the high seas, and complains that he is out of sight of the haven, stands here before you. To me it was told: Come, *egredere de terra tua,* leave thy home and thy land, leave everything. And I was led to the port —that is, to the religious life, which is the safe and sure haven for all who seek their salvation. I came to this port when I was twenty-three years of age. Two things I loved beyond all others, and it was they led me to this port: freedom and peace. To keep my freedom I never took a wife, and to obtain peace I fled from the world and came to this port of religion, where I found freedom; and here I was able to do just as I wished, for I wanted and desired to do nothing but that which was told or commanded me.

I would not have wished to be a priest merely for my own greater peace; but because I wanted to do as I was told, for this I felt to be my freedom and my peace, I was led to become a priest. And so having reached that happy haven, I looked upon the waters of the sea of this world, and I saw that many fish swam around there, and, desiring to fish for them, I began to take a few small ones with my hook—that is, to draw with my preaching some souls to the port and the way of salvation. And because this pleased me well enough, the Lord set me in a ship and took me to fish in the high seas, and gently and gradually he brought me here, as you see; so that, since I have come into the high seas, I see no port to which I might turn back, and where I may again find peace. *Undique sunt angustiæ*: troubles surround me on every side, and I cannot see what I should do. . . .

O Lord, whither hast Thou led me? I say with Jeremiah: *Seduxisti me, Domine, et seductus sum*—Lord, thou hast deceived me, and I was deceived. *Fortior me fuisti et invaluisti*—Thou art stronger than I, and hast prevailed. I, for wanting to catch these fish for You that they might be Yours, find myself on these high seas, and I see no port to which I might return to find my peace again. *Væ mihi, mater mea*—woe is me, O my mother. *Quare me genuisti virum rixæ et virum discordiæ in universa terra?*—wherefore came I forth out of the womb to see labour, and sorrow throughout the world? I was free and at peace. Now I am everyone's slave. I see everywhere war and discord coming upon me. . . .

You see our ship where she is now, and yet the end of the voyage on which the Lord takes her is not in sight. Last night I disputed with Him, and I will tell you part of our discussion. He exhorted me to keep on my course, and I said: 'Nay, Lord, take me back to the port and give me back my peace.' And He answered: 'There is no turning back: dost thou not see the contrary wind that drives thee on?' and I said: 'Because Thou, Lord, dost not wish it, yet Thou art just, tell me if I may dispute with Thee awhile, though I am dust and ashes and Thou art Lord of all. Tell me, if I must go on over the seas of the world fishing for Thee, why here rather than elsewhere? What have I to do with Florence? I was born, as Thou knowest, in Ferrara and brought up there, and not in Florence.' The Lord answered and said: 'Dost thou not remember having read of the man who came down from Jerusalem to Jericho, and was assailed and wounded by thieves on the road, and there passed by men of his own people, and none of them helped him, but only the Samaritan, a foreigner and a stranger, cared for him? Dost thou not know also that it is written "*quod nemo propheta est acceptus in patria sua*"? That is why thou, a stranger, hast come to preach here, outside thine own country.' I answered the Lord reverently, and said: 'Lord, I am not satisfied with this. I am happy to preach in the ordinary way to reprove vice and further the cause of virtue, here in Florence or wherever

Thou wilt. But what have I to do with the state of Florence, to preach on it? . . .'

Then the Lord showed him how, while attending mainly to things of the spirit, he must 'establish all those things that preserve and sustain the spirit, and the things by which the spirit is governed'; and how he must do this in Florence: 'to make her virtuous, create for her a state that will preserve her virtue.' Savonarola then asked Him what would be his reward in the next world for such great labours, and he was given a wonderful promise. But when he asked further what his reward would be in this life, the Lord answered: 'The servant is not greater than his Master. Thou hast read how after I preached to the Jews, they crucified Me. This and no other shall be thy fate.' 'Oh Lord,' I said then, "*da mihi hoc martirium*—grant that I may die for Thee, as Thou didst die for me.'

Once again a divine revelation or miraculous human foresight had rent the veil of his cruel destiny; and once again, without shrinking, he went towards it with brave and Christian determination.

Chapter 12

THE STRUGGLE AGAINST THE
ARRABBIATI AND THE TIEPIDI

‹ON the 1st of January, 1495, the new Signoria took office: and it was a joyful sight to see the whole of the Piazza de’ Signori full of citizens, unlike on previous occasions, thanking God who had given this popular government to Florence, and delivered them from servitude; and it was all the work of the Friar.’ This delight in their new-found liberty, in a people greeting the entry of their freely elected Signoria ‘as a wondrous thing’, is noted in the diary of Landucci. The whole population no less than he acknowledged their debt of gratitude to Savonarola for all this, or at least for the possibility of celebrating it so happily. Yet, from this same new Signoria, Fra Girolamo received his first affront and his first bitter reward.

The head of this government, as gonfalonier of justice, was Filippo Corbizzi, ‘a man of little worth, authority and virtue’, who had been elected by the Accoppiatori precisely for his pusillanimity, a quality then much appreciated. This man, whom we shall soon find among the leading Arrabbiati, immediately gained a following of the precursors of this sect and of those who were dissatisfied with Fra Girolamo’s authority. Such discontent, at first entirely negligible, germinated in the minds of some citizens at the beginning of 1495. We can distinguish between the true causes of this discontent and the pretexts that were falsely put about to cover them up and to blacken the reputation of the Friar among those who otherwise would have been

106

inclined to praise, rather than blame him for his efforts, which aroused the hatred only of a few factious people.

Among the true causes of hatred for Savonarola, besides the suspicion and displeasure with which some people began to view the considerable influence of a friar in matters of state, was the bitter disappointment that Savonarola with his 'universal peace' not only deprived them of their longed-for revenge against their enemies, but intended to give a full pardon to the supporters of the Medici, whom they would have preferred to punish and remove from office. Another source of discontent was a reform that Savonarola warmly promoted and almost dictatorially imposed: which was to qualify with a right of appeal the authority of the so-called 'six beans' whereby, with only six votes, the Signoria could tyrannically, at their pleasure, dispose of the life and possessions of any citizen. Finally, we must also mention the dislike of the *ottimati* [rich and powerful citizens] for that broad popular government of which the Friar was the principal initiator.

Among the pretexts were rumours of understandings between the Friar and Piero de' Medici, though these were neither true nor even likely, and quite obviously arose from a wickedly false interpretation of his Christian and civic generosity towards the Medici faction. Savonarola's adversaries had to put this interpretation on it because they could not have gained popular support against him by condemning his programme of 'universal peace'. Then there was the calumny, arising from the same sources but even more absurd, that Savonarola had hidden in San Marco the treasures of the Medici family and of their partisans, treasures that the magistrates were seeking in order to confiscate them. Substance was given to this rumour by the fact that, according to information extracted by torture from a witness under interrogation, fifteen hundred florins had been found in the convent, which had been put there by the hated Ser Giovanni delle Riformagioni before the entry of the French. Yet all the citizens habitually deposited their possessions in the convents when disturbances were feared, and Savonarola could not know about every individual deposit made, nor, in all probability, was he under any obligation to report them if he did. He was even accused by some of having enriched himself with these treasures, he who wished never to possess anything of his own, and who had even refused alms from his friend Giovanni Pico to relieve the poverty of his family!

Such were the causes and pretexts. Now the effects. At first the expressions of discontent were hardly noticeable and did not go beyond the various malicious rumours, which grew louder and more frequent as Savonarola, who had resumed his sermons in the cathedral at Epiphany, insisted on painful subjects, especially the 'six beans' and 'universal peace'; so much so that many citizens began to be scandalized, and to say: 'This wretched friar is going to ruin us all.' The gratitude of the Florentines had lasted so long! And Savonarola in his sermon of January the 11th, commented bitterly: 'You may know in your sorrows how fleeting are the things of this world, and how soon the glory of this world passes away. Take the example of myself, who a few days ago was called the father of this city and its prophet, and now suddenly I am called its robber.'

At that time the Arrabbiati (we may now begin to call them by this name, which suits them all too well, although it had not yet been used by writers), plotting how they might diminish the authority of Fra Girolamo, had the idea of getting another friar to oppose him (thus applying a Medici maxim under a popular régime). There had recently arrived in Florence as a kind of envoy of the Duke of Milan a preacher of a certain reputation—that Fra Domenico da Ponzo who, as we saw, assured the people of the saintliness and prophecies of Savonarola during Lent 1492. 'They applied to him, therefore—and as he was not a monk of very holy life, they had little difficulty in suborning him and rousing him against Fra Girolamo.' With brazen impudence, and in spite of his former expressions of enthusiasm which the Florentines must still have remembered, he began to preach against Savonarola, inferring that he told untruths out of factiousness and prophesied falsely because 'there were no longer prophets, nor could ever be'. Perhaps here Ponzo was speaking from experience, for he himself had prophesied in Lent 1492 that within a particular month blood would flow in the streets of Florence, saying that he would stake his life on this happening. Fortunately for him, the Signoria did not take him at his word; instead of holding him as a hostage, as he had suggested, it deported him from Florentine territory. Yet the risk he had run must have made him detest and disbelieve prophecies ever after.

Together with him the Arrabbiati approached the gonfalonier Corbizzi, who, as he was a man of the type we have described, and foolish into the bargain, was easily won over to their designs. This man, then—and here we may discern the influence of Ponzo—ordered for the 18th of January a disputation before the Signoria, calling to it, besides Ponzo and Savonarola, Fra Tommaso da Rieti, Prior of the Dominicans of Santa Maria Novella (conventuals, and consequently opposed to those of San Marco), a theologian of some reputation, and also several other priests, and those citizens who had a hand in the affair. Tommaso da Rieti spoke first. Proposing as his text the passage of St. Paul: '*Nemo militans Deo implicat se negotiis sæcularibus*' ['No man that warreth entangleth himself with the affairs of this world'], he reproached Savonarola for his interference in matters of government, and then went on to attack him for his prophecies. But Fra Girolamo—whom the Signoria had sent for 'on matters of great importance', without further explanation, hoping to catch him unprepared—replied briefly in his usual quiet manner. Turning to Fra Tommaso, he said that he, a Dominican, proved the truth of the words of the Scripture: '*Filii matris meæ pugnaverunt contra me*' ['My mother's children were angry with me']; and he added dryly that he knew very well what he was saying, and that the future would bear him out. The pseudo-Burlamacchi has him say many other things that he probably did not say, but I believe he really did quote those words of the Evangelist, which were so often on his lips: '*Ego palam locutus sum mundo . . . et in occulto locutus sum nihil*' ['I spake openly to the world, and in secret have I said nothing'], adding that this was also what he would continue to do, and that he would answer everything in his next sermon. Then, bowing his head and wrapping himself in his cloak, he departed.

Two days later, on the feast of St. Sebastian, he went into the pulpit to answer his opponents. After the exposition of the psalm that was his text, he suddenly said: 'Now, Florence, I want to say something to you. Florence, I will not preach to you any more about the six beans.' Then, without any direct allusion to the improvised disputation in the Palace or mentioning any names, he began to say in a polite way what a fool the gonfalonier Corbizzi was, remarking: 'You know that in that office we do not always find the wisest citizens.' This must have been very amusing for the Florentines, who knew Corbizzi all too well. He then went on to deal with the great theologian of Santa Maria Novella: 'You of the Order of St. Dominic, who say that we ought not to involve ourselves in matters of government, you have not read aright. Go and read the chronicles of the Order of St. Dominic, read what our founder did in Lombardy in matters of state. And read, too, what St. Peter Martyr did here in Florence, when he intervened to unify and pacify this state, so that the conspiracy to murder him was made in this very city. And the Cardinal Messer Latino of our Order was the one who made peace between the Guelphs and the Ghibellines. St. Catherine of Siena made peace in this state at the time of Pope Gregory. How often did the Archbishop Antoninus go to the Palace to prevent the enacting of iniquitous laws? But tell me, who are those who must give peace and unity to the city of Florence? Certainly not those whose passions are involved. Therefore, it must be someone in between, and not swayed by passion.'

He ended by proposing that there should be a conference of citizens and also of priests, but that they should be good ones; for, he added with another stab at the two who had opposed him at the Palace, 'there really are good men who love the truth'. Finally, alluding to his forthcoming sermons in Lucca, he said, that in the meantime, as he saw many who were angry with him, he intended to give their anger room and imitate Jesus, who on occasions, for similar reasons, left one city and went to another.

In the next sermon, on Sunday the 25th of January, having again uttered his prophetic threats as in the past, and again recommended the conclusion of universal peace and the completion of the reforms of the state, he took his leave of his people, not without a sense of sorrow: 'I want to be a friar; I give up the state, and no longer wish to concern myself with the six beans. I will go away to my cell, and do not send again for me, for if the King of France comes, or the Emperor, I shall not come. You in your councils, do as God inspires you, and do not draw me in in any way, for now I must cede to anger. I shall go to Lucca, and then perhaps farther afield. Pray God to give me grace to go and preach to the infidels, for I greatly desire to do so.'

It is easy to believe the diarist Landucci when he remarks, with his usual diligence, that this announcement 'displeased the people greatly'. Was the reformer of Florence to depart, then *re infecta*? Everything at the time seemed to indicate that he would, as no satisfactory answer, perhaps none at all, had been received to the Signoria's pressing entreaty to the Pope on the 28th of December, 1494, which we referred to above. No better fate seems to have befallen, at least up to the 25th of January, the fresh approach made by the *Dieci* [Council of

Ten] in a letter written to the Florentine ambassador in Rome on the 8th of the month. But Savonarola did not go to Lucca.

Nardi writes that the revocation of the order from Rome was easily obtained, and we are very willing to believe him because, whoever had asked for that order, the Pope could not then have had motives or commitments pressing enough to make him resist the importunate requests of a government and an entire people concerning such a trifling matter. It is true that the elders of Lucca, having heard something of the opposition of the Florentine Signoria, renewed the struggle over the disputed Prophet of San Marco by writing agitated letters to their fellow-citizen Giovanni Gigli at the Court of Rome, and to Felino Sandei, asking that the order contained in the Brief should be upheld in spite of all the efforts to have it revoked. At any rate, whether easily or not, the revocation came, leaving the Lucchese still with their strong desire to hear Savonarola preach.

With the sermon of the 25th of January there came to an end that brief and fervid mission in which the Friar had attempted to give final perfection to the reform of the state, and had had least fortune with the most important issues. In twenty days he had given seven sermons, the most notable being that of the 13th of January, called the sermon of the renewal of the Church, in which he had retold in detail the story of his prophetic preaching. This sermon enjoyed considerable fame, and was the first of the Friar's sermons to be printed, and that practically at once. The two preceding it, on the other hand, and the four that followed it were not published until 1515, collected in a single volume with all the others given by Savonarola during the various religious festivities of the year 1495: that is, those given before and after the Lenten sermons, which were published by themselves. These sermons of the feasts throughout the year go under the title, consecrated I am not sure whether by use or abuse, of *Prediche sopra i Salmi* [*Sermons on the Psalms*], which shortens unduly and distorts the title given them by the sixteenth-century editor, *Prediche sopra alquanti Salmi e Scritture* [*Sermons on Various Psalms and Scriptures*].

These sermons are perhaps the first to have been collected at the actual time of their delivery. The notary Ser Lorenzo Violi is supposed to have taken them down in shorthand, according to his own statement, and from now on he becomes the faithful recorder of the Friar's sermons. In fact, however, the texts of many of these sermons on the

Psalms seem too incomplete, and in particular too short in comparison with what we know to have been the length of Savonarola's sermons; and Violi himself apologizes for this in his *Giornate,* saying that he was not expert enough at the beginning, and had not then sufficiently applied himself to the task. This may very well be true; but I think it is equally true that his later efforts would not have been better, had not the preacher himself helped to perfect them.

Throughout the whole of February Savonarola really did withdraw into the seclusion of his cell, as he had promised or threatened to do on taking leave of his people. But on the 1st of March, Quinquagesima Sunday, he went again into the pulpit of the cathedral to begin his Lenten mission. During these sermons he began to preach on the Book of Job, the prophet of patience and tribulation. Nothing could have been more appropriate for the Florentines, who had just been through the hard trials of the loss of Pisa and so many other of their possessions, than to exhort them to bear these tribulations with patience and await with faith the reward that God would give them.

According to the text of the Lenten sermons as it has come down to us in the only existing edition of 1545, it appears that Savonarola in the first few days kept to the promise he had made at his disillusioned farewell and did not occupy himself with public affairs. It is true that we know enough about this text to treat it with some reserve; for we are told, as usual, that it was taken down in Latin by two disciples and later translated. We cannot tell why Violi did not take it down, as he had recorded immediately before and after it the sermons on the Psalms—a very curious state of affairs which makes us doubt both the texts. Other causes for doubt are not lacking, and make us think of a compilation based on the original Latin drafts, made immediately after the sermon, if not by Savonarola himself, by some one of his friars. This is not the place to enter into the details of these causes. Here we must take it that the text in which we have these *Prediche sopra Giobbe* [*Sermons on Job*], though in a shortened form, is substantially complete and faithful.

One likes to think, and it is very likely, that Savonarola either out of real disdain, or to make a show of it to the people, abstained from making any reference to politics in his first sermons. Indeed, such a sorrowful and angry silence seems clearly confirmed by some words of his sermon on the 18th of March: 'O Florence, though I have implored the Lord with all my strength, yet, O ungrateful people, seeing your obstinacy, I too, like Moses, have broken the tables of the law, and have given up your state so as not to be involved in your affairs, since you yourselves cannot deal with them.'

When, however, he delivered himself of this outburst, his irritation had passed, and he came back in those same days to stressing in almost every sermon the necessity to conclude rapidly the universal peace. At the same time, as the chronicler Parenti tells us, although there is no trace of it in the text we possess of these sermons, it appears that Savonarola also concerned himself with the question of the appeal against the 'six beans'. As usual, Ponzo opposed him fiercely from the pulpit of Santa Croce; and this was one of the bitterest and most memorable oratorical duels that Florence saw in those years. The victor, and it could not have been otherwise, was Savonarola. The 'Law of Peace and of the Appeal against the Six Beans', as it was entitled, was passed first in the Council of Eighty on the 19th of March, and then finally approved by the Great Council.

While Ponzo, who, as someone said, could have done with a rope to hang himself, was telling the people that they had been deceived, Savonarola triumphed in his sermon of the following day, the eighteenth of those on Job: 'I tell you, Florence, that God cannot be withstood; you see that you have not been able to resist Him. Do you not know that I told you that God wanted you to do what you have now done, and yet you have done it, many of you, against your will?' In other words, what he had predicted had come true: that the Florentines would make that law in spite of themselves, and that in the voting-urn the white beans would turn into black ones—that is, the votes against would turn into votes in favour. Certainly, considering the powerful opposition he had had to face, this was one of the most memorable victories won by the Friar with the power of his personality and his words; 'it seemed as though everything he proposed had behind it some superhuman force.' All the same, the law had gone beyond his suggestion in giving the right to appeal to the Great Council, whereas he had more wisely preferred it should be to the Eighty.

Although this much debated matter had now been dealt with, Savonarola did not lack material for his other sermons as the Lenten mission continued. As in the previous Advent, he recommended that trade should be revived to give work to the lower classes, and that relief should be found for the poor and unemployed; he insisted that the churches should melt down their gold and silver to provide bread for the hungry; he demanded modesty in social customs, and especially in the ornaments of women. In this way he set in motion his moral reform, which was to be no less spectacular than the political one.

The sermon he preached on the 1st of April, in the octave of the Annunciation, created a great stir among the people, and its fame spread rapidly throughout Italy. In this sermon he told at length, and one might say with great prolixity, of an imaginary embassy he had made to the Virgin on behalf of the Florentines. The text had better fortune than the others of this series, for it was published by the preacher himself, who put it complete in his *Compendio de rivelazioni*. But it was attacked bitterly and at length by his adversaries, who reproached him for his pretension to having been in Paradise: a ridiculous criticism, as it is obvious to everybody that, rather than a vision, it was a spiritual fantasy of the Friar. The modern reader, who can hardly credit that so great a man with so powerful a mind could pursue such fantasies and lose himself in such minute descriptions of ingenuous or downright puerile allegories, must consider that the taste for such things, both in sacred and in profane matters, had by no means disappeared, and Savonarola was much inclined to them by his education and his own scholastic tendencies. Nor should we be surprised at the excitement with which the sceptical Florentines listened. Savonarola, who was able to hold the minds of his hearers with his terrible eloquence, was equally well able to enchant them by colouring these fantasies of his with ingenuous delights.

Suddenly, at the beginning of April, another matter begins to dominate the Lenten sermons: the perilous conflict which the *Tiepidi* [the lukewarm]—that is, the bad priests and bad monks—had decided to wage, and were at that moment preparing, against Savonarola. It is not easy to say what the obscure beginnings of this were. While we see the struggle with the Arrabbiati break out suddenly and openly, and can date its beginnings with remarkable precision, this other battle eludes any attempt to establish the chronology of its beginnings, both on account of its more astute nature, and because its causes, unlike those of the political conflict, are to be sought in a slow process of fear and resentment, jealousy and suspicion.

Looking closely into the sermons and writings of the Friar, we find at first only a clear presentiment, or rather a prophetic vision, of this struggle: first, when he had begun *nova dicere novo modo,* in the Lent sermons at San Gimignano in 1487, then in those in Florence in 1491 and, with greater certainty, in 1492. I would not put among the first signs the suborned opposition of Fra Mariano (though this will have some echo in the bitterness of the final struggle) and other rivalries and jealousies with preachers, nor any single acts of opposition on the part of bad priests. Though in the days of Lorenzo, Savonarola wrote: '*scribæ et pharisei pugnant contra me*' ['Scribes and Pharisees fight against me'], the Pharisees of 1495 are different from those of 1491, and the struggle we are now dealing with is quite another thing.

Even so, in the drafts for the sermons on the Ark, for Lent 1494, we find certain statements that surprise by their early date: '*Certum est non esse hæreticum quia semper paratus sanctæ Romanæ Ecclesiæ emendationi*' ['One is certainly not a heretic if one is always ready for the reform of the Holy Roman Church']. This is a somewhat obscure allusion, but not so obscure that it does not give us clearly to understand that even at that date someone had accused him of heresy. And in the sermons on Haggai for Advent that same year he utters a judgment on his future enemies and future struggles which is extraordinarily precise and clear: 'The lukewarm [priests] of the Church are barren: they are barren because they have no spirit, they speak well of the Church and are of the Church, but have no devotion. God will move them, and they will come against me and against you [Florentines] and speak against us, and you will have a greater battle with them than with any armies. Already they have begun to arise, and to write letters.'

It is hard to say what those letters written by the Tiepidi may have been—whether they were libels in letter form, like those that soon were to abound in print all over Italy, or, which is more likely, reports defaming him at the Court of Rome. Even the best-informed biographers do not dwell on these early forms of opposition. This much is, however, certain: even when political opposition and party hatred grew bitter against Savonarola as he followed his chosen path, he always knew and always said that the last and hardest battle was not this one, but the one which he would have to fight against the race of the Tiepidi, the direct descendants of the Pharisees.

And now, during the early days of April, ecclesiastical opposition took concrete form; from words it passed to deeds. The Friar announced this in his sermon of the 4th of April, in which, after once more going back over the beginnings of his prophetic preaching and exclaiming against the Tiepidi, he went on to say: 'I want to tell you something this morning: in this city, in a certain place, they have gathered together and conspired against me, and they have agreed to do many things against me, and not only here in the city, but also outside. These are no longer references to the empty shouting of Ponzo from the pulpit of Santa Croce; he is referring to a real and actual conspiracy of bad priests and bad monks ('of priests, monks, and laymen,' Savonarola specified in a later sermon) to concert the downfall of the hated scourge of their shameful ways. The Friar shows that he had specific information of such a gathering and its deliberations, quite obviously through someone who had been present and betrayed its secrets. I think, too, that Ponzo, not without some previous understanding with his friends the Arrabbiati, must have had a very big part in this 'council'. I believe this for the following reasons.

On the 31st of March a League had been formed by the Pope, Lodovico Sforza, the Venetians, the Emperor Maximilian, and the King of Spain, under the guise of a defensive pact, but with the intention of passing to the offensive against Charles VII; and these allies were making every effort to draw in the Florentines. Sforza, the moving spirit and brains behind the League, must have thought it wellnigh impossible to bring in Florence unless the authority of the Friar were first brought low; he realized that this authority was itself sufficient to hold the city firm in its allegiance to the King, and in that same Lenten mission Savonarola had been urging the Florentines to adhere to the French alliance. Some time before, on the 25th of January, Somenzi, the Milanese agent in Florence, wrote to the Duke: 'I am doing what I can to rouse the enmity of this people against him'; and again on the 8th of February: 'The arrangements against the Friar are going well.' It is clear that these arrangements were with the Arrabbiati; but Somenzi, the devilish instrument of a devilish master, was not the man to overlook Savonarola's other enemies, the Tiepidi.

It is therefore extremely likely, if not absolutely certain, that, as the need grew on account of the demands of the League, the intrigues of Somenzi and the Arrabbiati at once made contact with Ponzo, who was virtually another agent of Sforza in Florence, and incited him to work among the priesthood as they were doing among the citizens. This would be the 'council' alluded to by Savonarola in his sermon of the 4th of April. Biographers, who had not succeeded in putting together various documents and pieces of information, have hitherto been unable to give the necessary account of this meeting and its earliest effects.

In this council it was decided, according to the information that had leaked out to Savonarola, to influence against him as many monks and priests as possible in Florence, and particularly to defame the Friar at the Court of Rome, with the assistance of the enemies he already had there, such a Genazzano and Mei. They also had means of hiding the real causes of their campaign under reasonable pretexts. He was accused at this very time of the heresy of the Fraticelli[1] (he was falsely said to have denied possessions to the monks); he was maliciously charged with having wanted to levy a tax on the clergy; he was reproached with having proposed, in the name of charity that is beyond all law, that the sacred plate of the churches should be melted down to feed the poor. They knew that such accusations had had, and would have, little success at Rome, but they also knew than an Alexander VI and his Court would not be able to put up for long with the terrible things the Friar was saying about their vices, especially when reasons of state were also involved. It was therefore enough to give, as the need arose, either a true or a malicious version of what he said. They also knew that Savonarola, warmed by the struggle and carried away by his sincere and generous nature, would run his head farther and farther into the trap they were so cunningly setting for him.

When he learned of this understanding, Savonarola, who had so often spoken of the fearfulness of ecclesiastical persecution, realized at once how great the danger was, and how much more serious than the anger of the Arrabbiati, which from now on he was to fear primarily as the instigator of those persecutions. In almost every sermon—in those of the 5th, 7th, 8th (given in the Palace before the Signoria), 14th, and 15th of April, and again in that for the 24th, which was the last in Lent, he spoke repeatedly about the campaign raised against him by the Tiepidi, and about their secret council, telling the people, even

---

[1] [A sect of ascetic Franciscans declared heretical in 1317 by John XXII, whose authority they challenged on the matter of the poverty of Christ.]

at that early date, that soon orders and surreptitious excommunications would come to remove him from the city.

About that time, a rumour was spread that a command to report to Rome had in fact reached him; and although this proved to be untrue, it was true that, probably in that very same secret council in Florence, they had tried to get such an order from the Pope, as the ambiguities of some Milanese letters suggest. It is astonishing to find so soon, in one of the Friar's sermons, words that anticipate the terms of offence and defence of the final battle: 'They [the Tiepidi] go about shouting at the moment, and declare that I have said that excommunications have no power [over me], and they quote to the simple people the text which says: "*Sive iusta, sive iniusta, timenda est*" ["Just or unjust, it is to be feared"]. O lukewarm priest, do you not know that this is to be understood "*nisi contineat mixtum errorem*"? That is, excommunication is to be feared when it is not mixed with error; but when error is evident in it, you know well that it has no power.'

Things and times have now come to this pass. Between what we can see and what we can readily imagine, there is enough to make us believe that already, as the Friar said in the sermon from which we have here quoted a good deal, 'things are beginning to boil in the spiritual war'. With that secret council, of the utmost importance and yet until now almost unknown, we pass from the prologue of the opposition to the first act of the drama.

Chapter 13

THE KING AGAIN IN FLORENCE; FLORENCE, THE CITY OF GOD

❖❖

CHARLES VIII, who in the meantime had acquired the whole of the Kingdom of Naples with unheard-of ease, taking cities and fortresses 'merely with his presence', as Savonarola had prophesied, was already anxious to return to France; but he was much more anxious and eager to return when he saw so many states and armies gathering in alliance to oppose him.

In Florence, too, fears were again rising. With all their traditional friendship towards France, and the allegiance that the Friar strove to arouse in them, with all the pleasure felt at the conquest of Naples, the Florentines, having experienced Charles at close quarters, now loved that unlovable king only when he was far from their territory. On the 9th of April, it was being said in the city that Charles had asked for the whole of the Oltrarno as lodgings; and when on the 28th the rumours of his return grew stronger, 'everyone awaited him with the fear he might sack the town: no one trusted in his friendship'.

On the 1st of May, with the city in this state of trepidation, Fra Girolamo began to preach again, and continued to do so on Sundays and other feast days. The return of the King placed in his hands a powerful weapon with which to overcome much opposition and to rout out vices and abuses, and he used it very cleverly. Not wanting to frighten the city more than it was already, but at the same time wishing to use its terror for its own improvement, he alternately encouraged the citizens not to fear, promising them every good fortune, and threatened them with imminent punishment if they did not rid themselves of their wicked habits and superfluous vanities. In this regard it was not enough for him to admonish the citizens and especially the women for their clothes and their fine coverlets worked with gold thread; even the Signoria did not escape the criticism of the terrible Friar: 'You too, Signori, who have up there in your chambers so many vanities, so many womanish things: I am willing for you to be decently set up, as befits Signori, but with a little more simplicity. "Friar, are you asking to be knocked on the head one of these days?" I believe you are quite right. But come, let God's will be done. The death of martyrs is not called death, but birth; it is not death to go and live with Christ.'

Everyone knows that these last words came true exactly three years later; but they almost came true in the days when they were spoken. On Sunday, the 24th of May, as he was returning to the convent in the evening after his sermon by the Via del Cocomero, he only just managed to escape from the violence of an attacker. As the registers of the Council of Eight for the year have not been preserved, it is impossible to say who the criminal was, and what was his motive in attacking the man to whom the city owed so much. As far as conjecture goes, it is a doubtful choice between private hatred (and the Friar had no lack of such enemies especially among butchers, gamblers, and sodomites) and political hatred, possible engineered by the diabolical Somenzi; conceivably, it may have been a bit of both.

In the sermon of that very same day, with the King already on his way back to Florence, Savonarola had said something that must have displeased Lodovico Sforza and his agent, whose every effort was employed to bring the Florentines into the League: 'Make no league except with Christ!' But first he followed his usual method of doling out favours and prophesying tribulations, to keep the Florentines on a short rein. They would get back Pisa on the one hand, or war on the other, if they did not do penance, and if the butchers' shops were not closed until Whitsun; otherwise, '*ecce gladius Domini super civitatem florentinam, cito et velociter!*'

The sword, even if sheathed in a somewhat doubtful friendship, was indeed on its way. Savonarola would dearly have liked it to come out of its sheath and lay about, but in reprobate Rome—whither Charles was headed with a good half of his army, having left the other

half to garrison Naples—and not in the beloved chosen city of Florence.
For this purpose, he wrote a long letter to the King, probably on the
25th of May, in French; and to make sure, fearing that in such unsettled
times and amid so many enemies it might not be delivered, he wrote
him another, exactly the same, also in French, on the 26th. Earlier we
find that he had written him three other letters, one which may have been
sent in February by the hand of the Cardinal of St. Malo, and one by
Philippe de Commines. Both these men had passed through Florence
during the preceding months on the service of the King, and had gone
to visit the humble friar who was regarded almost as the master of
the city.

All the addresses of Savonarola to the King, either in speeches
or letters, are substantially alike and repeat one another. In this letter of
the 26th of May he told him that the God who had revealed to him the
coming and the victory of the French armies, now revealed and commanded him to tell the French King that, if he did not treat the Florentines well on his way back and did not maintain his solemnly sworn
promises, giving them back the lands he held in forfeit, God would
withdraw his mandate, send many tribulations, and raise the peoples
against him. After this, Savonarola put him on his guard against Piero
—without, however, mentioning him by name—and cleverly dangled
before his eyes the many promises the League had made to the Florentines; he added, however, that the latter, held firm by his preaching,
would not turn against the French Crown.

While the city was in tumult, the Friar was working quietly at
his *Compendio di rivelazioni*; and so as to have absolute quiet on the
days when he did not have to preach, he stayed at the convent of San
Domenico, where amid the beauties of the country around Fiesole he
was 'better able to attend to spiritual affairs' and to this work of his,
which he proposed soon to publish.

On the 1st of June, Charles entered Rome. Savonarola's hopes were
high, as were those of all good Christians, on this ocassion. And in fact the
King was worse disposed towards the Pope on his return than he had
been on his way out. He had good reasons for distrusting the Pope's
'wicked nature', particularly as Alexander's son, Cardinal Caesar
Borgia, who, as Charles's hostage, was supposed to assure him of the
Pope's doubtful loyalty, had secretly fled, leaving Charles empty-
handed. At which Charles exclaimed: 'What a nation of rascals these

Lombards are, and the Holy Father is worst of all!' The King's displeasure had been increased by the League the Pope had helped to form against him, by the Pope's continual ambiguities, and by his refusal to crown Charles King of Naples. I do not know whether he believed the rumours that attributed to the Borgias' poisons the death of the young brother of the Sultan, who was another valuable hostage given him by the Pope. He must, however, have heard all kinds of stories about the Pope from those who constantly pressed him to reform the Church. Among these, in his own Court, was Cardinal Peraud. Savonarola was not inactive either. He must have told Charles a good deal when they met in Pisa and Florence, and also through the medium of the Cardinal of St. Malo. Then, in his letter of the 26th of May he addressed Charles as minister of God 'in this ministry of the renovation of the Church, begun in these days'. Only the day before, he had said in a sermon: 'You will see how Rome will be confounded'—probably in the hope that they would not have long to wait after the King arrived there.

In fact, if by these words he meant that Alexander and the Court of Rome were about to receive at least some part of the punishment they deserved, the Friar this time let himself be deceived by his desire for justice and his religious zeal. The Pope, having held out some hope of his awaiting the King in Rome, had taken refuge at Orvieto two days before Charles's arrival; and then, giving him hopes of a meeting between Orvieto and Viterbo, as Charles drew near to this town he withdrew to Perugia, intending, if he were followed, to go on to Ancona, where the sea gave him fresh opportunity for escape. Luckily for him, Charles had little time and more pressing troubles while the armies of the League were preparing to cut off his retreat. He put off his displeasure to a more suitable time, and hastened on his way to Tuscany.

'"Alas, nothing will now be done to Rome! He has passed, and nothing more will happen!"' This is what Savonarola makes an imaginary speaker say in his sermon of the 8th of June, thereby expressing his own disappointment and that of all good folk. But he added: 'I tell you that Rome will be confounded; doubt not one instant, for it must be.' It was indeed to be, but not until the memorable sack of Rome in 1527. Meantime they must think of Florence, with the dark and threatening stormcloud drawing near. While the city was preparing arms and defences, the Friar was still urging her to arm herself, above all, with prayers.

As the fears of the Florentines grew with the approach of the King, who had now entered Tuscany, so too did their love and support for Savonarola. He needed now nothing more than their terror to obtain from them the good works and penances he demanded, and, feeling compassion for them, he strove to give them courage with affectionate words: 'O my people, I see you full of fear and dismay . . . you shake like a reed in the wind. . . . My people, have faith in God, for those who trust in Him have nothing to fear in this world. Put aside such sadness!' And in the preceding sermon he had said: 'Florence, see if I am not mad; for when things were well with you, I foretold evil, and now when they go ill, I promise you good things.'

On the 12th of June Charles was already in Siena, and one can imagine the consternation in Florence, where meanwhile, besides Savonarola's spiritual armaments, soldiers were being drilled and streets barricaded, when it was heard that Piero de' Medici was coming with the King. A letter of Piero's had been intercepted, expressing his intention of returning with the French army. Nor could Florence have been pleased with the answer given by the King to her ambassadors when they inquired of him what route he would follow, so that they might arrange for the necessary victuals for the army. He bluntly replied that they should prepare for him the whole dominion.

Florence now turned again to Savonarola. He had realized, even when the King was still far from the walls of Siena, how things would go, and had said in his sermon of the 9th of June: 'If I have to go somewhere on your behalf, pray God every day for me, that I may do what is best for you.' He went, in fact on the 15th of June, as 'procurator and advocate of the Florentine people', accompanied by Fra Antonio di Olanda and Fra Tommaso Busini, together with an armed escort under the command of Bartolommeo Ridolfi, a member of the College of the Signoria The next day the Ten sent a letter after him reminding him of the great faith the city had in him and begging him to go to Siena, where it would be easier for him to have audience with the King. But, either because the King was already on the point of leaving Siena, or because Savonarola thought it dangerous to leave Florentine territory, or because his previous experience in Siena had been enough for him, he preferred to await the King at Poggibonsi, where the vanguard of the French army had arrived in the meantime. Charles did not arrive there until the 17th.

When Savonarola went to his lodgings, the King was at table, but he rose at once and went to meet him at the head of the stairs, which the Friar was already climbing. The King 'showed him great respect', says Guicciardini; and we cannot but believe this testimony and others that we possess, for these demonstrations of respect by a great king to a humble friar were made in the presence of many townspeople. Perhaps the Frenchman's reverence for this extraordinary man had been increased by accounts from some of his ministers and officials and, above all, by the Cardinal of St. Malo, who, as we saw, had gone to visit him in February, and by Philippe de Commines.

Commines, who had just come back from his legation to Venice, where he had seen almost before his very eyes the formation of the League against his master, had been astonished by Savonarola's penetrating mind and by his knowledge of worldly affairs, particularly of the manœuvres of that League, 'of which', Commines writes in his *Mémoires*, 'he could speak better than I myself, who had but lately come from there'. And when he had asked Savonarola whether the King would be able to get past so many enemies without danger to his person, the Friar had replied 'that he would have to fight on the way, but that he would come out of it with honour . . .; but because he had not done his duty in the matter of reforming the Church, and because he had allowed his men to pillage and plunder the people, even those who were his allies, who had opened their gates freely to him, as well as those who were his enemies, God had given a judgment against him, and soon a blow would fall upon him. . . . And he told me that he would go personally before the King and tell him so.'

Now Savonarola was again before the King. He spoke 'modestly but forcefully' and said those very things: that he should treat kindly the faithful Florentines, keeping the treaty he had sworn to, and restoring their property; that he should in no wise support Piero de' Medici; that his men should not plunder the people; and that he should attend to the reform of the Church. Otherwise, he would soon be severely punished by God.

The King listened patiently to these admonitions, and answered kindly. He argued a little about Piero, whom he said he wished to put back in Florence as a private citizen; but then he dropped the matter.

As for his passage through the city, we hear that Savonarola resolutely refused it, threatening retribution. I would not attribute to this refusal a force it did not in fact have, even though others have done so, because I believe that the Frenchman had already decided to take a different route. Some historians say that his reason was resentment of the great defensive preparations made in Florence, but I think it was rather fear. Furthermore, he could not delay longer while the armies of the League were massing in the territory of Parma.

It did not, therefore, cost him much to assure the Friar of his good intentions towards the city of Florence, and to show that he no longer felt any animosity against her. But, as for restoring lands and fortresses wrongfully withheld, he gave, according to his nature, his ill intentions, and the conflicting advice of his ministers, contradictory answers, both in that first conversation and in two others he had with the Friar: one in the collegiate church of Poggibonsi, and the other at Castelfiorentino, whither Savonarola accompanied him on his way to Pisa. Meantime, Fra Girolamo had reported on his progress to the Ten, and received from them through the Florentine ambassadors, prayers and encouragement 'to continue this holy mission, in which this city and this people have the greatest faith'.

The King would have liked Savonarola to go with him to Pisa, holding out hope of its restitution when he got there, but the Friar took his leave, protesting that he must return to his flock. Once again he showed clear-sighted wisdom; if he had gone, he would not have been able to do anything, he would have suffered much bitterness and indignity, and he would have fallen considerably in the people's estimation. Instead, he went back to Florence, in reality empty-handed of everything but vain words, but with the reputation of having averted the King's descent on Florence and of having silenced his anger, and with a great crop of the usual good promises—goods of low price and even less value, but always acceptable to anyone in difficulty and need.

With these gifts he returned to the city on the 20th and presented himself to the people, who came to his sermon in vast numbers, estimated at between thirteen and fourteen thousand. He told them of his threats to the King and of the King's kind answers, and said that he had sown good seed and that in good time they would gather and eat the harvest. All except his enemies, who said that the city had lost rather than gained from his mission, once more saluted him as the saviour and father of their country. According to Landucci, 'the Friar was held in such great esteem and devotion at that time in Florence that there were many men and women who, if he had told them to go through fire, would certainly have obeyed him'.

The popularity and following of Savonarola were truly extraordinary at that time. Even the Arrabbiati, a minority that seemed greater because of the violence of its passions, appeared to have been silenced, though actually they were working secretly while waiting for more favourable times and occasions. An instance of the almost boundless authority of Savonarola at this time was the resigning of the Council of Twenty, who were blamed by the public for having elected certain worthless and incapable Signorie, for their disunity among themselves, and for persisting in an office that was merely an impediment to the new government. They hung on obstinately to their title, notwithstanding the hatred and suspicion of the entire people. The Friar cleverly made a veiled allusion to the subject in a sermon, but in such a way that the people clearly understood it; and then he had a word in private with Domenico Bonsi and Giuliano Salviati, who were members of that council. Whereupon the latter spontaneously gave up his office before the appointed time, and all the others followed his lead. This was on the 7th of June, while the King was on his way to Tuscany. Only then did the city feel itself truly free. And this was another benefit that the Florentines fully acknowledge they had received from Savonarola.

A further event increased the reputation of Fra Girolamo. Pandolfo Rucellai, one of the foremost citizens, who was one of the Ten and the appointed ambassador to the King of France, gave up office and took the habit in San Marco, having been converted by Savonarola's teaching. Sanuto, commenting on this episode, says: 'Savonarola was regarded as a saint in Florence.' The case of Rucellai was only one of many. Innumerable proofs were seen of the fame and veneration that surrounded the convent of San Marco, where famous men and young sons of the noblest Florentine families flocked to ask for the Dominican habit. We have already seen how the dying Giovanni Pico della Mirandola took that habit from the hands of the Friar himself. Shortly before, it had covered the mortal remains of Politian. At the beginning of this year, 1495, the famous Greek and Latin scholar Zanobi Acciaioli had become a friar of San Marco; and, not long after, he was joined by that other good humanist Giorgio Antonio Vespucci and Fra Malatesta Sacramoro, both canons of the cathedral, Maestro Pietro Paolo da Urbino, and many other men of great worth.

Thus that Dominican cloister, since the time the 'barbarous' friar from Ferrara had entered it, had become more and more the House of Knowledge. Even after Pico's death the flower of Florentine intellect and learning continued to frequent the 'Accademia Marciana', and some of them, such as Benivieni, actually had keys to the convent so that they could come and go freely whenever they pleased. Those who gathered there, besides the resident scholars, were Crinito, Fonzio, the Aristotelian Arduino, the Platonist Nesi (who had perhaps then already begun his *Oraculum de novo sæculo,* full of enthusiastic praise for the Friar), and the young Giovan Francesco Pico, who had inherited from his famous uncle a devotion to Savonarola as well as a love of study. The company was, therefore, pleasant and learned; even pleasanter was the peacefulness of the surroundings, so favourable to study; while the store of books collected there by the generosity of Cosimo de' Medici was extremely rich. Lately an even greater treasure had been added to this store: the Medici library had been preserved from pillage after Piero's departure and handed over to San Marco by the city, first of all for safekeeping and then in pledge for 2,000 gold florins, which the brothers scraped together by the sale of their last possessions. Then, in 1497, poor as they were, they pledged themselves to pay another thousand florins in order to ensure permanently to the city and the convent (so at least they hoped) that priceless treasure of learning. This was the work of Savonarola, of the man who for so long, owing to the ignorance of the learned and unlearned alike, had the reputation of being a vandal destroyer of manuscripts!

It is true that he loved and honoured human knowledge only as a means to attain the final end: God. More than ever now there burned in his mind that old ambition to make San Marco a centre of Oriental language study, a nursery of apostles for the conversion of the infidel. He used to say with pride from the pulpit that in his convent, besides Latin and Greek, they had three other languages: Hebrew, Arabic, and Chaldaic. The first of these was taught by the Jew Blemmet, and the eminent Hebrew scholar Sante Pagnini was formed in that fine Savonarolan school.

It would not, however, be fair to suppose that Acciaioli, Vespucci,

Sacramoro, and others like them came to take orders in San Marco attracted more by the smell of old books than by the odour of sanctity. We know enough of their lives to judge that, if the lure of study was an additional bait, they were caught, no more and no less than many others, learned and unlearned, noble and poor, Florentine and foreigner, with the bait of the eloquence and the example of Savonarola, in the miraculous nets of this great fisher of men.

What he had sketched out when he began his work, was day by day taking full shape, and the whole city began to mirror the gentle and peaceful life led at San Marco. A sudden and wonderful change had taken place in Florence, like a change of scenery in a theatre. Wishing here to give only a brief account of this in keeping with the character of this biography, we prefer to quote the dispassionate prose of Guicciardini rather than the words of Piagnoni apologists and biographers. 'The things he [Fra Girolamo] did for the observance of good behaviour were both saintly and wonderful, and there never was in Florence such goodness and religion as in his time. . . . There was no more gambling in public, and in the home only with fear and trembling; the taverns were closed, these being usually the home of unmannerly youth and of every vice; sodomy was put down and greatly chastised; the women in great part gave up their unseemly and lascivious garments; and boys were weaned from bad habits and brought to live a moral and seemly life. . . .'

So greatly was the Friar loved and revered by the Florentines, so great was his authority with the magistrates, that when, immediately after his return from his embassy to the King, he pressed the city in one of his sermons to sacrifice one of its best-loved customs, the annual spectacle of the Palio di San Giovanni, it did so. The money usually spent on these festivities was instead distributed to the poor. 'Nor was it deemed unfitting, at his instance, to give up this ancient custom and national feast, so great was his authority with us. . . .' Thus writes the chronicler Parenti, who goes on to enumerate other signs of the miraculous renovation of the city (remember the frequent exhortations of the Friar to revive commerce and industry) and adds: 'They began to revive the silk and wool industries throughout the land, and everyone felt that they should help one another . . . and all blameworthy customs were banished. It is a wonderful thing that suddenly there should be such a great change in the behaviour of the people.'

So even at that time Florence fully justified those lines in which Marietta Rucellai was to sing of the great Savonarolan reformation:

Un'arra di Paradiso
questa città pareva;
sendo ciascuno unito,
gran pace si vedeva.[1]

Yet already against the author of all this good work, against the restorer of morals and the Christian religion, the very man who usurped the name of Vicar of Christ was preparing to strike the first blow.

[1] This city seemed an earnest of Paradise; all were at one, and great peace was everywhere.'

Chapter 14

THE FIRST PAPAL BRIEFS

◇◇◇

THE farce of the restitution of Pisa and the fortresses, which the King had clumsily played before the Florentines, was now going into a second performance. Charles had departed without restoring Pisa, in spite of all his assurances, and in fact promising the Pisans he would never hand the city over; yet he now gave fresh promises to the Florentine ambassadors that he would do so when he reached Asti. At this, some enemy of the Friar raised his head in Florence and jeered: 'Go on, trust the Friar, who says he has got Pisa back for you.' None the less, on the 6th of July, the Republic sent two new ambassadors to the French camp to negotiate; and it is probable that Savonarola, perhaps at the request of the Signoria, gave them a letter for the King. This may be the one of which we have a sixteenth-century copy that bears no date. In this letter he repeated his injunctions and threats on the subject of the shameful non-observance of sworn treaties, adding, not without strong words appropriate to the gravity of his theme: 'God is much displeased with these things, wherefore the tears of His servants have come before Your Majesty, and He has begun to give you some token of his disapproval.'

The same day, the 6th of July, the French were met at Fornovo by the armies of the League. Though they managed to fight their way through, they lost most of their transport and artillery, and the honour of the day remained doubtful. The King himself was in great danger of being killed or taken prisoner. I believe that in the height of that danger, when he, as we are told, despaired of human aid, and turned to implore God's help, he must have remembered the obscure words heard a few days before from the lips of the Friar, that proud and mysterious friar whom once more he had found in the path of his victorious army, prophesying his misfortune. He must have remembered them even more clearly shortly afterwards when he got the news that, while his armies had been fighting the League, the French fleet had been defeated outside Rapallo, and that Ferdinand of Aragon had retaken Naples from the sea with the same ease with which he had lost it not long before.

These disasters to Charles were bound to have repercussions on the fortunes of Savonarola. As long as the King's armies were running through Italy unopposed and the population saluted him with '*Benedictus qui venit in nomine Domini*', neither the Pope nor the Arrabbiati would have dared to touch the man who had prophesied Charles's coming, who seemed to be so much his friend, and who received from him demonstrations of respect. But now that the expedition of the 'new Cyrus' was about to end in ridicule and shame, there would not be slings and arrows enough for him who was still the King's supporter, who, right in the heart of Italy, held firm to the King's side the wealth, fortresses, arms, and territories of the Florentine Republic.

The Friar realized and sensed this danger. Though ill with fever and dysentery, in addition to his habitual stomach troubles, and though given strict warning by his doctors not to preach, after barely ten days' rest he went into the pulpit on the 5th, and again on the 12th and 15th of July. He poured derision on the Tiepidi and their broken hopes that this illness might close his mouth for a long time and perhaps forever. But that his illness was still with him is borne out by his own words: 'I shall try to go gently, if I can, so that the doctor may not reproach me.' He also chastised the wicked priests, and once again repeated ('"Brother, you are asking for another pain that no doctor will be able to cure"!'): 'I have told you, Florence, to make no league except with Christ.'

Just at that moment, in order to draw the Florentines into their League, Sforza and the Pope were making fresh approaches, thinking to find them better disposed after the King's disillusionment of their hopes and his military failure. After the action at Fornovo, Maestro Alberto da Orvieto, the Pope's ambassador, came to Florence for this purpose, and was joined a little later by Bishop Francesco Soderini. Having found the Signoria still obstinately of the same mind, he told them it was a great shame that so great a republic as the Florentine should allow itself to be governed by a friar. He also wrote strongly against Savonarola in letters to the Pope, certainly not without some understanding with the Arrabbiati; he gave a bad report of Fra Girolamo's sermons, suggested that he be called to Rome, and added that there was no hope of Florence changing her mind while the Friar remained.

Then from Rome came the blow that had been about to fall in April after the secret council in Florence, and that may only have been withheld in view of the imminent passage of the King. It took the form of a Papal Brief bearing the date July the 21st, 1495. Savonarola, who was on his guard and had faithful friends near his enemies even at the Court of Rome, was already aware of what was being planned, and, cleverly taking the initiative, he had promptly written to the Pope himself.

It is a strange fact, and one which deserves a chapter to itself in the curious history of erudition, that among so many students of Savonarola, some of great intellect and many of great diligence, none has noticed that the Brief of July the 21st is quite clearly a reply to a letter of the Friar, and precisely to that preventive letter just referred to, written 'proximis diebus'—that is probably early in July. This letter, unfortunately, is now lost; but the Brief itself and a letter of Savonarola's written a short time after, indicate what must have been its content and purpose: to protest that the Friar preached 'only those things which he knew to be in the service of God, being always ready, however, to submit them to the correction of the Holy Roman Church'. It is obvious that Fra Girolamo, knowing that the Pope was angry with him for his sermons as they had been misrepresented by enemies, had hastened to justify them in that letter, taking the opportunity also to tell him of the remarkable fruits they had borne. This was an easy task, for the almost miraculous reformation of the Florentines was now well known to everyone, and the Pope, as a good Christian (had he been one), would have been obliged to judge the sermons and their preacher by that change, in accordance with the infallible precept of the Master: 'A fructibus eorum cognoscetis eos.'

By anticipating the blow in this way, Savonarola perhaps hoped

THE FIRST PAPAL BRIEFS

to ward it off again or at least to soften it. And perhaps in this latter
sense he succeeded. The Papal Brief was a very strange document that
one might figuratively liken to the famous poisoned sweets of Borgia.
Although basically (not only in my opinion, but in the opinion of all
who have written about it) a sentence of death, it was from beginning
to end a wonderful eulogy of Savonarola. The good Pope, 'having
heard from the reports of many people that Fra Girolamo laboured
exceedingly among the other workers in the vineyard of the Lord',
was much pleased and thanked God for this, being sure that Fra
Girolamo would thus be able 'to sow the word of the Lord among the
Christian people and harvest a hundredfold'. At this point Alexander
VI, still more admiring and humble, added that, as Savonarola declared
in his sermons that the future events he prophesied appeared to him
by divine revelation, he wished to hear these things from Fra Girolamo's lips, so that, understanding them better in this way, he might
do what God willed. These are his words: 'Ut quod placitum est Deo
melius per te cognoscentes peragamus.' What a marvellous document of
curial duplicity! Anyone ingenuous or foolish enough to believe these
words sincere should first reflect that this is nothing more than the
application of the political counsels of Maestro Alberto, and then
should read the next Papal Brief, which throws off the useless mask of
pretence and is the best gloss on the first.

But the Friar was neither ingenuous nor foolish, and had no need
of supernatural insight to know that if he obeyed the Brief and went
without delay to the Pope, he might never reach Rome; he would certainly never return to Florence. He repeatedly stated, and proved by
his actions, that life mattered little to him; but his great work, which
he had fostered in the dreams of his youth and now saw in miraculous
flower, mattered a great deal, and he could not leave it.

He had always said and preached that the aid of human prudence
was not to despised, and so he replied on the 31st of July, adopting the
same tone as the Brief: he had long wished to see Rome and do reverence to the relics of the Apostles and His Holiness the Pope, and still
more did he wish it now, having been summoned, he the very least of
mortals, by His Holiness himself. But he was prevented by physical infirmity, in consequence of which his doctors had forbidden him to
preach and even to study; by the grave danger to his life if he ventured
outside the Florentine dominions; and by the harm his absence would

bring to the city, which was not yet well established in its new reforms. For these good reasons, directed rather at the intentions than at the actual words of the order, he asked to be allowed to put off his visit. In the meantime, as His Holiness wished to be informed of what the future held with regard to the scourging of Italy and the renewal of the Church, he could learn all these things, as though from Savonarola's own lips, from a short work that he had recently sent to press; as soon as it appeared, he would send it to His Holiness.

The Pope appeared perfectly well satisfied with this letter and these reasons, even if the closest and most virulent enemies of the Friar were not. Either the Pope was merely putting a good face on it, or, in keeping with his frivolous nature, he did not much care. This caused Somenzi to write dejectedly to the Duke of Milan: 'It seems that His Holiness did not have the courage to make a friar come to Rome against his will.' For his part, Fra Girolamo, 'to give anger room', as he used to say, decided with wise and prudent moderation to give up preaching for a while, the more so because his poor health and his doctors demanded treatment and rest.

But on the 28th of July, before replying to the Pope, he had wanted to speak once again to his people; and his farewell sermon had a special solemnity, being honoured by the presence of the Signoria and all the magistrates. He demanded fresh severity against sodomites and blasphemers; it was madness for the magistrates to show them clemency [Savonarola puns on *clemenza* and *demenza*]. He urged them to hasten the building of the hall for the Great Council, and to make a law to abolish the *parlamento* [popular assembly], which had always been in Florence an instrument of violent and tyrannical change. He suggested other wise provisions, among them one for use during times of plague, 'because the plague is certain to come'. He had begun by saying that he preached that day inspired by love rather than by medicine, for he would not be preaching if he had listened to his doctors. Later, drawing towards his conclusion, he suddenly came out with these words, which sum up the character of this great preacher: 'When I am up here, I am always well. And if out of the pulpit I could be as well as I am in it, I should always be well; but when I get down from here, I know I shall have my troubles, and for this reason it shall be a little while before I see you again, for I must attend to getting well. Then I shall start preaching again, if I am still alive.'

In the peaceful atmosphere of San Marco he set himself to correct the proofs of that 'libellus' which he had promised to send the Pope, and to which he had also made a reference in his farewell sermon of July the 28th. This book was none other than his *Compendio di rivelazioni*, written first in the vernacular and immediately afterwards translated into Latin by the author himself, so that it might be the more appreciated by churchmen and the learned, and have a wider diffusion outside Italy. It did in fact have a tremendous fortune both in Italy and abroad. In the space of six weeks there were five editions: the first and second in Italian, both dated August 18th, 1495 and printed by Bonaccorsi; the third, dated September 1st, printed by Lorenzo Morgiani, also in Italian; the fourth, dated September 5th, printed by Bartolommeo de' Libri, likewise in Italian; the fifth, in Latin, dated October 3rd, printed by Bonaccorsi. Four other editions came out in the following year, among them one in Paris and one in Ulm.

Such a great success is easily explained by the widespread curiosity, not only in Italy, to know those prophecies of the famous friar which had already come true, and the others whose outcome was still to be seen. How eagerly the work was awaited before its publication is apparent from correspondence between the Duke of Ferrara and his ambassador in Florence, Manfredi, who was ordered to have a manuscript copy made if the printing was going to take a long time. But there was no need of this, for on the 20th of August the Friar sent to Ercole a copy printed on 'good paper', and refused the offer of the Duke's ambassador to reimburse him for the expense of this special copy.

The Duke, in thanking the donor, praised the book greatly as being 'composed with great elegance and order'. Really, it hardly appears so to us. Valuable as it is for its biographical content, on which we have already drawn a good deal, the material is not well digested or proportioned (nor, indeed, does it claim to be so), as the book is almost entirely taken up by the immensely long sermon of Ascension Week, preceded and followed by a brief summary of the prophetic sermons of the Friar up to the date of writing. At the end are included summaries of threatening prophecies made to the King of France in recent months, among them the one about the people revolting if he did not observe the agreements made with the Florentines.

It is very likely that Savonarola sent a copy of the *Compendio* to the King about the 20th of August, at the same time as he sent copies to the Pope and the Duke of Ferrara. We have, in fact, a copy of a letter to the King, undated but certainly written about that time. There is no reference in it to the sending of the book, unless one wishes to see one in the words: 'You see here that which I prophesied to you—that is, the rebellion of your people'; but this interpretation, if there are no mutilations in the text, seems rather far-fetched. At all events, on the 27th of August Charles concluded fresh agreements with the Florentine ambassadors in Turin by which, with certain safeguards, all the territories and fortresses then in the hands of the King were to be restored. In effect, only Leghorn was given back. As for the others, whether the cause was obstinacy, corruption, or caprice of the French officers, or secret instructions from the King, the long-drawn-out comedy was degenerating into a dreary meaningless farce. This placed a weapon in the hands of the Friar's enemies.

Thanks to his sagacity, things seemed to have quietened down in Rome. Then, like a bolt from the blue, another Papal Brief reached Florence. It was dated September 8th, and was of a completely different character from the preceding one. But its clumsy authors did not realize, or did not care, that if, as I said earlier, this second brief was the best gloss on the first, the first was still a terrible gloss on the second. In this one the Friar, who had been praised before as the hard-working sower of the Divine Word, now suddenly becomes 'a certain Girolamo Savonarola', scandalous propagator of new dogmatic errors, of heretical propositions, of nonsense, of false prophecies!

The Brief formulates and exemplifies in detail the above accusations, together with the utterly false ones of disobedience to the Brief of July the 21st and, further, of the 'scandalous separation from the Fathers of Lombardy, obtained through the underhand cunning of perverse friars'. It then orders the following penalties: Savonarola's case was entrusted to Fra Sebastiano Maggi, Vicar General of the Congregation of Lombardy, to be decided, judged, and punished according to the statutes of the Order, and Fra Girolamo was ordered to recognize and obey the judge who had been chosen. In the meantime, while his case was being considered, he was suspended from teaching and from preaching in public; the convents of San Marco and San Domenico in Fiesole were again attached to the Congregation of Lombardy; Fra Domenico da Pescia, Fra Tommaso Busini, and Fra Silvestro were to go to Bologna within nine days, where they would be assigned to some convent of the Congregation outside the Florentine dominion.

The enemies of the Friar—among whom we may include the Pope, although he was probably the one who had the least part in this affair and this Brief—had at last come to the realization that the only way of dealing him a death-blow was to deprive him of the independence that he had so cleverly and laboriously achieved; and now here was the Brief that took it away from him. But if the blow was well aimed, it was clumsily delivered, so that once more Savonarola's task of parrying it, and showing that the Pope had been misled, was easy, as he had found in the papal letters 'no less than eighteen mistakes'.

The first and strangest of these errors was addressing the letters 'to the Prior and Convent of Santa Croce of the Preachers' Order' instead of to San Marco. This is so absurd that one is tempted to attribute it to low cunning, aimed at guaranteeing the delivery of the Brief by the Friar's enemies and the diffusion throughout the city of the news of the disaster about to befall him. But if it was intended to be clever, it was still absurd, because the only result must have been to delay considerably the formal delivery of the Brief; the friars of San Marco would not have been so foolish as to accept it straightaway in that form when it was sent on from Santa Croce, knowing or being able to imagine that it portended nothing good, and especially in the absence of their own Prior, Savonarola.

He, as we learn unexpectedly from the receipts given to the papal couriers when the Brief was at last accepted, was 'gratia recuperandæ valetudinis absens'; but we do not know to what more salubrious spot he had gone to regain his health. Conjectures, though worth little, cost even less to put forward, and one of the least improbable is that he had gone to the hospice of Santa Maria del Sasso in the Casentino, which had been joined to the Congregation of San Marco barely four months before, at the time when Savonarola became Vicar General of the Congregation. Such a choice would have given him, at one and the same time, a healthy stay in a convent of his Congregation, and an opportunity to pay it an official visit as Vicar. This is not an entirely gratuitous conjecture because it explains a letter from the Friar to Maruffi, which may have been written then.

During this month a confusion of difficulties and chronological uncertainties beset the biographer of Savonarola, due to the evidently wrong dating of certain documents. This is not the place to go into the details.[1] Here we can only take the road that seems best; in any case, the error will be only a matter of a few days either way and will affect only details of little importance. We may, therefore, suppose that the Brief, which reached Santa Croce about the middle of the month because of the usual delays of the chancelleries, would not have been formally received and accepted at San Marco, owing to the error already mentioned, before the 28th of September. In the meantime, after the letter had been opened at Santa Croce, the friars of that convent or their friends had divulged its contents, giving the Signoria occasion to write to the Pope on the 17th a general defence of Savonarola, and allowing the latter time and opportunity to compose a full reply. Then, on his way home, Savonarola went to Arezzo, anxious to reply to many things that Ponzo had said there against him the previous May, and probably to fulfil a promise he had already made. There he preached one or two sermons. From Arezzo he wrote to assure Fra Silvestro 'that he would not be late' in returning to Florence and in sending his answer to the Pope, which had already been greatly delayed. Finally, on the 30th of September or the morning of the 1st of October, he sent off his letter to the Pope, antedating it September the 29th. All this seems (and I am the first to admit it) too complicated. But—apart from the Arezzo episode, which could be cut out—I do not see any other solution to all the complications unless one changes the date of his answer to the Pope; and this I certainly would not feel able to do. It is now high time we considered this reply.

In this very long letter Savonarola replied to the accusations contained in the Brief, one by one and point by point. It is an answer that is at times too involved, at others oversubtle, but on the whole conclusive. It says, in substance: the matters for which he was accused had been falsely or inaccurately reported to His Holiness; he could not be blamed for his prophecies, of which many had already come true, until the others were proved false; he could not be accused of having disturbed the peace of the Church, when all he had done was call the people to repentance; it was untrue that the separation of San Marco had been 'the work of perverse friars', as it had been accomplished by

---

[1] [This sentence has been substituted for a phrase in the original referring the reader to a long note discussing the problems referred to.]

the entreaties of the Cardinal Protector after long and grave consideration; in any case, the friars of San Marco, who were well known for
their exemplary life, could not be called 'perverse'; it was also untrue
that he had refused to appear before the Pope and to obey him, for he
had merely asked, for good reasons, to defer his visit. Finally, the Vicar
of the Lombard Congregation was suspect to him as a judge on account
of the great differences between them in the past: every law, human
and divine, forbade an enemy to set up as judge of his adversary. For
similar reasons, the friars of San Marco could not readily accept their
former adversaries and persecutors as their superiors. When the cause
is absent, its effects must also be absent; and in his case the accusations
falsely made against him were shown to be baseless calumnies. Therefore, Savonarola signified that he would take no action on these
superior orders until His Holiness, having recognized his innocence,
absolved him of all blame.

The most effective part of the letter was that dealing with the
separation from the Lombards, because it corresponded to the most
dangerous but also the weakest part of the Brief, which incautiously
stirred up the wasp's nest of the upper hierarchy of the Order, and gave
no little offence to the Cardinal Protector and the other cardinals who
had supported Savonarola. To obtain a clearer understanding of the
views of his superiors in Rome, and to distinguish his friends from his
enemies, the Friar wrote at this time to a Dominican prelate, probably
to be identified as Fra Lodovico da Ferrara, Procurator of the Order,
begging him to support his cause with the Protector. By so doing, the
prelate would show that he had no part in that council of Pharisees
and Herodians who were filling the Pope's ears with so many lies
about Savonarola. This letter, which was sent together with a copy of
the letter to the Pope of September the 29th, bears the date September
the 15th in the late copies from which it is known. As this is
impossible, I would correct this date to October the 15th.

In the meantime the Friar, while waiting for the Pope's decision—
which he declared both in writing and by word of mouth he had no
intention of disobeying, being resolved not to sin in this respect even
venially—again went into the pulpit on the 11th of October. He had
two things to say to his people: how he was faring with the Pope; and
a recommendation to fortify the state and make it safe, because news of
intrigues within and preparations abroad by Piero de' Medici was

again about in the city. Two very different things, it would seem; but, as the Pope was the prime supporter of these preparations, one is tempted on closer inspection to regard them as one and the same.

On the first matter, which in his sermon he treated last, he said: 'They [the Arrabbiati] have conspired together: I know them, these affairs of yours, in so many different ways that you would be astonished if I told you. *Inierunt concilium cum Herodianis.* They have conspired with your enemies, and they have said what the Pharisees said of Christ when they asked him if it were lawful to give tribute to Caesar or not. They said: "We shall catch this fox." . . . So these have said: "We will speak so much evil of this man to the Holy Father that we will fetch him from this hole; and if he will not go, we will accuse him of disobedience, and this way he will be caught in any case." Do not think that these people care whether I go to Rome; they merely want to have me on the road. It would be enough for them to get me out of Florence. They say: "If he obeys, we shall have caught the fox; if he does not obey, we shall get him excommunicated; the people will be scandalized, and he will lose favour." But you know that we shall obey the Holy Father, and that I and my brethren would rather die than commit a sin.'

As for the second matter, he who had so often from the same pulpit called for the exercise of mercy when the country was in danger, cried out against the traitors: 'What are you doing, Council of the Eight? It is time to take up the sword: show them no mercy. Make a law that anyone who speaks ill of this state should pay fifty ducats; *quia est crimen læsæ maiestatis,* it is a crime of *lèse-majesté.* I tell you that Christ intends to rule here, and any who fight against this government fight against Christ.' For the usual grumblers he jokingly proposed instead a lighter punishment: 'I would that you, Signori, when you have some difficult matter to decide, should call in these gossips and say to them: "Tell us, what is to be done in this affair?" And I'll wager my cloak that they would not know what to say; or if they did say something, it would be something stupid. Then you should take a measure of millet and say to them: "Here, take this and go and feed the chickens."'

In this sermon and in that of the following Sunday, the 18th of October, also devoted almost entirely to matters of state, he proposed many wise provisions to give greater perfection to the new government. He also asked in the sermon on the 18th that they should speed up the building of the great hall and set (as was later done) a tablet in the wall with the following famous lines carved on it: '*Chi vuole fare parlamento, vuol torre al popolo il reggimento.*'[1] He further said: 'If you find any one of those who speak ill of this state and this government, set him down as an enemy and rebel against Christ. So I told you recently that you should cut off the head of anyone who works against this state. "O friar, you have preached and still preach peace!" Brother, you seek to destroy the peace.' Again there was no lack of critics of this fresh interference of a friar in the city's affairs. Others, as Parenti notes, praised him, seeing that the citizens themselves did not dare to speak out and put forward the needs of the people: 'This Fra Girolamo did openly and without fear, the sole champion and pillar of popular goverment.'

And indeed that humble friar appeared now more than ever to rule alone over the destinies and people of the city, while almost all the rulers of other Italian states were hostile and threatening in their attitude towards the Florentines. It was perhaps shortly before the point our narrative has now reached, that Lodovico Sforza gave Leonardo da Vinci the strange commission to find out 'what forms the reverend father called Fra Girolamo used in ordering the state of fortifications: *item,* the orders and the exact form of all his dispositions'. So Savonarola was also believed to concern himself with the fortifications as well as with the government of the Republic—he who wanted only to build a fortress against the enemies of Christ!

Meanwhile, on the 16th of October the Pope had sent another Brief, which, as usual, took some time to arrive; yet through the usual mysterious channels the Friar had already had some advance news of it. On the 25th, knowing that he would now have to give up his preaching, he wished to take leave of his faithful people before the actual order arrived. On this occasion, without giving any explanation, he said: 'Fra Domenico will come back to preach to you on the Apostle's day. Pray God that he may inspire me when I shall preach again.' And the day after, in conversation with the Ferrarese ambassador, he told him he had good hopes, 'from information received from his friends in

---

[1] ['Those who want a parliament seek to destroy democratic government.' The *parlamento,* or popular assembly, need not be called, but when summoned was omnipotent and could resolve any matter with a two-thirds majority. Such popular decisions were feared by experienced men, as they were open to the influence of demagogues and armed intimidation.]

Rome', that the Pope would suspend action against him and 'silence the whole affair'.

This was, in effect, the substance of the Papal Brief of October the 16th, which, after the preceding sweet and bitter ones, might be termed bittersweet. Having learned the good reasons advanced by the Friar, and having had good reports of him from the Protector of the Order, from other cardinals and perhaps even from the very man whom he had appointed as judge of the accused, the Blessed Fra Sebastiano Maggi—who, like the saintly man he was, would only have been able to repeat what he had always said of Fra Girolamo, that 'he had heard his confession innumerable times in Lombardy without finding even a venial sin in him'—in these circumstances what could the Pope do? The crafty lawyer from Barcelona quickly realized that his advisers had once again led him into a thornbush, and he made haste to extricate himself as best he could, with his usual coolness.

Without openly admitting that he had been deceived by others, this is what he said in this Brief: He had been much displeased by the disturbances among the Florentine people (a fine confession!), especially as they were due to the sermons of Fra Girolamo. These, rather than rooting out vice (a remarkable contradiction of what was said in the Brief of July the 21st), strove to predict the future. It was not, therefore, without mature consideration that he had called him to justify himself against the accusations brought against him, which *should they be true,* would call for punishment. Yet, having now heard that Fra Girolamo was willing to submit to the corrective authority of the Roman Church, he had been well pleased and had begun to believe that Fra Girolamo had preached these things not out of wickedness but out of a certain simplicity and zeal to labour well in the Lord's vineyard. He ordered him, therefore, in holy obedience, to refrain from any further preaching until he was able to present himself before the Pope, or until some other decision, after mature consideration, should be made in his case. If he obeyed, the former Brief would be suspended together with all the clauses they contained.

To take away the Friar's freedom to preach was like taking his life, and for the city it meant dismantling its most powerful bastion against enemies within and without. So they and the Pope, having aimed at a greater victory, could be happy at least in this. Piero de' Medici, meanwhile, was busy raising an army on the border of Florentine territory nearest Perugia. On the other hand, Savonarola too had some cause for satisfaction and for regarding himself as victorious, having forced the Borgia Pope to withdraw more or less openly his unjust accusations and, above all, to countermand those orders for punishment which would have meant the ruin of all the Friar's work. Because of his love for this work, and because he had already declared that he was unwilling to sin even venially in this matter, he shut himself up in a longer and more productive silence.

Chapter 15

THE FIRST INTERVAL OF SILENCE

‹✕✕✕›

ON the 8th of September, the same day on which he sent to Savonarola that unfortunate Brief, the Pope also addressed to the Florentines a sharp letter instructing them, under threat of excommunication, to refrain from giving further assistance to the King of France. Such a coincidence will not surprise the reader after so many similar ones which I have been at pains to note in these pages. At the same time, the Pope ordered Charles to leave Italy within a few days, requiring him, if he did not do so, to appear before him in Rome, under pain of excommunication. Borgia was not very happy in these Briefs of his; for he gave the King the opportunity to reply sarcastically that he would very much like to come to Rome, but he would like first to be assured that the Pope would not run away, as he had done on Charles's previous visit to that city.

We may be sure that it was not on account of the Briefs of Alexander VI that, at the time of which we are speaking—i.e. the end of October—the King crossed the Alps again to France, 'more like the vanquished than the victor, despite the victories he had won'. He left the Florentines in a sea of troubles, though they alone had remained friendly to him in an otherwise entirely hostile Italy. Savonarola was even worse off, though he had firmly held his people to that alliance in spite of threats and entreaties from the Pope and Sforza, and in spite of the shameless bad faith of the King, who still kept the lands he had taken from them, with the exception only of Leghorn. To no avail, the Friar wrote to him again after he had left Italy, reminding him that he had suffered the misfortune Savonarola had predicted because he had been unwilling to believe the Friar's prophecies.

The King's misfortunes were not limited to the unsuccessful Italian venture. He was to suffer a more painful disaster in France, for shortly after his return he learned of the death of his only son, the Dauphin Charles Roland. This was the blow that the Friar had predicted in Poggibonsi. When Commines heard this prophecy, he had thought at once of the Dauphin: 'When he spoke of this judgment of God, there came into my mind the death of the Dauphin, for I could not imagine any other thing that the King might so take to heart.' The King may not have thought of this at the time, but the prophecy must have come back to him when the misfortune occurred, or at least when he was reminded of it in the letter of the terrible Friar.

The correspondence of Savonarola with Charles VIII was one of the things that most irriatated the Pope, Sforza, and the Arrabbiati. Savonarola's long letter of the 26th of May, which was printed through the inopportune zeal or the vanity of some follower, or perhaps through the venality of some publisher, was bitterly attacked by the supporters of the League. Savonarola complained of this in his sermon of the 28th of July: 'That letter which I wrote to the King of France was printed without my knowledge, and contains many errors. I beg the reverend Vicar not to permit these things to be published unless he has first examined them, and that the printers should not take them without the Vicar's stamp and licence.' He must have been annoyed less by the errors in the published text (there is no question of falsification) than by the reproaches and bitter invective to which it gave rise on the part of his enemies, who had published in Bologna a lengthy and embittered commentary (a fact that hitherto seems to have escaped Savonarolan scholars).

Fra Girolamo must have found his correspondence with the Duke of Ferrara, at this time quite frequent and regular, a good deal more satisfactory than that with the King, who does not seem ever to have answered his letters. With the Duke he corresponded either directly or through the letters of the ambassador Manfredi, who often reported to his Duke what the Ferrarese Friar had said, and passed on to the Friar the expressions of reverent esteem of the lord of his native city. This relationship had begun when Duke Ercole, having heard great things of the Friar, grandson of the former chief physician at his

Court and now practically the leader of the Florentine Republic, had charged his ambassador, on the 13th of May, 1495, to question him on the affairs of Italy, on the great threats he uttered against its princes, and especially on the subject of Ferrarese politics. On the 18th the ambassador reported the Friar's answer, which was a very general one, with a promise of a more detailed reply which Savonarola himself would write, and which in fact he sent on the 20th or 21st in a letter that is now lost. We may gather, however, from the Duke's delighted answer that in it Savonarola gave him 'advice full of prudence and charity', promising to send him the *Compendio* as soon as it was ready. On this matter of the *Compendio* the letters became more frequent, and we have already quoted some of them; others were received and sent during the period of the most recent Papal Briefs.

At that time the Duke of Este was in Lombardy, where he had witnessed the short-lived truce between the King of France and Sforza. The famous humanist Pandolfo Collenuccio, after a short stay in Florence, there gave the Duke an account of how he had enjoyed every day the company of 'our Fra Girolamo of Ferrara, truly a holy man, even greater in person than in his writings'. It is worth mentioning here, as an instance of the Friar's clairvoyance, that when Collenuccio discussed the truce with him and spoke of certain letters newly received from Sforza referring to it as a true and fruitful peace, as it was generally believed to be, 'he, still smiling, called it a treacherous affair, unworthy of the name of peace'. Later, when Collenuccio called on him again to take his leave before returning to Bologna, and asked him for his final opinion on the truce, Savonarola replied: 'Messer Pandolfo, I will answer you with the words of the prophet Ezekiel: "*Eo quod deceperint populum meum, dicentes pax pax, et non est pax*" ["Because they have seduced my people, saying, Peace; and there was no peace"].' That the truce was in fact a deception was shown soon afterwards by the ambiguous behaviour of Lodovico Sforza.

In the same letter in which Collenuccio related these things about the Friar, he also told the Duke that Savonarola was sending him in a few days 'that book of his done into Latin',—that is, the first edition of the *Compendio* in Latin; 'it was already printed, and he told me that we must wait for it to dry.' He sent it off on the 29th of October, and with it a letter, to which his noble correspondent sent an affectionate reply.

Yet, as he proudly boasted later, Savonarola was never willing to take advantage of this close relationship with the Court of Ferrara and the reverent and kindly disposition of the Duke, to obtain some relief for his family, which, apart from his brother Alberto the doctor, was suffering the hardships of poverty. Rather than say a word on the subject to the Ferrarese ambassador, Savonarola wrote to his brother Alberto on the 28th of October, scolding him and exhorting him to aid with money and a few bushels of corn his other brother, Ognibene, sore laden with children and poverty. 'It is no use expecting anything from me, *quia mortuus sum mundo* ['for I am dead to this world'], and I cannot help any of you, except in spiritual matters,' he wrote; nor had he ever written in any other tone to his poor mother.

In those days the Friar was endeavouring, as he always did when silenced by illness or his enemies, to sow the good seed by means of his writings, since he could not do so with his sermons. On the 26th of April he had published his fine prayer, *Diligam te, Domine;* and on the 24th of October the *Operetta sopra i Dieci Comandamenti* [*Treatise on the Ten Commandements*]. He was now drafting his treatise *De simplicitate christianæ vitæ,* with which—now that he had perfected the political reform in his city of Florence which should serve as an example to the whole of Christendom—he intended to begin his religious and moral reform. This work in substance was a full exposition of all Catholic doctrine, written with that clarity and intelligibility for the general public which is one of the finest qualities of many of his writings; and it gave the lie conclusively to those accusations of heresy and schism made against him by the Tiepidi, with the Pope at their head.

In the meantime, as his enemies were again raising their heads and his supporters were losing courage, Savonarola published between November and December a brief apologia in the form of a letter, in which he said what he could not then say from the pulpit, and refuted the many reports about him circulating in the city. In this *Epistola a un amico* [*Letter to a Friend*], whose immediate popularity is attested by the appearance of three editions almost simultaneously, the author rebuts the charges against him of heresy, false prophecy, schism, and dis-obedience ('If this were true,' he replies, 'it would certainly not have gone unpunished, but His Holiness the Pope, having heard my ex-planation, in his wisdom remained perfectly satisfied'). He also rejects the accusation of having disturbed the city, which he had in fact paci-fied, and of having put in power a 'senseless government', whereas it was the best that could have been devised. Finally he replies to other charges and refers the reader also to his *Compendio di rivelazioni*.

These apologetic writings, which the Friar was to employ more and more in his enforced silences, incited his opponents to reply in the same form. This gave rise to the vast number of works for and against Savonarola, which occupy a unique position in the history of fifteenth-century printing; though equally remarkable is the number of editions of his own works. The *Epistola a un amico* was immediately countered by the Arrabbiati with an *Epistola responsiva a frate Ieronimo . . . da l'amico suo;* it is hard to say which is most tedious, its length, its stupidity, or its gratuitous insults.

But if these and similar libels could do little harm to the Friar, neither his own apologies nor those of his followers (e.g. the *Epistola a uno amico* of Domenico Benivieni in answer to the last-mentioned work), however compelling and conclusive they might be, could ever have the force and effect of his sermons. These were now urgently needed, not only for the work of moral reform which had already been begun, but also for the very safety of the city while Piero de' Medici was still biding his time on the border nearest Perugia. On the 2nd of December he was to come as far as Cortona, where, it was rumoured, he had some understanding with people in the town.

The Signoria, therefore, decided to do all in its power to get permission for Savonarola to preach in the following Advent. To this end they wrote on the 13th of November a pressing letter to the Pope in which after saying much in praise and defence of Fra Girolamo, the eloquent Chancellor Scala burst forth with these words: '*Indigemus, Beatissime Pater, indegemus isto viro Dei atque prædicatione*' ['We need this man of God, Holy Father, and his preaching']. On the same day and with the same urgency of expression they approached Cardinal Carraffa, and wrote again to him on the 17th, so that he might obtain the permission for the Friar from the Pope *vivæ vocis oraculo,* as time was now running short and it would take too long to obtain a Brief in the usual forms.

In spite of these moves, the first Sunday of Advent passed without the requested permission being received; and on the eve of the second Sunday the Council of Ten sent still more pressing representations to Becchi, the Florentine ambassador in Rome, asking him to refresh the Cardinal's memory and, if necessary, to speak urgently to the Pope himself in the name of the Republic. No answers to these letters survive, but that an answer, and in no uncertain terms, was received, is shown by a comment in Landucci's diary under the date December 11th: 'We heard that the Pope sent orders to Fra Girolamo that he should not preach'—which is obviously a popular version of the contents of a letter from the Protector or from Becchi to the officers of the city, now lost, like so many of the answers to letters from the Signoria and the Council of Ten.

The Florentines, by now so used to hearing their prophet preach, especially at Advent and Lent, were mortified at the news and could not resign themselves to it. The faithful Fra Domenico da Pescia did what he could to fill the gap with his sermons. He had come to be called the 'Fattoraccio' [the 'rotten bailiff'] in the contemptuous terminology of the Arrabbiati, on account of his devotion to Savonarola and his frequent standing in for him. Following in the footsteps of his master, Fra Domenico devoted his sermons from the pulpit of Santa Maria del Fiore at the end of that year to the reform of the boys of Florence, who were more vicious and badly behaved than those of any other city in Italy. To gain their interest and at the same time control them better, he ordered them into groups by quarters, and made them elect their own officers. They agreed to give up their brutal game of throwing stones, while the 'pole game', which consisted in barring the streets, was turned to good purposes: the tolls taken from passers-by were distributed as alms instead of being spent on riotous living as before.

The year 1496 opened gloomily for the city. They were expecting to have Pisa restored to them with the arrival from France of Monsieur de Gemel, who had been sent by the King for that purpose or with the pretence of it. Instead, they lost the city completely. The French commander of the fortress, disobeying the King's apparent orders, treacherously sold the fort and handed it over to the Pisans. Naturally, the Florentines were furious, as Landucci tells us; and as a result, led by the Arrabbiati, the ignorant and vulgar people 'turned against the Friar in hatred, and roamed about San Marco at night, shouting and uttering insults: *That pig of a friar, we'll burn him in his house. . . .* And some wanted to set fire to the convent gate'. To meet this situation, the Eight decreed 'that nothing should be said in public about the Friar, nor about the government, under pain of severe punishment'. Certain crude sonnets by Tommaso Baldinotti attacking the Friar must have been written at this time. On his side, it is doubtful if the Friar got much consolation from the letters written in his defence, and in defence of the friendship with the King of France, by that 'sinning Angel', the anchorite of Vallombrosa,[1] who sent out a tedious procession of wishy-washy writings in print and in manuscript. The city was divided and full of quarrels, and, owing to the treacherous behaviour of the French, not a few who had previously been favourable to them, were now beginning to incline towards the side of the League; among these we shall soon find the chronicler Parenti.

It was, therefore, more than ever necessary that the Friar should preach, at least during the following Lent, and the Signoria and the Council of Ten again began to do battle to obtain the permission of the Pope. The Signoria wrote urgently to the Cardinal Protector on the 28th of January, and the Ten on the same day sent pressing letters to the ambassador Ricciardo Becchi and the Cardinal of Lisbon.

While in Florence letters were being written, in Prato prayers were being said. Special prayers for this purpose in the convent of San Domenico had been ordered by Savonarola in a letter to Fra Antonio di Olanda, the Prior. This convent had only recently been joined to the Congregation of San Marco—which is remarkable evidence of the great esteem in which, in spite of the Papal Briefs, the superiors of the Order continued to hold Fra Girolamo. Their General himself, who had come to Florence about that time, had given him personal demonstration of that same high regard.

However, on the 5th of February the Signoria was still pressing the case with Cardinal Caraffa to get for the Friar that blessed permission to preach—and to preach 'in our city', they were careful to specify, aware of the demands made from Lucca. The same day the Ten wrote to the Cardinal of Lisbon, who with the cardinals of Perugia and Segovia was active on behalf of the Signoria in seeking to weaken the Pope's determination.

The Pope's persistence, in the face of so much opposition, in a matter that cannot have seemed to him of great moment, as he had not yet conceived for the Friar the hatred he ultimately would have, would be hard to understand, if it were not for certain words he let fall which throw light on the motive. A few days later the Pope said frankly to the Florentine ambassador that 'the League did not want him

---

[1] [His writings appeared as the work of 'Frate Angelo peccatore Anachorita del heremo di Vallombrosa.' His name was either Angelo Fondi or Angelo Leonora.]

to allow Fra Girolamo to preach': a truly wonderful admission for its pure effrontery! Not zeal for religion, then, but dirty politics was at the bottom of it all.

In the end, however, being assailed from so many quarters, the Pope, while not consenting to countermand the Brief of October the 16th, did go so far as to give his permission *vivæ vocis oracula* to Caraffa and Becchi for Savonarola to preach again. But, as was characteristic of the nature of the man, he probably did not give this permission unconditionally; because then, if it suited his purpose, he would always be able to deny that he had given it, as in fact he eventually did. However, if it is easy to trick individuals and peoples, it is more difficult to deceive history; and this is borne out by the fact that, of this almost silent consent obtained by Cardinal Caraffa, of which there was to remain no record, we have enough evidence today to prove absolutely that it was given, enough to prevent any historian worthy of his profession from asserting, as some did, that Savonarola preached against the ban of the Pope.

This ambiguous consent, which even Borgia did not dare to deny in principle (an eloquent confirmation that he gave it) when he was reminded of it by the bishop Niccolò Pandolfini at the time of the first papal reprimands, must have reached Florence between the 14th and 15th of February, allowing the necessary time for the latest letters from the Florentine government to have had their effect. On the 16th the Friar openly declared that he had had permission from the Pope to preach in Lent. But even before this, on the 11th, the Signoria, still without replies to its letters from the Cardinal and from Becchi, had decided to wait no longer. With a unanimous vote it had ordered Savonarola, who asked for nothing better, to preach during Lent in Santa Maria del Fiore, under pain of their grave displeasure.

When the news of this decision spread throughout the city, it changed the anxiety of recent days, when all were in suspense as to whether the Friar would preach, into great rejoicing and eager expectation. Since the floor of the Duomo, despite its immense size, was not considered capable of holding all the congregation, they set to work in great haste labouring day and night, to put up tiers of wooden steps as in an amphitheatre—a thing never before seen in any Florentine church.

On the 16th of February some 4,000 boys between the ages of six and nine, and another 6,000 between ten and fourteen, in groups according to quarters of the city, and each quarter with its own flag, headed by the pipers and mace-bearers of the Signoria, marched in procession through the city with olive branches in their hands, singing hymns specially composed by Girolamo Benivieni and Savonarola himself. It was such a moving spectacle for those who saw and heard it, that the good townsfolk wept with relief and said: 'Truly, this change is the work of God.' It is Landucci who tells us this, adding: 'We seemed to be looking at those crowds in Jerusalem who walked before and behind Christ on Palm Sunday saying: "Blessed is he that cometh in the name of the Lord."' These were the same boys who not long before had been practising sodomy, the same who before had molested and frightened passers-by, the same who had often injured or killed some of their own number and others as well with their stupid game of stone-throwing, the game which, writes Nardi, was so rooted in long tradition that 'not even the severe and terrible proscriptions of the magistrates had been able to repress it, let alone stamp it out.'

Finally on the morning of Ash Wednesday came the time for the Friar's sermon. The streets were crowded through which he passed on his way to the church, accompanied by a large group of his followers bearing arms beneath their cloaks. 'The women up on the walls looked on him as if he were a saint, or at least as the man in whom lay the salvation of this people.' The immense church was even more crowded, and had been since daybreak, with about 15,000 people; the wooden tiers were packed, too, with children singing, before the Friar came, some of those sweet hymns in the vulgar tongue. They sang:

> *Viva Cristo e chi gli crede!*
> *Su, Fiorenza, all'operare!*
> *Che Gesù vuol coronare*
> *chi morrà per questa fede.*[1]

'At that time,' wrote Landucci, 'there was such feeling in that church, and such sweetness from those children singing, some above, some below, some on this or that side, that it did not seem to come from children's mouths. . . . Truly the church was full of angels.' When the preacher arrived and the singing stopped, every murmur was silenced among the waiting crowd, and finally in the vast silence he spoke.

---

[1] 'Long live Christ and those who believe in him! Come, Florence, set to work! For Jesus will crown all who die for his faith.'

Chapter 16

THE SERMONS ON AMOS; THE QUIET
AFTER THE STORM

<><><><><><><><><><><><><><><><><><><><><><><><><><><><><><><><><>

As always, Savonarola returned from long meditation with himself and with God, more ready and ardent for his work. He was a preacher to the marrow of his bones, and after that long silence his heart was full of sermons, as the heart of a poet is full of song. After his exordium he went straight into the fray, conversing as usual with an imaginary interlocutor: '"What does it mean, friar, that you stayed so long to rest and did not enter the field to help your soldiers? Were you perhaps afraid of being killed?" Certainly not, my children. If I had been afraid, I should not have come back now, for I am in greater danger now than before. "Was it your conscience pricked you, and made you stop preaching?" Not I. Why should it? "Oh, we understand that an excommunication came, and you were forbidden to preach." Did you read that excommunication? Who sent it? But, even supposing it was so, do you not remember that I told you that even if it came, it would be worthless?'

He demonstrated this with a parable: 'Tell me, if you had a business in Bruges and it was well managed by one of your men, and if out of jealousy your rivals wrote slandering him, and you, disturbed by these letters, recalled him, telling him what you had heard about him, and he came back and let the business go to ruin, then would you not be angry with him and say: "Fool, did you not see how I wrote to you? On no account should you have come back." No one, he continued, should obey the commands of a superior when they run counter to the commands of God. 'Oh, you who write so many lies in Rome, what will you write now? I well know what you will write. "What, friar?" You will write that I said one should not obey the Pope, and that I will not obey him. That is not what I said. Write down what I did say, and you will find it does not suit you.'

And yet a scruple of conscience had held him back from preaching: this he recognized and explained with the words of the psalm which he had taken as his text that morning: '*Dixi: custodiam vias meas*' (Psalm 39). 'Seeing so much opposition, from so many quarters, against a poor man not worth three pence, I said in my heart: "Perhaps you did not take good heed to your ways, and your tongue has erred." And so I looked carefully at my ways, one by one.' He was not concerned with the ways of the mind. As for the ways of faith, he knew that he had always believed everything that the Holy Roman Church believed, and had submitted and still did submit to Her. Likewise, he did not find that he had erred concerning the good life, or in pride or envy. So, having found all his ways blameless, and recognizing the need of the good and the wicked, he began to preach again, though not without placing on his mouth a good bridle, as the psalm says; the bridle of Prudence, which he put on out of consideration for the wicked, 'for if only the just were listening, there would be no need of such a bridle'.

This is how he began his Lenten sermons, 'the most eloquent that ever issued from his heart'. They were collected by Lorenzo Violi and, what is more important, published with the consent and collaboration of Savonarola himself. With a shortening of the title given them in some sixteenth-century editions, they are usually known as the *Prediche sopra Amos* [*Sermons on Amos*], from the book that provided the text for all except the first. I can find no other reason for the Friar's choice of this prophet, than that Amos was killed as he himself was to be killed. He made a reference to this when introducing the text: 'So, good people, do not marvel at our persecutions, do not be dismayed, for this is the end of prophets: this is our end and our reward on this earth.'

This, then, was his exordium of this Lenten series. And for the first few days, the prudence that the preacher had set as a bridle on his mouth, appeared to be keeping good guard. But, as Savonarola often said, he was one man in the pulpit and another out of it. 'This is a terrible place,' he said one day; 'one cannot do up here as one does down there.' And truly, when he was up there, it was no longer Savonarola who spoke, and there was no bridle capable of stemming the flood of words which overflowed from his heart. We know what had been his dominant preoccupation from the days of his childhood, what had brought him to the cloister, what had governed his whole life, inspired his every action: the renovation of the Church. No human force, certainly not his own, could have removed this preoccupation from his heart; nothing could have induced him any longer simply to weep in silence, as he had written in his youthful poem.

In the seventh sermon, on the 24th of February, the symbolic bridle set upon his tongue had already allowed a good many words against the prelates of Rome: '"*Ne prophetetis.*" They do not want anyone to prophesy. Tell me, why do you wish to drive out this divine faculty from the Church? . . . Jeremiah and Amos were ready to die rather than not prophesy and not obey God. . . . We only say what is true; it is your sins that prophesy against you. It is not I, but all earth and heaven that prophesy against you. . . . We lead men to simplicity and women to live in decency, you lead them to lust and pomp and pride, for you have spoiled the world and corrupted men with lust, women with indecency, and children you have led to sodomy and filth and turned them into prostitutes. . . . No, God has told us to prophesy; we will therefore obey God and not men.'

On the 27th he compared the pious Florentine carnival with that of Rome. On the 28th he gave his famous bold sermon on the kine of Samaria—i.e. the concubines of Rome, 'concubines of priests and friars': 'Come, leaders of the Church, come, priests, come, friars, come, novices . . .; you go at night to your concubine, and the morning after, you go to take the Sacraments'—words that, though used gener-ally, everyone must have applied to Borgia, a disgraceful fornicator. Every day, almost without fail, Savonarola made some attack on the Roman prelates: 'Look at the Court today, where they sell benefices and even the blood of Christ and the Virgin for money . . .; they talk only of evil, of women and boys; they waste their time on dogs and mules; the Lord has allowed these gardens to be ruined.' It would seem that at this time there had come to Savonarola's ears some information, beyond what he already knew, about the scandalous behaviour of the Pope and some cardinals, and that it had greatly aroused his anger;

this is perhaps the secret to which he alludes darkly with the metaphor of the little key.[1]

The Pope was not unaware of the true but terrible things that the terrible but veracious Friar was shouting from the pulpit. The Arrabbiati assumed the task of reporting them to him, suitably amplified and distorted (as one of them confessed), almost day by day. Borgia was not slow, therefore, to complain bitterly to the Florentine ambassador, and to threaten some demonstration of his anger against the preacher and the city. Once again the pretended reasons seemed more persuasive than the real causes; but, whatever the cause of this anger was, we can be sure that neither zeal for the reverence due to his office (in this he was extremely tolerant) nor personal resentment could have overcome the splendid indifference of Borgia. The truth lay elsewhere: in one of his conversations with the Florentine ambassador the Pope let slip the astonishing confession, which we have already quoted, that the League did not want Fra Girolamo to preach.

This also explains very well the sporadic nature of the Pope's anger. As it was not based on reasons or pretence of apostolic zeal, nor, up to this point, on strong hatred or fear, it rose and fell according to the prevailing political winds or according to the inspiration received from Sforza, the Venetians, the Arrabbiati and the other enemies of the Friar. And so, after the angry demonstrations of the beginning of March, his wrath subsided; so much so that the Florentine ambassador could report: 'His Holiness seems somewhat reconciled with us, for he was very ill-disposed on account of the bad reports and advice about Fra Girolamo given by the ambassadors of the League ... complaining that you allow him to preach against the will of His Holiness, and that he holds you to allegiance with the Most Christian King against your will.' Always that same sore point!

It was precisely this irregular and ambiguous behaviour of the Pope that more than anything else aroused the indignation of Savonarola. Shortly before, he had seen contradictory Briefs arriving, volubly ordering and countermanding. Now he saw the Pope's anger boil up and subside merely for political reasons and in response to the reports of his enemies; he saw all his great work of Christian and moral reform depending on these unsavoury manoeuvres. Then these words came from his sincere and passionate heart, in an outcry against all such intrigues: 'I am ordered by Christ to defend this truth, and to stay

1. See Note on page 165

here as long as I draw breath. . . . Go, write to Rome and say: "That friar says that Rome may do what she pleases, she will never put out this flame. . . ." I tell you that this flame is lit in bishops, prelates, and cardinals, for there are cardinals too who defend this truth, and it is lit in many parts of Italy, and in many great secular leaders; and when the time comes, this truth will burst forth; and I have letters too from certain great men, of which I will not tell you at present. . . .'

With these words he was stirring up a wasp's nest. The Pope knew very well how many sovereigns, princes, and, in his own Court, cardinals, bishops, churchmen wished to set their hand to the reform of the Church. He could not fail to be suspicious and displeased that they should turn to that indomitable friar with whose ardour, dangerous zeal for religion, mysterious fascination, and great following he was well acquainted. The protests started again. Or perhaps this is where they really began as the direct expression of Alexander VI's own feelings. From words, it seemed, he had the intention of passing to deeds. Someone remembered that Fra Girolamo had once been accused in Bologna of having criticized the Pope, and the records of the proceedings were looked up. At the same time, the Pope thought of putting Savonarola's case in the hands of two cardinals, two bishops, the General of the Order, and some masters of theology.

In the meantime it was said that he had sent an order either to the Signoria or to the Friar himself that he should stop preaching, and that the Council of Eight had had the papal runner escorted out of Florentine territory before he could execute his mission. There is no proof of this, and such rumours were often spread by the Arrabbiati to ruin the Friar's reputation and discourage his followers. On the 14th of March the Friar denied from the pulpit that any such order had come. I cannot say whether, playing on words, he simply meant that it had not come *to him*. He added: 'But I have written to him'; and he said the same thing two days later. Again we are groping in the dark. But, by the glimmer of light those words seem to shed, it would appear that there must have been another letter from Savonarola to the Pope, so far unsuspected by any biographer, and lost, like the one of July 1495, at least to us, if not also to the addressee. We have already seen, and shall have occasion to see again, that it was an habitual recourse of the Friar (and a sign of good faith) to turn directly to the Pope when clouds gathered in the direction of Rome.

Now, as we have already seen, a storm was gathering in those parts. In Florence, too, where opinions were divided, the atmosphere was becoming heated, though it was only a pious hope that made Somenzi forecast 'that this people is going to see confusion; that is, they are going to fight among themselves'. But he added sadly: 'I believe that when it comes, the Friar's party will win, because it is a good deal bigger: two-thirds of the people are for the Friar.' No truer than his forecast was what Sforza's agent wrote in the same letter about the influence of Savonarola in the elections of the magistrates: 'He is the one who makes the Signoria as he pleases, *et similiter* all the other offices and magistrates.' This did not occur even indirectly, as far as the Friar's own desires went. Indeed, during those very days he had reproved from the pulpit those who gave their votes to his followers solely because they were his followers.

On the other hand, it was quite true that the magistrates, interpreting the will of the people, upheld the cause of their prophet with obstinacy and courage, and even rashly. I have already said that there is no proof that the papal messenger was deported by the Eight; but the firm resolution of the Signoria at this time is shown by a letter sent to Becchi on the 12th of March, in which they constitute themselves observers and guarantors of the Friar's preaching; and also by the way they called to order the Augustinian Fra Gregorio da Perugia, who, preaching against the Friar at the instigation of the Arrabbiati, had gone beyond the limits of decent antagonism. Then, as always, the zeal of the Ten was heroic. Strong in the greater length of their tenure and the important functions of their office, on which the foreign relations of the Republic depended, they multiplied encouragements and exhortations to their ambassadors on behalf of the Friar, particularly in Milan and Rome, where poor Becchi, a man of little weight and not very enthusiastic about the Friar, found himself between the hammer of the magistrates and the anvil of the Pope. The Ten hustled and pestered him to get the Pope to allow Fra Girolamo to preach during the rest of Lent. So as to keep hidden this extreme support of theirs, but much more not to reveal the increasingly vigorous threats being made in Rome against the Friar, they repeatedly told the ambassador to write information on matters of this kind on separate sheets, so that they might keep them secret when the letters of the ambassador had to be read out in the councils. These contained many, among them some of the Friar's supporters, who were more prudent, or richer and hence more afraid of the interdicts out of concern for the effect on trade, and consequently disinclined to break with the Pope.

One of these was the courageous Piero Capponi, who in the deliberations of the 10th of March said of Savonarola 'that, in view of the great work he had done and was doing in the city, it would be a good thing to use all means possible to get him to preach while there was no prohibition from the Pope; but, as there was such a prohibition, he considered it advisable to call together some doctors and citizens learned in the law to meet Fra Girolamo and discuss with him what was best to be done for the interests and good of the city, so as not to go against the will of the Pope: because *"reddite quæ sunt Cæsaris Cæsari at quæ sunt Dei Deo"*. On other occasions the interdicts of the Pontiff had done great harm to the city, and particularly to her merchants.'

In short, in spite of the favour of the Florentine government, in spite of the fact that a great majority of the people followed him, the affairs of Fra Girolamo were in the long run to be attended by some danger, if the storm that threatened from the direction of Rome were to burst and damage with its spiritual thunderbolts the thoroughly temporal interests of the Florentine merchants. Tempers were heated, and arguments embittered and driven to extremes by those preachers who, like the aforesaid Fra Gregorio, inveighed against Savonarola; while he, attacked with so many false accusations, was obliged to defend himself; and there can rarely be defence without offence.

He was free from jealousies and petty monastic feuds, and gave proof of this in his Lenten sermons, when he supported with all the weight of his great authority the proposals of the Franciscans, his bitterest rivals, for the establishment, in the public interest, of a Monte di Pietà[1] to combat the odious usury of the Jews. But when the Franciscans, envious and angry at the following of the great preacher, went about saying that everyone who went to hear him would be excommunicated (with what grounds the reader has seen for himself), then he could not avoid joining battle with them. And one knows that in battles, even battles of words, people fight to win. Naturally some of the blows delivered by the Friar also reached the shoulders of the Roman Pharisees, and so tempers rose. On the 23rd of March when

---

[1] [Municipal pawnshop or city loan-agency.]

Bishop Pandolfini met the Pope's remonstrances with a reminder that Savonarola was preaching by his permission granted through Cardinal Caraffa, the Pontiff, who could not deny this, cut him short in a threatening tone: 'Very well, we will not speak now of Fra Girolamo; the time will come when we will speak about him to better effect.'

The Friar found himself on especially slippery ground in his sermon of the 24th of March. He had come to the end of the book of Amos with his thirty-second sermon, and had begun to expound the prophet Zechariah, and had now got to the verse that says: 'Et ostendit mihi Dominus sacerdotem magnum' ['And he showed me (Joshua) the high priest']. He then spoke of the Pope who would reform the Church: 'God will send a saintly Pope: this one or another, because He can make this one saintly if He wishes. . . .' And he went on to describe from his text the qualities of a good Pope, which formed a strange contrast, between tragic and comic, with those of Borgia. 'The Pontiff must be very chaste . . .' and so on. Not many days before, he had given a portrait of the virtues of one of the most glorious figures in the history of the papacy, St. Gregory, adding: 'I leave you to draw your own conclusions. Everything now is the opposite. Why, therefore, should I not persist in my prophecy?'

Already on street corners, indoors, in the confessional, the Tiepidi were urging women and timid menfolk: 'Hurry to communicate now, for the interdict will come before Easter!' Instead, just when it seemed as though the storm were about to break, the clouds suddenly dispersed. Those famous records of the proceedings in Bologna against Savonarola turned out to be 'trifling matters'. The theologians whom the Pope had convened—without, however, the cardinals and bishops —to examine the case, did in fact meet. Most of them, to curry favour with the Pope, spoke against Savonarola, but, in addition to one Maestro Niccolò who spoke 'quite decently', a courageous young Dominican 'most nobly' took up his defence. At this council, among the list of accusations was this very strange charge: 'that Fra Girolamo has been the cause of all the ills of Piero'! In conclusion, no conclusion. Well might Savonarola say, alluding to this tribunal in a sermon shortly afterwards: 'Scrutati sunt iniquitates, defecerunt scrutantes scrutinio' ['They examined my crimes, and the judges abandoned their inquisition'].

Lent was now over, and with it the sermons. In the last of these, on

the 10th of April, he had made a solemn act of faith and submission to
the Roman Church: 'The keys with which the Church binds and looses,
I say they have power to command everyone ... and so, as I have told
you, I am always ready for any obedience to the Roman Church,
except when its commands are against God or against charity, which I
do not believe could be; but if they were, I should say: "You are not
the Roman Church, you are a man and not the Shepherd, for the
Shepherd does not give orders against God or against charity." And
I should say: "You err."' He had also addressed the Pope with dignified respect: 'We will now speak to the Pope. It has been said and
written to His Holiness that I have spoken ill of him, which is not true.
It is written in Holy Scripture: "*Principi populi tui non maledices,* thou
shalt not curse the ruler of thy people." This I have never done. I
have never named anyone from this pulpit.' This did not mean, however, that he had not, without naming him, criticized the vices of the
Pope.

On the 13th of that month the echoes of that sermon could not yet
have reached the Court. Ricciardo Becchi, the Friar's supporter in
Rome, was then urgently begging the Ten for a letter from them or
from the Signoria, which he could show to the Pope and the cardinals,
giving some demonstration of good will on the part of the Florentines
and Fra Girolamo towards the Pope and towards the Sacred College.
They replied on the 16th with a letter that was not very formal, saying
merely that, as far as the Friar was concerned, his attitude was blindingly
clear, as he had preached in public and spoken 'very respectfully' of
the Pope. Now everything seemed fine, and Becchi wrote back on the
23rd: 'The Pope is very well pleased with the matter of Fra Girolamo.'

It is difficult to believe that the relative failure of the committee of
theologians and the fresh demonstration of respect towards the Roman
Church could have worked such a change in the Pope's feelings. Still
less could it have been due to that recent feeble letter from the Ten,
after so many others of much greater vigour had been sent. The Roman
clouds that had threatened Florence and Savonarola had been blown
away by a wind from beyond the Alps.

The King of France—continually urged by the Florentine ambassadors and by Cardinal della Rovere, but more especially by the need
to rescue his men whom he had abandoned in the Kingdom of Naples
with little hope of survival, not to mention victory—was getting ready

to march into Italy again. It was being rumoured already at the beginning of April, and about the 20th was being described as certain and imminent. Sforza, the Venetians, and, above all, the Pope were terrified. Besides their common fear of the enemy, they regarded one another with all the suspicion that each of them richly deserved. While the first two were seeking to have the Emperor enter Italy to offset the French, soon it was being said that 'the Pontiff was hinting to the King ... that he might come to some agreement with him, and leave the League'. In such circumstances, it was certainly not the moment for Borgia to quarrel with the Florentines and with the friar who was virtually their overlord.

Even Lodovico Sforza, who also had some idea of allying himself with Charles, came very near to making up his quarrel with Savonarola. The friar had written to Sforza first on the 11th of April, as it was his custom to write to all the princes of Italy to exhort and admonish them, strong in the authority of his ministry and the reputation of his great name. We may here recall, for example, the fine, grave, and prophetic letter written at this time to Galeotto Pico, Lord of Mirandola, exhorting him to mend his ways and predicting his early death. In the letter to Sforza he begins quite frankly with the Duke's harsh criticisms of him and his sermons, and then writes that he has done nothing more than invite all the princes of Italy in general terms to repent. He takes the occasion also to address to Sforza a piece of personal advice: 'to repent of his sins, because the scourge is drawing near.' And he concludes: 'I have not written this out of fear of men, nor out of concern for temporal goods, since neither from you nor from any other prince do I desire gold or silver or favour or fame or any other transitory thing, or any reward. Rather, I expect nothing from these words of mine other than infamy, opprobrium and persecution, and finally death. This do I await with great longing as my last and most perfect joy, *quia mihi vivere Christus est, et mori lucrum*' ['for Christ is my life, and death is my reward'].

He handed this letter to Somenzi so that he might send it to the Duke with the first messenger. To the cunning agent this seemed a good occasion for an attempt to gain the favour of the hated but overpowerful enemy; and so he advised his master to answer Savonarola kindly, considering 'that the said Friar could be a good means of bringing all this people into alliance with yourself, since the Friar has all the populace of this city in his favour'. The Duke liked this advice, and, congratulating Somenzi on it (both were cunning rogues, but only effective when dealing with men of their own stamp), he answered Savonarola in a letter, in which pride and former rancour almost disappear under several layers of unctuous compunction. The following passage gives some idea of this: 'If we have offended you and done anything to your displeasure, we are sorry, and from now on we shall refrain from so doing. . . . And you may be sure that your recommendation and opinion will be prized by us; and we shall not fall back from doing penance and deserving well with God.' Savonarola answered this letter of Sforza's with great sympathy on the 25th of April —on his return, that is, from a short journey out of Florence, or perhaps, though the letter is dated from the convent of San Marco, while he was still away.

Leaving Florence on the 16th of April, he had preached the next day at Prato, 'standing on the steps of the presbytery' in the church of San Domenico, and had given a sermon on the prophet Joel which was greatly admired. Landucci remarks: 'There were so many people there from Florence and the country around, practically everyone had descended on the place.' He preached again on the following days, once in the refectory of the convent before the professors and students of the Studio of Pisa, which had been transferred there on account of the rebellion in that city. Among those present were Marsilio Ficino and the then no less famous philosopher Oliviero Arduini: the Plato and the Aristotle of Florence! The sermon he gave greatly pleased that unusual audience, and when it was finished, Arduini said to his pupils: 'Let us go and carry that man's books, for we are scarce worthy to do even that.' According to the early anonymous biographer, 'he spoke so wonderfully that all were caught like fish in a net'. Among the converted were three doctors and many students, among them the young German Niccolò Schönberg, who later, when he had gone to Rome, found himself unable to forget the figure and the words of the prophetic friar. Coming to Florence at the time when the Friar was irregularly excommunicated, he went and threw himself at his feet and received from his hand the Dominican habit. He later became Procurator of the Order, archbishop, and cardinal, and carried into the papal councils and into those of the Florentine Republic something of the spirit of Savonarola.

Of other sermons at Prato—if indeed he gave any, as we are led to believe—we know no details except that in one of them he is supposed to have prophesied the dreadful sack of the town which occurred in 1512. This prophecy he repeated in private to the nuns of San Niccolò, in so far as it touched them closely. These things I repeat on the authority of the old biographers, who dwell at unusual length on the work of Savonarola in that part of the country, and describe the crowds who travelled thither day and night, singing sacred hymns, to be present at his sermons. On the other hand, they tell us nothing of what he did at Pistoia, where he had intended to go when he left Florence. But on the evening of the 25th of April two magistrates of the Eight took the trouble to ride out to Prato to ask him to preach on the following day at the Palace, for the election of the new Signoria. That night they all returned together to Florence. Such was the esteem in which the Friar was held at that time! However, either because he was indisposed or for some other reason, he was not present for that election, and it was Fra Domenico da Pescia (who always took his place when a substitute was needed on important occasions) who said Mass and preached that day in the hall of the Great Council.

At this election it was discovered that some people were trying to rig the voting, and a number were arrested and put in the Bargello. Among these were that Filippo Corbizzi whom we have already come across as gonfalonier, as a fool, and as a member of the Arrabbiati, and two of his accomplices. They were convicted of plotting, particularly out of hatred for the Friar, to overthrow the state, and were condemned to prison for life. A strange thing happened that day. Shortly before the plotters were unmasked, Fra Domenico in his sermon had spoken of a vision that had appeared to him in the night: 'how he thought he was among a crowd of angels and devils gathered together, and on the left were the devils, and on the right the angels.' This came true directly afterwards, when it was seen that the conspirators had in fact been sitting on the left of the altar.

It cannot be supposed that Savonarola went back to Prato in the following days. One scholar supposes him to have been there on the 1st of May; but we have a letter to the Duke of Ferrara dated the 27th of April at San Marco, congratulating him on the decrees he had made in Ferrara to purge the city of vice and bring it back to a Christian way of life, according to the suggestions and the example of the Friar. This letter has an autograph signature, while that of the 25th to Sforza, of which I have spoken, is entirely, including the signature, in the hand of Fra Niccolò Seratico. It could, therefore, have been copied by the chancellor from a minute sent to him from near-by Pistoia or, even nearer, from Prato.

On the 28th of April, at the printing-house of Bonaccorsi, the last sheets of a new short work by Savonarola, the *Expositio psalmi 'Qui regis Israel'*, went to press. This was at once translated by a close friend and immediately reprinted several times. On the same day, the 8th of June, two different editions of it were published. The fame and immense following of Savonarola ensured for all his works an unprecedented sale; in a short time he made all the Florentine printers rich, without counting the crumbs that fell to other Italian printers. These were not few in the fifteenth century, and in the sixteenth they would have filled the seven baskets of the New Testament.

Note

[Savonarola made frequent allusion to a 'casket' and its 'little key', to symbolize certain secret information he kept locked in his heart; and he constantly threatened to open it and reveal the truth about the Church. At first he seems to have used it with reference to the political machinations of the Arrabbiati with Rome; but later he related it exclusively to the corruption of the Papal Court.]

Chapter 17

THE SERMONS ON MICAH;
THE GREAT CALM

✕✕

AFTER Lent a decree of the Eight had commanded that within the city and a radius of a mile around its walls, there should be no preaching for two months. The reason given was fear of the plague, which had been a hidden threat for some time; but it was believed that the real reason was to silence the Tiepidi, who were preaching bitterly against the Friar, and particularly one Franciscan from San Miniato. This bitter feeling on the part of so many friars was generally attributed to their uncontrollable jealousy of the devotion that the whole city had for Fra Girolamo and San Marco, and also of the rich alms that resulted from such devotion, while the other Orders lacked both the devotion and the alms.

Yet, hardly a month had passed when, on the 8th of May, Savonarola again went into the pulpit of the Cathedral. What forced him to break the ban (Parenti says that he was believed to have been given permission, if indeed Fra Girolamo needed to have permission) and to begin preaching again after barely a month's rest, he explained himself that day: it was the abusive outcries of the Arrabbiati and the Tiepidi, the intimidation of the good, confused and discouraged by those continual attacks, and the fact that Whitsun was drawing near. At the end he added: 'I will tell you truly that preaching will serve me well, for when I do not preach I cannot live.'

Very true reasons, for the faith and favour of that changeable people needed, if they were not to dry up, to be continually irrigated

166

by the words of its prophet, 'because when the waters of eloquence fail, everything dries up'. And really the rumours spread about him by his enemies, even when he had gone to Prato and Pistoia, had been so many and so absurd, that it would have been hard to refrain from answering them, if only to hold them up to ridicule. Among other things, it had been said that he had pretended to be going to preach in order to take money out of the city and make his escape: they even quoted the figure of 60,000 ducats! So Savonarola could begin, jokingly: 'Well, here I am, and I have not run away. Some people have told so many lies, that it ought by now to suffice them. They say that I took away a lot of money: the worse for you, Florentines, who were not able to catch me!'

The reasons, then, were overwhelming. But perhaps there was also another reason. On that 8th of May, after the sermon, the great bell of the Palace rang for the Great Council, as Corbizzi and other criminals recently condemned for offences against the state, had appealed to the Council under the new law. Savonarola, who had so strongly called for mercy for the followers of the Medici, knew how important it was for a young and as yet not well established state to repress with just severity any attempt to subvert it. Before this case arose, he had said in a sermon: 'Whoever he is, cut off his head.' On this occasion, when it was not a question of capital punishment but only of imprisonment, he could only say the same. He repeated, in fact, though in general terms: do what is just. And the appeal of the criminals was rejected.

The same reasons that had moved the Friar to resume his sermons, induced him to continue them with remarkable assiduity, giving them not only on Sundays and prescribed feast days, but also on ordinary saints' days and weekdays; so that between the 8th of May and the 3rd of July he gave seventeen sermons. These and the following ones, given up to the 27th of November, were collected by Lorenzo Violi as diligently as he had collected those of Lent; and like those, they did not go to the press without being revised by the preacher himself. From the Biblical text on which most of these sermons are based, this collection was given, from the sixteenth century, the title of *Prediche sopra Ruth e Michea*.

The Friar took Ruth as a symbol of simplicity, and he preached nothing but simplicity during that period. At the same time, he was working on a new version of his treatise *De simplicitate christianæ vitæ*, of which he had sent the first version to Duke Ercole on the 10th of January. He fitted this work in during the hours he was free from preaching and giving audiences, which had become a particularly heavy charge since he had become counsellor not only of the Republic, but of the entire Florentine people. For the love of that simplicity, he demanded more and more in his sermons the moral reforms he had proposed, particularly in the dress of women. Up to then he had obtained everything he asked for from the pulpit, but this was to be, at the height of his authority and fortunes, his first defeat. The pardoning of the adherents of the old government, universal peace, popular government, the law of the six beans, all had seemed hard sacrifices to some Florentines; not, however, as hard as this one, which involved making their women look less attractive.

After much controversy, early in June, a statute on this subject was approved; but the Friar was not at all satisfied. His own recommendation had been for a somewhat broad reform to begin with, regarding the use of silks and jewels. But he was strongly opposed to what seemed to him excessively low-cut dresses, and he set up as an example the women of Genoa: 'I tell you to your faces. You are trying to spoil your beauty, rather than to improve it. So I tell you, mend this error, or I shall go on decrying it from this pulpit.' And he did go on protesting vociferously; but even in a watered-down version, the law did not get past the Council. *Inde iræ.* In his sermon on the 24th of June, St. John's day, on which the Florentines had again given up their Palio for love of him, he inveighed against the members of the Great Council: 'You are unworthy to enter that hall of Christ: you were unwilling to put through that reform. You say: "Oh, it is full of silly things". . . . I can well believe it, because you put them in to ruin it; and there are lots of things in it which seem foolish to you, but they are not. You say that it is not a good thing to include in the reform the prohibition of curled and waved hair for women. Tell me, did not St. Paul include it in his? *Non in tortis crinibus, et cætera.* . . . ["Not with braided hair, etc . . ."] But if I had been at that Council, and had read out to you that reform, they would not have seemed frivolous matters, and I should not have laughed. You well know that things are debased when they are laughed at.' But his outcry was in vain, though he kept it up in almost all his subsequent sermons. The Florentines stood firm. The reform of their womenfolk did not pass.

There were some who criticized Savonarola for his insistence on these laws and others that seemed of small importance, or at least not urgent, while magistrates and citizens were preoccupied with more serious and more pressing concerns: first that of making money, since the funds of the Republic had fallen so low that it was finding difficulty in paying its soldiers. The Friar, while blaming them for giving their thought and care exclusively to such temporal matters, made great efforts in his sermons to persuade the richer citizens to make free loans to the Commune, instead of charging interest as they usually did.

He spoke often and with passion of these and other spiritual or temporal affairs in the city, lamenting the fact that he did not find among the magistrates, in the councils, and among the people that readiness which he desired. He then refreshed the memories of the forgetful, speaking with pride of his achievements:

Find another who has done these things, predicted events so far in advance, created such enthusiasm, and reformed so great a city, and by preaching in one city has spread his fame all over Italy and outside Italy, one who has had to fight so many and such powerful opponents in so many struggles within and without the city, and caused so many to turn to the monastic life. And when he has done all this, then believe him. I have spoken to you like a madman. '*Vos me coegistis*', as the Apostle says, praising himself to the Corinthians, who were deceived by false apostles. But I tell you, it is not I who have done it, but the power of God. . . . O Italy, O Florence, '*quæ occidis prophetas et lapidas eos qui ad te missi sunt*'. You seek to slay your prophets, Italy; and you, Florence, to kill those who are sent to you by God. You jeer at the prophets, you laugh at the things that are told you by the spirit of the Lord. . . . O stones, cry out, cry out, you who have so often heard my words, since these men do not wish to hear them! Stones, remember those words, so that on the Day of Judgment you may bear witness against these men, who have not been willing to believe.

He also spoke *pro domo sua,* as the convent of San Marco was no longer large enough to hold the multitude of friars who gathered there; until, in June, he received from the heirs of Niccolò da Uzzano the unfinished building of the University, which was later linked with

San Marco by an underground passage. The nuns of the Order had benefited no less than the friars from the preaching and the example of Savonarola. Just at this time the convent of Santa Lucia, where there were only a few Dominican tertiaries, was reformed as a closed house, and immediately was filled by more than a hundred sisters. Another two hundred would have come if there had been room for them. The General of the Order, in a letter of the 26th of June, commissioned the Friar to carry out the reform and to give the veil to the nuns. Thus was fulfilled a prophecy made by the Friar when he first became Prior. Standing at the window of the Greek library of San Marco, he had said to Fra Roberto Ubaldini: 'Do you see that convent of Santa Lucia? There will be built a great convent, and many people of all the noble families of Florence will come there, and they will come with great spiritual devotion.'

The other themes of the Friar's sermons at this time are those which are common to all his preaching. He expressed himself with his usual vehemence against the vices and lack of spirit of the prelates, the priests, and the monks—possibly slightly less strongly than in the previous Lent. And no remonstrances came from Rome against him or against the magistrates of the Republic.

Even though we may without too much difficulty discern the causes of this calm, it cannot fail to surprise after the recent storms. This curious phase must be carefully considered when judging the past and future moves of the Pope. His benevolent attitude did not appear to change even when, at the beginning of June, news came that the King's enthusiasm for the new Italian expedition had cooled. The fact is that Borgia was only then beginning to understand, and perhaps to fear, the greatness, strength, and following of that man whom not only the Florentine Republic but 'all the princes in and outside Italy' believed and revered; all of them 'sought from him with letters and embassies a remedy for their misfortunes, and advice on how they should act'. The Pontiff, therefore, thought he must win his good will. So, between May and July (according to Parenti, who as a chronicler was as well informed of Palace secrets as he was of the street-corner gossip, and who was not at all favourable to the Friar) the Pope secretly sent one of his sons to Savonarola on the pretext of seeking his advice (but probably to tempt him) as to 'whether there was some means of placating the King of France, so that he should not proceed against him, and thus preserve him in the Apostolic See'. The Pope certainly did send, as Savonarola tells us, one Lodovico da Valenza, a master of theology, to persuade him to gain for the Pope the favour of the Florentines.

Finally, about the 15th of August, on which day the Friar again began to preach after a silence of six weeks in obedience to another ban imposed by the Eight for fear of the plague, the Pope sent to Florence Fra Lodovico da Ferrara, Procurator of the Order (could this not be the same occasion referred to above?). He was commissioned to discuss with Savonarola the matters on which he had preached, and to offer him a cardinal's hat on condition that he withdraw discreetly from some of the things he had said. This Fra Lodovico did. The Friar's reply was gentle, and similar to that which he usually gave in such circumstances: that he had never sought honours of any kind, but, as he had a vocation from the Lord, he wished to ask Him before replying; the messenger should, therefore, come next morning after the sermon, when, enlightened by prayer, Savonarola would be better able to give him an answer.

The papal envoy came next day to hear him, confident perhaps in the counsel that sleep can bring, and confident too, through his experience in Rome, of the miracles that the promise of a red cardinal's hat could usually work. The Friar began well. It seemed that he wished to justify all his past preaching, his moral and political reforms in Florence, his invectives against wicked prelates, his attitude towards the League, his relations with the King of France. However, the justification, which at first appeared to be the peaceful continuation of the previous evening's discussion, became more and more vigorous and impassioned, and finally burst forth in a great cry: 'I want no hats, no mitres great or small: I only want the one which Thou gavest to Thy saints: death. A red hat, a hat of blood: that is what I want.' It is recounted that when the Pope was told of Savonarola's refusal, terrified at such greatness of spirit (or perhaps merely annoyed), he ordered that no one should mention Savonarola again in his presence, either for good or evil. The story is borne out by what happened, for, although the Friar went on undeterred with his regular sermons, without toning them down in any way, there was, at least for the time being, no more interference from the Papal Court.

This might have seemed a good time to try to break the obstinacy of Savonarola and his Florentines, as his fortunes at home were showing signs of declining somewhat. There were various reasons for this decline, but they all depended ultimately on the recent coolness of the King towards Italian affairs. It seemed to many even among the Friar's partisans, that the city, surrounded as it was by so many enemies, could expect no help from one who had been either unwilling or unable to rescue even his own troops left behind in the Kingdom of Naples, all of whom had by then surrendered or been killed. Thus, in Florence the murmurings and dissensions increased; and at this time the Piagnoni did not have the best of it.

It was not that the partisans of the Friar, who, as we know, were the majority of the people, had suddenly become opposed to him. An incautious reader might be led to think so by some biographers who are inclined, in order to digest the very last crumb of erudition, to generalize on every document, every libel, every factious piece of information. But it is true that the misfortunes of the Florentines, almost all of which bore the seal of the lilies of France, gave great strength to the voices of his opponents and weakened those of his followers. The latter, though still faithful, did not know how to oppose the eloquence, not of the Arrabbiati, but of events. A prime cause of the instability and changeableness of Florence was the short terms of certain key offices: the Signoria was elected for two months, and the Eight for four. In fact, at the time of which we are now speaking, neither the Signoria nor the Eight were particularly favourable to Savonarola. And when he began to preach again at the end of August, he suffered another misfortune.

On the 23rd, Lodovico Sforza called before him the ambassadors of Ferrara and Florence and, in the presence of the whole Council, caused to be read aloud, as the work of the Friar, certain letters that he said he had intercepted on their way to France. One, which seemed directed to the King in person, though addressed to a certain Fra Clemente, simply begged him to come to Italy. The other, addressed to a Messer Niccolò, using guarded words and without naming anyone, sought to give a warning against the Archbishop of Aix, the French ambassador in Florence, whose actions seemed of doubtful loyalty to the King and hostile to the Friar. These letters, which in their brevity would be better described as notes, were the most inept fabrications imaginable. But, whether Sforza himself had written them, or whether someone in Florence had done so with the express purpose of having them intercepted, they furnished the Duke with a good pretext for a demonstration of indignation. After uttering scorching words in the presence of the two ambassadors, he had copies sent, not without suitable comments, to all the Italian states, and also (with notable perfidy) to the Archbishop of Aix, who was accused in the letters, if not of treason, of using little zeal in the service of his king.

The effects of these communications from Sforza were varied. The French ambassador was most vociferous of all. He had come to Florence on the 22nd of May and had gone at once to see the Friar, hoping to gain his assistance in his mission. However, as this consisted in mulcting the poor Florentines of another large sum of money in return for the usual empty promises, and as the Archbishop, a partisan of the Duke of Orléans, was at the same time promoting on his own account some court intrigue or other, he found the Friar not disposed to listen. Seeing Savonarola's coolness, he began to speak ill of him and intrigue against him, without worrying whether it was to the King's advantage to undermine the most solid pillar of support he had in Florence. It is, therefore, easy to imagine how much fuss he made about those wonderful letters. But the Signoria gave him little satisfaction. When he went on spouting fiery words and threatening to go into the pulpit to unmask the Friar's hypocrisy, they told him that he ran the risk of being torn to pieces by the populace.

Among the other Italian rulers, Bentivoglio and the government of Bologna listened gladly to this 'contumely'. But the Duke of Ferrara hastened to inform Savonarola through his ambassador Manfredi of what was being plotted against him, using affectionate words and begging him, as usual, to enlighten him on Italian affairs. The Florentine Signoria, when the agent Somenzi showed them the *corpus delicti,* replied coolly that they did not know whether the letters were really the Friar's; and that even if they were, they could only agree with them. But Sforza's worst disappointment came from the Pope. Basing his remarks on these letters, he had written to the Pope attacking Fra Girolamo and expressing his confidence that 'he would soon make him repent'. Alexander VI, who a few months before would have breathed fire and slaughter for much less, did not react at all.

As for Savonarola, he flatly denied both to Manfredi and to Somenzi that the letters were his. He said that when he wanted to write to the King of France he did so openly and not under cover; he had not, however, written for some time, both because he saw no purpose in doing so, and because he feared that the letters would be intercepted by the agents of the Duke of Milan. In any case, if they had examined the originals, it would have been easy to confirm that they were not in his hand nor in that of his chancellor. Today we cannot make such an examination, but there is really no need for it. The form is enough; it is certainly not Savonarola's, nor is the substance, which is, as I have said, unbelievably stupid and inept. It is not a matter for surprise that the Friar, speaking on the subject from the pulpit in his sermon of the 4th of September, after having denied explicitly that he had written that rubbish, did not insist further in his denials, which might not be believed. But with a certain note of defiance he let it be understood that to solicit the King's return and to denounce the ill-doing of his ambassador was a thing 'that should gladden every Florentine's heart, unless he be his country's enemy'—just, in fact, what the Signoria had told Somenzi.

At that time Sforza was continuing his intrigues for an invasion of Italy by the Emperor (as they called Maximilian, though he was not yet Emperor). The latter's ambassadors came to Florence on the 20th of August to invite the Republic to join the League or to declare its intentions, and went away with nothing but delaying assurances. The Florentine ambassadors, who after a long delay went to answer His Imperial Majesty, said much the same things, which were very much like a refusal. He in the meantime passed into Italy and hastened his preparations against the city.

In Florence, fear of this enterprise and the bad seed scattered by the Arrabbiati and Sforza, increased disunity and agitation among the people. The enemies of the Friar grew bolder, as, after preaching again on the 11th of September, he had let Fra Domenico replace him and lapsed into silence, because of either fatigue or anger. Even Angelo, the talkative hermit of Vallombrosa, forgetting that shortly before he had declared Fra Girolamo a true prophet, now attacked him in an *Epistola contro ai moderni profeti*.

On the 9th of October, for the solemn celebration in the cathedral of the anniversary of the taking of Pisa, there was an attempt to give the sermon to a Franciscan from Santa Croce instead of to Savonarola's deputy. Perhaps this was done to show that, as the Friar himself once

said in jest, 'he had not taken a lease on that pulpit'. Having made sure
that it had not been done on orders from the Signoria (although it was
later clear that it was not done without their knowledge) Fra Domenico
insisted on preaching himself. He cried out against those who spread
it about that Fra Girolamo's credit was declining, and said that the
elements, the earth, and the sky were more likely to fail first. The
matter did not, however, pass off without some demonstration of displeasure from the magistrates; and it seemed to some a sign of the
times.

But then the Emperor, who was contributing to the enterprise
little more than his name and his person, appeared before Leghorn with
the ships, men, and money of the League. The Florentines were thrown
into confusion, as the situation was thought hopeless. They could find
no other refuge than the usual one: Savonarola. The Signoria solemnly
ordered him to preach, and this time there was no question of getting
the Franciscan from Santa Croce.

Leghorn was already besieged on land and the navies of the League
were patrolling the sea, when on the 28th of October Fra Girolamo
went again into the pulpit. He was obeying the Signoria and, much
more, the dictates of his own heart. Once again his hour had come;
once again he felt himself almost the natural father of that people which
clutched at him in its trials and tribulations. His enemies, and with them
the fearful and the waverers, had been going about in those days shouting and saying at every street corner: 'Do you see now that the Friar
has deceived us all?' And he, mocking them, replied with the same
words all through that memorable sermon, which was later called by
his followers the sermon of *Se' tu chiaro?* (*Do you see?*):

Do you see now? Because I do.'Oh, you are laughing, friar!'
Yes, I am laughing because I have good news from heaven. You
can be as distraught as you like. 'We have no news to laugh about.
But if what you say turned out not to be true and you were a false
prophet, then you would have nothing to laugh about either.'
And if it is true, shall I not be able to laugh? Tell me, then, how
will you see clear? Believe me, I know what I am saying, and if I
did not see, and had any doubts about our affairs, I am not so
stupid that I would not be able to make a decision and get out of
the situation by human means. Believe me, I can see where I stand,

and if I were not sure that this is the certain truth, I should by now have taken remedial action. But you cannot trifle with the affairs of God. . . . Do you see? Because, I do. 'What do you see?' I see that God is addling the brains of the Italians. Many will be deceived. Tell me: have you ever seen it happen, or has it ever happened to you to go to market to do some errand and you do another instead? Have you ever seen a barber go somewhere to shave someone and then shave another instead? So I tell you that this time you will not have understood. . . .

But his feelings would not allow him to continue always in this vein.

My son, turn back. Since I came into this pulpit and saw you here, my heart has changed. I am changed, and I want to weep, for I feel compassion for you. You must remember, on All Saints' Day two years ago, how many tears were shed in this church; so today, seeing you all here, I am moved to compassion. I do not wish that you should suffer. . . . Fear nothing, for when the great tribulations come, '*transferentur montes in cor maris*'—the mountains shall be carried into the midst of the sea. The sea means the armies, which will be storm-tossed like the sea. Therefore, when the great tribulations come, God will take the mountains and carry them into the sea.

These dark words seemed to come true not many days later. But in the meantime some French ships carrying soldiers of the Republic and grain, of which there was great shortage in the besieged area and in Florence itself, arrived in Leghorn from Marseilles with miraculous speed, helped by favouring winds. They successfully avoided the navies of the League, which, because of storms, had been obliged to stand farther out towards Meloria. This assistance greatly encouraged the Florentines no less than the besieged city, seeming to be a sign that 'when human forces failed to succour them, divine aid would provide, as . . . Savonarola had affirmed in his sermons to the people.'

His predictions seemed to come true even more happily shortly afterwards, for it was destined that the hopes kindled by favourable winds should also be fulfilled in the same way. On the 16th a stiff wind rose from the south and dispersed and battered the ships of the

League. The flagship, which Maximilian had left only shortly before, went down before the new fortress with all her men and guns, while two Venetian galleys met the same fate off Sant'Iacopo. All the other ships suffered some damage from the dreadful storm, so that the enterprise had to be abandoned. We find that, after Iacopo Salviati had carried the news to Florence that Leghorn could hold out no longer, and then that night the fleet had been dispersed by the storm, Savonarola is reputed to have said early the following morning to the discouraged Fra Malatesta: 'At this very hour the Emperor is routed and in flight, as you will hear this morning by the first news which comes to the Signoria.'

When the fleet was forced to raise the siege, the army immediately did likewise on land. The Emperor retired to Pisa, whence, ill-provided and shamed, he went off to Lombardy. On the 27th news came to Florence that he was already there 'and going as fast as he could'. The authority of the Empire, at a low ebb in Italy and especially in Florence, certainly acquired no greater lustre through his efforts.

On that same day, the 27th of November, Savonarola again spoke to the people. He had preached for All Saints' and on the 2nd of November, when he gave his sermon known as the *Predica dell' arte di ben morire* [*Sermon on the Art of Dying*], famous both for its contents and for the very fine engraving that he himself ordered for the printed edition. In the sermon on the 27th, which was his last on Ruth and Micah, he did not crow over the victory nor attack his enemies, but merely gave thanks to God and called on everyone to give thanks for such a great gift and for so wonderful a sign wherewith He had made good His promise. 'From this the good took much comfort, and Fra Girolamo's reputation rose of being a man of God and preacher of the truth.'

Chapter 18

THE TUSCAN-ROMAN CONGREGA-
TION; THE SERMONS ON EZEKIEL

✧✧✧

WHILE the Emperor was besieging Leghorn by land and sea, a great web of political intrigue was being spun around Savonarola. It seems as though Sforza and the Pope, probably suspecting the suspicious behaviour of the Venetians, were doubtful of the success of the enterprise even while it appeared to be going well. On the 7th of November, just as though all the insults, threats, and intimidations over the affair of the intercepted letters had never been, Sforza made Fra Girolamo great offers and professions of affection and esteem through his ambassador Somenzi, begging him to use his influence to win the Florentines over to the Emperor—that is, to the League. Somenzi also cleverly gave the Friar to understand that this would gain him the favour of Cardinal Ascanio Sforza, to whom the Duke had already written recommending Savonarola. He received kind words from the Friar in reply, which again kindled the hopes of the Duke's agent, and deceived him in such a manner that on the 13th he wrote again to his master assuring him 'that there was no better means of bringing these matters to a successful conclusion'.

As for the Pope, we have seen how for six months he peacefully bore with the constant preaching of the Friar, which previously had caused him so much irritation. Nor apparently was he to change his mind for several months to come. On the 7th of November he addressed a Brief to sixteen convents, among them San Marco, San Domenico at Fiesole, Santa Maria del Sasso, and San Domenico at Prato. Savonarola is not even mentioned in it, nor any of the charges expressed and withdrawn in previous Briefs, nor are any of these Briefs referred to. The convents were ordered to join together in a new Tuscan-Roman Congregation, whose Vicar should be elected for the first two years by the General and Cardinal Protector of the Order. In justification of this union, geographical reasons were adduced, and also the 'pious wish' to spread to all those convents devout customs and regular observance. And as in no convent of the Order was observance so perfect as in San Marco, the implication was that the union was desired so that all might mirror that perfection. Against anyone who might hinder or object to the Brief, the document itself contained the threat of excommunication *latæ sententiæ*.

This time Savonarola's enemies had been more skilful. To achieve the same end—that is, the Friar's downfall, either through his removal or his enforced revolt—they had now chosen a more suitable means, cleverly avoiding the mistakes of the past. It would appear that the compiler of the Brief took good account of the valid objections raised by Savonarola. There is no frontal attack against this adversary who had shown himself too well armed, no unjust reunion with the Lombards, no suspicious expression of opinion. Under colour of doing good, and with the greatest probability of doing spiritual harm, there lay simply the purpose of removing Fra Girolamo. This was later confirmed by Pope Alexander himself. In the meantime that 'pious wish', in fact most impious, covered all with its hypocritical cloak.

The inspiration for the Brief had come from an astute Florentine, Francesco Mei, who, although he had at first shown himself devoted to Savonarola, had always been his enemy. Savonarola once told him to his face that he was like the staff of reed of the Bible. Ambitious and clever, after the recent death of Lodovico da Ferrara he had become Procurator of the Order, and he at once took advantage of this to strike a terrible blow at his former superior, having first turned the Protector and the General against him. These changed quite suddenly from enthusiasts into enemies. The General gave Mei the charge of organizing the new Congregation, and appointed as his coadjutor the good and saintly Iacopo da Sicilia, perhaps to lend respectability to the affair or the better to ensnare Savonarola, as he knew Fra Iacopo to be very devoted to him. Finally, the Pope, in a further Brief issued on the 6th of December, gave the new Congregation power to admit monks from other convents.

All this remained a dead letter. Savonarola, who was not directly addressed in these Briefs, replied only indirectly and some time later in his *Apologeticum fratrum Congregationis Sancti Marci,* in which he proved that the union with the new Congregation would have been harmful and impossible, and that the superiors of the Order could not issue commands against the constitutions of the Order, against charity, against the good of men's souls. The two hundred and fifty brothers of San Marco, however, answered the Pope directly and more effect-ively. They declared with unanimous resolve that they held the Brief to be irregular, and that they objected to passing from close observance to a more lenient one, as they would do in the new Congregation. These reasons were found to be so conclusive in Rome that, as the Friar was informed by his usual friends at the Papal Court, 'some would have liked to find an answer, but they could not . . . , and they became so angry that they tore up the papers'. And in fact neither Savonarola's apology nor the friars' letter were ever answered. No superior had the courage to remove Savonarola from his post as Vicar, or to order him to be transferred, as a simple monk, to another convent. No one approached him about creating the new Congregation; and there could be no question of disobedience when he had been given no precise instruction. Everything, therefore, remained as before, and no blame can attach to Savonarola for that.

He thus went on with a quiet conscience in the way he had chosen, the way of charity, though he knew that it would take him straight to martyrdom; he continued his work, and went on, in that Advent, spreading the good word. In the last of the sermons on Micah, given on the 27th of November, he told the people that on St Andrew's Day he would begin his exposition of another prophet. On the 30th, from the pulpit of the cathedral, he began his sermons on Ezekiel, which he continued on the feast days of Advent. These were published clandestinely in 1515 from the transcript made by Lorenzo Violi, to-gether with those of the following Lent, though both series are brief and faulty, as they were not corrected by the preacher.

The choice of so terrifying a prophet gave promise of a terrible series of sermons. Savonarola was indignant at the recent Brief and at so many intrigues, and his last illusions about the Pope's good faith had disappeared. In the very first sermon—in which confirming all that he had already said, he often repeated, like a refrain: 'Say no more: "The Friar has deceived me"'—he holds an imaginary dialogue with the prophet, in which Ezekiel admonishes him thus: 'You are not a Jew, you are a Christian, and the veil of the temple was rent when Christ was crucified; so that you must not speak *sub nube*; you must speak the truth openly, though some may take it ill.' These words did not augur well for the Court of Rome.

During this Advent he also spoke a good deal about civil and political affairs. On account of the Pisan war and bad weather, scarcity of food was increasing in the city, and he needed to persuade the rich to bring out their hidden stores of grain, and the magistrates to punish the hoarders; he wanted to ask all good men to give alms. Then there was the Great Council to be 'polished' by removing some defects in its constitution and some of its less worthy members. Although the Friar was a man of the people and devoted to their interests, he was wise enough to recognize the necessity of holding them a little in check. Then, too, he wished to introduce sumptuary laws regulating the dress of women and children, the excessive elaboration of wedding processions. Above all, he constantly pursued people and magistrates alike with his refrain: 'Do justice, Florence, do justice, do justice.'

He hammered away at this theme more often and more energetically still in his sermon on the 13th of December, and it came to be called the 'sermon on justice'. Justice against the sodomites, against the gamblers, against those who conspired against the state 'with priests and friars, at their fine dinners and suppers, their talk is always of the Friar; here they eat bread and Friar, meat and Friar, wine and Friar'. They all should be punished for the harm they did to the city, not for what they said against him. Only the day before, asking for justice against the whisperers of evil, he had said: 'Leave them alone, those who speak ill of the Friar, for he is in his cell. Pay no heed to the Friar, but to those who constantly slander your government and your citizens.'

Et iustitia de cœlo prospexit—justice is up there in heaven, and looks down here on earth. Justice, what are you doing? Where are you looking? Come, come, why do you delay? Come down to us, O justice. And she answers: 'I am ready to come, but I look

for who might receive me, and I see no place prepared for me.'
O people, do you want this justice? Prepare her a fine chamber,
make it possible for her to come, do not prevent her coming. O
Consuls of the Guilds, do you desire this justice? O magistrates of
Florence, O Council of Eight, which of you desires to welcome this
justice? No one replies. My Lords, it rests with you; it is your duty
to receive her; you must take her. Prepare her the chamber, make
ready the road so that she may come. Justice does not come without the sword. Begin therefore to keep the sword beside you, so
that you do not have to fear to do justice. Keep ready two or three
hundred armed men, and when you know of an evildoer who
deserves justice, straightway have him taken, and if these men are
not enough, enlist the people; make yourselves feared, and see
justice done.

After he had given, on the 28th of December the eighth and last
sermon in Advent, Savonarola took a rest—if we can describe as rests
his hard-working intervals of silence between series of sermons. During
that time he was working assiduously at his most important book, the
Trionfo della Croce, and the final pages of his Lenten sermons on Amos
were being printed. These sermons had a very wide sale at once, and
would have been more popular outside Italy if it had not been for the
language difficulty. Some English merchants offered a large sum for
them to be turned into Latin, and a copy of the book was taken to the
Sultan in Constantinople, who ordered that it be translated into
Turkish.

The curve of the fortunes of Savonarola was now reaching its
highest point. Everything seemed to turn in his favour at the beginning of that dangerous year 1497. The Advent sermons had also passed
without any protest from Rome, and no one had come about that
blessed Tuscan-Roman Congregation. In Florence the election of the
Signoria, for which special prayers had been requested by the Friar
in his recent sermons, had carried Francesco Valori, the most energetic
if not exactly the most devout piagnone, to the highest position in the
Republic.

Francesco was a courageous and fine-looking man, a lover of his
city, without any taint of corruption in public affairs, but ambitious,
haughty, impetuous in anger and in his decisions, 'so heated and lively

in his opinions that he pursued them without respect for others, hustling and abusing anyone who opposed him'. On account of his character and manners, few liked him. Fra Girolamo, privately, did not much like him either, especially objecting to 'his nature, for he was the sort of man to frighten away all his friends'. Savonarola would have preferred the wise Giovambattista Ridolfi as the head and standard-bearer of his party, 'but he was put off by his great family relations', particularly since one of his grandsons had married the Contessina, youngest daughter of Lorenzo the Magnificent.

The election of Valori as gonfalonier produced results that at first seemed excellent, though later they proved harmful to the Friar's cause. On the one hand, it finally gave the Piagnoni a leader, and therefore unity and strength, where before they had been said to be a tail without a head (unlike Francesco, who was called a head without a tail). On the other hand, however, it gave the form of a faction to something that before was merely a great moral and religious idea. In the same way, Valori 'polished' the Council; but, against the advice of Savonarola, he broadened it and opened it to the young men, among whom the Arrabbiati were strong, and very soon the Friar and his supporters had to bear the consequences. Further, he managed to push through laws, as dear to the Friar as they were odious to the citizens, by wearing down all opposition with his arrogance, 'threatening that he would bring in the laws repeatedly until they were passed'. These odd methods gave a factious colour to many good laws, besides driving away from the Friar's party as many orderly and peace-loving citizens as were regularly alienated by Valori's personality.

For the time being, the Friar triumphed, and his name stood above all things. Some part of the reform of women and children was approved after great difficulty, but it remained a dead letter. Gambling and sodomy were pursued with terrible laws. That these were not issued merely 'for show', as Parenti at first sourly insinuates, is shown by the effects which this chronicler himself has to record a few pages later. Any man who insulted Fra Girolamo was punished promptly and not without a certain factious severity; this happened to one Girolamo Muzii for a crude *frottola* [poem] disparaging the Piagnoni and their prophet.

Then came the Christian festivities of the Savonarolan Carnival and the first 'burning of the vanities', celebrated in the Piazza de'

Signori on the 7th of February, 1497. There had been erected a wooden construction in the shape of a pyramid with eight sides rising in steps, on which were displayed the 'anathema' that the Friar's lads had gone from house to house collecting: obscene books and pictures, lutes, women's false hair, cosmetics, perfumes, mirrors, dolls, playing-cards, dice, gaming-tables. A Venetian merchant tried to buy up all these beautiful things for 20,000 ducats, but all he achieved was that a fine picture of himself was put on the top of the edifice to share with the effigy of Carnival the rule of the vanities.

The procession of boys formed at San Marco and came down to the square, each quarter of the city represented by a group with its own banner. They took up their positions on the steps and in the loggia of the Signori, singing *laudi* (hymns) in the vulgar tongue recently composed in praise of Jesus Christ and against Carnival. Finally they set fire to the wooden structure, which was full of brushwood, straw, and gunpowder, and with a joyful mingling of the music of the fifes and trumpets of the Signoria, the ringing of bells, the crackle of the flames, and the songs of the children, the burning was celebrated amid the great enthusiasm of the entire population. This has sometimes been exaggeratedly represented as the symbol of iconoclastic barbarism; it appears rather to us to symbolize the triumph of Savonarola and of his civil and religious reforms in the city of the Medici.

The next day, the first of Lent, the Friar began to preach again, taking up the text of Ezekiel at the point where he had left it in the last sermon of Advent. Immediately, angry voices of other preachers were raised against him. The harshest was that of Fra Iacopo Grumel, a Franciscan Minorite, preaching in San Lorenzo, and in consequence his authority to preach was taken from him that same day. The same was done to other friars of that Order—a move which showed too clearly Valori's factiousness. Before Lent he had called to the Palace the preachers of the convents of Fiesole and San Miniato, and, having threatened them he dismissed them in his usual arrogant fashion. When, later, authority to preach was restored to the four preachers of that Order, they did not change their tune, and were again deprived of permission. The only one left inveighing from the pulpit of Santo Spirito was the Augustinian Fra Leonardo da Sarzana, who was later to express in other ways his jealousy of Savonarola.

During Lent Savonarola did not fail to repay these Tiepidi in good coin, but in general terms, scorning to descend like his enemies to individual insults. His criticisms of prelates and the Court of Rome became more frequent, his expression harsher. After the just but hard punishment he gave them in the sermons of the 13th, 14th, 21st, and 22nd of February and others, came the more violent scourges of the 4th of March: 'There is a proverb among friars: "He comes from Rome, don't trust him." . . . O wicked Church, listen to me! In the courts men are always dying [spiritually], they are all finished. Wretched people! I do not say this is true for everyone, but few remain good. When you see that they gladly stay on in Rome, you say they are cooked. He's cooked. You understand me.' I believe that when he passes from the plural to the singular, and particularly with his pointed 'you understand me', he was alluding to the Pope. If I am wrong, then I think that many of the Friar's audience that morning made the same mistake, even though the preacher added at once: 'I am not speaking of anyone in particular.'

He went on: 'You, harlot Church, you used to be ashamed of pride and lasciviousness. Now you are ashamed no longer. See how once the priests called their children "nephews"; now they are called sons, not nephews: sons everywhere.' This is the infamy that attaches to Borgia, the first of Roman Pontiffs to do such a thing. In that very year 1497, or at the end of 1496, the last son of Alexander VI was born, and it is likely that Savonarola, always well informed, knew something about it. This would account, better than the so far harmless plan for the Tuscan-Roman Congregation, for his disgust and the sudden violence of his language.

It seems that this awesome sermon caused an uproar in the city, and that some people were scandalized by it. On the 5th of March he returned to the charge with another imaginary conversation, this time with one such timid soul: '"Oh, you said that the Church is a harlot. Oh, Father, the Holy Church! What have you said?" You are a fool. Look as St. Jerome on this point in Ezekiel, where he says: "*Ista ad Ecclesiam referre possumus*" ["We may apply this to the Church"]. Now go and study, and then speak of these things.'

If the harshness and roughness of the form and, even more, the substantial truth they expressed were remarked on in Florence, it is not to be supposed that they went down easily in Rome. The Council of Ten had sent their own secretary, Alessandro Bracci, there, as a man of greater trust both to them and to the Pope than poor Brecchi. On the 13th of March the Pope listened to Bracci's speech with its general offers of service, its usual requests on the subject of Pisa, and its expression of the Florentine refusal to leave France and join the League, and then answered with these words: 'My Lord Secretary, you are as fat as we are, but, forgive my saying so, you have come here with a very lean commission; and if you have nothing more to say, you may go back as you please, since your Signori have got no further than the usual fine words and justifications. . . . We do not know how you come to be so obstinate and stubborn. We believe it may arise from the trust you place in the prophecies of that soothsayer of yours. But if we could speak in person to your people, we think that, with the true arguments that we could put forward, we could completely induce them to see their own good, and cure them of that blindness and error into which the Friar has led you. But what pains us even more, and gives us a just cause of complaint against you, is that your Signoria and citizens permit him to rend and insult, to threaten and trample on us, who occupy, *licet immeriti,* this Holy See. . . .'

After so long a calm, the waters were now again becoming stormy. And we shall not have much difficulty, on this occasion either, in finding deep and hidden causes that were probably no less effective than those sermons of the Friar which were beginning to sting too much. On the 25th of February a truce had been negotiated between the King of Spain, representing the League, and Charles VIII. Although the French King had wanted to exclude Italy from the truce, he had been obliged to include her. And so the Pope and his allies no longer feared a French invasion, and could once more harry and threaten the dejected Florentines, again left high and dry by their faithless ally. Their disillusionment was indeed great, and many of them—again losing faith in supernatural aid, although they had so recently had proof of its efficacy, and in the supernatural vision of the Friar—once more let themselves be influenced or intimidated by the insults and sneers of the Arrabbiati. Savonarola's reply to these gossips who went about saying 'We are for the natural' was to mock them in a sermon that was one of his strongest, repeating that very phrase of theirs at frequent intervals. He criticized the King no less harshly, 'calling him foolish and weak', and adding that, as he had accurately predicted the rebellion of the people and the loss of the King's son, he would now predict Charles's own death. Exactly a year later this prophecy came true with the King's miserable end, as foolish as his whole life had been.[1]

The Friar used to say: 'My Florentines' faith is like wax; a little warmth and it melts: *in tempore credunt, et in tempore tentationis recedunt*' [sometimes they believe, and in time of trial they do not]. The faith of the Duke of Ferrara appeared stronger on the occasion of the truce. As soon as it became known, he wrote to his ambassador, Manfredi, telling him to ask Savonarola what policy he should adopt. Savonarola replied on the 7th with a memorandum in his own hand, advising a cautious trust in the King, which it seemed to him dangerous to give up; but he recommended the Duke communicate with the King through some trustworthy person and open his eyes to the truth. Meantime he should steer a prudent course, so as not to fall into any danger. If there can be no doubt that Savonarola was sometimes struck by a tremendous illumination, it is equally true that he could not always, and as he pleased, look into the future. On these occasions he had to turn to natural lights, which sometimes, between exaltation of spirit and physical exhaustion, he may have confused with supernatural revelation; in consequence, he moved uncertainly under the guidance of one or the other.

Everything now seemed to go wrong for him. Valori had been followed by Bernardo del Nero, leader of the Bigi, partisans of the Medicis; he was strongly opposed to the Friar, although Savonarola had saved his life and the lives of his family after the upheavals of 1494. This election aroused the suspicions of the popular party, and increased disunity and restlessness in the city. This is how it is described, not by factious enemies, but by the friendly Ferrarese ambassador: 'The city is more divided than ever before, and it is feared that great disturbances will arise; if they do, it will be very bad and very dangerous for the city. The Friar is doing what he can to prevent it, but he has opponents, indeed enemies, in plenty, and especially since we had news of this blessed truce. His rivals have raised their heads and become so bold that things could not be worse.'

Savonarola's health and strength were also declining. Although he had purposely preached almost every day much more briefly than

[1] [Charles VIII accidentally hit his head against a gateway at Amboise in April 1498 and died nine hours later.]

usual, on some occasions he could only finish his sermon with great effort and difficulty, begging the people's indulgence. One morning he was forced to break off without finishing. Although ill and weak, his courage was not shaken by the resurgence of his enemies, or by the loss of the support of the Signoria, or by the flashes of lightning portending fresh storms from the direction of Rome. There, as Becchi wrote to the Council of Ten, there was already talk of excommunication, but the Friar did not desist from his customary bold words. Manfredi confirms this, but the sermons of those last days of Lent are more eloquent: '"O Father, you are so alone!" Alone? I tell you, there are others in every city, castle, and village; and in every order there are hidden some who have this same fire within, but they remain hidden. They whisper something in my ear, and I reply: Stay hidden until you hear *"Lazare, veni foras!"* I am here because the Lord God has put me here. I am waiting for the day when He will give me a great blow, and then I shall cry out in a loud voice: *"Lazare, veni foras!"* Pray, therefore, because I can see that one day we shall be constrained, and I shall give a shout that will be heard throughout Christendom. . . .'

Meanwhile, Lent was drawing to an end. On Good Friday, Savonarola gave a wonderful sermon, full of piety, on the Passion of Christ. As usual, the Augustinian Fra Leonardo preached from the pulpit of Santo Spirito, mingling insults against the Friar with the most dreadful rubbish. 'He said the most childish things,' writes Landucci, 'while Fra Girolamo had more listeners than ever: he continually had more than 15,000 people at his sermons.' The Augustinian fared no better when he put up in his church a list of thirteen *Conclusions* that he had already proposed in his sermons. They were answered, point by point, by a Franciscan, Fra Paolo da Fucecchio, master in theology. To tell the truth, he was not the only member of that Order to do justice to the great Dominican. At that very time, on the Monday after Easter, were published the *Propheticæ solutiones* of the Minorite Giorgio Benigno (the Bosnian Giorgio Drachisich), one of the finest and most reverent testimonies to the Prophet of San Marco.

To return to the Augustinians, one of greater calibre than Fra Leonardo preached at that time a terrible sermon against Savonarola. He was Fra Mariano, the same Fra Mariano with whom we became acquainted in the days of Lorenzo de' Medici, and the oldest enemy of the Friar. He had recently been conspiring in Rome with Ponzo and Mei to procure the downfall of his hated adversary. One day while preaching in the Consistory he had several times cried out to the Pope, who was present and asked nothing better: '*Abscinde, abscinde hoc monstrum ab ecclesia Dei, Beatissime Pater*' ['Cut off this monster from the Church of God, Holy Father']. Savonarola from his pulpit in Florence at once replied to that ambitious flatterer, 'who (he said) had always run after the great lords and masters', and predicted his early demise. And Fra Mariano did die the following year.

Over and above the petty jealousies and mediocre monastic differences, Fra Girolamo appealed in that same sermon to monks of all Orders to unite with him in the great work of reform...

Come, for Christ wishes to revive His Church. Come, I call on you, but I will cry in a loud voice and name no names. O priests, *Magister adest*—the Master is at hand, He is come, and He calls and desires you to reform His Church. He calls you to prayer, for the axe is laid to the root. O monks, black, white, or brown, all of whatever colour: the Orders have been abased. *Magister adest,* the Master is here, and calls for reform. O mendicant friars, the Lord wishes to renovate His Church: *Magister adest,* the Master is here. O nuns, *Magister adest.* You who cannot believe, pray, for the Master is here and will renew all things. Go to all the priests, monks, and nuns, and speak in their ear this good news: soon there will be reform, and they must pray. . . .

The body of the Church was rotten, but he had courage enough to revive it:

You who are in France, in Germany, who have friends in those parts, send letters everywhere, write that they should go to their churchmen and say: 'That Friar says that he bids you on behalf of God to turn to the Lord and pray, for the Lord is coming.' Come, send off messengers, for this dead body cannot be revived otherwise! . . . Many of you say that there will be excommunications . . .; do you not know who they are that seek them? Last year it did not succeed. Did I not tell you that, though it may come, those who do this, seek to do worse harm than merely excommunicate? I pray God it may come soon. 'Are you not afraid?' Not I, for they would excommunicate me because I do no evil. Bear it upon a lance, open the gates to it. And I will answer it; and if I do not astonish you, then say what you will. I will cause so many faces there and here to turn pale that you will be well pleased, and we shall utter a great cry, like that of Lazarus, and you will see the whole body tremble. . . . Lord, cause me to be persecuted: I ask Thee this favour—that I may not die in my bed, but that I may shed my blood for Thee, as Thou has done for me.

It is clear that now the last desperate hope is born in the mind and words of the Friar.

Chapter 19

THE ASCENSION DAY RIOTS AND
THE IRREGULAR EXCOMMUNICATION

<><><><><><><><><><><><><><><><><><><><><><><><><><><><><><><>

IN the city torn by dissension and impoverished by the long war
and even more by the decay of industry and commerce, shortage
of food was now increasing. To make the situation worse, innumerable peasants and beggars flocked in from outside the city,
perishing with hunger. The hospitals were full of them, and also all
the other places recently set aside for this purpose. Many of these
wretches collapsed in the streets or were found dead on the embank-
ments. Through Advent and Lent Savonarola had implored the citizens
to succour all those in great need, and, inspired by his exhortations, the
city had made many provisions and the people had generously given
alms. But something more was needed. The poor crowded into the
Piazza del Grano, where the Commune had bread and corn sold at fair
prices, so that in the crush men and women often died of suffocation. On
the 19th of February there was a great riot there, the public store was
pillaged, and cries were heard of 'Palle, Palle' (the Medici device), 'as if
the former state had been better'. On March the 21st it was rumoured
that Piero would enter Florence secretly and, after distributing grain,
would rouse the city in revolt. There was another disturbance on
April the 18th in the Piazza dei Signori.

In these conditions, and knowing that he was favoured by many
of the important citizens and even for a few days by the gonfalonier
himself, Piero de' Medici decided to try his luck. Collecting funds with
the help of the Pope and his relations the Orsini, he raised as secretly

as possible a large band of armed men in the territory of Siena. He had promised the Sienese in return (as is shown by a secret document I have recently discovered) Ponte a Valiano, a much coveted stronghold of the Florentines. It cost him little to give away other people's property, and he was not new to this kind of generosity. Thus, with six hundred horse and a few more than the same number of well-chosen infantrymen, he left the territories of Siena on the 27th of April and moved rapidly forward.

The Florentines received news in good time of the army that was being collected, but they realized too late that this was not just another of Piero's vain manœuvres. People were probably more afraid then of the enemies and intrigues within the city and of the character of the gonfalonier, than of the soldiers marching so boldly towards them. Fresh news continued to come in: Piero was at Tavarnelle; he was at San Casciano; he was at Certosa. The gates were barred, artillery was put in position, and suspect citizens were imprisoned. Filippo Arigucci, one of the few Friar's men in the current Signoria, sent the poet Girolamo Benivieni to tell Savonarola in what straits the Republic now was, with Piero having already passed San Casciano, and with the Signoria full of dissensions and suspicions among its members. He found the Friar in his cell reading, and told him at once, in great agitation, what he had been sent to say. Savonarola raised his head quietly from his book and replied: '*Modicæ fidei, quare dubitasti?* Tell the Signoria that we will pray to God for the city, and that they should not fear Piero, for he will come right up to the gates and then turn back without doing anything at all.'

And that is what happened. Caught on the way in a tremendous downpour, Piero had to stop more than two hours, with his men soaked and exhausted. This heavy rain, according to Guicciardini, made up for the lack of preparation in the city, to which once again the inclemency of the weather was clement. Instead of surprising the city at daybreak as he had intended, Piero reached San Gaggio near the Porta Romana when the sun was high, and those within had already taken many precautions. He waited there for some hours, sheltering behind the wall of the fountains, which may still be seen there, while the inhabitants ran to the city walls to enjoy the spectacle of the small army that did not know what to do with itself. In the end, seeing that the city was not rising in his favour and that no one came to open the gates to him, and afraid lest the armies of the Republic should arrive, re-directed from the war against Pisa, he went back to Siena humiliated as usual.

On the 28th of April, while Piero was at the gates, the new Signoria was elected. It turned out even more hostile to the Friar than its predecessor, having as gonfalonier of justice Piero degli Alberti, a leader of the Arrabbiati. The new Council of Eight, who were beginning their four-month term of office, did not differ in quality from the principal magistrates. So the supporters of the League and the other enemies of the Friar became bolder than ever.

The times were really becoming threatening for Savonarola. The Arrabbiati, now sure of the Signoria and the other major officers except the Ten, demanded that he be prevented from preaching. This seemed such a terrible thing to do, that the Signoria, though many of its members would have liked nothing better, found itself in disagreement and hesitant to act, with the result that there were threats of riots and excesses. In the end, there was a general prohibition of all sermons; the excuse given was fear of the plague, and also 'other just causes', as they put it. These were in fact unjust causes.

On the 3rd of May, therefore, by order not of the Eight but of the Signoria itself, it was decreed that except for the following day, which was Ascension Day, all preaching in public was forbidden. Immediately after that day, all benches and tiers of seats 'erected in some churches for hearing sermons' were to be removed. This was a strangely roundabout way of indicating—for there were no others—the tiers built in Santa Maria del Fiore for the sermons of Fra Girolamo.

One might think that the Arrabbiati would have rejoiced and felt satisfied with their victory. On the contrary, living up to their name, they got up and said that the Friar ought not to preach even on the following day. More dangerous was a band of unruly young noblemen recently formed in Florence, called the Compagnacci. They used to gather together for gay supper-parties and joyful orgies. Some of them had first joined together in a conspiracy in favour of Giovanni de' Medici, but since then one can say that all they wanted was to enjoy life and get rid of the Friar, who constituted the chief enemy and impediment to their dissolute ways.

With these people becoming more violent in their bold pretensions, and the Friar's supporters outraged at the decree of the Signoria, the whole city was at fever pitch. Wagers were being made in public on whether the Friar would preach the next day. The Signoria, in order to salvage some of its dignity, was obliged to issue a statement that such wagers were void, and to decree that no one should dare to interfere with the next day's sermons. But at the same time it warned the Friar, through certain citizens and for his own good, that he should not preach. In this way, as he alone would be silenced, the Arrabbiati would have complete victory. To these zealous counsels Savonarola replied that he did not wish to leave the people without a sermon on the very day when our Lord commanded the Apostles to preach his doctrine to all men.

At this point the Compagnacci considered setting fire to the tiers and the pulpit in Santa Maria del Fiore, but, realizing that this crime could cost them their lives, they adopted another scheme, less dangerous but much more disgusting. At night they laid over the pulpit the skin of a donkey that had been dead for several days, and with this and the rotting innards of the carcass and other worse filth they smeared the pulpit all over, right to the base of the crucifix. They also drove nails, with the points sticking up, into the edge of the pulpit where the Friar was in the habit of hammering with his fists in the heat of his sermons. However, this revolting sacrilege was discovered early in the morning, and the sacristans had time to take action, so that the pulpit was already cleaned and planed smooth by the time Savonarola went into it.

His preamble was on the power of faith, with which it was necessary to be armed, for the time of tribulation had now come, as he had often predicted it would. Then, saying that that morning his hopes of rising up to heaven with Christ had been disappointed, he proposed to speak on the words of the psalm '*Domine Deus meus, in te speravi*' (Psalm 31), addressing his words first to God, then to the good, and finally to the wicked. He called on God to bear witness to his innocence. To the good he confirmed all the things he had already told them, and gave them encouragement for the road of the tribulations soon to come. He had hardly begun addressing the wicked, reproaching them with having tried to prevent his preaching, when a great hubbub broke out in the church. It was the signal for the beginning of the riot organized by the Compagnacci. Many of them, suddenly throwing open the doors, began to shout and rush outside with the panic-stricken mob at their heels. This was just what the Friar's enemies wanted, hoping that in the general confusion they could seize and kill him. But they did not succeed. The bravest of his followers surrounded the pulpit, determined to protect him. Bartolommeo Giugni, a member of the Eight, who had come near the pulpit (probably not to kill the Friar, as was then believed and as was later written by the Piagnoni—although he was most hostile to Savonarola—but to exercise the authority of his office), received a blow in the face, 'a thing unheard of in past times'.

Savonarola had tried at first to dominate the uproar with his mighty voice: 'I hear noises: the wicked do not want to hear their share. Wait, you there! Be patient a little; for if you knew what I know, you would weep. Have no fear, you others, for God is with us. . . .' But his words were drowned, lost in the infernal uproar. He knelt and prayed; then, rising to his feet, he showed the people a small crucifix, crying that they should put their trust in that. But the faithful, mistaking his meaning, held up their own red crosses, which were almost the badges of the Friar's followers, crying: 'Jesus.' Not a few of the Arrabbiati were recognized and hustled out of the church, some of them receiving blows in the process.

In the end the preacher departed, surrounded by a band of armed men fiercely devoted to him, and accompanied by a great multitude of the people. 'Among them was Giovambattista Ridolfi, carrying a lance on his shoulder' and shouting: '*Viva Cristo!*'—and Ridolfi was one of the most prominent citizens, a grave and prudent man! They escorted the Friar safely to San Marco, where after supper, in the garden, he finished the sermon, or, rather, just the exposition of the psalm.

Such a riot could not fail to leave its mark on the city. On the one hand, the Friar's party gained by it, as they were joined by many good citizens who were incensed at the sacrilegious licence of the Arrabbiati. These, on the other hand, gained much more strength from having that day finally cast aside all scruples and made an extreme demonstration of their force, and especially from having dared to offer a public outrage to a man who up to that time had been venerated by the majority of the citizens and respected by nearly all. Now the spell was broken; and this was very important. Besides, for the first time the Friar had been the subject of a scandal that formed an excellent pretext for attacking him in Rome (and we shall soon see the effects of this), and for bringing pressure to bear on the magistrates to remove him from the city as the cause of all disorder.

The movement for this grew from day to day with the vehemence of his enemies. We have evidence of this from Manfredi, who cannot be suspected of bias. On the 6th of May he sent news of it to his Duke, adding that Fra Girolamo, with whom he had held conversation shortly before, had expressed his determination not to preach, and to do everything possible for the good and unity of the city. I do not believe, however, that Savonarola would ever have abandoned Florence and his good work. Besides, his followers desperately opposed such a step, and they were still the great majority of the citizens, if not the most active. We find an echo of their opposition and brave resolve against the Arrabbiati in certain Piagnone sonnets by Giovanni Terrosi:

> chè se 'il Fattore e 'l Maestro va via,
> tal fie lion che ti pare uno agnello.[1]

Indeed, in the councils the Piagnoni rejected any suggestion that the Prophet should leave the city.

Yet this was still talked about, some urging for and others against. I do not know on what Manfredi, writing on the 12th, based his belief that things would settle down as a result of these negotiations. With this letter he sent the Duke a copy of the *Epistola a tutti gli eletti di Dio e fedeli cristiani* [*Epistle to all the Elect of God and Faithful Christians*], composed by Savonarola on the 8th of May, and published in great haste with the object of exhorting his followers to stand firm in their present tribulations. Forbidden to preach, he had no other means of comforting his friends and refuting his enemies. The Ferrarese ambassador was, therefore, quite right when he foresaw that the Friar would be writing and publishing other similar works. Meantime, four editions of the *Epistola* came out within a very short time.

Manfredi's confidence that the two parties would come to some agreement seems already somewhat weaker in a letter of the 16th of May. On the 20th a crowded and noisy council was held in the Palace, and it achieved nothing, for the Arrabbiati persisted in demanding the Friar's exile. Yet, while they were being rebuffed in Florence, their hopes were revised by assurances from outside the city.

[1] 'If the Bailiff and the Master leave, those who seem lambs will turn out to be lions.'

As early as the 19th of March the ambassador Becchi had warned the Ten that at Rome there were threats of excommunication against Savonarola. These, unfortunately, came from Cardinal Caraffa, who formerly had been his most influential supporter; and even from Becchi's letter it appeared quite clear that at the bottom of everything was that 'Holy League', which, between Sforza and the Pope, could have little that was holy about it. In Rome, the prelates had waited awhile to see what might come of Piero's attempt to reinstate himself, and then the election of a favourable Signoria, the riots of Ascension Day, the bitter dissensions among the citizens, the insistent demands of the Arrabbiati, and, above all, the money of Tanai de' Nerli and Alfonso Strozzi (of which I have been able to discover trustworthy evidence) all combined to convince the Roman prelates that the moment had come to give the Friar the finishing stroke.

The blow came in the guise of a packet of Papal Briefs bearing the dates of the 12th and 13th of May. One of them, which was addressed to the Signoria and was intended to lead the way for the others, has not been preserved, and we know nothing of its contents. It may never even have reached the Signoria, for reasons that will soon be apparent. The others, addressed to various churches and convents in Florence, were simply identical copies of the papal excommunication. This began with the usual excuse—which now had been said, unsaid, and said again—of the pernicious heretical doctrine, recapitulated the history of the Briefs and the Tuscan-Roman Congregation, etc., and then ordered the recipients to publish in the usual forms that Fra Girolamo da Ferrara was to be regarded as excommunicated, as were all those who listened to his sermons or conversed with him or favoured him in any way. Which was as good as saying two-thirds of the Florentine people.

Gherardi's statement that the ultimate causes of the excommunication were Savonarola's refusal (but there was none) to join the new Congregation, and his fulminating sermons, is a restrained and clever way of covering up the prime reasons, which were a good deal less respectable. Becchi, who certainly does not appear to be devoted to the Friar, states baldly and clearly that the Brief had been demanded by the enemies of Florence—i.e. the allies of the League—in conjunction with the Friar's private enemies, particularly Genazzano, Ponzo, and Mei, who by now had the General and the Protector under his thumb. Becchi might have added what we know now to be true, and in fact did add it a few days later : 'with the backing of certain private citizens' —that is, with the influence and the money of Nerli and Strozzi.

The dangerous task of delivering the Briefs was entrusted to a certain Maestro Giovanvittorio da Camerino, who had been banished by the Eight the previous March for his outspoken hostility to the Friar. Put on his guard by his friends the Arrabbiati, and fearing to end up at the Bargello (the jail) instead of at the Palace, he stopped at Siena and remained there for a long time without giving any sign either to Florence or to those who had sent him. In Rome, Pope and cardinals, who had lost all trace of him, constantly sought news of his whereabouts from the Florentine ambassadors. The Ten, replying to Braccie on this subject on the 5th of June, advanced the conjecture that he must have 'changed his mind about his coming here, knowing what sort of brief he had round his neck'—with which they mockingly alluded to the Briefs he carried and the Eight's ban against him.

The envoy and his charge were, therefore, both lost, and meanwhile in Florence and in Rome there was great talk of these Briefs of excommunication. It was even thought that they might find their way back to Rome. Savonarola, hoping to ward off the blow again, wrote a very dignified and humble letter to the Pope, regretting that His Holiness should have believed the calumnies of his enemies, protesting his innocence, and calling to witness the many thousands of his hearers, and his own sermons, whose message had been spread abroad by printers and booksellers. Because he knew that among those who accused him of speaking evil of the Pope there was a famous preacher (meaning Fra Mariano), he was much surprised that this person should dare to accuse another of a crime of which he himself was guilty : many worthy people were ready to testify to having heard that preacher inveigh quite openly against the Pope. Then, after again offering his submission to the correction of the Holy Roman Church, Savonarola concluded:

What do I preach, then, with all my strength and the power of my voice, but repentance of sin and the mending of our ways, for the sake of Our Lord Jesus Christ, while I labour to revive that faith which is almost extinguished in men's hearts? Soon, by the grace of God, I shall publish a work *De Triumpho Christi* in defence of the faith, from which it will be apparent whether I am a sower of heresies (that may I never be!) or of the Catholic truth. I beg Your Holiness, therefore, not to lend faith to the envious and the slanderers, without first having assured yourself of this, as they could already be shown openly to have been guilty of many lies. If human aid should then fail me and the wickedness of the impious prevail, I shall trust in God, my help, and make known their wickedness to the whole world, so that perhaps they will repent once and for all of their undertaking.

The Pope was pleased with this letter, so much so that he began to be sorry he had sent the ill-fated Briefs. Once again he showed himself in some respects better than the other enemies of Savonarola who had urged him on. Not that he was not the man and the Pope he was; but his pleasure-loving nature disposed him to a certain magnanimous tolerance and indifference. He wanted to live and let live; he loved his own good too well to waste himself in the pursuit of others' ill, unless it were to bring more good to himself. Besides, situated as he was, knowing himself to be in the wrong and in danger of losing his throne, it seemed to him that to persecute that terrible friar would be to stir up a wasp's nest. Also, he was both extremely intelligent and well versed in Curial affairs, and understood perfectly well the good reasons that Savonarola put forward in his reply. Finally, even in his abject sinful state, it is quite clear from several indications that he had a certain reverence for, or at least an obscure terror of, that great and uncorrupted man.

The Cardinal of Perugia and the Bishop of Capaccio, who had again become strong supporters of the Friar under pressure from the Council of Ten (still well disposed to Savonarola, even to the extent of writing to Bracci on May the 20th, in the teeth of the hostile Signoria, a letter full of his praises), noted the changed attitude of the Pope and gave good hopes of success. Cardinal Carraffa still remained hostile 'because he was continually being got at by the General and the Procurator'—that is, Torriani and the perpetual Mei. But on the 14th of June (a whole month had gone by, and there was still no sign of the messenger and the Briefs) Bracci was able to report that he had 'finally improved the mood' of the Cardinal as well. In any case, the Cardinal had already shown himself repentant, if not of having worked against Savonarola, at least of having done it in that manner. He asked Becchi yet again about the missing papal envoy, and when Becchi replied that he had not yet reached Florence, the Cardinal said: 'And if he is wise, he will never arrive: we must use other methods to exact obedience from Fra Girolamo.'

At last, on the 16th of June, Maestro Giovanvittorio da Camerino gave signs of life from Siena. He sent a letter to the Signoria asking for a safe-conduct to come to Florence 'to put certain matters before them' on behalf of the Pope. He took care not to mention the real subject of his mission, hoping that it was not yet known. As, however, everyone knew it all too well, the safe-conduct was refused. So great was the authority of the Friar still, even with a majority of the Signoria hostile to him! Not knowing which way to turn, the Apostolic messenger decided to send the Briefs by someone else, although such a procedure invalidated their delivery and publication. For this reason, or an even more honourable one, 'since the publication was procured by certain citizens to serve their own private ends', many churches refused to accept them. In any case, as though to symbolize their irregularity, the proper forms had not been observed even in drawing up the text.

On the 18th of June, therefore, in only five churches of Orders extremely hostile to Fra Girolamo, the excommunication was solemnly promulgated to the tolling of bells and between two lighted candles. In Santo Spirito 'it was read and published by the hand of a Fra Leonardo', the same one who had so often and so ineptly attacked Savonarola in words and writing. Savonarola could not delay his answer if he did not want his adversaries to get too bold and his supporters too discouraged. He replied without delay and very effectively.

In a letter *Contro la escomunicazione surrettizia nuovamente fatta* [*Against the Recently Published Irregular Excommunication*], addressed to all Christians and beloved of God, and dated the 19th of June, he showed the excommunication to be invalid because founded on false premises maliciously put forward by his enemies—namely, on an absurd accusation of heresy and a nonexistent disobedience. Such disobedience (he went on), if it had existed, would not have been reprehensible, as the Tuscan-Roman Congregation had been created not out of religious zeal but merely to persecute him. He had only obeyed the wishes of his bretheren, who refused unanimously to enter the new Congregation, and had written to the Pope to that effect.

This letter in Italian, aimed at the general public, was in print by the very next day. It was followed immediately by another in Latin, for the benefit of ecclesiastics and learned men, in which, with a wealth of scholarship and citations from Pietro da Padule, St. Antoninus, and Jean Gerson, he proved that it was not true that obedience to the Pope was always obligatory, even when his commands were unjust (this, according to Gerson, would be showing 'the patience of the ass and the timidity of the hare'); it was not true either that all the interdicts were to be observed. For the unlearned, the original text of this letter was accompanied by a translation made by Cioni.

We could have no more reliable evidence of the validity of the Friar's arguments than that of persons learned and competent to judge, and of the opposing party. That these arguments also seemed valid to the Pope himself, as long as he considered them without prejudice and until he saw them appear in print to the great detriment of his own honour, we shall have occasion to see shortly. In the meantime, the following developments were taking place at the court of Milan.

On the 25th of June the Duke called before him the ambassadors of Florence and Ferrara, and, in the presence also of his counsellors, he had the papal excommunication and the Friar's reply read out. Then, as was his habit, he gave a display of eloquence and sarcasm at the expense of the two ambassadors as supporters of Savonarola. When he and some of his obsequious consellors had said of the Friar's justification 'that they never had seen so foolish a thing', Fra Vincenzo Bandelli, a master of theology and later General of the Order, who usually was given to flattering the Duke, could not refrain from observing that, on the contrary, 'they were very good reasons'. The ambassador of Ferrara and, still more, his colleague from Florence, who was ready with his tongue, said the rest. If we want still further confirmation of the validity of Savonarola's reasons, suffice it to say that even a Franciscan theologian found them excellent, and wrote and told him so.

In Florence, with its deep political divisions, the results of the excommunication and of Savonarola's personal apologies followed exactly the party alignment in the city. The Piagnoni considered the excommunication to be invalid and the Friar's arguments valid. The Arrabbiati thought just the opposite. The Arrabbiati breathed fire and slaughter, and the Piagnoni went on frequenting San Marco and the religious offices celebrated by the excommunicated Friar as though nothing had happened.

But, in effect, something very serious had happened. In canon law the excommunication was not valid, both because of the absence of any formal disobedience on the Friar's part, and because of the *error intolerabilis* which quite plainly marked the papal decree. This has been definitely established by the opinion of many learned men and of many canonized Saints of the Church; and they did not know, as we do today, that this Brief had been paid for at so many ducats per word. Politically speaking, however, the Arrabbiati now held a powerful weapon in their hands. From the excommunication and the contempt shown for the power of the Holy See, it was a short step to an interdict on the city, which would mean also its economic collapse. And then there was the scandal to be considered, and the consciences of those people who regarded the excommunications as valid. If to demand the prohibition to preach or even the banishment of the Friar had seemed, before, an intolerable abuse of power by a turbulent minority, the excommunication now at last gave the Arrabbiati, who had become more papist than the Pope, an excellent pretext —in some ways, even, more than a pretext.

It cannot be doubted that the effects would soon have been seen if the Signoria elected for the months of July and August had not turned out to be the exact opposite of its predecessor, and so unfavourable to the Arrabbiati hopes, for it had a majority of the Friar's supporters. 'For this reason it is thought that the Friar will not have to go after all,' observed Somenzi sadly in a letter to the Duke of Milan on the 29th of June. He put it down to the change of front of the Bigi, who, having been let down by the Arrabbiati over Piero, had again joined up with the Friar's followers.

Savonarola had had a narrow escape. Somenzi, who as instigator and accomplice in the mischief was in a good position to know, wrote in that same letter: 'Almost everyone thought that when this new Signoria came in there would be some great change; and nothing has come of it, so the *Disperati* have been deceived.' *Disperati*, 'the Desperate'—this is what he calls the Arrabbiati. And that is, in effect, what they were.

Chapter 20

THE PLAGUE OF THE SPIRIT AND
THE PLAGUE OF THE BODY

<><><><><><><><><><><><><><><><><><><><><><><><><><><><><><><>

On the day after the excommunication was published, news reached Florence that the Duke of Gandia, the Pope's eldest and favourite son, had been stabbed to death and thrown into the Tiber. This seemed to all the devotees of the Friar a prompt and terrible sign of the wrath of God. Savonarola himself wrote to Giovan Francesco Pico: 'The punishment has come: thus does it go hand in hand with transgression.' And it must have seemed so to the Pope too. He felt that he had brought that punishment on himself with his scandalous living and by the outrage he offered to the Church of Christ by his unworthy occupation of the see of His Vicar, if not, indeed, by sending that Brief against all conscience. It is a fact that, overcome with grief and remorse, he proposed and declared in the Consistory that he intended to change his manner of living, and deputed six cardinals to reform the Court and ecclesiastical customs.

While the Pope was in this frame of mind, Savonarola, his heart full of compassion and hope, wrote to him on the 25th of June a letter of consolation. In it, after exhorting him to partake of the ineffable comforts of the faith, the only source of peace for the human heart, he even asked him, inspired by his own ingenuous hopes, to grant him not only absolution from the unjust interdicts, but also his assistance in the work he had undertaken, for which, like St. Paul, he had suffered *usque ad vincula*. And I believe that, with the Apostle, he intended what follows also to be understood as an allusion to the prohibition on his preaching: '*sed verbum Dei non est alligatum*'—'but the word of God is not bound.'

The strangeness of this letter written by the excommunicated Friar to console the Pope and invite him to repent, has rightly been pointed out. Its reception, however, has been misrepresented, because we know, in fact, nothing about it, and the text that has been quoted as evidence is not relevant. All we know for certain is that, before he received the letter, the attitude of the Pope towards Savonarola had been improving. He had read and approved in Consistory that other letter of the 20th of May; and he had even told the Cardinal of Perugia that the publishing of the excommunication displeased him, '*et erat omnino prætor mentem suam*' ['it went beyond his intentions']. Indeed, in conversation with Bracci he had shown himself disposed to revoke the interdicts.

However, after his first remorse had passed, the Pope's good intentions went up in smoke. Guicciardini writes that, dispensing first with his good intentions and then with his sorrow, he went back to behaving worse than before. It was not difficult for the Friar's enemies to lead him back to his far from friendly thoughts. In fact, after having received certain letters from Florence, he first placed Savonarola's case in the hands of the six cardinals for reform; though this did not destroy all hopes at least of the suspension of the excommunication. Then, when other letters came, and as his good intentions faded, his anger was again kindled. He told Bracci that, as the Friar was making a mockery of the excommunication even in published letters, he intended to proceed against him with every means permitted by the canons against the rebels of the Church. And he began again to ask that Fra Girolamo should appear before him in person.

The new Signoria, which entered upon its term of office on the 1st of July, was headed by Domenico Bartoli of the Friar's party, and was, as Somenzi wrote, largely favourable to Savonarola. The Council of Ten, which up to now had been alone in its efforts to defend Savonarola, was now joined by the more authoritative voice of the Signoria in urging the ambassadors to work for the Friar's cause. Unlike the Ten, the Signoria could write directly to the Pope, and it did so in the warmest terms on the 8th of July.

Being, therefore, besieged on two sides, Bracci and Becchi went on pressing the Roman Court to revoke its interdicts; but already it was a lost cause. The allies of the League and certain Florentines were busy every day undoing the work of the two ambassadors. Among them was Iacopo Nerli, to whom Alexander VI communicated his gratitude for everything he had done 'in these matters of Fra Girolamo, much to his satisfaction'. The poor ambassadors were sent by the Pope to the cardinals, and by them back to the Pope, as from Herod to Pilate. On the 19th of July the conditions for the revocation were still the same: either Fra Girolamo must come to Rome, or he must join the Tuscan-Roman Congregation. In other words, he must resign himself to abandoning his work or losing his skin.

In the meantime, however, those continual good offices, those demonstrations of the veneration of a whole people for Savonarola, those enthusiastic praises of the ambassadors speaking *nomine publico* to the Pope and the cardinals (one, the Cardinal of Perugia, received letters of deep gratitude from the Signoria) were able at least to prevent more serious measures from being taken. It was strange to see how, as a result of the peculiar Florentine constitution, the Signoria in office gave the highest priority in the negotiations of the Republic to the absolution of a friar whom only a few days before the same council had been trying to have banished from the city.

They might not perhaps have got as far as banishing Savonarola even then without serious disturbances, in view of the great following he had. But if another hostile Signoria had been elected, or if the excommunication had been published without that providential one month's delay, the violence of the Arrabbiati would have become unbearable. In the short interval between the Ascension Day riots and the end of Piero degli Alberti's term as gonfalonier, and particularly after the excommunication, the factiousness of the Signoria and the Eight was apparent not only in their own attacks against the Friar and his party, but also in the way they permitted others to offend him with impunity. The Convent of San Marco was the object of many insults and shameful tricks, done at night-time while the brothers were at matins; and pictures of the Friar in obscene guise were broadcast in the streets.

Against this persecution and contumely of the Prophet and his followers, the voice of a Piagnone poet was raised in lament:

> *Voi dite pure spina a questa rosa,*
> *e parvi ogni ora cento, un punto un anno;*

e tante pappolate attorno vanno,
e credon fargli male, e lui si posa.

   Deh, Gesù dolce, non tenere a tedio
da poi che tanto ben non è accettato:
tu sai e puoi, se vuoi pigliar rimedio!

   E priegoti, se ignun fusse cascato,
(perché rinforza tanto questo assedio,
noi siam feriti e punti in ogni lato!),

            pel sangue del costato,
sparso pe' peccator, di pietà fiume,
mostra al popolo ingrato el vero lume![1]

'*E tante pappolate attorno vanno*' ('and so many slanders go around')
—indeed, there were published and sent out in streams at that time
'many sonnets and *canzoni* and letters of invective, in Latin and Italian,
attacking the Friar and his doctrine'. Many of these printed invectives
were refuted in the same way by Savonarola's followers, adding continually to that mass of pamphlet literature already referred to. To
satisfy the requests of the Franciscans and the Augustinians, the Signoria
ordered the friars of San Marco not to take part in the procession on
St. John's Day. The procession of the feast of Corpus Domini was upset
by sacrilegious demonstrations against the Friar. 'Everyone gave themselves up to gambling, and permitting all kinds of evil.'

A petition was got up at this time by the most fervent Arrabbiati,
and sent to Rome (where the Friar's opponents asked for nothing
better), 'testifying that Fra Girolamo preached false doctrines'. Because
of this, two letters were at once addressed to the Pope by the Piagnoni,
bearing witness to the opposite, and asking that the interdicts be revoked. One of these was signed by all the friars of San Marco, and the
other by a large number of citizens. While signatures were being collected by a notary (Filippo Cioni, translator and editor of some of
Savonarola's writings), and the Signoria was also debating as to whether

[1] 'You call this rose a thorn, and every hour seems to you like a hundred, every
moment a year; so many slanders go around, and think they do him harm, but he stands
firm. O sweet Jesus, do not be weary that such great good is not accepted: Thou knowest and canst, if Thou willst, find the remedy! And I beg Thee, if anyone has fallen [for
thy cause] (for the siege grows stronger round us, we are wounded and assailed on every
side!), by the blood of Thy side, spilled for sinners, a river of love, show to the
ungrateful people the true light!'

these petitions ought to be permitted, the plague came to add itself to the other tribulations of the Florentines, and silenced everything.

The disease had long been dormant, but had become more serious towards the beginning of June. Landucci remarks that the poor were not sorry to die, as they suffered from 'spiritual and bodily starvation', owing to the scarcity of bread and of the Word of God. Every day, ten or a dozen died, perhaps a few more. 'Everyone was saying: "This is a mild plague."' But it had become quite the opposite of mild by the end of the month, when up to sixty people a day were dying. On the 2nd of July, twenty-five died in the hospital of Santa Maria Nuova alone. The city was emptying. The rich fled to their country houses; anyone who could sought refuge in the country. On the 9th the disease came to San Marco, where the first to die was Fra Tommaso Busini, a man of saintly life and one of the best in the convent, and very dear to Savonarola.

In the midst of all this trouble Savonarola never faltered. The youngest friars and those of greatest importance or promise for his work, he sent out of Florence to certain villas generously offered by some of the citizens. He himself remained in the convent to direct the healthy, attend the sick, and comfort the dying. On the 15th he wrote and had printed a brief letter of consolation, which was later entitled 'Against the Plague of the Spirit'. On the 24th he wrote these words to his brother Alberto:

The pestilence now raging here is not yet very great; but it is a terrible beginning, if God does not help us. More are dying of high plague-like fevers than of true plague, so that some days fifty or sixty or seventy have died, and sometimes as many as a hundred, so they say; whether it is true or not I do not know. And it is not abating; indeed, we see nothing in Florence but crosses every day and corpses. We are well, by God's grace, and I have not left Florence, although I have sent away more than seventy brothers, because I am not afraid, hoping that God's grace will be with us. I also stayed in order to console the afflicted.

He wrote to him again on August 14:

All our company is merry and leading a holy life. It is true that I have sent away the more important brethren, particularly the young ones. The citizens here are so full of charity that they have given us their palaces and paid all our expenses. The brethren are divided into four groups. One citizen provides for more than thirty, another for fourteen, another for fifteen, and another for eighteen. There are still more than forty of us here, and the citizens buy for us everything we need and let us want for nothing. Though we do not go outside our walls, they send and bring us everything. If Rome is against me, know that she is against Christ, not against me, and is fighting against God. *Sed quis resistit ei et pacem habet?* [Who shall resist Him and yet have peace?] Doubt not but that God will triumph. Fear not that I remain here in Florence in the midst of the plague, for the Lord will help me. I stay to comfort the afflicted, friars and citizens alike. Although both have begged me to go away and I have been offered many places of safety, nonetheless I have not wished to abandon my flock. It is quite unbelievable how joyful are the spirits of those who believe, in life as well as in death. *Et tam fratres nostri, quam cives et mulieres reddendo animas Salvatori commendantes, dormiunt, non moriuntur* [And our brethren and the citizens and women alike, commending their souls to the Saviour, fall asleep, they do not die]. So that the living not only no longer fear death, but welcome it.

Fearless, burning with zeal, he found it difficult to appreciate the weakness of others. To Fra Paolo del Beccuto, who, having seen ten of his brethren die, wished to take refuge in some safer place, he wrote on the 18th of August, reproaching him violently for his timidity, and holding up to him the example of so many brethren who had died joyfully, as though going to a feast, and especially a Fra Battista da Faenza, who the day before had begged as a favour that he should order the monks to let him go to heaven, as their prayers were preventing his departure.

At that time, strengthened by the joy and conviction which he observed in the words and the eyes of the dying, Savonarola was working hard at his spiritual writings. He was still correcting, perhaps already on the printer's proofs, his *Triumphus Crucis*. He was writing the dialogue *De Veritate prophetica*, designed to dispel any doubts that his claim to prophecy was a deception or a mere illusion of his own.

He composed other short works too, and among these, in all probability, the second version of the dialogue *Solatium itineris mei*. He must also have written in this fruitful period of leisure a great number of letters, for his correspondence, of which much has been lost, suddenly at this point becomes far less meagre. Besides the letters we have just quoted on the subject of the plague, and another to Giovanni Cambi in July, there are two to the Duke of Ferrara of the 1st and 29th of August. The first of these begs him not to be discouraged if the things predicted are slow in coming, and the second advises him what reliance should be placed on the King of France. After this doubtful reply of the Friar to his letter full of faith of the 8th of August, the Duke considered it prudent to join the League. There are also two letters to Lodovico Pittorio of the 3rd and 13th of August; and of the 13th, too, is a letter to Giovanna Caraffa, wife of Giovan Francesco Pico. He wrote other letters on the 4th and 14th of August to comfort and exhort the friars who were away from San Marco, and those of the convent at Fiesole. He also visited the friars away from his own convent, and there 'read the prophet Jonah, and explained the story of Samson'. On the 14th, too, he wrote a kind of encyclical to all the friars of the Congregation. Another letter to his friars, whose date is unknown, might perhaps be justifiably included here.

Also at this time, which was so propitious for spiritual comfort and consolation, in that greater peace which had come upon San Marco with the plague, Savonarola invented a new manner of singing psalms. Going in procession with his new friars round the convent, he alternated the verses of the psalm '*Te Deum*', and perhaps sometimes of other psalms, with those of the psalm '*Ecce quam bonum*', so dear to the Friar and his companions that it became almost the symbolic song of Savonarolan doctrine. It is perhaps not too daring to suppose that this 'new manner', which spread with the fame of the Friar himself, may have given rise to new musical forms.

Finally, if not in mid-August as the pseudo-Burlamacchi says, then in the last days of the month, the plague burned itself out. It left behind it only the aftermath of pestilential fever and the grief of so many deaths. Another sad business, and the death of five citizens that arose out of it, left an even more painful scar on the city.

Following on their denunciation by a certain Lamberto dell'Antella, which was begun out of revenge and greed and ended in the torture chamber, five citizens were arrested at the beginning of August and subjected to examination. Among them were Bernardo del Nero and Niccolò Ridolfi, who were leaders of the Bigi and among the most prominent men in the city. When they had confessed to certain intrigues with Piero de' Medici, they were condemned to death by a council of two hundred citizens. The relatives of the condemned men appealed to the Great Council, as the law allowed them to do, and when the Council met again to decide the question, opinions were divided. On the one hand, the death of such men as these would be a dreadful thing, and yet it seemed wicked not to observe the law. On the other, it was felt that public safety demanded a prompt and severe punishment for such a crime as this. Finally, Francesco Valori burst out in a rage, cursing the Signoria, and saying that 'they must die or he would'; with this he practically forced them to refuse the appeal. The same night the five criminals were executed.

Some writers, both old and more recent, have laid this act of exemplary justice at Savonarola's door, blaming him for not having moderated the zeal of his followers, who were indeed those most determined to refuse the appeal. They reproach him with having thus been the first to violate a law that he had been the first to support. The truth is that he did nothing to make the criminals' fate any worse. Nor could he have decently intervened on the side of leniency after he had repeatedly shouted from the pulpit that, especially in matters regarding the state, justice should be rigidly enforced. Under pressure from the relations, he recommended to mercy, but coldly, the young Tornabuoni, one of the convicted men. Not a word did he say in favour of Niccolò Ridolfi, brother of Giovambattista, who with Valori was virtually the standard-bearer of his followers. There is rather a note of coldness towards the criminal apparent in the letter of consolation which, on the 19th of August, two days before Niccolò's final sentence and death, Savonarola addressed to 'his' Giovambattista:

True Christians may be recognized in great prosperity and in great adversity: for in the former they do not exalt themselves, and in the latter they are not downcast, but with greatness of spirit they preserve at all times their equanimity. This they do in virtue of their faith, through which they rate of no great value, nay even as nothing, this life on earth with all its desires of the flesh, but constantly think of the life to come. And although sometimes the senses may rebel, nonetheless reason, with the grace of God, stands firm, and never moves from its proper place.

Therefore, my Giovambattista, in this adversity of yours, arouse the virtue of faith and the greatness of your spirit, and consider that riches and the honours of this world disappear like a puff of wind, and our time on earth grows daily shorter. There is no shame to man save in his own guilt, and the sins of others do not harm us; no one is offended save by himself. So we must put aside sadness and everything else, and think only of your brother's soul, if it should be God's will that he should die: for by gaining his soul, you will have gained him forever, and nothing will be lost. Perhaps God has ordained this penance for his salvation: often tribulations save those who would be ruined by prosperity.

I have wanted to write you these few words as a friend, for I know that the wise need few words, and that without me you will know how to console yourself. The Grace of Jesus Christ and the consolation of the Holy Spirit be with you always. Amen.

San Marco, August 19, 1497.

Ridolfi did not bear malice for this coolness of the Friar's, and we shall find him at his side in the hour of misfortune and danger. But while he hid his feelings for love of the common cause, he did not forgive Valori for the ferocious outburst which brought his brother 'an end not consonant with his prudence and his manner of life, nor with the nobility of his family, nor with the honours, dignity, authority, and power that he had enjoyed, equal to any other citizen of his times'.

At that time the followers of Savonarola again increased in strength, and on the 10th of September Somenzi could well write to his Duke: 'Now one can say that the Friar's party hold the government of the state freely in their hands, without any opposition.' After the gonfalonier Bartoli went out of office, they had three further Signorie in their favour. The effects of this were soon apparent: never was the Florentine legation in Rome so vigorously pressed in Savonarola's favour, not so much by the Ten (whose zeal for the Friar had been somewhat impeded by Becchi, especially when they wrote to him practically behind the Signoria's back) as by the Signoria itself. When

Cardinal Caraffa himself approached the Signoria for some favour connected with the property of Nofri Tornabuoni, confiscated after the trial of Bernardo del Nero, they were not slow to ask him in return for the absolution of the Friar.

Success seemed to be within their reach. It was a question of a large sum, which the Cardinal claimed was owing to him, and one can well imagine that the Signoria would have been glad to order the Ufficiali dei Ribelli [commissioners for dealing with traitors' property] to give him satisfaction if he could bring himself to obtain the revocation of the interdicts. At the end of the preceding June it was being said that citizens of Florence had offered a large sum to Roman prelates to obtain this revocation. It was also said that Cardinal Piccolomini had asked for 5,000 ducats for this favour, but it would be disagreeable to accept this rumour as true merely on the authority of the pseudo-Burlamacchi, involving as it does a serious slur on the character of the future Pius III. It is, however, given some colour by these words used by the Friar himself in his letter of the 13th of August to Lodovico Pittorio: 'As for my excommunication, I should consider it a much greater censure, were my absolution to be obtained at a price.'

It is apparent that Cardinal Caraffa had good hopes of success, and that he communicated them to the Signoria: for he advised them to get Savonarola to write to the Pope in a conciliatory manner. The Signoria took his advice, and replied on the 13th of October through Bracci: 'We believe that Fra Girolamo will now have carried everything out.' In fact, another humble and dignified letter was written that same day by Savonarola to the Pontiff, which, translated, begins: 'As a son grieved by his father's anger seeks every way to placate him, and no rebuff causes him to despair of his father's usual compassion, since it is written: ask and it shall be given unto you, knock and it shall be opened—so I, more afflicted at the loss of Your Holiness's good graces than at any other misfortune, unceasingly throw myself at Your Holiness's feet, begging that in the end my cry will be heard, and that you will no longer suffer that I should be torn from your bosom.' And, in anticipation of being able to throw himself at the feet of the Pope to cleanse himself of every false accusation, he concludes this virile act of submission, begging forgiveness for any fault which, out of ignorance or inattention but never out of malice, he might have committed.

It was said that the Pope may never have had this letter. If he had previously shown himself so sensitive to every profession of reverence and homage from Savonarola, it is hard to see why he should have been deaf to this one, which went far beyond all the others. I do not think that doubts of this kind are permissible; for, if the letter had been intercepted, the deception would soon have become apparent, as it was written at the instance of the Signoria and therefore was being watched for by the Florentine ambassadors.

The reason is quite different. Once again the politics of the rulers of Italy came to weave their web around the Friar's affairs in such a way as to appear one and the same thing in the eyes of the Pope. Now that the truce with the King of France had lapsed, and there were thoughts and rumours abroad of a French invasion, the League, with the exception of the Venetians, was making every effort to buy the support of the Florentines with the promise of the restitution of Pisa. Knowing how much this meant to the Florentines, Borgia thought the absolution of the Friar might be another counter to offer in the bargain. In any event, hopes were still alive on the 19th of November, for Manfredi, after a long conversation with Savonarola, wrote to the Duke of Ferrara: 'The Father hopes that his affair with the Pope will soon be put right, as the matter is in a fair way and His Holiness inclined to agree.'

In the meantime (as Parenti, with some gnashing of teeth, is obliged to record), 'the credit of Fra Girolamo having greatly improved here in this city, his portrait was cast in bronze medals, on one side of which was his head surrounded by this inscription: *Hieronymus Savonarola ordinis prædicatorum doctissimus*; and the other side showed Rome with a hand holding a dagger above it, and the words: *Gladius Domini super terram cito et velociter*.'[1] Florentine art could not fail to feel the influence of one who had made so great an impression on the life and politics of the city, and could not deny him its homage. After the great Michelangelo, a swarm of lesser artists who were enamoured of Savonarola's teachings, from Botticelli to Lorenzo Credi, from Baccio della Porta to the Della Robbia brothers, were among his followers. Some designed the beautiful engravings which adorn his works, others portrayed him in paintings or medallions, such as the one which had the honour of being described by the Arrabbiato Parenti, or in precious stones, as Giovanni dalle Corniole did; it is said that Michel-

---

[1] [Attributed to Ambrogio della Robbia].

angelo, gazing at his jewel engraved with the portrait of Savonarola, exclaimed that Art had reached its highest point and must now perforce decline.

The deadly year 1498 was just beginning. Early in January the Signoria had sent Domenico Bonsi to Rome to negotiate on Pisa, and included in his instructions that he was to treat for 'the complete and free absolution' of Fra Girolamo. Shortly before, in a letter to Bracci, they had given similar orders: 'When you receive this, go to the Pontiff, to the Cardinal of Naples, and to all those places where you think you may have favour to achieve this object, and insist, make a fuss, and bring pressure in every possible way.' Both Bracci and the new ambassador probably did as much. But, so long as the Florentines did not join the League, no amount of outcry would make the Pope hear, and in fact, right up to the 6th of February, he gave the ambassador nothing but a 'cold reply'.

In the meantime, the Friar's patience was at breaking-point; his anger was ready to overflow. He had filled that long sad silence with the composition of new works and the correction of their proofs. To the nuns of Annalena, and to all those who sought from him letters of exhortation, he wrote a long and beautiful letter explaining that he had written enough by now on the perfection of the spiritual life. But this did not prevent him shortly afterwards from writing a *Tractatus de vitæ spiritualis perfectione,* which he published together with a translation by Filippo Cioni. A letter, which may perhaps be dated around Christmas 1497, is addressed to the monks of San Domenico in Bologna, congratulating them on not having been scandalized or dismayed during his tribulations. His *Triumphus Crucis* had already appeared in its Latin version, and perhaps also in the Italian translation. It is a sober and lucid treatise in four books, designed to demonstrate the truth of the Christian faith, and it is considered to be his greatest and finest work. Many editions were made, right down to the beginning of the eighteenth century, and it was used in the Roman schools of *Propaganda Fide* at least until that time. At the beginning of 1498, 'at the request of the illustrious Signoria', while Giuliano Salviati was gonfalonier of justice, he wrote in a brief space of time his *Trattato circa il reggimento e il governo della città di Firenze* [*Treatise on the Rule and Government of the City of Florence*], which is a systematic digest, not lacking in qualities of style, of all he had said in his sermons on this subject, but treated on

general lines and without going into the details of the Florentine constitution. His *Trattato contra gli astrologi* was written at the end of 1947,
and published then or at the beginning of the following year. This
work was a pitched battle against people with whom he had been
skirmishing all his life.

Writing, however, was not enough for him: he must preach. He
could no longer contain the fullness of his heart, nor his anger at the
evil life of the Pope and the wicked prelates, and at the political hag-
gling on which, coming after earlier bargaining of another kind, he
now saw his absolution depend. Perhaps, too, that useless act of submission to which he had brought himself against the dictates of
conscience, for the sake of his mission—that act of humble submission
at the foot of the august throne of Peter, while trying not to look at
the infamous creature who sat upon it—perhaps it was this which now
gave him the bitter assurance that the time had come to utter one 'of
those great cries of Lazarus'.

He had behaved with extreme caution while he still kept some
hope that Borgia would change his mind. Although he was himself
convinced that his excommunication was invalid, and determined not
to obey it, he had abstained from celebrating Mass in public and
especially from preaching. But the first Sunday of Advent, the 3rd of
December, seeing that his letter to the Pope had not borne the promised
and desired fruit, he is reported to have said at a gathering of friars and
citizens 'that the woman was already heavy with child, and the time
for giving birth was nigh'. Then, on Christmas Day, he solemnly
celebrated the three sung Masses, giving Communion with his own
hand to his friars and hundreds of laymen, and walked in procession
around the square of San Marco.

Savonarola's credit rose even higher, and the effectiveness of his
excommunication further declined, when at Epiphany, following an
ancient custom in the city, the Signoria went to San Marco to make
their offering and, what matters more, kissed Fra Girolamo's hand at
the altar, to the great astonishment of the more knowledgeable present,
and of the Friar's friends more even than of his enemies. He was
already being urged by his followers to start preaching again. There
were not only the children, who had gone to the Signoria the previous
September to ask that the tiers of benches should be put back in Santa
Maria del Fiore, but the men too, who came to Fra Girolamo hungering

after the Word of God, and saying: 'Father, when are you going to preach again? We are starving for it.'

Finally, there was a rumour that he would preach for Candlemas, and at the end of January the tiers were rebuilt in the cathedral in great haste. To find out what truth there might be in these rumours, the ambassador of Ferrara went to see Fra Girolamo at the Fiesole convent, where he was staying. He replied that, come what may, he was 'ready and determined to preach for this Quadragesima, and perhaps even before, when he received the sign from those who could command him'. When the ambassador asked him if he were waiting for the order of the Pope or the Signoria, Savonarola answered that he would do nothing on the orders of the Signoria or of the Pope, whom he saw still persisting in wicked ways and refusing to cancel the unjust excommunication, but that 'he was waiting for the command of One greater than the Pope or any living creature'.

In spite of this, he did not preach for Candlemas. He did not want to throw the fatal dice before the final decision came from Rome. But letters came from Bonsi to him and the Signoria, according to which it was clear that the Pope made Florence's joining the League a condition for his absolution, and that (the ambassador added) 'once this was agreed to, he would do anything in his power to please you'. Then, losing patience and filled with anger, 'seeing that his work was being ruined', Savonarola abandoned all restraint and waited no longer. The Cathedral Chapter, egged on perhaps by one of the usual fairy tales addressed to them by that awful bore the 'Angelo peccatore', or fallen angel of Vallombrosa, sent representatives to the Palace of the Signoria to remonstrate about the risks they were running—but all in vain. In vain did Leonardo de' Medici, Vicar of the Archbishop, issue a ban on anyone who attended the sermons of the excommunicated priest. The Signoria replied by threatening him with banishment as a rebel if he did not quit his office within two hours—which he hastened to do immediately, and he was then replaced by a certain Peter Martyr, a fervent Piagnone. On the 11 of February, Septuagesima Sunday, the intrepid Friar went up again at last into the pulpit of Santa Maria del Fiore and began his pitched battle.

Chapter 21

THE SERMONS ON EXODUS AND
THE DEPARTURE FROM THE PULPIT

◇◇◇◇◇◇◇◇◇◇◇◇◇◇◇◇◇◇◇◇◇◇◇◇◇◇◇◇◇◇◇◇◇◇◇◇◇◇◇

THAT 'hidden guidance of God' which, according to Savonarola, had since ¦1492 guided his prophetic preaching, once again seemed to be in evidence. He took as his text for¦ this last Lenten series of sermons the book of Exodus, meaning, as he said, that the chosen people—i.e. the Florentines—would go forth with him to the promised land in spite of the hostility of Pharaoh—i.e. Alexander VI. However, as those sermons also signified his own exodus from the pulpit, from his mission, and from life itself, one might say that on this occasion, too, he was guided, if not by a secret presentiment, at least by a strange destiny.

It is true that ordinary human foresight sufficed to show him the extreme danger to which he exposed himself. This time there was no equivocal consent as there had been in 1496, there was no favourable attitude on the part of the Pope, but instead only a silent hostility, against which the most pressing appeals of the Signoria, the constant requests of the Council of Ten, and the respectful protests of the Friar himself had availed nothing. This time there was the excommunication, which he had not obeyed. And a Pope such as Alexander VI could not in the long run safely permit governments, ecclesiastics, and laymen to make mock of him, even though at first he had evidently disliked the excommunication and regarded it as a mistake. It was to be foreseen, therefore, that he would take matters to their logical conclusions. The Friar could not depend, either, on the temporary advantage he held from the political point of view, for he knew too well the precariousness of tenure of the magistrates, and hence of the entire political situation in Florence.

Nonetheless, if he must have known the mortal dangers of that unequal struggle, I do not think that he was yet in the frame of mind of the good soldier who seeks death on the battlefield when all hope of survival is lost, nor that his immediate aim was that martyrdom which he had so often invoked. Although it may seem hopeless to us today, the Friar, as he began to preach that February, was still trusting to human aid, before turning, with greater faith, solely to the help of God.

When he appeared in the pulpit, the people in their joy at his return sang the psalm '*Te deum laudamus*'; and he opened his sermon thus:

Lord, I who am mere dust and ashes wish to speak first this morning with Thy Majesty. Thou hast set me upon a great sea, I am out of sight of the port and cannot turn back; and I would not turn back even if I could. I cannot, because Thou art not willing; and I am, therefore, not willing either. I am content to remain here where Thou hast set me, but I beg Thee, Lord, to remain with me. These my enemies say that Thou art not with me. I beg Thee, Lord, to stay with me. I ask Thee not for gold or silver, nor for peace and tranquillity, but only to give me light. Grant me the natural light of reason and the supernatural light of faith, that I may not think anything contrary to the Scripture and the teachings of the Church. Grant me also the supernatural light to know things that are hid and to come, that I may not deceive myself nor deceive the people, as I have not deceived them heretofore. And I beg Thee now to start a new era, and that this may be the beginning of great things. . . .

Coming next to the excommunication, he said:

God governs the things that are in nature lower, through superior agents. Men are by nature all equal, but because man is by nature a civil being and they live together, it has been necessary to make one of them governor of the common good, and such governors are the instruments of God, moved as second causes by the first cause, as the saw is moved by the hand of the craftsman. If a saw is taken to a carpenter and he buys it and then throws it down among the broken tools, then this instrument is no more than the other tools. So it is with the prince: if he is not used like a tool by the agent—that is, by God, whose instrument he is—then he is no greater than any man, and has no one who moves him; he is like the broken tools which are all alike, and you may then say to him: 'You do not well, for you are not guided by the supreme agent.' And if he says: 'I hold the power', you may say to him: 'That is not true, for there is no hand guiding you, and you are a broken tool.'

At another point he said:

Now on whose side art Thou, Christ? On ours or theirs? You have seen that our side has always told the truth, and we have always stood firm, and our teaching has brought in clean living, religious fervour, and prayer. And yet we have been excommunicated, and they are the blessed, although it is evident that their doctrine leads to evildoing, and giving themselves up to eating and drinking, to avarice, to concubines, to the sale of benefices, and to so many lies and wicked ways. On whose side wilt thou be, O Christ? On the side of truth or of lies? Christ says: 'I am the truth, and I wish to be on that side which is true, and on the side of those whom you say have been excommunicated, and the devil will be with the ones who are blessed.' Lord, I turn to Thee. Thou didst die for the truth, and I am content to die for Thy truth. I offer myself to Thee as a sacrifice: here I am, I am happy to die for Thee, and I beg Thee to grant that I die only in defence of Thy truth.

A great crowd of people came to this sermon, in spite of the papal excommunication and the Vicar's ban, but fewer than used to come, 'and many stayed away out of fear . . . saying: *iusta vel iniusta, timenda est* [just or unjust, it is to be feared]'. On the 15th of February, 'Fra Girolamo preached in San Marco, and invited only priests and monks', Landucci says, adding: 'and, as one of them told me, he revealed all their rottenness.' A few days later the sermon could be read by every-one, for it was taken down, like the one before and those that followed, by Lorenzo Violi, and immediately published. He did the same for many other sermons, publishing them at intervals before collecting them in one volume some years later.

The Friar preached again in the cathedral on the 18th of February, Sexagesima Sunday. 'Still more people stayed away' as fear grew among the apprehensive citizens. It was to encourage the timid that on that day he undertook to prove the invalidity of the excommunication, and to show that anyone who believed it valid was guilty of heresy. Before entering on this demonstration, he—who rebelled only against wicked customs and the wickedness of prelates—submitted it 'to the determination of the Holy Roman Church'. After prefacing his sermon in this way, he went over the history of the Briefs, the better to explain the errors they contained, and other things contrary to the common good, with the pious object of proving that the Pope had always been got round. Similarly, he preached on the 25th of February, Quinquagesima Sunday, 'still arguing that the excommunication was invalid and untenable'.

It is easy to imagine how hard to stomach these sermons were for the Pope, especially as they were promptly served up to him by the Arrabbiati, poisonously seasoned by the ambassadors of the League. Already on the 17th of February, when he could only have had the merest indication that the sermons had been started again, or at most a brief summary of the first one, he had shown some signs of anger, On the 22nd, when Bonsi and Bracci had a long conversation with the Pope on the subject of the League, that perpetual sore point and the crux of the whole story, the Pope, after complaining that the Florentines did not really want to abandon their alliance with the King of France, walked out of the room in disgust, and from the doorway sent them this parting shot: 'Let Fra Girolamo preach, if you like; I would never have believed that you could treat me thus.' This is a clear indication that in striking this bargain he did not intend to separate the two matters, as he knew very well how attached the Florentine government was to the Friar.

But things got worse and, indeed, quite changed their aspect when the contents of the sermon of the 18th of February became known in Rome. If the Pope had resented the letter published by Savonarola after the excommunication in which the Friar argued its invalidity, we may well imagine what he felt at hearing that the same thesis had been preached from the pulpit! It was no time for Alexander to demonstrate his customary generous indifference. And the more so because at that same time a very full apology by Giovan Francesco Pico had just been published, expounding in two books and proving with a wealth of learning the same thesis. If this was not pernicious to the papacy, it certainly was to the Pope, considering also the standing of the author and even of the person to whom it was dedicated: none other than the Duke of Ferrara, a vassal of the Church.

The Pope's anger burst out. Perhaps from this moment the affairs of Fra Girolamo ceased to be a commodity with which to barter with the Florentines; perhaps even then, though he still dissimulated, Borgia made up his mind irrevocably, League or no League, to destroy the Friar. On the 25th of February he called before him Bracci and Bonsi, and reminded them how he had used his influence for the city in the matter of Pisa (was he now using Pisa to barter with them over the Friar?). He deplored the open contempt they had shown him, and complained of the Signoria and of Fra Girolamo, 'speaking with the greatest indignation, and using very strong words about him'. He told Bonsi to send a messenger post-haste to the Signoria with a letter notifying them that if, when they received it, the Friar was not silenced at once, 'either by constraint or any other method', he would impose 'a universal interdict on the whole of the city'. He added that he had wished to say these words in the presence of the Cardinal of Perugia and other Prelates 'so that it might be understood that he had no intention of changing his mind'. Then he had read out certain sonnets which had come from Florence, mocking him; and he repeated several times— he who was so tolerant of the satires of Pasquino—'Am I to be derided in sonnets like that!' The ambassadors were not allowed to make any reply, or even to complete a sentence; the words were always cut short on their lips by the Pope and the other high dignitaries present. There could be no persuading them, as the Council of Ten had suggested to the ambassador, of the excellent qualities of Fra Girolamo 'and that his works went far beyond human capacity'.

The Pope proved the next day that his anger was not transitory, by sending off two Briefs by messenger, one to the Cathedral Chapter, and the other to the Signoria. To make sure that this second one reached its destination, two copies were made, and one was sent to the Chapter together with the first, with the order that they should pass it on. The other copy was given under seal to Bonsi, who forwarded it with his own letter to the Ten on the 27th. The Brief addressed to the Chapter is now lost, and we do not know what it contained, but it appears to have been an order to the canons not to allow Fra Girolamo to preach in the cathedral. The one to the Signoria, which is the more important, again recapitulated the story of the Briefs directed at Savonarola—who is called the 'son of iniquity'—deplored his disobedience and public contempt of the interdicts, expressed strong dissatisfaction with the favour accorded to him by many citizens, and ordered them to send him to Rome under strong escort, or at least to segregate him, as a 'rotten limb', under guard in a safe place; otherwise the city would be placed under ecclesiastical interdict for having favoured a man so pernicious and suspected of heresy.

While the riders carrying the Briefs were galloping full tilt towards Florence, the city was celebrating Carnival, but a pious and decent one: the last Savonarolan Carnival. These were the pleasures and junketings of that day, among a people once so licentious and pleasure-loving. In the morning Savonarola celebrated High Mass in San Marco and with his own hands gave Communion to 'all his brethren and several thousands of men and women'. Then he went up into the pulpit erected near the door of the church, with the Sacrament in his hand, and there he stood, as he had said in his sermon on Quinquagesima, praying fervently in silence that heaven might strike him down if his work were not of God and his words inspired by Him.

In the afternoon the procession of boys, divided in groups according to the quarters of the town, with candles and olive branches in their hands, went as they had done the previous year into the Piazza dei Signori. There a wooden construction, like that of the previous Carnival, had been put up, and it was laden as before with precious vanities. And again, after the recital of a dialogue (*contrasto*) between a Florentine and Carnival, and after the singing of vernacular hymns (*laudi*), the burning was celebrated to the sound of bells and trumpets. Then the procession formed again and returned to San Marco, where the Cross was set up in the middle of the square, and three circles of boys, friars, and laymen danced around it. The Compagnacci did their best to break up the procession and the bonfire, throwing stones, pulling the crosses out of the children's hands and breaking them in pieces, and throwing filth. Then a doctor of law, Messer Luca Corsini, was seen to throw off his cloak and throw stone for stone at those trying to hinder the procession.

The revival of such boldness in the Arrabbiati and the Compagnacci may perhaps be explained by the election of the new Signoria, which this time had turned out in their favour. Four out of eight priors were hostile to the Friar, and the new gonfalonier, Piero Popoleschi, was strongly opposed to him—like the Germans to water, to quote the effective image used by the poetaster Giovanni 'sarto'. Only three priors were convinced Piagnoni; the other one, Piero Fedini, was less reliable. On the eve of this Signoria taking office—probably on the 28th, the first day of Lent—the dangerous Papal Brief, of which we already know, arrived at the Palace.

That morning the Friar had preached, threatening the wicked of Florence, who had behaved so badly during the procession, and the wicked of Rome: 'O clergy, clergy! O Rome, Rome! You will have so many tribulations that you will be sorry you ever fought against our work. You say you are the blessed and we are the excommunicated, and yet you fight as the damned and the infidels. Fight, I say, like Christians, if you wish to be believed! Write to Rome and say that that Friar who is in Florence, with his followers, will fight against you as against the Turks and pagans, and that we desire to die and be martyred, and that I have a great wish to be martyred by you. O Lord, grant me this favour! You think, Rome, to frighten me, and I know no fear.'

He preached, too, the following morning, March the 1st, the first day of office of the new Signoria. As he came near the end of his sermon, he said: 'Briefs have come from Rome, have they not? They say they call me *filius perditionis*—that is, the son of perdition. Write to them this: "He whom you call thus says that he keeps no concubines nor boys for pleasure, but devotes himself to preaching the faith of Christ. . . . He works to exalt the Church of Christ, while you seek to ruin it."' He concluded by saying that he would give way before their anger, and would preach no more from the pulpit of Santa Maria del Fiore, but in San Marco. Obviously, aware of the mood of the Signoria and the Chapter, he wanted to leave before being ejected. It was the first step in his exodus from the pulpit, and God knows how painful it must have been for him.

On the next day, as he had announced, he preached in San Marco, and women were not admitted, as the church, though large, was not able to hold all his listeners, now that people were flocking back to him. Lost in the throng was Niccolò Machiavelli, who, as always incredulous and sneering no less towards the Pope than towards Savonarola (about whom he was later and on maturer consideration to write with reverence), made some amusing comments on the occasion in one of his letters: 'Then he began to recite your blessings, priests, and to treat you so that even the dogs would turn up their noses at you.' Addressing Borgia without naming him, the Friar had said that morning: 'Listen here, before you condemn us: I want only that men should lead a virtuous life. Why then do you oppose me so violently? But if you are against the good life, and if you do not live like a Christian, I do not want peace with you. "O Friar, say not so! Friar, he is a great master." However great he may be, I do not want peace with him if he does not live virtuously. If you want to fight against me, you live like a pagan, because I live like a Christian, and your way of life is against Christ. If I am martyred, you will be the tyrant.'

In the meantime an answer was needed, written rather than oral, to the Papal Briefs—truly a difficult task. For this purpose the Signoria called together a *Pratica* [grand council] on the 3rd of March to seek advice. The gonfaloniers were divided among themselves; the Buonomini and the Ten (for whom Giovambattista Ridolfi spoke, reminding them 'that the Pope had changed his mind suddenly on account of letters from the Duke of Milan, not of the sermons') all declared themselves in favour of the Friar and of a dignified rebuff to Alexander VI. Most of the other citizens whose opinion was sought, gave a similar answer. Among others, it is pleasant to read the answer given by Giovanni Cambi: 'As for the Brief, he might well send it to Perugia, but not to us. It would be dishonourable to obey'; and as for Savonarola, 'it would be rewarding him with ingratitude. We are very obliged to him for what he has done. . . . We have a treasure that anyone might envy. . . .'

As such was the opinion of the Pratica, the Signoria could not have run counter to it without the danger of being tried and punished when their brief term of office came to an end, if they were followed by a Signoria favourable to the Friar. This was always a powerful restraint on the officers of the Republic. Then, all alike had their pride as Florentines: jealous of their freedom, which even with the Arrabbiati counted more than their hatred of the Friar, they could not easily tolerate that the Pope should issue orders to them, as though they were his vassals, with his imperious Briefs. 'Let him send them to Perugia' was often repeated in the Pratiche of the succeeding days.

These things have not been properly considered by the historians of Savonarola, even the greatest of them. They were surprised that the Friar should have been strongly defended at that time even by a Signoria which was thought by contemporaries, and by themselves in the light of what subsequently happened, to be thoroughly hostile to him. I am surprised by their surprise. They did not understand that, besides the opinion of the Pratica to which they had to be reconciled, the Arrabbiati then controlled only five firm votes in the Signoria, including the gonfalonier. So only later, after the defection of Fedini (of which the historians were not aware), were they able to count on the 'six beans' necessary to checkmate the Friar's party.

For all these reasons, plus, if one likes, the typically Florentine desire to aggravate the Pope by throwing his offensive Brief back at him, the Signoria on the 3rd of March sent him a dignified but negative answer. This cannot have been a Machiavellian ruse to make him even angrier to the detriment of the Friar, as Villari and Schnitzer asserted on the authority of the always Machiavellian Somenzi. In that reply, after praising the truthful prophecies and the achievements of the man 'who in this Brief is called the *son of iniquity*', they concluded that the Pope had been misled by false accusations; and they declared that they could not obey him without committing an act unworthy of the name of Florence, a monstrous ingratitude towards one who had deserved so well of the city. They also told him bluntly that they were more concerned with the good of their Republic than with other people's convenience. As though this were not enough, the Ten did not wish to lose this opportunity of adding their voice to that of the Signoria in support of the Friar. On the 3rd they sent the ambassador a letter to show to the Pope, in which, naturally, they hit even harder.

Savonarola went further still. On the 1st of March, in the sermon from which I have already quoted, he had said, referring to the Brief of the 26th of February: 'I hear . . . that you have received official letters addressed to the Republic. You are too kind and respectful in sending a reply. Let me answer: I will buzz in their ears in a way they will understand.' He replied, in fact, on the 3rd of March, the same day the Signoria and the Ten did, with a letter which, translated [from Latin,] runs as follows:

Holy Father, as it is the duty of the Christian to defend the honour of God, the faith of Christ, and the rectitude of virtuous living, and as I see the flock strayed wholly from the path owing to the evil example of many of their shepherds, and therefore I preach the truth of the Gospels, to confirm and strengthen men's faith, in teaching the Christian life and predicting by divine inspiration what will come to pass, so that men may repent, and seeking with all diligence to further the cause of peace in this city, and yet having for this reason been persecuted, and still suffering persecution from evil men, I certainly did not deserve that Your Holiness, at least, should have always opposed me on these matters, but rather that you should have lent me all aid and favour.

You, on the other hand, having heard and read my all too obvious excuses and justifications, and likewise understood the truth of what I have preached, which only the impious and enemies of Christ shamelessly denying it pretend mendaciously not to understand and continually attack—you, I say, having known and understood all these things, have yet always listened to all my calumniators and detractors; and in thus depriving me of that help which it was not only your duty as a Christian to give, but which your high office should have compelled you to give, you have opened the way to the wolves, and given them all strength and facility to hinder the work of Christ.

But God, who chose the humble and weak creatures of the earth to confound the strong, has answered the prayers of His poor children. He is ready to prove this truth, for which we now suffer so many ills at your hand; to prove it, I say, against you and against all His other enemies, both with natural proofs and with supernatural signs. These things shall be shown in this manner, and proved with these arguments to those who hinder God's work. We do not seek thereby the glory of men, but only that of Christ, for which we dearly long to die. Therefore, Holy Father, delay no longer in providing for your salvation. Farewell. From San Marco, Florence, March 3, 1497.

Here was a full-scale challenge, open, ingenuous, and dignified, and in every way worthy of Savonarola. A contemporary rightly described it as a 'terrible letter'. As Fra Girolamo had promised in his

226

sermon, it was such that the Pope understood it. He understood well enough that he must make an end of this, and quickly. He really had no need any longer of the incitements of Fra Mariano, who had meantime become General of the Order for his anti-Savonarolan services. On the 4th of March, the first Sunday in Lent, he had been ordered by the Pope to refute Savonarola's doctrine, but he did nothing but pour forth, in the presence of the Sacred College and of the Pontiff himself, a stream of abuse. He inveighed against the Friar, shouting: 'The great Jew, the robber! . . . Pope Alexander has pissed less than he has had medals struck in his honour,' and so on with other insults, vulgarities, and stupidities. 'Do you know, wicked knave, when you see those visions of yours? When you have put down a lot of that good Trebbiano wine? . . . O Sacred College, O Pontiff, do something: you do not know what he is plotting; he will say things that will darken the sun. But you do nothing. People can make figs to your very faces; and, if it were not for the reverence I owe you, I would do it myself to you now.' And, so saying, he actually did make that indecent gesture before the very eyes of the cardinals and the Pope. Those eyes had seen, and moreover were yet to see, worse things.

In the meantime the Court was waiting for the answer from the Signoria. Bonsi, who (as often happens to ambassadors) from always having the same things dinned into him, was himself inclined to agree with them, was on tenterhooks. He well knew the risk his country was running, and he was also in some personal danger, having been mysteriously set upon one night. Furthermore, it was extremely difficult for him to steer a course between his superiors, who wrote to him about the Friar's supernatural work, and those Roman prelates who based themselves only too firmly on the natural aspects of life. Finally, the answer that we have already seen arrived. Not surprisingly, when it was given to the Pope, 'it was not very acceptable to him', and 'he went so far as to say that he found it a wretched letter'. He added that he was not ill-informed, as the letter said, about the sermons of Fra Girolamo, because he had read them in print. He ended by saying that he might well now proceed to impose the interdict on the city, but that he was nonetheless willing to give the Signoria a further warning that, if the Friar went on preaching after retiring to San Marco, and if they did not stop him, he would certainly place them under the interdict. The letter from the Republic displeased him, but he was more angered by the letter 'of an evil nature' which he had received from Savonarola.

Bonsi tried in vain to pacify him and convince him of the Friar's virtues. When he had gone, Borgia gave vent to an outburst of Hispanic rage, as the Bishop of Parma later recounted, still trembling with fright. The latter also told Bonsi, on oath, that all the Pope wanted was for Savonarola to stop preaching and humble himself to ask for absolution, but Savonarola would not do so. This was quite untrue, because the Friar had sought absolution in his letter of the 13th of October, 1497.

In his first access of rage, Alexander had written, and perhaps also sent off, to the Signoria the terrible Brief '*Nunquam putavimus*': 'We never thought that things would come to such a pass that you would dare to contend with Us on the subject of Fra Girolamo, as in a dispute, or in a lawsuit. . . .' It went on in the same vein, insinuating that the Friar himself had inspired the Signoria's letter; in fact, in his interview with the ambassador the Pope had actually said that he recognized the Friar's style. '*De bono opere non lapidamus Hieronymum*', the Brief went on, without considering that these words, modelled on those which the Pharisees said to Christ [John x, 33], created a strange parallel not at all to the Pontiff's advantage. Finally, after pouring out his indignation at the behaviour of Fra Girolamo and the Florentines, who had made him 'almost their Delphic oracle', shutting out all other preachers so that they might worship him alone, he ended with the usual injunctions and threats of an interdict.

However, either this Brief was never sent, or, if it was, its delivery was arrested in time. It was thought, on maturer reflection, that by offending the Florentines still more deeply, it would have the opposite effected to that intended. The Signoria received merely a Brief dated the 9th of March, beginning '*Expectantibus nobis*', which said the same things, more or less, but in a milder form. It was a rude awakening for the Ten when it reached their hands. While the Pope demanded actions, they had been sending poor Bonsi nothing but words, and he finally complained of this on the 16th of March; in a letter full of realism, he asked to be relieved of his charge.

When the Brief arrived, the Signoria summoned a great Pratica on the 14th. As the danger grew, opinions were more divided than on the previous occasion, but there was still a majority in favour of standing out against the Pope's demands, or at least against a substantial part of them. The Friar was spoken of with the highest praise. Lorenzo Lenzi said that before mentioning him 'he felt he ought to wash out his mouth'. As the question remained undecided and the Signoria was not convinced, on the 17th it asked further advice, this time from a very limited committee of citizens—'as it were, the heart of the city', the official report says. They agreed that Fra Girolamo should be persuaded to stop preaching entirely. The Pope's other demands were judged unworthy of the Republic. These decisions were communicated to Savonarola, and on the 18th Bonsi was commissioned to inform the Pope orally of this hard-won partial victory.

In the meantime, the Friar had preached every day in San Marco to men, and on Saturdays to women only. Every day he spoke of the corruption of Rome, and the need not to obey the Pope's orders against the commands of Christ and of charity. On the 7th of March he cried out:

'O Friar, what do you say of the Briefs that have arrived?' I tell you that those Briefs are not from the Pope. Let us examine the case. You who have judgment, stand forth and consider all the circumstances and judge for yourself. They say that the Pope, as Pope, cannot err. They think that is saying something wonderful. It is a plain man's proposition, and it is true in itself, but what they infer from it to attack me is not true. This other proposition is also true: that a Christian, as a Christian, cannot sin; and yet many Christians do sin, inasmuch as they are human and every human can err. I, as a Christian, cannot err, and, as a monk, I cannot disobey my Rule, and it is as good as saying: '*Homo, in quantum homo, non est albus*' ['A man, as a man, is not without sin']: ask any philosopher, or even a logician, and he will tell you that it is true. Thus the Pope, as a Pope, cannot err, because he is then acting according to his great office, but when he errs, he is no longer Pope; and if he orders something which is in error, then he is not Pope. . . . It follows, therefore, that that Brief, which is so ill conceived, was not written by the Pope.

And on the 14th:

'O Friar, he is God on earth and the Vicar of Christ.' That is true; but God and Christ tell us that we must love our brother and do good. So, if the Pope ordered you to do something contrary to charity, would you do it? You raise your head too high. Do you want the Pope to do more than God Himself? He is not to be called Pope, and he is not to be obeyed, when he commands against the will of God.

On the 17th of March, as we have said, they came to forbid him to preach. The following morning, going up into the pulpit for the last time, he described how he had received the messengers of the Signoria:

Yesterday, about the third hour of the night, *quoniam qui male agit odit lucem,* an embassy came from the rulers of the city and told me that I was not to preach any more, for various reasons. I said to them: 'Have you done what your Signori told you to do?' 'Yes.' 'I also have a Master, and I will hear what He has to say, and tomorrow morning I will give you your answer.' And I gave them no further answer at that time; and so this morning I will answer from here.

But there could be no doubt of the answer, and he took his leave of his people with heartfelt words, recommending them to God's care.

O Lord, I commend to Thee the good and pure in heart, and I beg Thee to overlook the omissions of the good, for human weakness is great. The good and the pure in heart must be commended to Thee. *Benefac, Domine, bonis et rectis corde.* Lord, I pray Thee to delay no longer in fulfilling Thy promises.

This was the end of the sermons on Exodus; this was the next stage in the Friar's exodus towards the promised land.

Chapter 22

THOUGHTS OF A CONCILIUM:
THE ORDEAL BY FIRE

◇◇

O F the human assistance on which Savonarola had relied when
he entered on his pitched battle, part, the favour of the
Signoria, had already failed him to some extent, and was to
fail him more as time went by. In any case, this was a weapon of
defence, rather than offence, and without the latter a war can seldom
be won. The weapons that might have destroyed the enemies of his
ambitions were primarily those of the King of France. There was much
talk of his coming before the Friar began to preach again, and at the
beginning of March news of the expedition was still being received.
When these resources failed, too, there remained one more: that 'cry
of Lazarus' which was to arouse the governors of the peoples, the good
prelates, the true monks, all those who desired to purify the See of
Peter of its scandal. He had already hinted at this, as we have said, in
the Lenten sermons on Ezekiel. But he had always hoped that the
Pope would change his mind, or perhaps for some human or divine
punishment that would achieve the same end. Now, as every other
road was closed to him, and as his work was in danger, he finally
decided to utter that great cry which would shake the entire Christian
world.

Then, as you may remember, he had cried out: 'You who are
in France, in Germany, who have friends in those parts, send letters
everywhere. . . . Come, send off messengers, for this dead body cannot
be revived otherwise. . . .' During those early days of March messengers

were indeed sent off. At the Friar's request Domenico Mazzinghi wrote to France, to the Florentine ambassador at the King's Court; Giovann Cambi wrote to Germany, directly to the Emperor; Simone del Nero wrote to his brother, ambassador in Spain. These letters, each of which included a copy of that challenging letter to the Pope of the 3rd of March, were intended to clear the way for other letters that Savonarola had in mind to write to them, 'because it would be primarily their responsibility to deal with these errors through the appropriate Concilium'. The Concilium! 'I should not be surpirsed,' continued Simone del Nero in his letter, 'if the Father should one day write something of this to those princes, inspired to do so by the will of God.'

Not for nothing had he exclaimed in his sermon of the 9th of March:

'*Veneruntque simul et congregaverunt cunctos seniores filiorum Isdrael....*' ['They came and gathered together all the elders of the children of Israel.'] This is a good point, but I want to save it up awhile yet, and I shall put it here in my satchel; it is not yet time. I shall say only this: Tell me, Florence, what does Concilium mean? Men have forgotten what a Concilium is. What does it mean that your children know nothing of it, what does it mean that today no one does it? 'O Father, it cannot be summoned.' Perhaps you are right in saying that it could not be summoned; but I am not sure if you understand it in the same way as I do. Concilium means a gathering together of the Church—i.e. of all the good abbots, prelates, and important men and good laymen of the Church. Observe, however, that it may not properly be called the Church where there is not the grace of the Holy Spirit: that is the true form of the Church, and where there is not the form of the Church, there the Church may be said not to exist.... And for this reason you might say that the Elders of the tribe of Israel cannot be gathered together, and that there can be no Concilium. Likewise, in the Concilium reformers must be appointed who shall reform what is rotten. Who shall these reformers be? Those who reform must first be reformed themselves, and so it would be necessary to set a guard upon the guard. Likewise, in the Concilium the wicked priests are punished, the bishop is deposed who has been guilty of simony and schism. How many then would be deposed! Perhaps none would remain.

We have some evidence that while he was saying these things from the pulpit, he was already preparing to send those first notifications to France, Germany, and Spain, and had begun to work out the letters to the princes about the Concilium. In the meantime he made the drafts in Latin (and we have a copy of these) of the letters for the Emperor, the King of France, and the King and Queen of Spain, employing in each of them words appropriate to their particular conditions and ambitions. He reminded Charles VIII of the mission for which he had been chosen, and that, because he had neglected it, he had received a salutary punishment from God, by the death of his son. To all of them he declared in somewhat similar terms that 'this Alexander VI was not really a pontiff, nor could ever be, not so much because of his simoniacal and sacrilegious election, and his publicly committed sins, as because he was not a Christian, and lacked any kind of faith'. For these reasons, on which he would write more fully at a more convenient time and place, he begged them to order a solemn Concilium in a free and safe place so that the Church should no longer remain without a shepherd to the great danger of the souls of men. If they did not do this, it would be held against them as a grave misdeed, and they would provoke the anger of God.

He proposed writing similar letters to the kings of England and Hungary, but his weary hand stopped short already at these first drafts. Although, as was shown, the conditions were satisfied for the summoning of a Concilium even against the will of the Pope, the Friar's Christian heart was unable to overcome its last scruples and to overturn, even for a most pious end, the Church of Christ. Perhaps even when things were so bad, and even in the heat of the battle, before taking that last way out for his own work and the Church, he remembered that the ways of the Lord are infinitely varied, and that (as he had said himself on this very theme in his last sermon but six) 'this is the way of the things of God: to move gently and slowly.'

At Rome, meanwhile, poor Bonsi was sweating worse than in the summer sun, and spring was just beginning. The letter written to him by the Signoria on the 18th in answer to the Brief of the 9th reached Rome on the 22nd. In the interval the fury of the Pope had increased further with the news he had received of Savonarola's last sermons—so much so that on the 17th, in a conference including the Pope and Cardinal Sforza and some others, it was decided not to limit

233

their demands any longer to the silencing of Fra Girolamo, but to get him handed over to them at all costs. Not only would the interdict be applied, but all the Florentine merchants in Rome and their goods would be seized; then the Signoria would be asked to hand over the Friar within a certain time, and if it refused, the merchants would be imprisoned and their goods confiscated.

Needless to say, the threat frightened the merchants, especially those who had dealings with the Curia. They hastily sent a courier with a letter to the Signoria on the 18th, informing it of the extreme danger to their persons and, what probably seemed to them worse, to their money and possessions. This letter was not without its effect in Florence, both at the Palace and at the Calimala.[1] The letters that these merchants sent to their families and friends must have been even more influential.

The Florentines, up to a point, might defy ecclesiastical censure, but they would never risk their trade. In the last of the Pratiche of which we have spoken, that of the 14th of March, Messer Enea della Stufa had sung the praises of 'that blessed Fra Girolamo' and of his convent so full of holiness as to invite comparison with the early cenobites', and had said that they could not, to satisfy the Pope's wicked desire, take so great a man and 'send him bound under guard'; as for the merchants, they should have no fear for them. To which Giuliano Gondi replied: 'If Messer Enea had something to lose in the affair, he would speak differently.' Savonarola might well have repeated to the Florentines the words he had uttered in a sermon of the days of triumph: 'If I wager my life, why will you not risk your goods?'

It was evidently just at this time that Fedini went completely over to the enemy, and thus gave the death-blow to the Friar and his followers by placing in the hands of the Arrabbiati the six fatal votes. 'Però el Frate ne farà ancor lagno' ['The Friar will bitterly regret it'] is the comment on this key episode of the poetaster Giovanni 'sarto', who hitherto has been unknown to the biographers of Savonarola.

Another deserter, more illustrious if less decisive, was the Duke of Ferrara. The young Giovan Francesco Pico had dedicated to him his *Apologia,* demonstrating the invalidity of the excommunication which Savonarola had unjustly suffered; and this work was certainly not published without the Duke's knowledge, and possibly with his consent. But, having news from Rome that the Pope had taken it ill, and seeing

---

[1] [The principal cloth Guild in Florence.]

things were going badly for the man he had so much admired and courted in the days of his prosperity, Duke Ercole hastened to write a lying letter of excuses on the 26th of March. Let us hope that it recommended him to Alexander VI better than it does to us.

On that same day the Duke also wrote to thank Felino Sandei for advising him to take this step. This Sandei was the same man who in 1495 helped Savonarola to defend himself against Alexander VI; but he had recently passed over to the opposing camp on the eve of realizing certain of his ambitions, and had been responsible for drafting the powerful Brief 'Numquam putavimus'. While we are on the subject, I must mention here another defection among the many which must have saddened the Friar at this time: that of the famous philosopher Oliviero Arduini. It was he who had said in 1496 that he was not worthy even to carry Savonarola's books for him; and now, lately, he had ranged himself among the members of the Chapter most hostile to the Friar. The rats were beginning to leave the sinking ship.

The Pope, meantime, after being somewhat soothed by the oral communication made to him by Bonsi on the 23rd of March on behalf of the Signoria (though he complained that it had not replied directly to the Brief), now began to protest that other friars of San Marco, preaching in the Friar's stead, were saying the same things he had said. The ambassador had some difficulty in obtaining an audience of the Pope in those days. In the end, on the 30th, he heard from the Cardinal of Perugia 'that His Holiness had decided to put an end to all this', and was thinking of sending a prelate to Florence to bring Fra Girolamo to Rome, with great promises that he would be treated 'humanely'.

Of the 'humanity' of the treatment prepared for Savonarola, all Rome was talking at that time. We have an echo of this in a letter long attributed to Michelangelo, which contains the sarcastic comment: 'He must come to prophesy in Rome for a bit, and then they will canonize him.' The ambassador replied with some heat that the Pope was not keeping to his bargain, since he had already obtained one of the alternatives he had demanded, and that 'to attempt to remove Fra Girolamo . . . would be to throw the city into a tumult'. When he asked to speak with the Pope, he was told that 'it was not the right time'; he was put off till the next day, and then, after waiting four hours, he was sent away. The ambassador concluded: 'I deduce that His Holiness is being influenced by people who would like to cause some unrest in our city.' Influenced and convinced, I would say, for this was, in effect, the Pope's intention from now on. And fortune served him better than the secretaries of his chancellery could have done with their Briefs.

After Savonarola had been prohibited altogether from preaching, his place in the pulpit had been taken by Fra Domenico da Pescia, who was most vehement on all matters affecting his superior and master, and no less violent and bold than Savonarola in his sermons. Opposing him from the pulpit of Santa Croce, and returning blow for blow, was the Franciscan Fra Francesco di Puglia. Things went so far that the Franciscan in his enthusiasm, preaching on the 25th of March, the Feast of the Annunciation, incautiously challenged to ordeal by fire anyone who sustained the validity of Savonarola's doctrine and the invalidity of the excommunication made against him.

It was no new thing for him to issue such barbaric challenges. Only the year before, in Prato, he had offered to maintain through the ordeal by fire his accusations against Savonarola. And at once Fra Domenico, who was preaching in Prato at the same time, took up the challenge, for he was also much inclined to things of this kind by his simple nature and his great faith. But the Franciscan, with the excuse that he had been recalled to Florence, had thought it prudent to leave the city with all haste, *re infecta*.

The fresh challenge, therefore, opened up again an old contention between the two preachers, and Fra Domenico did not pause to consider before taking it up. This he did in his sermons on the 27th and 28th of March. It is difficult to say whether the Franciscan had again spoken merely without serious reflection, or because he had been urged to do so by the Arrabbiati. Schnitzer, who was very sensitive to the suspicious, if not exactly suspect, Piagnoni biographers, inclined towards the latter alternative. For my part, I favour the first possibility. What is not at all in doubt is that Fra Francesco, after throwing the first stone, would have been very glad to withdraw again.

Unfortunately, they were not in Prato now, and the controversy had become so heated that the fire would almost have lit itself. Fra Domenico's enthusiasm was fired, and the opinions of the citizens were inflamed and divided. The Arrabbiati, if they had not actually put the Franciscan up to it, saw at once that this was a wonderful opportunity to get rid of the Friar, and immediately threw themselves into it with all their might. On the one hand, they urged the Franciscan, perhaps even on the pretext of the public good, to press on manfully, while assuring him (as Doffo Spini, the leader of the Compagnacci, later confessed) that they would on no account let him go into the fire. On the other hand, the Signoria, being on their side, was easily persuaded to allow the ordeal and, under pretext of removing the divisions among the citizens, to promote and prepare for it. Thus, on the 28th of March, 1498, in the Palace of the Signoria of the most civilized and refined city in Italy, the notaries registered the conclusions that were to be proved, just as in the times of the barbarians, by one of those judgments called 'divine' but also, and much more justly, termed 'common judgments'. Briefly, these conclusions were as follows: that the Church needed to be reformed; that she would be scourged and reformed; that Florence too would be scourged, but later would be revived and would flourish; that all this would take place in their times; that the excommunication recently issued against Fra Girolamo was invalid, and those who did not observe it did not sin.

These conclusions were at once signed by Fra Domenico, who in his simple faith could now have been held back by no one, although we know that he was severely reproved by Savonarola. On the same day, and not without hesitating and protesting (a remarkable and most valuable piece of evidence) that he was only doing it 'at the instances and request of the Florentine Signoria', Fra Francesco di Puglia also signed them. But—and this was probably suggested to him by the Arrabbiati—he said that he wished to try the ordeal with Fra Girolamo. With Fra Domenico, with whom he had no quarrel, he expressed the willingness to pair off for the ordeal one of his brethren. This was a most impudent innovation, shuffling the cards after they had been dealt; he had said in the pulpit that he was ready to try the ordeal with anyone, and it was obvious that his adversary must be Fra Domenico and no other, as it was he who had taken up the Franciscan's challenge.

As a result, the affair remained in doubt and suspense while the two friars failed to agree. But after this rather lame subscription, there came immediately to sign the conclusions, in the presence of the Signoria and the Vicar of the Archbishop, another of Savonarola's friars, Fra Mariano Ughi, undertaking 'to make the ordeal *per ignem*' if a Minorite friar would come and oppose him as the preacher had promised. He was accompanied by Fra Domenico, who, while signing, requested his challenger to be content with him, 'because Fra Girolamo has yet to be the protagonist of other, greater affairs'. Earlier he had said of his master 'that his time was not yet come'.

Intermediaries in good and bad faith went to and fro between Santa Croce and San Marco, and also between the Palace and the two convents. Then on the following day, the 29th of March, the irresolute Fra Francesco di Puglia, realizing that he had made a poor showing, and not knowing which way to turn, went again to the Palace. He admitted that 'he could not compare himself with Fra Girolamo either for scholarship or virtue', but because 'he was the principal person involved, he wanted him'. He said vaguely and in general terms that he would have three or four friars ready; but when pressed by the Signoria, he finally offered Fra Giuliano Rondinelli, though he was not present. Fra Giuliano came to subscribe to the document the next day, the 30th of March, under the signature of Ughi, protesting nevertheless, as Francesco di Puglia had said and continued to say, that he believed he would burn. As these signatures stood, Ughi and Rondinelli should have faced each other. But Fra Domenico was not the man to miss a feast of this kind. He demanded his rights, and was given them.

By now it was the Signoria who led the dance. On the same day, it called a meeting of the citizens of the Pratica to hear their opinions. They were contradictory and not very firm opinions, in which we can detect a sense of shame and disgrace; but to the modern reader the proceedings of that council seem far more disgraceful. So much so that it is almost refreshing, among so many wretched words, whether favourable or inimical to the Friar, to dwell for a moment on those of Carlo Canigiani, a violent opponent of Savonarola, with their crude realism and Machiavellian flavour: 'It seemed to him, he said, that it was more suitable in the Palace to talk of war and finance.' Also, as a revulsion against the barbarous trial, it is not unpleasing to hear the irreverent and typically Florentine attitude expressed by Filippo Giugni: 'I think fire is an odd thing, and I am not inclined to go for it. We might try getting him [Fra Girolamo] to go into water, and if he did not get wet, I would be one of the first to ask his pardon.' Giovanni Canacci, who was also strongly opposed to the Friar, put it even better: 'If our forefathers who founded the city had thought that such a thing would be debated here . . . for sure they would have been indignant.' If these individual attitudes appear honourable, the general conclusions arrived at were most dishonourable, wavering between indifference, uncertainty, and the dominating wish to see the trial held, to finish it one way or the other. Friends and enemies of the Friar all concurred in this opinion for opposite reasons, and with the pretext that it might promote unity in the city. Among the friends who supported the opinion—persuaded, it is true, by their great faith in the Friar—we are sorry to find men like Giovambattista Ridolfi, held to be one of the wisest men in the city, and Piero Guicciardini, father of the historian. The Pratica was then dismissed, having turned out very much as the Signoria had hoped, and a decree was issued establishing that, when the ordeal was over, the head and principal agent on the losing side should be banished from the city. However, if the champions of both sides were burned, then only Fra Girolamo should be regarded as the loser, and he alone should be banished.

He, in the meantime, remained in his cell, very ill-pleased with the affair. As he later confessed in his first trial, he had been most annoyed that the simple-mindedness of Fra Domenico had given rise to such confusion. Although he understood that he could not now withdraw, and might indeed rejoice in the fervour of his friars and of many citizens as well, this kind of thing was repugnant to him and seemed to be tempting God. He was intelligent enough to see where all this would lead him, with the Signoria against him and opponents of such a stamp; and he was unable to use his strongest weapon to defend himself: his sermons. As he could not do otherwise, therefore, he wrote on the 1st of April, and at once had printed, a brief apology, in which he sought to justify himself for being compelled to accept that trial, unsought by him, so that the truth might not be overthrown. He showed that he was in no wise called upon to enter the fire with Fra Francesco di Puglia, who had issued the challenge and had it accepted by Fra Domenico. The only comfort in so grave a situation was the great faith of his friars, of whom three hundred had offered to go into the fire, and also of many citizens, priests, nuns, and even children, who had all subscribed to the challenge. Further, on that same day, several thousands of people present at the sermon in San Marco became so exalted that they began to shout: 'I will enter this fire for Thy glory, Lord.'

On the eve of the ordeal, the 6th of April, the definitive act was drawn up embodying the material of the preceding ones, *mutatis mutan-*

dis—that is, once more setting the trial between Fra Domenico and Rondinelli. Two things are to be noted here: the challenge is recognized as being issued by Francesco di Puglia, and Savonarola appears only indirectly as the propagator of the doctrine to be proved by supernatural signs, and not in any way as a participant in this barbarous experiment. Another notable and capital feature is that the act lays down that whichever party refuses to enter the fire, or hesitates to do so, shall be declared the loser. On the same day the Signoria issued an appropriate order that, if Fra Domenico was burned, Fra Girolamo should be declared a rebel and should leave Florence within three hours. That morning the Friar had given a short sermon to encourage his followers, although really there was no need for it.

In Rome, as in every other city of Italy, wherever the affairs of the Friar had for a long time been followed with the greatest interest, everyone was in suspense at the outcome of this strange event. The Pope certainly could not be pleased with experiments of this kind, particularly as among the arguments to be proved by this judgment of God was the validity of the excommunication he had issued himself. The letter of the ambassador of Florence to the Ten on the 4th of April, shows him to be more afraid and embarrassed than angry and displeased. This would confirm the statement of the early biographer that Pope Alexander was afraid that, if the friars of San Marco won, he would lose his mitre.

At last came the memorable day of the ordeal, or of the miracle, as people were then calling it: it was the 7th of April. In the Piazza dei Signori a great platform had been erected, about seven feet high, ninety feet long, and sixteen feet wide, covered with rubble, earth, and bricks, so that it would not catch fire. On this was built a great bonfire of wood treated with oil, resin, and gunpowder, so that the fire might spread faster and more dreadfully. Down the length of the platform ran a narrow path through the bonfire, barely more than two feet wide, and through this the two friars were to pass, entering at the same time from opposite ends. The Loggia dei Signori was divided in half by a partition. One side was assigned to the friars of St. Francis, the other to those of St. Dominic; and each side had its own altar.

All the entrances to the square except three were barred with beams and planks. The foot soldiers of the Signoria were put on guard at the Palace and at these entrances. On the side of the Loggia were three hundred soldiers under the command of Marcuccio Salviati, a good captain and faithful to the Friar. The Compagnacci had turned out in armour and well armed, under the orders of Doffo Spini, to the number of about five hundred, and took up their position opposite the Loggia near the platform.

At the appointed hour the Minor brothers came first and took their places silently and without any ceremony. Savonarola, meantime, had celebrated Mass at San Marco before a great crowd of the faithful, and pronounced a short sermon, ending with these words: 'Thou knowest, Lord, that I did not undertake this mission out of my own pride. Thou knowest that it was Thy doing. This people has believed in me because I was sent by Thee. I ask Thee, therefore, this morning that Thou wilt show to this people that Thou reignest in heaven and on earth, so that they may believe that Thou hast sent me, and change their ways, and everything may be to Thy praise and glory. Lord, fulfil this morning our prayers, and show that we have told the truth.'

At that moment the mace-bearers of the Signoria had come to say that everything was ready for the trial, and the friars moved off in procession, about two hundred and fifty strong. They proceeded in pairs, in order of seniority, devoutly singing psalms. Fra Domenico followed, wearing a flaming-red pluvial, and after him came Fra Girolamo carrying the Host in a silver ostensory. Behind them was a countless multitude of men, women, and children with lighted torches and candles. When they all reached the square, singing the psalm 'Exsurgat Deus et dissipentur inimici eius', Savonarola and his brethren took up their places in the part of the Loggia set aside for them. The manner of their coming, as Guicciardini tells us, was so expressive of their wonderful courage 'that it not only reassured their own followers, but even made their enemies flinch'.

In fact, while Fra Domenico, on his knees before the altar worshipping the Sacrament, was waiting among his brethren praying and singing psalms, the other champion, Giuliano Rondinelli, was safely shut up in the Palace and did not come out all day. 'You can imagine,' comments the old biographer, 'how anxious he was to enter the fire!' His superior, Francesco di Puglia, did likewise, while the other Minor brothers, agitated but silent, 'walked up and down like the peripatetics'.

After a great interval of time, when the crowd was getting restive,

241

the four officials appointed by the Signoria came to beg Savonarola to begin the ordeal. The Friar answered that Fra Domenico was ready and waiting for his opponent. When they asked the Minorites in their turn, they immediately began to raise difficulties and endless captious objections. They objected first that the pluvial, then that all the clothes of Fra Domenico might be bewitched. So, with Savonarola's consent, Fra Domenico went into the Palace, stripped naked, and dressed in the clothes of one of his brethren chosen by the Minorites themselves, putting on a chasuble taken from the Palace chapel. Then they raised objections to his crucifix, which they said might be enchanted. So he put this aside and took up the Host; whereupon the arguments became fiercer, and this time with greater cause. By this time it had begun to get dark, and the Signoria sent the Minorites away, as perhaps had been planned right from the beginning; they decamped with all speed, and without any demonstration. Then Savonarola and his followers departed as well, and, although his opponents made some attempt to attack him, they returned safe and sound to San Marco under good escort.

While all these objections were being debated in the square, a storm broke with heavy rain, hail, and lightning, soaking the crowds and all the preparations for the fire. This seemed to the Friar's followers a sign of Fra Girolamo's saintliness, and to his enemies merely some magical and diabolical trick of his. To a large majority of the people it was a sure sign that God would not tolerate the ordeal.

Back in San Marco, where more than a thousand women had waited in prayer for six hours on end, Savonarola made a brief address to the people, giving them a faithful account of what had happened, and showing that, as the ordeal had failed not through any fault of his but through the inconsistencies of his opponents, victory was theirs. This was indeed perfectly true, according to the agreement. Parenti says that the Signoria reprimanded the Friar when giving him permission to leave the square. But we need not lend credit to this chronicler, who was by now extremely hostile to the Friar; and even if it were true, such a Signoria would not merit our confidence. It is worth noting that, if they had had a reasonable or at least a not too unreasonable excuse for declaring the Friar the loser, they would not have failed to banish him immediately from their territory, according to the terms of their earlier decision. As they did not do so, hostile as they were to him, it means that they had no grounds whatever for doing so. Any-one with a good knowledge of the Florentine constitution cannot accept Schnitzer's assertion that it was Lanfredini, a Friar's man, and provost on that occasion, who prevented the decision to banish him; the gonfalonier had the power to assume the provost's office when he wished, and we know very well what sort of man he was.

While, therefore, under the terms of the agreement he had won, Savonarola still seemed to many people to have lost; simply because he had not, in spite of everybody and everything, terms or no terms, accomplished the miracle that was expected, or feared, of him—perhaps even by going into the fire himself alone. Too simply, but not perhaps without a certain Florentine subtlety, it was argued that, if he was a saint and a true prophet, he could and should have done so; and if he could not do so, even in so extreme a necessity when his teaching and his mission hung in the balance, it appeared quite plain that he was neither a saint nor a true prophet. This failure to perform a miracle was not forgiven by the foolish multitude and by those among his followers who lacked a true and unshakable faith.

It may seem unbelievable and monstrous on the face of it, but in this blind resentment of the populace, there was beneath that greater disappointment another, which was that they had been deprived of the extraordinary spectacle they had greedily looked forward to. The proverbial Florentine curiosity, that perpetual urge for new and strange things, which was part of their nature and the mainspring of so many of their successes and honourable enterprises, had been waiting with unspeakable longing for that pyre to burst into flames. Their disappointment, as often happens with the mob, was soon changed into contempt, hatred, rage, and blind and cruel anger. That pyre was to be set alight not long after, no longer to test Savonarola's doctrine, but to celebrate his martyrdom.

Chapter 23

THE ASSAULT ON SAN MARCO; IMPRISONMENT AND TRIALS

<hr/>

THE next day was Palm Sunday, the 8th of April. Never, perhaps, had the city contained so much hatred and so many thoughts of violence as on that day, when according to Christian custom the symbol of peace is blessed. Already the previous evening, after nightfall, the Piagnoni could not show themselves anywhere without being insulted and jeered at. The Arrabbiati and the Compagnacci knew that their hour had come at last, the hour when they might deal the Friar a death-blow, shaken as he was by the papal thunderbolts, treated with hostility by the Signoria, his reputation with the people falling, and his power to preach gone.

In so imminent a danger the Frateschi did nothing, although they knew that Iacopo Nerli and Alfonso Strozzi still held in readiness the men and arms displayed at the ordeal by fire, and that during the night their enemies had gone about stirring up the mob. In vain did Luca degli Albizzi, seeing how things were going, try to persuade Valori and the other leaders of the Friar's party to arm and take the initiative rather than have it taken from them. Those good men did not wish to be the first to cause such disorder in the city. So once again the sons of darkness were wiser than the sons of light.

The morning passed peacefully: it was that brief and menacing calm that comes before the storm. Fra Girolamo, after saying Mass, went up into the pulpit, and with great sadness, almost as though sensing his coming doom, he spoke a few words, declaring that he

244

offered himself as a sacrifice to God, and was ready to die for his flock. Then he knelt down with all the congregation and, turning to the crucifix, said: 'Lord, I thank Thee for desiring now to make me in Thy image.' And in the week of Christ's Passion, Savonarola's own passion was to begin.

It was evident from the Friar's own words that he did not intend at all to begin preaching again. Nevertheless, the Arrabbiati protested violently to the Signoria, out of anxiety not for the honour of the Pope or the Signoria, but for their own cause, should he again take up the feared weapon of his sermons. They had to make an end of it. And the riots, which had been simmering for so long, suddenly broke out.

After evensong a great crowd of men and women had gathered in Santa Maria del Fiore to hear the sermon of Fra Mariano Ughi, one of the best and most trusted substitutes for Fra Girolamo. The preacher, accompanied and escorted by a devout throng, was arriving from the direction of the Via del Cocomero when a certain Antonio Alamanni began to hammer loudly on the benches, shouting: 'Get out of here, you damned Piagnoni!' So 'there arose a great tumult in the church, and those who could find the door were the lucky ones.' One of the Friar's supporters drew his weapon, but was disarmed, beaten, and chased away. The mob of boys in the pay of the Arrabbiati stoned everyone who came out, as well as the preacher who was just arriving with his party. These were driven back towards San Marco with the enemy on their heels shouting 'To arms!' and 'To San Marco! To San Marco!'

This cry roused the populace, people of the worst sort, hungry for loot, violent and bestial: the scum that rises to the top of every violent disturbance. 'To San Marco! To San Marco!' The quickest and most aggressive, converging from all parts of the town, met at the corner by the Sapienza a young boy from the Scuola de' Pecori who was on his way to the Annunziata, saying his prayers. They called out: 'Oh, the rascal! Saying his psalms, too!' and they chased him and ran him through with a lance. Then, reaching San Marco, they began to throw stones into the church, which was still full of men and women who had gone there for vespers. An artisan who came out to reprove with mild words those who thus offended the house of God, was stabbed to death. The mob, in its first rush, did not yet dare to enter the church, whose doors were immediately closed. They were waiting for night-fall, or reinforcements, or some encouragement to commit greater excesses.

To this end, people were gathering from all quarters at the Palace to bring pressure on the Signoria. The Compagnacci with their armed men, reappearing as if by magic, occupied the square. Finally the Signoria, despite the opposition of the provost Lanfredini, issued at 10 p.m. a sentence of banishment compelling the Friar to leave the frontiers of the Republic within twelve hours. At the same time they immediately sent a messenger to Bonsi to tell the Pope the good news. In the meantime, other armed men and rough elements came to swell the throng attacking San Marco. The Frateschi, 'as though stunned, shut up in the churches, looked at one another, and made no provision for their defence'.

In vain the Piagnona bell of San Marco sounded the alarm; in vain did it call to its aid the magistrates and the faithful. The magistrates were in league with violence, the faithful were deaf with fear and bewilderment. The defenders, unaware either of that complicity or of that cowardice, were preparing with manly courage to resist attack until help could reach them. The women left by a back door of the convent, followed by the cowardly men, among them the diarist Landucci. A few score brave men looked to the defences, some keeping the assailants off by throwing tiles and stones from the rooftop, others arming themselves with those few weapons which had already been used by the citizens to escort their prophet, and with a very few others collected without his knowledge in anticipation of what was about to occur.

Then Fra Girolamo, seeing what terrible things were happening and the blood that had already been shed, put on a pluvial and took a crucifix in his hand, intending to go out into the square, saying: 'Let me go, for *propter me orta est hæc tempestas* (because of me this storm has arisen).' But his brethren came behind him weeping, and the people barred his way, among them Giovambattista Ridolfi, who said: 'No, no, Father; what shall we do then?' But Savonarola protested: 'You are resisting the will of God.' Coming upon a friar who had taken up arms, he reprimanded him severely and made him lay them down. After which he went in procession around the convent and then rested for a while in his cell, alone with his grief. Later he went into the sacristy, dressed in his sacred robes, and entered the choir, where, kneeling before the Host, already detached from earthly things, he waited for his martyrdom.

It was getting dark. In the meantime, news of the ban of exile issued by the Signoria had been received. But it was not believed, for those inside San Marco thought it was a ruse of the enemy, not realizing that the Signoria and their enemy were now all one. Then came another 'terrifying' order, declaring that all laymen must leave the convent under pain of being proclaimed rebels; and as a result many did leave. The siege was now growing stronger, and with it the rage of the assailants. Already, in spite of the hail of tiles from the roof, they had put straw at the gates and set fire to it to burn them down.

At this juncture the leaders of the Frateschi took counsel. Francesco Valori said he would go out and gather his followers and raise the siege of the convent, as he had promised Savonarola from the very beginning of the riot. Although advised against it by Ridolfi, he had himself let down from the walls where they overlooked some gardens behind the convent, and made his way home. But things looked different to him once he was outside San Marco, and he did nothing but hide in an attic. The mob was already on its way to burn and plunder his house. They killed his wife and dragged him out from his hiding-place. While he was being taken to the Palace between two guards of the Signoria, he was met and killed by Vincenzo Ridolfi and Simone Tornabuoni, in revenge for their kinsmen who had been executed over the case of Bernardo del Nero. Iacopo Pitti, an Arrabbiato, also struck him, but he was already dead. It was then a little past the first hour of the night.

At San Marco the bells went on sounding the alarm. Savonarola was still praying in the choir. The defenders, reduced in numbers because still more of them had sought safety, were waiting for Valori and his promised reinforcements. The gates were already burning, and some of the enemy had scaled the walls on the side by the Sapienza, entered the cloisters, and looted the sick-bay and the cells. Having reached the sacristy, they were trying to force the doors to gain entrance to the chapel, where the friars were singing '*Salvum fac populum tuum, Domine*', oblivious of the noise and ignorant of how the battle was going; if any one of them turned towards the source of the noise, another said to him at once: '*Orate, fratres.*' Eventually, as the enemy

R   247

pounded on the doors, Fra Girolamo quietly commanded: 'Open and ask what they want, and reprove them for making so much noise.' Some of the friars left their prayers and beat back their assailants by hitting them in the face with crosses and lighted torches.

With the enemy within the walls, the fight became fiercer; according to Landucci, there were more than a hundred casualties, dead or wounded. The defenders of San Marco still had the upper hand. Many of those who had laid down their arms in obedience to their superior took them up again. Fra Luca della Robbia was seen pursuing the enemy around the cloisters with a drawn sword. But the man who became the soul of the battle, who passed from the defensive to the offensive and made a fortress of the temple, was a German. He was a certain Fra Enrico, a tall and powerfully built man, who threw himself into the thick of the enemy and seized from one of them an arquebus, which he proceeded to mount on the pulpit; then, from the place where Savonarola had for so many years spread the word of God, he spread death among the assailants, singing at each shot the verse 'Salvum fac populum tuum, Domine!' The church was full of smoke. The cries and groans of the wounded and the death rattles of the dying mingled with the slow singing of the monks. It was about the fifth hour of the night.

Savonarola had remained praying in the choir, where many stones had been thrown by slings and shots fired without anyone being hurt. But he could no longer bear such sacrilege, and, as he was unable to do anything to stop the combatants or to appease that riotous mêlée, he rose and said: 'It would be as well to seek some solace.' Then, taking the Sacraments, he went in procession with his monks to the dormitory, and from there to the library. Meeting Fra Benedetto, the miniaturist, who was coming armed from the battle, he ordered him severely to lay down his weapons and take up his cross. In the square there now appeared the soldiers of the Signoria, complete with artillery. Another decree had finally opened the eyes of those who still had some illusions about the Signoria, and they all sought to escape, leaving the convent without defenders. The enemy now occupied practically the whole of the convent and cloisters. It was the end.

The envoys of the assailants approached, bringing an order from the Signoria that Fra Girolamo should go to the Palace. Fra Domenico asked them to show him this order in writing, and they went back to fetch it. While they were waiting for the order and the safe-conduct, someone suggested to Savonarola that he should have himself let down from the walls of the convent and make his escape. Then Fra Malatesta, to whom Fra Benedetto assigns the role of Judas in this Savonarolan passion, said: 'Should not the shepherd risk his life for his flock?' Savonarola immediately embraced him without a word, and prepared himself to follow the guards of the Signoria, who were already returning.

But first he wished to say a few words of farewell to his brethren, gathered together in the Greek library. At the end he said that he suffered these tribulations gladly, knowing that the Christian life is to do good and suffer evil, and so to persevere until the end. After confession and Communion, he made his last farewells, exhorting his spiritual sons to the observance of their Order, and giving each a last kiss. He was just leaving when Fra Domenico said: 'I too would come to this feast.' And as Fra Benedetto also begged to come, Savonarola said to him: 'Fra Benedetto, if you would obey me, do not come; for I and Fra Domenico are going to die for the love of Christ.' It was now past the seventh hour of the night.

When the two friars went out into the square, a fearful clamour arose. Surrounded by guards, tied up like criminals, they proceeded amid the curses, the insults, and the spitting of the populace. So went the man who had so long been venerated as a saint and regarded almost as the master of that city; and in the dreary light of the torches he saw around him only faces ugly with hatred. Someone tried to burn his face with a torch; someone, in spite of the soldiers around, managed to strike him, saying as one said to Christ: 'Prophesy who struck you.' He had already entered the Palace gate through the wicket when someone kicked him from behind, shouting: 'There, there's where he keeps his prophecy.' This was the reward, these were the honours which the Florentines finally gave to Girolamo Savonarola.

He passed in this way into the Palace of the Signori, where he had so often been received with the greatest reverence. There the founder and legislator of that popular state saw assembled before him the fine flower of his enemies. Among them he must certainly have recognized Paolo Somenzi, the evil Milanese agent. At the ninth hour of the night this same person wrote joyfully to his Duke: 'When I was in the Palace I saw Fra Girolamo and Fra Domenico his companion brought in, and I saw them handcuffed and taken to prison; and this was at the eighth hour of the night.' Savonarola's prison was the famous one known as the Alberghettino, in the Palace tower, where Cosimo de' Medici had been confined before his brief exile. And so one might say that this small room saw the beginning of the Medici's greatness and the end of Savonarola's earthly glory. Fra Domenico and Fra Silvestro were put in other prisons. The latter has gone into hiding when he saw things going badly, but either gave himself up or was handed over in the morning to those who were already searching for him as one of the Friar's closest associates.

The Pratica was called together on that same morning, the 9th of April, to discuss what was to be done with Fra Girolamo and with his principal followers now held prisoner, and with those of the magistrates who supported him, particularly the Ten and the Eight. Not a friendly voice was heard. Just as a scene changes in the theatre, so the Florentine government seemed to have changed suddenly, though not a man in it had changed. Twenty-four hours before, in spite of the disappointment over the ordeal, the Friar still had in his favour the greater part of the people and the magistrates, apart from the Signoria, and consequently a large following in the Councils. Now these contained only his enemies. Through the efforts of a determined and powerful minority an almost silent revolution had taken place in Florence. What rioting there had been, had not occurred this time outside the Palace of the Signori but in the distant piazza of San Marco, where a handful of ruffians manœuvred by the Compagnacci attacked a convent out of hatred for a friar.

With Valori dead and the other leaders of the Frateschi in hiding or in prison, the Ten and the Eight, who had been almost entirely composed of them, virtually ceased to exist. Savonarola's followers in the councils were either not summoned or did not dare to put in an appearance. It was, therefore, decided to elect new magistrates, and out of these elections came a kind of quintessence of the Arrabbiati and the Compagnacci. As for the three friars, it was decided with a unanimity most unusual among the Florentines, to examine them diligently but to be in no hurry to send them to the Pope, as it was not desirable to let him know the city's secrets. Naturally, to examine them diligently meant torture, as that was the only way of getting the accused to say what they did not want to say, and what it was desirable they should say. It is true that one was not permitted to lay hands on the clergy without the Pope's express consent, under pain of excommunication, which could be raised only by the Pope in person. But the Florentines were not worried by this: in the Friar's case they felt they already had that absolution in their pocket.

So on the same day, Savonarola was twice examined by a committee of four citizens verbally elected. Although the official report says that he was given 'three and a half turns of strappado in two spells', the Friar 'remained resolute, and gave his replies with courage and arrogance'. The real commissioners for the examination were elected the following day, seventeen of them—'all his most bitter enemies', writes Guicciardini, which would in itself be enough to render his trial invalid. They included Piero degli Alberti, the notorious Doffo Spini, Giovanni Manetti, Giovanni Canacci, Benedetto Nerli, and Carlo Canigiani. A fine company! To adorn it still further, they appointed as its notary Francesco di Ser Barone, otherwise called Ser Ceccone, a hanger-on of Doffo Spini and recorder of the suppers of the Compagnacci, a wretched fellow who had been disinherited by his father and earned himself both imprisonment and exile.

These were the sort of inquisitors who again examined the Friar on the 10th. He was 'carried to the Bargello on a chair of hands, because he was in leg irons and handcuffs', and there was tortured with four great drops on the strappado. In the end he shouted: 'Let me down, and I will write you all my life.' He did indeed write. The examiners read and were not satisfied, so they jealously hid those autograph confessions. On the 11th and 12th he again behaved with great courage, if we may judge by some frank replies given in defence of his innocence and of his prophetic preaching. These replies were not recorded in the final text of that peculiar trial, but were reported by someone who saw the original draft.

News had already leaked out in the city that the Friar would confess nothing, and people were beginning to grumble. His most faithful followers were again raising their heads and frequenting San Marco, although publicly at least, the friars had renounced their master. They went on gathering there until the Signoria issued a decree that no one should go there under pain of being declared a rebel. For the leaders of the Arrabbiati, who had now gone too far to draw back, it was a question of life or death; and they were certainly worried to find that they had no grounds for proceeding against that innocent man. Then (according to one account, admittedly by a Piagnone) the notorious Ser Ceccone came out with the phrase: 'Where there are no grounds, you have to make them.' It is hard to say now exactly how the thing was arranged; we can only conjecture. But it is obvious that torture was the main ingredient used by the examiners in their forgeries. And later, when they had so maimed the Friar that his food had to be put in his mouth for him, the mere terror of torture was enough.

According to the 'authentic' account of the trial which was later published, the unhappy man had three and a half turns on the strappado on the 9th, and no more on the subsequent days of this trial. This is a lie. Quite apart from the fact that Somenzi says he had four on the 10th, and even supposing this to be the occasion described as taking place on the 9th (though the torture of the 10th is confirmed by others, and the mistake must then have been in the official record: a strange and serious error), we know from another source that he was given 'sometimes four and sometimes six'. We must reject the anonymous witness of one who saw him given one evening 'fourteen drops from the pulley right down to the ground'. Savonarola had delicate limbs and was highly sensitive, and it is not surprising that eventually, with daily examinations from the 13th to the 17th, he gave way under these tortures, which would have sent the roughest soldier out of his mind. To put it in another way, it would have been surprising if he had not broken down.

The rest was done by clever manipulation of the evidence thus extorted, which they had the Friar ratify day by day with the threat of further torture. Such manipulation was necessary, because even the text published by the Signoria admits that the hapless victim 'every day changed something, and sometimes said one thing, sometimes another'; that is, 'one thing' under torture, and 'another' when, gathering together his failing strength, he contradicted what he had said, and protested the truth loud and clear.

On the 18th the text thus 'put together and set in order' was read over to him by Ser Ceccone. In vain the poor Friar protested (as the old biographer tells us): 'If you publish this, you will die within six months.' It was easy for Ser Ceccone (who did in fact die within that time) to show him his own partial ratifications, which would have been sufficient in themselves to discredit him with the people. He could also point out that if the Friar refused to sign the text 'put together and set in order', it would be necessary to seek the truth more diligently. These were certainly strong arguments, especially when backed up with a few drops on the rope, for someone who had already had enough of such investigations. Nor, after so much suffering, could one blame Savonarola for coming to some compromise with his torturers and his own conscience.

Thus they came to the solemn ratification of the documents on the 19th of April; and even then he could not be induced to it without 'persuasion'—which is an indication that he protested about the text which had been compiled. After him signed two canons and six of his friars from San Marco. He had not seen any of them since the night of the riot, and they had been called in, to his confusion and their own. When he was given permission to address them, he told them to do three things: follow the doctrine of the good life he had taught them; take care of the novices; pray for him, since God had withdrawn the spirit from him. He meant the spirit of prophecy which led him to speak so courageously from the pulpit, and which, afflicted in mind and body, he had denied at his trial. In this he resembled Zechariah, 'who, when the light went from him, became as if stupefied'. He had recalled this example one day from the pulpit, as if prophesying what would happen to himself. The Judas of San Marco then said to him: '*Ex ore tuo credidi, et ex ore tuo discredo*' ['At thy word I believed, and at thy word I no longer believe']; but Savonarola, without answering, turned his back on him scornfully.

The report of this trial—to which Ser Ceccone put the final touches by adding a few poisoned words, after all had been signed, in the empty spaces at the ends of the paragraphs—was then read out in public in the great hall of the Council—in the very hall which had been built at Savonarola's instigation. He was not present, as was the usual custom. The Signoria was too afraid that, face to face again with the people, he might recover himself, and that the truth they had laboriously buried under that heap of lies, might suddenly come to life, if he called upon it with his 'cry of Lazarus' in that tremendous and fearful voice of former days. For this reason, and to make some gesture to the customs 'usually observed in such trials', they hit on no better device than the insertion, in the space before the signatures, of a few words declaring that the Friar had declined to be present out of fear. As though anyone in such circumstances could have refused anything whatever! Yet another obvious lie, therefore; but in the heat of the moment these words were believed by many, if not by all. And so, like the friars before them, the citizens also withdrew their belief in him.

The Arrabbiati, of course, boasted loudly of this trial and of the wonderful things that Fra Girolamo had confessed to. I shall be able to give a fuller account of these in the next chapter, when all the investigations have been completed, but I can say straightaway that if one takes out the most obvious interpolations, the sins of Fra Girolamo amount to very little—too little for a trial conducted by his mortal enemies and a shady lawyer by means of torture. The only real stain on Savonarola in this document is that he admits his prophetic mission to have been a pretence; and he soon retracted this statement. In any case, the Signoria was so dissatisfied with the trial that, when the account was published without their knowledge, they ordered by public decree that 'anyone who had bought it must hand it over at once to one charged to receive it, under pain of severe punishment'. Even before this, when sending an extract of it to the Pope, they wrote, in justification of its meagre contents: 'With great effort and difficulty, and with continual investigations, we have extracted very little from him'! As an excuse, they said the Friar was *patientissimi corporis,* thus glossing that mass of lies with another shameless lie that is denied by all the documents. They should have borne witness, not to an exceedingly resistant physique, but to a very great spirit.

As for the Pope—since we have mentioned him—after the Signoria had informed him through Bonsi of the Friar's arrest and asked permission to examine him, Alexander's immediate pleasure gave place to only one idea: to get him into his own hands. He expressed this desire at once in a Brief of congratulation sent to the Signoria on the 12th of April, accompanied by a Bull of plenary indulgence for those good Florentines, who, though they had once exalted the excommunicated Friar, had now been careful to put him in chains. The firm resistance of the Signoria to this request cast an immediate shadow over Borgia's joy. When, in addition to absolution for the torture already carried out, they also asked for the concession of ecclesiastical tithes, in return as it were for the arrest, the Pope sent off the absolution at once; but he let it be understood that the matter of tithes would be discussed after the friars had been handed over. From this position he would not budge.

While the Pope and Signori were negotiating on these matters, Fra Girolamo was subjected to a second trial, with the hope of extracting better evidence from him, while the effects of the first on body and spirit were still strong, and while the pains in his left arm, which had been dislocated by the tortures, ensured the efficacy of further torments. On the 21st, 23rd and 24th of April, therefore, the Friar was again examined—'without torture or any bodily harm,' the text of the trial affirms, though quite falsely, for Landucci noted in his day-to-day record: 'On the 23rd of April they tortured the Friar.' It becomes progressively clearer how little reliance can be placed on these accounts of the trials, which are full of lies at every step.

In this second document the skill and cleverness of Ser Ceccone appear to have been improved by experience. Having completed the rough draft, as usual, with the help of torture, he was much more crafty in putting the finishing touches to it. Instead of the poisonous phrases inserted at the end of the paragraphs, which even a child would have suspected, he put in here and there a few innocent marginal notes. So that on the 24th of April, when it came to the final ratification of the report, Savonarola added this caution: 'Although in some places there are marginal notes in the hand of Ser Francesco di Ser Barone.' These words, written with a caution that turned out to be imprudence, or, what is more likely, at the perfidious suggestion of Ser Ceccone, under pretext of good legal practice and open honesty, amounted in effect to ratifying blindly in advance anything that his bitter enemies might choose to add. And yet even from this second falsified trial, which in its turn was read in the Great Council on the 25th, Savonarola appears quite guiltless, particularly if we take out a few words which were most certainly introduced into the text by means of those ingenious marginal notes.

Tedious though it is to discuss any further this subject of the falsifications, because of their very obviousness, I would like to recall the words spoken by one of the Friar's examiners to Iacopo Nardi, a man of impeccable honesty, and admirable in this part of his *Histories* for the equanimity of his judgment: 'It is true that, for a good purpose, something had been taken out, and something added to the trial of Fra Girolamo.' It was perhaps during these days that another and more infamous examination of the martyr was carried out, at the instigation of Giovanni Manetti. He had been told by an astrologer that a hermaphrodite prophet would come into Italy, and he desired, with the Signoria's permission, to pursue this investigation with Savonarola.

The same examiners, meantime, dealt with the cases of Fra Domenico and Fra Silvestro and other lesser accused, with much more speed. The report on Fra Domenico bears the date of the 16th of April, but contains indications of earlier examinations. Written entirely in the hand of the friar himself, it is a unique document of his simple, fervent soul, clear as crystal and full of piety, faith, and devotion to Savonarola. His inquisitors had told him that Savonarola had confessed to goodness knows what transgressions, and primarily to having pretended to be a prophet, but he, 'become stupid in this matter', refused to believe them. Tortured, perhaps more savagely if not as often as Fra Girolamo, he ingenuously sought to persuade that evil set of examiners that he could never have told a lie or kept something from them, knowing that to do so was a sin. He added that he had spoken as though he were about to die, 'which could easily happen if you torture me, for my body is racked and my arms are broken, especially my left arm, which I have now had broken twice'.

An all too different spirit is shown in the examination of Fra Silvestro, a rather gossiping, intriguing friar, the politician of San Marco, quite absorbed in his sleepwalking visions. Nevertheless, in his depositions made on the 25th and 27th of April there is nothing that could harm Savonarola. Only in a sort of addition at the very end of the last paragraph, all in praise of the Friar, do we read this contra-dictory conclusion: 'Finally, I tell you that Fra Girolamo has deceived you.' As another part of the text says that only two pages of the reports are autograph, and as this queer conclusion comes after the signature of Fra Silvestro, it is clear that the same hand which wrote the other pages had every opportunity to add this phrase.

Finally, on the 5th of May, seeing that no more could be extracted from the Friar or from the ingenuity of Ser Ceccone, and considering that some decision should be taken, the Signoria called another Patrica to discuss what answer should be given to the Pope's renewed request, and whether or not they should satisfy his great desire to get Fra Girolamo into his hands. Once again the Pratica was strongly opposed to such a step. The reasons given were the usual ones, but Piero Popoleschi, who had just retired from the office of gonfalonier and knew all too well the secrets of the trials, added this comment, which is the most authentic recognition of their falsity: 'As for examining them [the friars] again, I consider the matter should be allowed to close here, *seeing how the investigation was made,* and for the peace and quiet of the city, for *if these things were all gone into again, it might give rise to scandal'*. One could hardly ask for a more eloquent confession.

On the following day, therefore, the Signoria wrote to the Pope, telling him of the city's ardent desire to witness the punishment of Savonarola, which would be an example and a warning to the many who still believed in him, as well as a powerful means towards the complete uprooting of that noxious plant. If His Holiness wished to examine the Friar on matters regarding the Church, he should, therefore, send someone to question him in Florence. But Alexander VI had already given in on this matter, perhaps feeling reassured by the temper of the new Signoria, which was more Arrabbiata than the last. On the 3rd of May, Bonsi wrote that the Pope was disposed to give way to precisely the kind of arguments which, before they had even received the ambassador's letter, the Signoria put in their letter of the 6th.

Alexander, in his reply to this letter on the 12th of May, gave the Florentines the glad news, which Bonsi in previous letters had already anticipated. He would accede to their requests and grant that Savonarola should be examined and punished, according to the law of the Church, in Florence. He was sending thither for this purpose the General of the Preachers, Giovacchino Torriani, and Francesco Remolines, judge of the Governor of Rome. They would come 'with orders to make a public example of them'—which means (and there is other evidence to support it, as we shall see) that before the Friar was examined, before the judges had even left Rome, the verdict had already been pronounced.

Chapter 24

THE LAST WRITINGS AND THE
LAST TRIAL; THE STAKE

✧✕✕✕✧

E VER since he was taken there on the terrible night of the
riot, the walls of his prison had been for Savonarola a sad
but peaceful refuge. Every evening he went back there
from the inquisitions, the tortures, and the sneers of his enemies, body
and soul torn and aching, broken and infinitely weary. It was not his
beloved cell in San Marco, full of books, of heavenly visions, of great
thoughts; but the solitude and the silence were the same. Here that
miserable wreck could at last recover himself again, find the man who
had once been Girolamo Savonarola; he could again unite himself
with God in prayer.

Even better than in his cell at San Marco, where we felt him to be
too far removed from our human condition, now that we see him shar-
ing our own wretchedness, we may draw near to him and ask him the
secret of his heart, and hear his answer. He will tell us the whole story
of his tragedy, briefly summed up in the words addressed to his friars
after the ratification of the first trial: 'Because God has withdrawn
his spirit from me, pray for me.' He will tell us finally why he denied
his prophetic mission under torture. That denial, which defiled the
record of all his labours, cannot be explained away as a falsification
of the words written in the report, but only as a falsification of the
Friar's spirit. This was brought about by torture, which his delicate and
sensitive constitution could not resist, and was helped by other torments
within him, perhaps no less effective than those of the executioners.

From the time when Savonarola had seen all human assistance fail him, as he was abandoned one after the other by powerful men, by prelates, and by friends who in the days of his triumph had been so generous in their praise and encouragement, he believed that in the end God's help would never fail him. In the greatness of his faith he believed firmly that a sign from heaven would finally reveal to all the holiness of his work, and confound his own enemies and those of the Church. This sign, which for some time had been his only hope, and which he had announced with ingenuous ardour in his last letter to the Pope, he perhaps thought for a moment might be revealed in the ordeal by fire. Perhaps this was the reason why he did not refuse to permit it, although at first it had been abhorrent to him. Even more desperately did he invoke such a sign in the horrible night of the riot, during the endless hours of prayer in the choir of San Marco, surrounded by the battle and yet in spirit so far removed from it.

His prayer had not been heard. God had not wished to take away the bitter cup from his lips either. With his enemies victorious, his labours all gone for naught, and himself reduced to unspeakable misery, he began to doubt the truth of his visions and of his prophecies. Perhaps he had been deceived; perhaps, without meaning to, without knowing it, he had deceived the people. Where formerly he saw only the greatness of his work, the renovation of the Church, the triumph of faith and Christian morals, he now saw in himself motives of presumption and pride, and the scandal, the dreadful scandal he had caused. Thus, he faced his examiners with his mind full of doubts and scruples, and heavy with sins he had not committed. Torture, maltreatment, insults, and fatigue prepared him for any retraction that did not inculpate others besides himself.

Yet, when the first and second trials were over and the moral and physical torment they entailed was at an end, he recovered a little in the solitude of his prison. Faith again took him by the hand, and set him on a better road. His life in prison was wonderfully edifying, as his life in the convent had been, though he was treated harshly and, according to the old biographer, had no other bed than the hard stone floor and no light at night. His gaoler, a wicked man and very much his enemy, was so moved that he was converted and became most humane with him. The Friar rewarded him by writing for him a *Regola del ben vivere* (*A Rule for Leading the Good Life*), and also gave to his small

259

daughter others of his compositions. 'Give thought to live well' he always said to him, 'and all your labours will be rewarded by God in Paradise, where you and I shall meet again.' These and many other pious words and sayings that leaked out through the walls of the Palace, edified, comforted, and confirmed in their belief those who still had faith in him. He had said in a sermon some years before: 'I shall be silenced when you put me in prison; and yet I shall not be silent, for I shall speak with him who brings my food.' At this time, to those few citizens who were permitted, with precautions, to visit him, Savonarola appeared serene, almost joyful. At intervals at least, there-fore, he had found the equanimity of the just man facing death—for he had no illusions about the clemency of his enemies.

It was in these moments of light, between hope and despair, that the Friar, having been given writing materials, composed in Latin his *Expositio ac meditatio in psalmum 'Miserere'*, which begins:

Oh, unhappy wretch that I am, forsaken by all, who have offended heaven and earth, whither shall I go? To whom shall I turn? In whom may I seek refuge? Who will have pity on me? I dare not raise my eyes to heaven because I have sinned against heaven. On earth I find no refuge, for I have here given cause for scandal. What then shall I do? Shall I despair? No, surely. God is merciful, my Saviour is full of pity. . . . I come therefore to Thee, most merciful God, I come full of melancholy and grief, for Thou alone art my hope, Thou alone my refuge. But what shall I say to Thee? Since I dare not raise my eyes, I will pour out words of grief, imploring Thy mercy, and say: '*Miserere mei Deus secundum magnam misericordiam tuam.*'

In this way, expounding the words of the psalm, he gives ex-pression to his own wretchedness and the hope that is his refuge. At one point he remembers Peter, who denied Jesus thrice when he was merely asked by a servant girl; and with that great example he com-forts the shame of his own weakness in denying, under the agonies of torture, his prophetic illuminations: 'But these questions [to Peter] were mere words; what would he have done if the Jews had come to blows? . . . He would have denied again if he had seen the whips got ready.' Just as he himself had done ! Therefore, he concludes with some consolation, 'If Peter, to whom Thou hadst given so many gifts and

THE STAKE

favours, fell so miserably, what could I do, Lord?' These are revealing words, which have escaped modern biographers. For, if in those pages the Friar justifies his having denied his prophecies, as though that denial were a sin, and does so in that prison where he is alone with God, it means that, when the torture ceased and he climbed out of the abyss of misery, he retracted those evilly extorted confessions—which is a clear demonstration of the falseness of the trials, the truth of his prophetic illuminations, and the sincerity of his whole life.

As he concludes this remarkable revelation of his soul with the words of the penitential psalm, there opens out for the condemned man, beyond the dark walls of his prison, a consoling vision of the Church at last renewed: that same vision which appeared to him as a child, and led him to the peace of the cloister, and thence to the war of his preaching: the vision for which he was suffering *usque ad vincula,* for which he was going towards death. And once more he offered himself as a sacrifice for its sake, praying the Lord to hasten that renovation: 'Then the Church will flourish, then she will enlarge her frontiers, then Thy praise will resound from the ends of the earth. . . . Do unto me now, I pray, what must be, so that Thou have mercy upon me according to Thy great mercy, so that Thou mayst receive me as a sacrifice to justice, as an offering to holiness, as a holocaust to the religious life.'

On the 8th of May this short work was finished and was already being talked about in the city. The Friar then began an exposition of the psalm '*In te, Domine speravi*', which is rather the description of a soul still torn between hope and despair: 'Sorrow has beset me, and sur-rounded me with a strong and numerous army. It has already seized all my heart, and fights ceaselessly against me day and night with clash of arms and noise of battle. My friends fight under its standard, and have become my enemies. Everything I see and hear bears the marks of sadness. The memory of my friends saddens me, the recollection of my children afflicts me, the thought of the cloister and the cell torments me, meditation on my studies gives me pain, consideration of my sins greatly oppresses and perturbs me. Thus, as to those who are ill with fever, every sweet thing seems bitter, for me everything is changed to bitterness and grief.'

Sorrow comes to attack him with its army of despairing thoughts; but hope smiles on the good soldier who has fallen, and raises him up

261

again: 'O knight of Christ, in what heart and spirits are you now; what strength and virtue have you for this battle? . . . Can you ever doubt the Faith, you who have strengthened it with so many arguments?' In this way every fresh attack of the enemy is in its turn driven back. The writer was unable to announce final victory with the last verse of the psalm, because his exposition was cut short at the beginning of the fourth verse. It is written in the old editions that at this point the Friar 'had his writing-materials taken from him'. This would not seem improbable, considering the wickedness of his enemies and how they must have feared his writings. But I am rather inclined to think that his time was cut short.

He had been working on this only a few days when on the 19th of May the papal commissioners arrived in Florence. Poor Torriani was there for show; the young Remolines at once took command of the proceedings. As he came from Rome, the Florentines at once called him Romolino: 'A man fit to be a hangman more than anything else'; an executioner. Unscrupulous as he was, he had barely got off his horse on arrival, when he said in reply to the wild shouts of 'Let him die, let him die': 'Of course he will die.' When the Arrabbiati went to call on him, and one of them, Girolamo Martelli, brought him a beautiful girl dressed as a serving-boy, he said: 'We will make a good bonfire: I have the verdict already here in my bosom.' This only confirms the information sent days before to Girolamo Benivieni by the Florentine bankers at the Court of Rome, who were full of information, like all bankers. They said that the Pope's order was to take the Friar's life, no matter if he were another John the Baptist. Certainly the Pope was not much better than Herod.

No time was lost. On the 20th began the third trial, the ecclesiastical one, at which the Florentines, jealous and suspicious, wished to have five of their representatives present, sitting with the Pope's commissioners, to hear the replies of the accused and, more important, the judges' questions. Ser Ceccone, in spite of what has been written by historians, did not and could not take any part in this trial, in which Romolino's secretary played the role that had been his. In any case, the process this time was much more rapid. The report did not have to be published, and they were not obliged to give account of it to anyone. The verdict had already been decided on beforehand. A few turns of the rope were all that was needed to extort from the Friar the few things that really mattered to the Pope: particularly, with whom he had negotiated for the Concilium, and how far these negotiations had progressed.

Romolino's first questions were on this subject; and the answers he received were those of an innocent man. They then asked Savonarola if he used to hear his companions' confessions, and he replied in the negative; if he had failed to observe his excommunication, and he acknowledged himself here to be a sinner; if he had said that Alexander was neither a true Christian nor Pope, and he replied that he had never said so, but had written it in a letter (the letters to the Princes, he means, wrongly using the singular for the plural), which he had, however, burned. Up to this point things were going badly for the inquisitors.

Then Romolino ordered him to be stripped for the strappado. The Friar, seeing the preparations made for the torture, knelt down and said: 'Now, hear me. God, Thou has caught me. I confess that I have denied Christ, I have told lies, O Signori of Florence! I have denied Him for fear of being tortured: be my witnesses. If I must suffer, I wish to suffer for the truth: what I have said I have received from God Himself. God, Thou givest me this penance for having denied Thee: I deserve it. I have denied Thee, I have denied Thee, I have denied Thee for fear of being tortured.' When he was stripped, he knelt again, 'and he showed his left arm, almost completely destroyed', and kept on repeating: 'I denied Thee, Lord, for fear of being tortured.' As he was drawn up on the rope, he said: 'Help me, Jesus. This time Thou hast taken me.'

These things, which Ser Ceccone would never have set down in his collection of lies, are recorded in the report of the apostolic commissioners, and I have quoted them here word for word as the finest proof of the Friar's innocence and the falseness of the trials. What does it matter if after being bestially tortured he denied all that he had said? Maybe, while the rope tore at his dislocated arm, he thought again, as in his exposition of the psalm 'Miserere', of Peter's spontaneous denial. But, apart from the denial of that heroic retraction, they could get nothing of importance out of him, even by torture. Romolino came back again, but in vain, to the subject of the Concilium. He left the hearing with nothing to show for it.

The day after, the same questions were put to him about the

Concilium and his negotiations with foreign princes. These negotiations did not amount to much and mattered little to the Pope, as the princes had sharper claws than he. On the other hand, he was very much interested in the approaches made to cardinals; but these boiled down to the difficult Cardinal della Rovere, who had once sent a message to the Friar saying that there would come to Florence 'a team of cardinals to hold a Concilium'; to St. Malo, who had visited him and spoken with him of the renovation of the Church; to Gurgens, who had spoken ill of Pope Alexander to him; and to Caraffa, who was very ill-disposed to the Pontiff. Over this last name Romolino's questions became more insistent, and his tortures and threats increased; for this was a cardinal of the Curia who had no King of France behind him, and they could easily lay hands on him. Savonarola wept: 'O friar, whither hast thou been led!' As threats could not make him say what was not true—that he had plotted with the Cardinal for a Concilium—the tortures were renewed until they got him to say that he had had some such negotiation with him. Tortured again—'after he had been kept at it for some time', the text of the proceedings notes cynically—he confirmed and ratified the report.

However, when he was examined again on the 22nd at 11 p.m. and again questioned under oath, he confirmed everything 'except what he had said about the Cardinal of Naples, which he had said out of fear'; and he also denied that he had had negotiations with other cardinals on the subject of the Concilium. He added that, thinking of the sacramental confession, he did not see that he could be absolved, if he did not unsay what he had untruthfully said against others under torture, and so he wished to retract this.

Poor saintly Friar! Forced by iniquitous judges to inculpate himself and others, he wished and was able, once his tortures ceased, at least to exculpate the others. Himself he could not absolve, and perhaps no longer wished to. This third trial, which is as false as the others in substance, if less adulterated, gives us the key to understanding the falseness of the first two. While all the other accusations against him were groundless, or must even be set among the greatest titles to praise owed to the man who had vowed himself to a great and holy mission (as, for example, that he had interfered in the affairs of the Florentine state), there remained only his denial of his prophecies and of himself. But, after those secret pages written on the 'Miserere', the papers of

the ecclesiastical trial show that until the end the Friar protested that
his denial had been extracted by force, and continued to vindicate the
truth he had preached, until his butchers cast him again into that abyss
of misery from which he had just arisen.

The brief and rapid hearing of the 22nd of May, the last of the
trials, at which the other commissioner was not even present, drew to
its close. By order of Romolino, Fra Girolamo was commanded by the
papal messenger to appear the following day *ad concludendum et audiendam
sententiam*. He replied: 'I am in prison; if I can, I will come.' While
he was being taken back to his prison after his examination, the commissioners passed sentence, which was drawn up by Ser Ranieri di
San Gimignano. Its conclusion need hardly be told, having been anticipated by the Pope, the commissioners, and consequently by ourselves
in these pages. But it must at least be said that, for false suppositions
and juridical enormities, it was the worthy crown of these unworthy
trials. For, without Fra Domenico and Fra Silvestro having even been
heard, the three friars were sentenced (on the examination of Fra
Girolamo alone, where the other two are barely mentioned) to
be degraded and handed over to the secular justices 'as heretics and
schismatics, and for having preached innovations'. But, to speak of
Savonarola alone, no one ever succeeded in discovering any heresy in
him; and he contemplated schism even less than did his 'accomplice'
Giuliano della Rovere, who was later rewarded, not with martyrdom,
but with the papacy. And as for innovations, the Friar preached that
the Sacraments should not be bought and sold, that the Pope should
not keep boys for pleasure, or concubines, and other similar novelties.

At the same time, the Florentine magistrates were meeting. It
was their duty *pro forma* to translate into everyday terms the verdict
of the apostolic commissioners, which first passed to the secular justice
of the chancellor of the Eight, and ultimately to the executioner. This
civil judgment, too, was, at least for Fra Girolamo, a mere formality;
for the Signoria had already advised the Pope of the people's desire to
enjoy the capital punishment of the Friar, and the ecclesiastical verdict
given did not permit a lesser one. Yet free republics have this to be
said for them: that when they wish to commit injustices, they are
obliged at least to cover them—or, rather, display them—with the
observance of due forms.

Some days before, a Pratica had been held at which only Agnolo

Niccolini, a doctor of laws and a grave and authoritative man, got up to propose that the Friar should not be killed, but should be kept safe in prison 'and allowed to write, for he will compose wonderful works to the glory of God'; and he warned them that history 'rarely produces such men as he'. However, the majority opinion prevailed. They feared that if he were one day set free by a friendly Signoria, all their deceptions would become known and their crimes avenged. 'A dead man cannot fight back,' one citizen concluded. This opinion coincided exactly with that of Parenti, who, as he was a member of the Eight, may be regarded from this point on as the official historian of that conference of executioners: 'Our intention was that he should not come out of it alive.' And it was perhaps then that Bernardo Rucellai uttered the wicked phrase: 'Let us lay the evils of the city on the friar, and rid ourselves of them all.'

Therefore, after the verdict of the apostolic commissioners, all that remained for the Signoria was to deliberate concerning the execution, which had already been set for the following day, as was shown by the summons to Savonarola, and by the great constructions being raised in the square. It is said that at the last moment, to lend an appearance of justice to injustice, some wished to save Fra Domenico's life. His simplicity and innocence they had been unable to corrupt even by torture. But there were others who feared that in the voice of that just man Savonarola might live again. At this point Romolino, who took part in the debate, said: 'One damned monk more or less, what does it matter?' In great haste a blacksmith was set to make a third iron collar for Fra Domenico.

Fra Girolamo had hardly returned to enjoy the peace of his prison after the examination of the commissioners, when the door opened and five citizens came in, accompanied by the notary of the Signoria and the notary of the Eight—that is, the excellent Ser Ceccone. They asked him further questions *in extremis* about matters of State. It was about midnight. When they left him, he found rest and peace in prayer.

Finally they came to tell him that he must die. He was not perturbed, nor did he ask what sort of death was prepared for him. He said nothing, and returned to his prayers. The same announcement produced different effects on Fra Domenico and Fra Silvestro. The latter was completely shattered and overcome with horror; the former received it not so much with courage as with a joyful readiness typical of the man. And so the funereal wait of the condemned men began.

Their handcuffs were removed, but they still had their legs in irons. Each had with him in his cell, according to custom, one of the Compagnia de' Neri, a pious brotherhood of citizens who attended and comforted condemned men in their last hours. Savonarola was given Iacopo Niccolini, who is known to history for no other reason. He was a pious and good man, though chosen, on the express orders of the Signoria, from among those who did not believe in the Friar. After that night, however, he believed in him for the rest of his life. He brought the Friar his supper, but Fra Girolamo refused it, saying that, as he had to die in the morning, he wanted to prepare his soul and not be occupied with digesting food. He asked for a confessor, and they sent to him, as also to his companions, a Dominican from the Abbey. They were afraid to send friars from San Marco.

In his prison Fra Silvestro 'seemed more exhausted and shaken'; while Fra Domenico, having eaten his supper cheerfully, had written to his brethren of the Convent of Fiesole a brief and gentle letter of farewell. Its last words were that they should care for the doctrine of his venerated master: 'Collect from my cell there the writings of Fra Girolamo; have them bound and place a copy in the library, and another chained copy in the refectory, to be read at the second sitting; so that the serving brothers too may sometimes read them there together. *Dominus vobiscum.*' Then he went quietly to sleep.

At some hour of the night Savonarola asked Niccolini if he might speak to his companions before their execution. At once the good Iacopo went to ask the Signoria, and, having received permission, the three friars were brought together in one room. Then Savonarola said, turning to Fra Domenico: 'It has been revealed to me that you desire to be burned alive. Know you not that it is not permitted to choose one's manner of dying, but that you must joyfully accept that which is prepared for you by God? Who knows whether you will be able to bear that which is made ready for you, as that depends entirely on God's grace?' At these words Fra Domenico humbly bowed his head in token of obedience. Savonarola then turned to Fra Silvestro and reproved him more sharply: 'And it has been revealed to me that you intend before dying to protest to the people that we are innocent. You must not do that, for not even Christ published his innocence from the cross; and we must do likewise, *quia omnis Christi actio nostra est instructio*' [for every act of Christ is an example unto us]. Fra Silvestro too was quietened by the words of his superior. After these conversations Fra Domenico and Fra Silvestro knelt before Fra Girolamo and asked his blessing, and so he blessed them. Then the three friars separated, each retiring with his comforter to a corner of the room.

Fra Girolamo asked for a drink, and when they brought him water in a very dirty bowl he was disgusted and, like Jesus when about to die, *noluit bibere*. But when Niccolini had thoroughly washed the bowl for him, he drank at once. Then he asked Iacopo the favour of letting him rest his head upon his lap, as he was very tired. This he did, and Savonarola quietly went to sleep. When he awoke, he embraced his comforter, thanking him for the kindness he had shown him that night; and it is said that he rewarded him by revealing to him that the tribulations he had predicted for Florence would occur at the time of a Pope Clement. This prophecy, which was to be wondrously verified during the siege of the city by Clement VII, leaves us in some doubt and uncertainty, by its extraordinary exactness, although we have it on the authority of Nardi and other most worthy people.

Daybreak came, and the three friars came together again to hear Mass and receive Communion. Fra Girolamo was allowed the favour of holding the Host in his hands for a while, and he prayed thus: 'Lord, I know that Thou art the true God, Creator of the world and of mankind. I know that Thou art the perfect Trinity, indivisible and inseparable, distinct in three persons: Father, Son, and Holy Ghost. I know that Thou are the everlasting Word that camest down to earth in the womb of the Virgin Mary, and wast crucified to shed Thy precious blood for us miserable sinners. I pray Thee, Lord, I pray Thee, my Saviour, I pray Thee, my Comforter, that the precious blood shall not have been shed in vain for me, but shall be in remission of all my sins, for which I ask Thy forgiveness, from the day on which I received holy baptism until this present time; and I confess my sinfulness to Thee, Lord. And thus I ask Thy forgiveness for anything in which I have offended this city and this people, in spiritual and temporal matters, and for everything in which I may have erred without knowing it. And I humbly beg forgiveness of all these people here present, and ask that they may pray God for me, that He may give me strength at my last end, and that the Enemy may have no power over me. Amen.'

After the Communion the condemned men were permitted to converse together for a while; and after this last talk Fra Girolamo blessed his companions kneeling before him for the last time. It was time to go. As they came down the staircase of the Palace they were met by friars of their Order, conventuals of Santa Maria Novella, sent by the General to strip them of the habit. One of them was Fra Tommaso Sardi. 'Hand over the scapular,' they said roughly to Savonarola; and, taking it off him roughly, they made him groan with pain, for his limbs were crippled by torture. They allowed him as a favour to hold the habit a short while in his arms, and he said: 'O holy habit, how much did I desire you! God gave you to me, and until now I have kept you pure; and even now I would not leave you, but you are taken from me!' With these words, not in the presence of men but only of death and his own conscience, Fra Girolamo again affirmed his innocence. So, barefoot and dressed only in a woollen shirt or brief tunic, he led the way out into the square thronged with people. Here comes the Friar!

Before the eyes of the condemned friars there now appeared the apparatus put up for their last suffering. From the terrace of the Palace a long wooden platform, about the height of a man, ran out to a point in the square, where above a great bonfire of straw and wood was erected a tall post with a crossbar near the top, almost in the shape of a cross. Murmurs of 'They are going to crucify them' had been heard among the people come to see these preparations. And so those in charge hastily had the arms of the cross shortened, 'so that it should not resemble Christ's'; but, no matter how much they cut off, it still looked like a cross. To it were attached the three nooses and three iron chains, to hold up the bodies of the hanged men while the flames enveloped them.

On the terrace of the Signoria there sat *pro tribunali* the apostolic commissioners, and on their right the tribunal of the Eight. On the left, towards the gate of the Palace, was the Bishop of Vasona, who had been charged by a Brief from Pope Alexander, evidently written before the departure of Romolino and therefore before the Pope knew in law whether the accused were guilty or innocent, '*ad degradandos fratres morituros*'; this charge he was ordered to carry out, under pain of excommunication. The condemned men, therefore, presented themselves to him for degradation. He was a certain Fra Benedetto Paganotti of the Preachers' Order, once a friar of San Marco and admirer of Savonarola. As he accomplished his office, he said in his confusion: 'I separate you from the Church militant and the Church triumphant.' The Friar gently corrected him in his usual quiet voice: 'Only from the Church militant; the other is not your affair.' And the good Bishop corrected himself.

Proceeding then along the way of the cross, the three friars came to the tribunal where Romolino sat, and he read them the strange sentence he had compiled. To make it even stranger, we find that he added these words: 'It pleases His Holiness to free you from the pains of Purgatory, giving you plenary indulgence for your sins, and restoring you to your pristine innocence. Do you accept this?' And the 'schismatic and heretical' friars piously bowed their heads and signified their consent.

Their next stop was in front of the tribunal of the Eight, where they were led by the guards, as the sentence of the apostolic commissioners had now delivered them up to the secular arm. There they heard the sentence of the magistrates, which 'having heard and examined their wicked crimes', condemned them to be first hung and then burned.

Only that long, bare platform now separated the three martyrs from the cross. Down it they walked in their thin white tunics, each one accompanied by his black-robed monk and black-robed comforter. Some foul youths, getting under the platform, stuck sharp points through the gaps in the boards to wound the bare feet of the friars, but they went quietly on their way among the jeers and insults. When they reached the foot of the cross, Fra Domenico said to those who accompanied him: 'Why do you not tell me to sing "*Te Deum laudamus*"?' They replied that it might give rise to scandal; so he began to sing alone, in a low voice, the psalm of thanksgiving.

Fra Silvestro was the first to climb the steps of the gallows; then, smiling and ecstatic, Fra Domenico; and finally, after watching his companions die, and withdrawn in an otherworldly serenity, Fra Girolamo. He told his confessor to pray for him, and then, reciting the little Creed, mounted the steps. Having reached the top, he looked down at that multitude which from the pulpit he had so often seen cheering or weeping. The executioner put the noose around his neck and gave him the fatal push; he tried to light the pyre immediately, before life had quite left that poor body, so that Fra Girolamo might feel the torment of the fire; but, clowning and gesturing as he did so (and the Signoria afterwards reprimanded him for it), he dropped the iron ring that was to check the corpse, and when he found it and lit the fire the martyr was already dead. By modern reckoning, it was ten o'clock on the 23rd of May, the eve of Ascension Day.

Before he was given the fatal push, a jeering cry rose from the crowd: 'Savonarola, now is the time to do miracles!'—just as they had said to Christ: '*Descende de cruce.*' But in the crowd thronging the square there were others who repeated the same words to themselves, I do not know whether one should say with despair or with faith. For this sublime silent death of the Friar terrified his devoted followers all the more. They hoped until the end that their prophet would accomplish a miracle, or at least that he would speak to the people some memorable words on his own innocence in final salutation.

Hardly had the fire taken hold when a great wind, springing up suddenly, blew the flames aside so that they did not attack the bodies of the hanged men. Then a great clamour arose in the square, and cries of 'Miracles, miracles!' Many fled in terror. But when the flames rose up again and enveloped the three corpses, they raised Savonarola's right arm and drew it up with the palm open and two fingers raised, so that he seemed to be giving his blessing to the people.

Then a hail of stones thrown by a wicked mob of youths (and those who allowed it were no less infamous) showered upon the bodies of the martyrs, and that arm, raised in blessing from the pyre, fell. The sacrilege went on until the bodies were consumed. From the miserable remains many relics were collected by pious people; some ladies dressed as servants came with brass urns to gather together those ashes, saying that they wanted them for washing clothes, but soldiers on guard drove them away with blows with the flat of their swords. This was reported to the commissioners, who, in order to remove them from the veneration of the people, had all the ashes collected and thrown into the Arno. Thus there came true those prophetic words uttered by the Friar in 1491, when he was expounding the psalm '*Expectans expectavi*'; 'The wicked shall go to the sanctuary, with axes and with fire they will break down and burn its doors; and they will take the just men and burn them in the centre of the city; and that which the fire does not consume and the wind does not carry away, they will throw into the water.'

Thus ended Girolamo Savonarola. His ashes, dispersed in the gentle winds of a Florentine May, fell, as true ashes of repentance, upon all Christianity. Other barbarians overran Italy, as he had predicted, and Rome was thrown into confusion, and St. Peter's was made a stable for horses and a soldiers' bivouac. But three things above all others he had foretold in his famous propositions: that the infidel would be converted—and while he spoke a bold Ligurian was bearing towards unknown lands that Christ who was part of his name; that the Church would be scourged—and that scourge was indeed dreadful beyond belief; and that the Church would thereafter be renovated—and what the Friar could not accomplish in life, he probably hastened by his death. It has been said before in other words, but it is hard to avoid repeating what is true: had his voice been listened to, perhaps beyond the Alps Luther would not have risen, or his influence would have been less; and the Reform, of which every Christian heart felt the need, would then have been born in the very bosom of the Church of Rome.

Chapter 25

PORTRAIT

$\diamond\!\!\!\times\!\!\diamond$

SAVONAROLA was of less than medium height, slender but well proportioned. He was white-skinned, with rosy cheeks and thick coarse hair of a reddish-brown colour. He carried himself erect, and his bearing was at once proud and gentle. His face was neither thin nor full, with a great hooked nose, thick close lips, and a brow heavy with deep horizontal lines. Under bushy dark eyebrows and reddish lashes were grey-green eyes, sometimes flashing with light, at others smouldering with hidden fire. He had aristocratic hands, long, thin, and almost transparent.

His clothes were the oldest and most patched to be found in the convent, but they were always, like all his person, of the utmost cleanliness. Poor and worn as those clothes were, they did not seem grotesque as he wore them, but showed a rare propriety, even a kind of elegance. He had, too, this special gift: that his garments were never sweaty, and seldom got dirty. His shoes were all cobbled; and this was how he wanted his monks to wear them, so that the townsfolk, he said, need not be approached too often for alms. He used to say that, just as silk and gold brocades were the glory of the rich, so coarse and mended clothes must be the glory of the religious Orders.

He dressed so meanly for love of poverty, which he used to call his bride; and in this he was a continual example to all the members of his own Order and to those of every other Order as well. An old biographer tells how one day two abbots of the Vallombrosan Order

273

who admired his teaching came to see him, wishing to reform their convents. In the middle of their conversation Savonarola began to stare at their habits, which were of very fine serge, smiling to himself without saying anything. When the abbots noticed this and observed the mean patched clothes of the man who had the devotion of such a great city, they were ashamed. Not knowing how to excuse themselves, they said, blushing: 'Father Girolamo, do not be astonished that our serge is so fine, for we choose them thus so that they may last longer.' To which he answered with gentle humour: 'It was certainly a great pity that St. Benedict and St. Giovanni Gualberto did not know that these lasted longer, or they would perhaps have done the same.' At these words the two abbots, in their shame and confusion, were filled with remorse. It was perhaps at that time that the Camaldolese friars of the Monastero degli Angeli wanted to change their habit to be re-formed under his orders, and had their intention drawn up legally by a notary. But Savonarola replied that their founder, Romualdo, had been a most saintly man, and had laid down for them a most holy rule; and so it were better that they should reform themselves in accordance with that.

Not only in clothes did he love poverty. He never possessed nor used as his own property anything other than a Bible or a breviary. He used to fill the narrow margins of these books in his minute hand-writing with learned comments and 'things needful for preaching', as the old biographer tells us, and as we can see in some such relics which have come down to us, 'so that when he had to go to preach, he did not have to carry with him a load of books'. However, when he had in this way made them more his own and more precious to him, and realized that he had conceived for them a greater affection than he thought right, he immediately gave them away to his brethren or his pupils.

His bed was the meanest possible: a frame of wood laid across trestles, with a large sack of straw for a mattress, a piece of rough woollen material for a sheet, and a coarse square of bombasine for a coverlet. His diet likewise was very poor, even poorer and less plentiful than that of his monks, which was yet said to be insufficient for bodily needs. If at table the server set before him the whitest bread, he changed it and took for himself the darkest and worst pieces; he would give the piece put before him to some older brother or one of weak constitution. He ate so little that it was hard to see what he lived on.

We have already spoken of the obedience of this servant of God, who was yet accused of disobedience, while telling the story of his life. Of his humility we need to speak at greater length here, as it may have appeared a less obvious virtue of his in these pages of ours so far, and indeed in any others written about him; and as humility might seem in no way compatible with the apparent pride of so many of his attitudes. And yet it would be hard and unjust to deny this virtue to one who loved it so much and praised it in one of his most cherished works; to one who showed so great a perfection in his spiritual life that it is impossible that he should have lacked humility, the basis and condition of other virtues which he possessed in so high a degree. Savonarola was humble as only a proud man can become, for I am convinced that humility in him was the mortification of pride. In fact, the biographers recount many notable instances of this virtue in him. Once, hearing himself praised by a great preacher, he immediately left the church, and afterwards severely reproached him. Another time, when the convent was being spring-cleaned, he apportioned to each man a share of the work, and took for his own the privies, he who was so fastidious and clean himself and such an important person. On another occasion he did this same work at night so that none might see and praise him, though he was observed by some friars who were spying on him, hoping to discover something to his discredit.

Even more than by this humility, the view that has commonly been formed of the Friar through false prejudices and misconception of his real deeply moral outbursts, is contradicted by his equally true meek gentleness. There can be no greater mistake than one which is often committed: judging Savonarola the man by the angry outbursts, the awful threats and contumely of the preacher when, from the height of that 'terrible place', as he called it, he exercised his terrible office of prophet and reformer. He used to say, as the reader will no doubt remember: 'One cannot behave up here as one does down there.' And when he came down from the pulpit and spoke familiarly, not to sins but to sinners, whose who had heard him in the rostrum and been subdued by his eloquence were even more fascinated and astonished by his great meekness.

The biographers relate many instances of this virtue too, some of them illustrating the rare equanimity he showed in philosophical or theological or any other kind of disputation. Where his opponents would become angry and immoderate, he never on any occasion or for any reason showed anything but an impassive serenity, and never raised his voice. On one particular occasion he had been disputing with an abbot of the Vallombrosans as to which was the most perfect life, the contemplative, the active, or a mixture of the two. His opponent, on taking his leave, said: 'Though your arguments have satisfied me, your gentleness has pleased me more.' He never was angered by anything that was said or done to him. For example, one day, at the height of the agitations against him by monks of other Orders and in particular by the Franciscans, he met on the road to Fiesole some Minor brothers, who uttered many ugly and contemptuous words against him. He listened to them all patiently, and replied without the slightest sign of anger: 'Peace be with you.'

His patience was so great that once after a sermon, when he had gone, tired and unwell, to be attended to by the infirmary brother, the latter, who was busy with something else, said to him: 'Father, wait a little while.' As it turned out, he waited two hours or more without losing patience, without making any protest, and without calling anyone. At last the infirmary brother, who had completely forgotten about him, passed where he was waiting, and apologized in great confusion. Savonarola answered quietly: 'Just do what you have to do.'

It is not surprising if the fascination of so many virtues, added to that which emanated from his person and his voice, enthralled not only his own brethren and the Piagnoni but also some of his antagonists, especially when they were men of good faith and virtuous life. Even others, when he could speak with them quietly and alone, were filled with awe and respect for him. According to the pseudo-Burlamacchi, this is what happened with Piero degli Alberti, his deadly enemy; taken to see him by Francesco Valori, Alberti went with the intention of remonstrating with him, and remained instead for a long time silent, as if stunned, listening to him talk gently of spiritual things. We have as witnesses of this personal fascination some very famous men who, having first known Savonarola's spirit and intellect through his actions or writings, found his stature greatly increased when they came to converse or dispute with him in person. Among others, this happened to Collenuccio, who described him as 'even greater in person than in his writings'; Pico had the same experience, and so did Commines and many others.

Of the man of prayer, of the mystic and of the reformer, I have no room to write here, nor of the miraculous work he accomplished in the mystical vineyard of Christ. In any case, I could only repeat what has already been said perfectly well by others. His writings tell part of that story, and it is all summed up in the life of the man himself, as we have, I hope, made apparent in these brief pages. I recalled the evidence of the Blessed Sebastiano Maggi that he had often heard his confession without finding in him even a venial sin. These words echo strangely those of a very different type of man, Doffo Spini, his examiner in a very different kind of confession: that of the infamous trials. Of the many miracles which have been attributed to the Friar, and which are narrated in detail in three different collections, one of them prepared by the Blessed Maria Bagnesi, I shall likewise not speak at all, as these are matters to be dealt with in the place where Saints are canonized, and not by a writer of history.

Since the word *saintliness* was used about Savonarola, it is my duty to record the witness to it of many people, starting from San Filippo Neri, Santa Caterina de' Ricci, the Blessed Colomba da Rieti, the Blessed Maria Bagnesi, the Blessed Caterina da Racconigi, the Venerable Maddalena del Paradiso, and Santa Maddalena de' Pazzi, who all revered the Friar, obtained miracles from him, and saw him surrounded by the glory of the blessed; from all of which it would appear that not to believe in his saintliness is for a Christian tantamount to not believing in the sanctity of those witnesses. If the case for his canonization was never promoted, other conditions for its being done were not lacking, in addition to these testimonies and his miracles: the proclamation *vivæ vocis oraculo,* made by a Pope, Julius II (I am bound to reject as suspect and in every way unacceptable the declaration which Alexander VI is supposed to have made after he had martyred him); the common consent of the Church; a cult devoted to him for more than a hundred years, which is demonstrated by various Offices composed for him and for a long time celebrated in some Dominican convents, and by the images of him in glory, which were being sold even in Rome during the Jubilee of 1600, with the inscription: 'Martyr, prophet, virgin, doctor.' This evidence is all purely historical, and in no way a discussion or affirmation of the saintliness of the Friar. The biographer must withdraw from such discussion, satisfied with having recorded, beyond the few things we have just mentioned, the saintliness of his life and works. As we look back on them, we are comforted by the words of the Scripture: '*A fructibus eorum cognoscetis eos.*'

When it comes, however, to the prophecies of one who said he was a prophet and was generally believed to be one, the historian cannot and should not draw back. Rather is he under an obligation to distinguish between those which proved true and those which proved false, between those which were really uttered by the prophet and those which his followers, in their excessive zeal, falsely attributed to him. This I have tried to do in these pages, at least for the principal items. Now, as his work draws to a close, the historian cannot deny that Savonarola did have, at least in certain flashes of insight, the ability to foresee the future, and to see what was happening at a great distance, as in the case of the defeat of Maximilian. I could not say, nor would I like to try, whether in every case this could be attributed to the natural lights of a very acute mind, or to mere coincidence; though it must be said that prophets of woe like the Friar have less chance of failure than those who promise happiness.

By a facile and superficially attractive analogy, it has been said that the prophetic sermons of Savonarola are very close to those of Gioacchino da Fiore, and in a way derive from them. They are undoubtedly parallel; but, like parallels, they do not meet at any point. It would be useless to seek the origins of Savonarolan prophecy in that of the Calabrese divine. Some themes common to both preachers are also common to other reforming prophets. One might as well say, and with greater truth, that the Friar's prophecies derive from those of the Old Testament. He himself, in fact, always expressed small admiration, even contempt, for the Calabrese abbot, and confessed that he had read few of his works and none of his prophetic ones. Also, Savonarola's constant affirmations that he was inspired by direct divine revelation are sufficient to distinguish his prophecies from those of Gioacchino. And after all we have said about them, his account at the trials should not be taken as valid evidence that Savonarola's prophecies were simply interpretation of the Scriptures. Apart from the well-known falsifications that account contained, we are reminded of

Herder's objection: 'What manner of inquiry is that, to ask a man under torture whether he is a prophet sent by God?'. Besides, however one likes to explain it, it is an undeniable fact that Savonarola's prophecies constantly came true.

Among his most solemn prophecies, the one regarding the conversion of the infidels was denounced as being false, and seemed so even to Schnitzer, the most convinced supporter of Savonarola's prophetic gift; and on these grounds alone there were some who would deny any prophetic spirit to the Friar, in spite of the fact that some of the greatest Old Testament prophets are known to have made mistakes. But even this prophecy can clearly be shown to have come true (as I have pointed out at the conclusion of my life of the martyr) when we think of the new lands being opened up to Christianity in those very same years by the discoveries of Columbus and Amerigo Vespucci, who gave his name to the New World. (Incidentally, Vespucci's paternal uncle was at that time a friar in the convent of San Marco.) It is useless to object that if at times Savonarola spoke in general terms of the infidels, at others he specifically mentioned the Turks. If these were not the only pagans known to exist at that time, they were, of course, the infidels par excellence; indeed, *Turk* was just another word for *infidel*. It was, therefore, natural that he should not describe in any other terms the infidels of the New World, of which he knew nothing whatever.

It seems that several of his prophecies derived from visions, some experienced when awake, others during sleep. In these, the figures and words of the Old Testament with which his mind was filled, suddenly became alive in his imagination and made him clairvoyant. He apparently saw in one of these visions the pagan throngs hastening to be baptized, and spoke of it several times from the pulpit; from this vision he derived the prophecy we have been discussing, and of course he clothed it in terms of his own experience and that of his age. Such things are unreliable and unrewarding material for those (and I am one of them) who seek in history only the truth of things that are certain. But even today there are more things in heaven and earth than are dreamt of in our philosophy.

However that may be, Schnitzer is quite right when he says that Savonarola will always be an enigma to the historian who does not recognize or take into account the fact that he was, above all, a prophet.

He is equally right in saying that by *prophet* one should mean not merely an oracle of things to come, but a reformer, a mouthpiece of the divine will; and that 'the Friar was a great and authentic prophet, because he was a great and authentic preacher and reformer'. But he is wrong when he says, almost contradicting himself, that in the Friar the reformer grew out of the prophet. On the contrary, from the reformer, from the man who even as a child 'could not suffer the blind wickedness of the peoples of Italy', sprang the preacher, the prophet, the statesman, and everything that Girolamo Savonarola did or was.

If, therefore, the preacher arose out of the reformer and the prophet, it was the preacher who consecrated the fame of the prophet and reformer. I have already spoken many times of the quality of his eloquence, which was quite extraordinary when, freed from scholastic fetters, it came spontaneously from his mind and soul. History itself bears sufficient witness to its powers. Those are fine and very true words he spoke amid the depression and dejection of the trials, when he was sneered at for his bewilderment and reminded of the pride and courage he had shown in the pulpit. 'Then I was master,' he replied. Machiavelli wrote: 'The people of Florence do not regard themselves as ignorant or artless: nonetheless, they were convinced by Fra Girolamo that he held converse with God.' This was what the Friar's eloquence and his virtues could accomplish, and it is not a little. We may ask ourselves whether in the end this great rouser of men did not, with the power of his word, unconsciously rouse and seduce himself. Only a diligent and minute research into all his actions, all his sermons, all his writings, can convince one in the end that this was not so.

I would not like to assert that Savonarola's qualities of mind were equal to those of his spirit—not because the former were small, but because the latter were so great. Posterity is in agreement with his contemporaries in recognizing that he had a brilliant intelligence and very acute judgment, 'not only as regards letters, but in worldly matters, the general principles of which he understood extremely well'. Even the opponents of Savonarola are in agreement with this opinion expressed by one [Guicciardini] who himself knew a great deal about those 'worldly matters'. Even those who cast doubt upon his spiritual gifts and Christian virtues never dared to deny him those more apparent qualities of mind. He had a vast memory and, to the very end of his life, constantly applied himself to study.

Besides his classical studies, his knowledge of philosophy—which, in the words of Guicciardini, 'he possessed so completely, and so freely used for all his purposes, as if he had invented it himself'—gave him his precision of thought and expression. I cannot, however, see in his philosophical works the originality that Villari found there. Those which we have in print are books written for the training of friars, and he tore up some youthful writings he had done on the dialogues of Plato, when he decided at one stroke to abandon his philosophical studies and the world. He knew no Greek, and I do not believe he ever thought to learn it, even though there were some in San Marco who knew it very well indeed. He was quite content to read Aristotle, Plato, and other philosophers or commentators in the very common Latin translations. His ideas on the uses of learning are well known, and I believe that, in consequence of those ideas, his ambition was really to learn Hebrew rather than Greek. Hebrew was taught in San Marco, and I should not be surprised if he made a start on the language, without, however, getting very far. I am led to this conclusion by certain detailed comments on the Hebrew text of the Bible which he discussed with Blemmet, rather than by the commission given to his brother Alberto in 1497 to obtain for him some copies of the Hebrew Bible printed by Soncino in 1494; these were quite evidently intended for the school of San Marco. He must have had a very strong desire to read in the original tongue the Book in which he found his true nourishment, the Book that had made him a friar, a reformer, and a prophet.

Savonarola was also not without virtues as a writer, though for me his supreme virtue here is the fact that he did not pretend to any. In comparison with the artificial prose of the humanists, that of the Friar, when it does not fall into slovenly expression, pleases by its spontaneous simplicity, which occasionally achieves beauty and vigour. Similarly, his youthful *canzoni*, though marred by roughness of style, yet shine out for their strength and sincerity of feeling, among so many artificial compositions of the time. I am not afraid to say that Savonarola, with his great and passionate soul and his forceful imagination, was a true poet; or at least more of a poet than many of his contemporaries who professed to be poets, and perhaps also a better poet in certain sermons than in his few verses. We should not be misled by the many things he said from the pulpit against poets and their art, and which he then expressed better in his *Apologetico,* any more than we are led by his rough letters to his mother to doubt the great love he bore her. In the same way, because he was sure that poetry could never be of service to religion, and at most a mere ornament to it, he repressed the poetry in his heart, as he repressed everything that might distract him from the prime truths, and from the ultimate end.

Of his knowledge of the things of this world, for which we have praised him, he gave ample proof in founding the popular Florentine state. The democratic reforms introduced by the Friar seemed wise and good even to the aristocratic Guicciardini; and if, as Gino Capponi well said, 'Savonarola was of the people, as a man, as a friar, and as a saint', he was certainly no demagogue. He knew very well that in some circumstances it was necessary to limit rather than expand the councils; and some defects and mistakes in the reforms that go under his name are due to the fact that sometimes his advice was disregarded. We cannot here, in a portrait sketched in broad outlines, make a detailed examination of the political work of Savonarola. Suffice it to quote the opinions of the three princes of Florentine politics, Machiavelli, Guicciardini, and Giannotti. The first wrote those famous words in honour of the Friar: 'Of so great a man we must speak with reverence'; and Machiavelli was not in the habit of speaking reverently of unarmed prophets, while among friars he was better acquainted with the likes of Fra Timoteo than of Fra Girolamo. The second wrote so much in praise of the man and his political reforms that we would have no space here to repeat it all. Giannotti reminded those friars who meddled in politics that 'there is no longer anyone like Fra Girolamo, so greatly endowed with learning, wisdom, and saintliness', and therefore they should not 'presume to think they may imitate one who excelled them so much in every respect.' Giannotti also wrote that the man who introduced into Florence the Great Council was a wiser man than Giano della Bella, because Giano wished to abase the upper classes to strengthen the position of the people, while Savonarola tried to ensure freedom for all. And this is the highest praise, and the truest, that could be given to Savonarola's political achievement.

Yet politics for him were but an instrument in the service of God, like art and poetry and everything else; and he understood them in no other way. For that, and no other reason (assuming that these words from his second trial are not fictitious), he had wished 'to reign in Florence'; so that Christ might reign there, elected by the people as their King at his suggestion. This is much better expressed by Capponi: 'He could truly say that he had never liked interfering in matters of state, and that in founding the people's government he had no other object than the good of their souls and the reform of morals. He was the preacher of an idea, and never the organizer of a plan . . .; he showed his greatness in organizing the state of Florence, but he was not himself concerned to govern it. He was the prophet of that state, and he would never have wished to be its administrator. He never had any such ambition.'

Far from wishing to be the political head of the Florentine Republic, he never even had any ambitions to rise in the hierarchy of the Church. We know in what circumstances, and with what high-minded words, he refused the cardinal's purple—though this may have seemed to so great a man an ambition of no great importance. But not even the idea of becoming head of all Christendom tempted the Friar, unless it be in goodness, holiness, and religious fervour. He said it himself at his trials, and his own enemies recorded it in those infamous papers concocted to defame him. It was perhaps the greatest thing he ever said: would that we could know his actual words. He is reputed to have said: 'I did not think greatly of becoming cardinal or Pope, because if I could have achieved my purpose without being Pope, I should have been the most revered and authoritative man in the world'; and he added that he thought 'it was a greater thing to be the head of this work he pursued, than to be Pope, because a man without virtue can be Pope, but such work as this requires a man of the highest virtue.'

Such was Savonarola, a man certainly born to great things and great thoughts, and his enemies could not do otherwise than increase his stature by the light of the pyre that set a halo upon his martyrdom. But he was also a man of strife and dissension, and echoed the lamentation of Jeremiah: '*Genuisti me virum rixæ et discordiæ in universa terra*' —'Thou hast borne me a man of strife and a man of contention to the whole earth'; and he continued to be so down the centuries. About his great name there continued, and always will continue, to be violently opposed judgments, disputes, and passions—a sign of inextinguishable hatred and invincible love. The mysterious and powerful fascination which, as during his lifetime, the Friar's memory has continued to exercise for more than four hundred and fifty years over any unprejudiced person who approaches the subject, and studies his life and writings, has often been noted, and not only by those disposed in his favour. On the other hand, he had against him, and still has, those who knew little of his life and writings; the descendants of the Tiepidi, who thought—or think—they felt on their own shoulders the blows that fell on their forebears; the modern Pharisees, who are troubled by a disobedience that never in fact existed, and in any event would have been holy disobedience; the enemies of the Christian faith; those who believe in no religion; and the fanatics of humanism.

These last (including Carducci, which saddens, though it cannot surprise when one considers the man and his times) spoke of a retrograde Savonarola who tried to put out the great light of the Renaissance (I cannot imagine how) and reduce the world to the darkness of a second Middle Ages. This is both false and foolish. Savonarola was a man of his times, even if he seemed to have retained certain medieval characteristics, owing to education and the influence of his grandfather Michele, who belonged to that age. The truth is that these accusations spring from the fact that he kept to its high eternal principles, and that he placed God above all else in a century that placed man above God. I would not say that Savonarola deserves to be called retrograde on this account.

It is true that some of his strictness and severity is displeasing, as also the little allowance he makes for human frailty; this is especially displeasing to those who, like myself, admire in him the fullness of his humanity and value some faults even more than certain virtues. For the unbelieving, Savonarola is only a martyr who sacrificed everything, even his life, for a pious illusion. But anyone who believes in a Divine Being, if he wishes to be consistent as the Friar was, must agree that everything should be subordinated to that Being, whether they be only the consolations of art and poetry or the other rare and precious things that embellish this human interlude. This is just what Savonarola did: and this is what we must remember when we judge him or try to understand him; this is what people should bear in mind when they accuse him of not having upheld to the last the freedom of human thought—just the opposite of those who attribute to him a nonexistent failure in obedience.

How various and strange are human judgments! Savonarola, an Italian friar and Catholic to the very marrow of his bones, was criticized by one Italian scholar for not having had the same idea as the German monk of 'independent reason', and for having pronounced, before his martyrdom, a beautiful and memorable profession of Catholic faith and accepted the absolution of the Roman Church. Once again I will let Capponi speak for me, and he was not a partisan of the Friar: 'All he wished to do was to destroy evil with the power of words, not to raise an altar of his own against that which was profaned.' And as his quarrel was only with bad priests, he did not wish either to conquer or to die in opposition to the Church. If he withdrew spontaneously from his appeal for the Concilium, and if he suppressed his just anger and accepted final benediction, not from Rodrigo Borgia the man but from that holder (albeit a wicked one) of the See of Peter, it should be set down not to weakness of character but to the strength of his Catholic faith. And this was not the least of his victories, even if some people—the mean, the unfortunate, and the weak—would have preferred him to have rebelled.

Certain minor writers and thinkers of the present day who, seeking to be thought profound, have placed Savonarola halfway between disobedience and obedience, halfway between the old and the new, between Catholic faith and heresy, practically change Savonarola into a mediocrity. My answer of these people is to quote the resolute expression of his dilemma by Guicciardini: 'I am doubtful, and cannot make up my mind either way . . .; but my conclusion is this: that if he was a good man, we have seen in our time a great prophet; if he was bad, we have yet seen a very great man.'

I myself was long in doubt. I had the good fortune to discover, at the hopeful dawn of my life as a man and as a scholar, a handful of unpublished works of the Friar, against which at that time I was strangely prejudiced by my preoccupations with humanism. This very same dilemma arose in my mind, and at the same time the desire to resolve it. I have given twenty-four years to the problem, seeking out books and documents, and pondering carefully over them, alternately believing and doubting, and breaking down the great doubt into a hundred particular questions in as many different publications. Now in my conscience and my understanding there remains only one doubt: whether these pages now drawing to a close, which have journeyed all the way from early prejudice to a final and quite opposite judgment, are enough to demonstrate to others what is to me at last clearly proven: that Girolamo Savonarola was both the things suggested by Guicciardini, a great prophet and, if in a different sense than that intended by that historian, a very great man.

Appendix

SUMMARY ACCOUNT OF THE CULT
AND FORTUNE OF SAVONAROLA

◇◇

SAVONAROLA's death and, before that, his imprisonment and trials, aroused the most diverse passions in Italy and beyond the Alps. But it would take too long within the framework of this brief account, and would in any case be of little use, to report all the references (which are not always reliable) to them in the official papers of Italian rulers. Even in far-off Russia there were some who wrote of that iniquity, and wept for it.

In France, Charles VIII had died on the 7th of April, the day of the trial by fire, and his wretched end bore out the threatening prophecies of the Friar. As soon as Louis XII, who succeeded him, heard of the Friar's imminent peril, he wrote to the Signoria of Florence, begging 'for several good reasons' that they should suspend their sentence until further notice 'if they intended to proceed to one by some means or other'. But as the special messenger galloped off from the royal stables on the 4th of June, the wicked deed was already done, and the waters and the winds had shared the martyr's remains.

In contrast to the King of France, the ruler of Savonarola's native Ferrara, Ercole d'Este, uttered no word in defence of the man he had honoured and cultivated in more prosperous days. But the death of Savonarola so angered the people of Ferrara that when the General of the Order, Gioacchino Torriani, went there for the Chapter of the Order on his way back from the 'legal murder' in which he had been an accomplice, he was very nearly stoned by the populace.

In Rome, on the other hand, the Pope did not hide his satisfaction nor stint his praise, nor in the end did he deny the Republic the price of the blood of the just man: the permission to impose a three-tenths tax on the clergy. Hence it was said with typical Florentine sarcasm: 'This friar was sold for thirty pieces like the Saviour, because three times ten make thirty.' But the Republic could obtain from the Pope no more than this filthy reward of Judas. After all his promises, he did nothing for them in the matter of the return of Pisa; instead, he allowed his son, Caesar Borgia, to rob and extract ransome from the Florentines in his sorties up to the very walls of the city. The most infamous period of the papacy of Alexander VI begins after the death of Savonarola, as though with him there had fallen the last barrier to papal wickedness. Poor Friar! His famous sermon on the fat kine of Samaria —i.e. the whores of Rome—was small beer in comparison with the famous supper in the Vatican on the 31st of October, 1501, with its remarkable joust of the harlots, '*quæ fuerunt ibidem in aula carnaliter tractatæ arbitrio præsentium*' before the eyes of the Pontiff himself.

Following the example thus set by the masters in Rome, depravity and the Compagnacci in Florence were at last taking their revenge. On the day of Savonarola's execution one of the Ten newly in office was heard to exclaim: 'Praise be to God, now we can practise sodomy.' It is not difficult to imagine what deeds followed such words. Even the chronicler Parenti, a leading member of the Arrabbiati, and enemy and examiner of the Friar, feared the imminent punishment of God as he narrated the depravities and insults to religion of those times, such as the sacrilegious race run in the Duomo itself, on Christmas Eve, 1499, by an ass with a thick stick suggestively thrust into its rear. The good Landucci, horror-struck by such enormities, and re-reading in his diary what he had written in former days at the time of the Savonarolan reformation, commented: 'The wicked have overcome the good. God be praised that I saw that short space of holiness!' We can well understand, therefore, the devout cry of lamentation raised by a poet of the Piagnoni:

> *Che debbo dir, Signore*
> *se non gridare ahimè?*
> *Ohimè, che il Santo è morto!*
> *ohimè, Signore, ohimè!*

Tu togliesti il Profeta,
il qual tirasti a te.
Oh Geronimo santo,
che in ciel trionfò sè.

.   .   .   .

Ohimè soccorri presto,
ohimè, Signore, ohimè![1]

I do not, however, intend here to rewrite the history of the events and morals of Italy, or even of Florence, after the Friar's death; but to examine briefly the fortunes of his name and his teaching, and the fate of his followers. These, if they were Florentine citizens, were persecuted by the State; while, if they were ecclesiastics—that is, friars of San Marco or secular priests—they were harassed bitterly for some time by the magistrates of the Republic, and for much longer by the powers at Rome. Many of the citizens were questioned, imprisoned, or fined; others, such as Soderini and Ridolfi, were treated more leniently because of their eminence and important family connections, and were only obliged to lend money. Others were relieved of their office, including the poet Ugolino Verino, who sent the Signoria an abject attack on the Friar, but it did not serve to obtain their forgiveness for his former devotion and his Latin poem dedicated to Savonarola. This attack makes a pair with one written at that time by another former and more illustrious Piagnone: Marsilio Ficino. The others—that is, the ecclesiastics—had a harder time of it. Among them were two canons of the cathedral who had supported the Friar; they were first imprisoned, and later freed on payment of a fine.

The friars of San Marco had the worst of it. The city deprived them of many privileges both old and new, and took from them the Medici library, in spite of the money they had paid and the rights they had acquired. What was worse, they took from them the great bell, the Piagnona; because it was guilty of having sounded the alarm on the night of the riots, it was taken down from the bell tower, whipped through the streets by the public executioner, and handed over to the triumphant Minor brothers of San Miniato. Those of San Marco were

[1] 'What can I say, O Lord, but cry Alas? Alas, the Saint is dead! Alas, Lord, Alas! You took from us the Prophet, and drew him up to You. O saintly Girolamo, triumphant in heaven. Alas, succour us soon, Alas, Lord, Alas!'

harder hit by the loss of that bell than by the loss of Savonarola! As far as Rome was concerned, it was not enough that they had renounced their superior and master; it was not enough, among so many other humiliations, that they should send the Pope an abject letter of apology, written in the interest of the convent rather than of their own consciences. In spite of their supplications, they were joined to the notorious Tuscan-Roman Congregation. The brothers most devoted to Savonarola were banished by the Florentine government—among them Mariano Ughi and Roberto Ubaldini, Giovanni Sinibaldi and Tommaso Caiani, Maurelio Savonarola and Niccolò Seratico, the former Girolamo's brother and the latter his chancellor. The fine flock was dispersed among the convents of the new congregation.

It will seem to the reader that up to this point we have said little about the fortune of Savonarola himself. However, it was necessary to describe the persecution of his followers and of his spiritual relics, to show what must have been the state of mind even of those who had best received the Master's teaching, and should therefore have been its most faithful guardians and disseminators. To understand the dejection of these disciples, thrown into confusion by the false trials and the storm of abuse and insults which had broken over the Friar and themselves, and terrified at the persecution of the city and the Church, it is enough to think of the case of Fra Benedetto. He was perhaps, after Fra Domenico, the most devout and fervent apostle of Savonarola, and even he wavered for a short time, as he tells us himself:

> e come tordo auta la ramata
> sbalordito, a Viterbo me n'andai;[1]

that is, he went to the convent of Santa Maria della Quercia, where at that time not a few of the spiritual sons of Savonarola gathered together after the dispersal. However, his doubt and fear lasted but a short time. 'When he was able to think clearly again,' the lies and inventions of the trials became evident to him, and soon his enthusiasm was so roused that he began to assert against everybody and everything the saintliness of his Master, defying the prohibitions of his superiors and suffering for Savonarola many years usque ad vincula.

The drama of Fra Benedetto was repeated with slight variation in every follower of Savonarola; the devotion of each was revived in

[1] '. . . and, as a thrush stunned in the snare, I went off to Viterbo.'

the same way. When the first persecutions were over, the citizens were allowed freely to profess their own faith, and, if they had previously handed them over and now asked for them back, they were even given the works of the Friar which the papal commissaries had ordered to be surrendered under pain of excommunication. The friars, on the other hand, were for a long time persecuted by their superiors—first among them, as usual, Mei, who was not satisfied with having been the author of Savonarola's ruin. Thus, on the 3rd of February, 1499, he issued an order, which was shortly afterwards ratified by the General, 'that no one should speak of Fra Girolamo either in praise or blame, and there should be no disputations about whether he had erred or not'. It was likewise forbidden for preachers to criticize the life and habits of Fra Girolamo, or to praise or defend his prophecies; it was even more strongly forbidden to keep any relics. It was even forbidden to sing the psalm 'Ecce quam bonum' because it had been the favourite of Savonarola and his followers!

But the spark had been kindled anew in the hearts of his disciples, and could not so easily be extinguished. Knowing that the above-mentioned decree had remained a dead letter, and that the cult of the Friar was being practised secretly in the convents of San Marco, Fiesole, and Prato, the General issued a letter on the following 24th of May, ordering an inquisition into those convents, with the purpose especially of discovering who was the author of an exposition of the psalms 'Verba mea auribus percipe', which had recently been published. In this work the saintliness of Savonarola was affirmed, and all kinds of retribution were threatened to those 'whose hands were sullied with innocent blood'.

The fire was also spreading, fed by the disciples of the Prophet who had migrated to other convents in the Congregation. At San Romano in Lucca there was Fra Stefano da Codiponte, who, with his famous sermon 'Jerusalem, Jerusalem, quæ occidis prophetas', caused anger and terror at the papal Court. This convent was soon to become the nursery in which the best and greatest of the Friar's followers were to be bred, in rivalry with San Marco. At Viterbo, Santa Maria della Quercia was already a stronghold of Savonarolan memories. At Pistoia, Girolamo Giannotti, translator and editor of the sermons on the psalm 'Quam bonus' and probably of others, was, with his brother Alessandro, who had received the habit from the hands of the Prophet himself, the soul of the Savonarolan cult in the convent of San Domenico. At Siena, Cherubino da Firenze, joined later by Girolamo Giannotti and Cristoforo Peraccini, the compiler of the Savonarolan concordances, avenged the wrong suffered by the Friar in that city in 1494 by cultivating his memory and condemning in the Chronicles of the Convent of Santo Spirito the violence that had been done to him.

In the meantime, from Florence, where the fire had been kindled, came fresh fuel for the flames. In 1499 the sermons on Micah came out, edited by Violi and printed by Antonio Tubini; but even earlier a summary of the prophecies contained in the Lenten sermons of 1496 had been printed there, under the inaccurate title of *Sunto e registro delle prediche* (*Summary and Catalogue of the Prophecies*). This compendium anticipated by many years the summary made, probably in 1528, by the great historian Francesco Guicciardini, who listed the prophecies of the five collections of Savonarola's sermons then known (*Psalms, Amos, Micah, Ezekiel, Exodus*). Also in Florence in the last two years of the century, there were printed many editions of single sermons and short works by the Friar, which, as they were issued without typographical indications, were difficult to trace and prosecute. Some of these were printed in the same unidentified type used for the commentary on the psalm '*Verba mea*'; and I should not be surprised if they were the work of the very monks of the convents subjected to inquisition on account of this publication. In these convents, meanwhile, matters went on as before.

The General continued to issue his decrees, but to no avail: it was like talking to the deaf. On the 29th of June, full of indignation, he wrote to the Vicar, Fra Iacopo da Sicilia, and to all the priors of the Congregation, saying that he had heard that on the anniversary of the martyrdom of Savonarola they had 'celebrated *Totum duplex*'. Perhaps as early as those days one of those special Offices had already been composed, which were recited on the 23rd of May. 'Which practice,' Torriani exclaims in fury, 'I will in no wise tolerate. If the prisons, censure, or privations of the Order are not sufficient, I shall hand over anyone who falls into such error to the judge in ordinary of the Supreme Pontiff. . . .' He was certainly wasting his time, as the Vicar General, Fra Iacopo da Sicilia, to whom these orders were addressed and whose duty it was to see that they were carried out, was the first to do just the opposite. We know that he sought out the relics of Savonarola, but to venerate them, not to destroy them; and with his own hand set down the miracles obtained, after having investigated the evidence in each case. It was for him that Fra Placido Cinozzi wrote the oldest and least orderly biography of the Friar.

When it was at last realized that no violent persecution of the Piagnoni friars could be expected from this Vicar, he was replaced at the expiration of his office by Fra Malatesta Sacramoro, the 'Judas of San Marco', who immediately gave such proof of his zeal that the General, seeing that he could rely on him, gave him powers to extend or modify the ordinances made against the Piagnoni. Shortly afterwards Torriani died, but his successor, Vincenzo Bandelli, went on with his policy of attacking everything that recalled the memory of Fra Girolamo. He again forbade the singing of the psalm 'Ecce quam bonum', and even (which seems somewhat absurd) had the friars' habits lengthened and their scapulars made fuller, laying down the exact measurements they were to have, so as to destroy the last signs of that holy poverty introduced by Savonarola. In all this he had the enthusiastic support of Fra Malatesta. This friar, whether from hatred of Savonarola or love of his own comfort, did not like a rigid observance of the Rule, and did his best to weaken it; he even attempted, but with no success, to have San Marco joined again to the Lombard Congregation.

There are many indications, among them especially the subsequent orders issued by the Generals, that the cult of Savonarola was not in any way diminished by those measures. Indeed, like other persecuted causes, it seemed rather to flourish. The psalm 'Ecce quam bonum' continued to be sung as before. Soon afterwards, the fine musician Verdelot set in the canon of one of his motets the 'sweet song', that popular air to which the psalms had been sung since the days of Savonarola. Artists of all kinds, whose sensitive imaginations had been fascinated by Savonarola in his lifetime, were so shaken by his death that some of them put away their brushes and chisels for a while. This had happened to Sandro Botticelli even before Savonarola's death, so absorbed did he become in the Friar's teaching; but later he gave full expression to his grief by painting a symbolic 'Derelitta' weeping over the three martyrs. In a similar vein, the poet Marcantonio Flaminio later depicted Religion weeping over the pyre of Savonarola. Not long after, Bartolommeo della Porta took the Dominican habit, and Baccio da Montelupo in desperation fled into exile; Cronaca 'had become so obsessed with everything to do with Fra Girolamo Savonarola that he would speak of nothing else'; while the great Michelangelo, in the solitude of his genius, reverently pondered over the Friar's words. Many of these artists went on honouring his memory, representing him in paintings, medallions, and cameos. Sometimes it was done openly, as by Bartolommeo della Porta, who put on a brave inscription: '*a Deo missi prophetæ effigies*'—'portrait of a prophet sent by God'; sometimes he was portrayed in the disguise of some saint, most frequently in large compositions destined as altar-pieces, as was done by Fra Paolino del Signoraccio. He worked in the convent of San Domenico in Pistoia, where, as we have seen, the hidden fires of devotion for the Friar were still burning.

While in the convents of Tuscany (though not only in Tuscany) the cult of Savonarola was increasing secretly despite persecution from the General, in the Florentine Republic the Piagnone party had already raised its head again. In the autumn of 1499 the first signs had been seen: the brothers of San Marco were reinstated in their privileges, and those who had been banished were being repatriated. In the city the prophecies of Fra Girolamo were discussed openly, and they seemed all to be coming true one by one. For the months of November and December the Piagnone Giovambattista Ridolfi was elected gonfalonier; and it was not two years since his fellow-citizens had been on the point of burning down his house! The first thing that he tried to do, 'wishing to ensure the safety of the Friar's party, which was again flourishing', and to avenge the Friar, was to get rid of Doffo Spini by accusing him of sodomy. But he was not successful, for the Arrabbiati gave their full support to the former leader of the Compagnacci. A short time after, Giovan Francesco Poggio was banished. He had been the author of the libel against Savonarola which was reprinted after the Friar's death with the addition of a Latin translation of the first falsified trial.

At that period the Friar's party and his influence were assisted much more by the resounding victories of the King of France. He had marched into Italy and, with the utmost ease and dispatch, had taken the Duchy of Milan; a year later he took prisoner the Duke himself and sent him back to France, where he ended his days in a prison unworthy of so great a prince but richly deserved by his actions. Now

Parenti, and the Arrabbiati with him, were congratulating themselves
on not having given up their friendship with the King for an alliance
with the Duke, as they had once wanted to do and would have done
if Savonarola had not opposed it at the cost of his life.

Once again everything seemed to prove that he was right. What
caused even greater wonderment was that the principal authors of his
downfall had died one after the other within a very few years: Fra
Mariano (December 14, 1498), Ponzo (May 13, 1499), the forger Ser
Ceccone (1499), the General Torriani (August 1, 1500), Francesco
Mei (November 28, 1500). On the 29th of May, 1503, the executioner
who had ill-treated and mocked the body of the martyr was stoned to
death, and his own body was dragged through the streets by crowds of
youths. Finally, on the 18th of August of the same year, Alexander VI
died, and his body was also honoured in the fine way that history recounts. It really seemed that a prompt and implacable justice descended
upon the authors of so much injustice. We find that Lodovico Sforza in
his prison, where he had all the time in the world to think over the disasters Savonarola had predicted for him, is supposed to have said to
some Florentine merchants: 'Tell the Florentines that the Friar was
right, and that for me he was a true prophet.' As the news of this spread,
the memory of Fra Girolamo progressed in fame and veneration, and
his followers acquired new faith and inspiration.

Their hopes were raised especially when, after the short papacy
of Pius III, the throne of Peter was ascended by Giuliano della Rovere,
once an admirer of the Friar and a bitter enemy of Alexander VI, to
whose memory one might say the Bull of the 14th of January, 1505, is
dedicated. This Bull, which was ratified by the Lateran Council, declared null and void every simoniacal election to the papacy. It is not
surpising if the Pope, who thus condemned the man who had sent
Savonarola to his doom, said one day in Santa Maria della Quercia
near Viterbo, in the presence of several friars, that he would gladly
have canonized the Friar.

Canonization was again mentioned in 1511, but not by the Pope.
This was in Pisa, where a secret council of twelve cardinals inimical
to Julius II met with the pretext of considering the reform of the
Church. Cardinal Carvaial, who was the instigator of the whole business, tried to win over the Piagnoni, who were now most influential
in Florentine territory. Incidentally, Pisa, as Savonarola had promised,

had been restored in the meantime to Florence. Carvaial promised them the beatification of the Friar; but they, faithful to the teaching of their Master who had been unwilling to blot his allegiance to the Roman Church at any price, refused to join the schismatic cardinals, and in fact resolutely opposed them.

After the death of Julius II, he was succeeded by Giovanni de' Medici, who took the name Leo X. The Friar had so fiercely opposed the new Pope's father and brother that the question of canonization, naturally, was no longer mentioned, not even casually, as perhaps it had been by his predecessor. At the time of Leo X there was a great falling off in devotion and observance of the rule in that Congregation of which Savonarola was the ideal patron. In the convent of San Marco itself, many monks joined the Medici party and sought honours and office from that great and amiable corruptor of men, the only true son of Lorenzo the Magnificent. This caused the anonymous biographer to conclude his life of the Friar with a bitter lament, repeating with Jeremiah (Lam. v, 16): '*Mœstum est cor meum, quia cecidit corona capitis mei*'—'The joy of our heart is ceased, . . . the crown is fallen from our head.'

Before acquiring the papacy, Giovanni de' Medici had regained for his family the rule of Florence. And so, besides his religious work, Savonarola's political work in Florence was destroyed. Cardinal Giulio de' Medici, Archbishop of Florence, who was the spiritual and— what was more important to the Pope—the temporal governor of the city, behaved with great circumspection. He made a show of seeking the company of the chief Piagnoni, among them Girolamo Benivieni, who then and for a long time afterwards cherished the illusion of converting him to the cause of the Friar.

Nonetheless, in February 1515 the inquisitor Fra Gherardo, a conventual Franciscan from Santa Croce, ordered on behalf of the Archbishop that anyone who possessed 'ashes or bones or teeth or effigies or images or other relics of writings of the said Fra Girolamo, which had already been forbidden, should take them to the Vicar of the Archbishop; otherwise, after a certain number of days, it would be regarded as an offence and would be punished. . . .' Parenti, however, who tells us of these fresh persecutions, adds: 'In effect, it was impossible to extinguish here in Florence the belief in the saintliness of Fra Girolamo.'

In spite of this, or rather because of it, during a visit to the city in 1516, Leo X, either put up to it by his relatives and friends or perhaps by the old enemies of the Friar, ordered the Vicar and Chapter of Florence to proceed to a re-examination of Savonarola's doctrine. Before the case was brought before the Lateran Council, where it was defended and won by Savonarola's old devotee Giorgio Benigno, the Bosnian Minorite who had since become Archbishop of Nazareth, it was examined in the Florentine Synod, and on this occasion opinions were sought from many theologians, some of which have come down to us. There was certainly some disagreement, but Savonarola's doctrine came through the test once again uncensured and justified (and it could not have been otherwise). So much so, that a speech in his defence composed by Lorenzo Maccagnini was not even delivered before the Synod, as the adversaries, 'siezed with fear', had abandoned the field. A more extensive and efficacious *Opusculum in defensionis fratris Hieronymi . . . tempore Synodi florentinæ* was composed by that Fra Luca Bettini, a Piagnone and son of a Piagnone, who is already known to us as the clandestine editor of the Master's sermons. This, too, I believe, was never spoken, but was composed for the author's own satisfaction, or to assist the defence, or in some way to help the cause.

The year before, Bettini had rendered a great service to the Friar's memory, and to Savonarolan studies, by publishing in Bologna the sermons *On the Psalms* and *On Ezekiel,* of which he had borrowed the manuscripts 'for a couple of days' from the jealous Violi. The edition was in a sense furtive on account of this deception, but in every other respect Bettini behaved all too openly. Instead of hiding his part in the matter, as he might easily have done, he printed his own name in the front of the two volumes, and provided each of them with an introduction. As if this were not enough, he put in the preface to the sermons on the psalms that Savonarola was a prophet sent by God. His courageous action cost him dear: when he was elected Vicar General of the Congregation by the brothers in Chapter (perhaps as much for his devotion to Savonarola as for his other qualities), the Master General, at that time the celebrated Gaetano, vetoed the election. The reasons given were the extreme youth of the candidate (he was only twenty-eight) and principally, though mentioned in second place, the publications in Bologna. At first the friars objected to this veto, but

Gaetano, who had recently sworn not to allow any supporter of the Piagnoni to be elected Prior of San Marco, stood firm in his decision and openly declared that the cause of it was that introduction. He then gave express instructions to Bettini not to publish anything without special permission from the Master General—i.e. from himself.

However, whether his superiors had learned of other works of his circulating in manuscript (for instance, the above-mentioned opuscule *In defensionem* and another entitled *Oracolo della rinnovazione della Chiesa*), or whether he had sustained with the same frankness and imprudence ideas of a similar nature in sermons or disputations, he got into hot water with his superiors, and only flight saved him from the horrors of monastic prison. He was lovingly taken in by his companion in faith Giovan Francesco Pico. Expelled from the Congregation in 1526, he died in the following year.

A worse fate, but greater merit, was brought upon himself by Fra Benedetto Luschino. After his first faltering, his zeal rose even higher, and in 1500 he had written a short work entitled *De carnali homine et rationali,* praising the Master, which brought him endless misfortunes and miseries. The work circulated in manuscript and anonymously for several years until, finally, the name of the author became known; and at the time of which we are now writing, Fra Benedetto, after ups and downs which there would be no point in recounting here, was already languishing in a dreadful underground cell in San Marco, where he wrote, among other things, his short poem entitled *Cedrus Libani* (1510) and his *Vulnera Diligentis* (begun in 1515). The first of these tells in tercets of small literary worth the story of the life of the Friar and his own. The second is a somewhat long-winded but most valuable apology for the Master, even if, as a source, it must be used with caution, owing to the fanatical devotion of the author.

In the meantime, although the citizens were led astray or corrupted spiritually and materially by the Medici government (not so much, however, the lower classes and people's party), the profound devotion for Fra Girolamo continued to flourish in Florence. It was the refuge of all those who secretly nurtured the ideal of liberty. Already inclined that way were Boscoli and Capponi, who had conspired against Cardinal Giovanni de' Medici in 1513 on the eve of his election to the papacy. Another convert to the Friar's party, though inspired by less noble sentiments, was that unruly Battista della Palla, who in

1522 conspired against Cardinal Giulio and the Medici government. He took refuge in France when this cardinal, elected Pope in his turn with the name Clement VII, gave little hope of fulfilling the hopes of him nurtured by Benivieni and other Piagnoni friends. There Battista, who was already inclined 'to the doctrine, saintliness, and, above all, the prophecies of Fra Girolamo', made himself their apostle at court, and managed to convert and direct 'into the paths of truth and spiritual consolation' the King's sister, the celebrated Marguerite, later Queen of Navarre. In this way the Friar again made his influence felt at the Court of France.

The really triumphal return of Savonarola came in the year 1527 after the terrible sack of Rome by the imperial troops. Rome was in effect thrown into confusion, as he had prophesied; and while the Pope was a prisoner in Castel Sant'Angelo, the Florentines on the 16th of May threw off the Medici yoke for the second time and regained their liberty. 'It would be hard to describe and scarce possible to believe with what gladness . . . men and women, young and old, noble and plebeian, priest and layman, gave themselves to rejoicing, and how quickly the belief revived, nay, multiplied a thousandfold, that Fra Girolamo had been a saint and a prophet. . . .' In that time of joy, citizens fell into each other's arms, and the Friar's name was on everyone's lips, especially when, with the same urgency and pleasure as the last time, they all lent a hand to put in order the hall of the Great Council.

San Marco once more became the heart of the city, and the Republic was governed from the convent no less than from the Palace. But, now that there was no Savonarola at the convent (he had, in any case, never willingly interfered in the government), this could neither please the wiser citizens nor serve the best interests of the city. Niccolò Capponi was elected gonfalonier for a year, a convinced Piagnone despite the doubts of Varchi; and the Friar's reputation grew greater under his direction of affairs. So much so that on the 9th of February, 1528, after the gonfalonier in the hall of the Great Council had 'recited more or less word for word one of the sermons in which the Friar foretells and promises, first, great evil and then great good for the city of Florence', he threw himself on his knees, crying: '*Misericordia!*' and the cry was taken up by the whole of the Council. He then proposed that Christ should be accepted as King of Florence. The election, which repeated that proposed by Savonarola, was carried at once, and was recorded in a tablet placed on the façade of the Palace.

After Capponi's term of office the city remained firm in its devotion to Savonarola. Two Dominican preachers who were then very popular, encouraged that devotion every day with their eloquence. They were Fra Zaccaria della Lunigiana, of the convent of San Marco, and Fra Benedetto da Foiano, of Santa Maria Novella. Thus, even the convent that had so bitterly opposed Fra Girolamo was reconciled to him in the purity of a glory *igne examinata,* proved by fire, and in the name of liberty.

At the same time, the reviving power of Clement VII foretold difficult days for the Republic, and the rash, vainglorious conduct of the Florentine government brought them even nearer. The imperial and papal armies came and laid siege to the city, which had prepared its defences in high spirits, almost impatient to come to the final test. Whether it was true or false, great importance was attached to the prophecy which the Friar was said to have made to Niccolini on the eve of his execution, to the effect that the greatest tribulation would fall on Florence at the time of a Pope called Clement. Now the armies of Clement were at their gates, and the Florentines sang:

> *Oh quanto è gran dolore*
> *che a sì crudel destino*
> *meni la madre patria*
> *un papa, un cittadino.*
> *Ma di tener Fiorenza*
> *non avrai, papa, il vanto;*
> *o tu l'avrai morente*
> *per darle l'olio santo.*[1]

This strange and highly civilized people for ten months set an example of military and warlike virtues such as had not been seen in Italy for many years. And the banner of their heroic but unavailing defence bore the name of Savonarola.

In April 1530, as the city was almost at the end of its strength, Lorenzo Ridolfi, a doctor of law, proposed to the Council of Eighty

[1] 'Oh, how grievous that a Pope, one of her own citizens, should bring the mother country to so cruel a fate! But you, Pope, shall never boast the possession of Florence; or you will take her dying, in time to give her extreme unction.'

that the papers of the trial of Fra Girolamo should be removed from the records of the Camera del Comune as a shameful thing; 'and he explained his proposal, saying that everything that had been done by the Florentines against the Friar had been done against God'. This proposal was carried out, and I fear that I cannot feel grateful to that ancestor of mine, in spite of his noble intentions. Although the papers concerned were of that despicable falsified trial, yet an expert modern eye might have been able to discern in them, if not the distortion of the martyr's thought, at least the lies that were interpolated, after they were signed, by the hand of the cunning notary.

The fall of the city saw, too, the fall of the spirits of the inhabitants and of the fortunes of Savonarola; at the same time, public persecution began afresh. The most ardent lovers of liberty were exiled, despite the terms of the capitulation. Few of these were not also among the Friar's most ardent supporters. Fra Zaccaria died, it was said by poison; but Fra Benedetto da Foiano was imprisoned in Castel Sant'Angelo on the express order of the Pope, who there let him die of hunger. It makes one think this was probably the 'humane' treatment that his predecessor Alexander promised to give Savonarola if he had been sent to Rome. Yet, not even the tyrannies and violent revenges of 'Papa Che-mente' ('the lying Pope'), as the Florentines called him, sufficed to destroy the illusions of the now eighty-year-old Girolamo Benivieni, who addressed to the victorious Pontiff that long letter which is a statement and exposition of the Friar's prophecies, designed to prove to him that the Friar was a true prophet sent by God.

Naturally, it was wasted ink. Not many years later the Piagnoni were able to rejoice in the death of the Medici Pope (1534), and even more in the killing of his bastard son Alexander, to whom he had given the rule of Florence. These rejoicings of the Piagnoni in particular, and the Florentines in general, are recorded by historians. They were not too discouraged, in their great faith, by the election of Cosimo, who was as great an enemy as any of the memory of the Friar and the convent of San Marco. As this convent had remained the city's last refuge and stronghold of all ideas of liberty, Cosimo one day had the friars ejected (1545); but he was firmly opposed by Paul III and forced to restore them, with no small loss to his prestige. To no avail did he remind the Pope through his ambassador Alessandro del Caccia that Fra Girolamo had been burned by one of Paul's predecessors; that Savonarola's doctrine was supposed to be heretical; that his exposition of the '*Miserere*' had been reprinted in Germany with an introduction by Luther (1523), who regarded Savonarola as a precursor; or, finally, that there was an idolatrous cult of the Friar in San Marco. Had he but known it, he who was usually so well informed, he could have told the Pope of the idolatrous cult being practised at that time in San Vincenzo at Prato by Santa Caterina de' Ricci. She celebrated his feast every year on the 23rd of May, since she had twice attributed her recovery from serious illness to the miraculous intervention of Savonarola, whose intercessions she had sought. But to return to San Marco: the Pope stood firm, and Cosimo had to be content with minor acts of revenge.

If I have spoken at such length of the fortunes of Fra Girolamo in Florence, it is because these political vicissitudes are the most obvious and well-known expression both of the increasing veneration for the Prophet of San Marco, and of the fears which that cult aroused. It is also because San Marco and Florence were still the centre from which that veneration was unceasingly spread abroad. It must not, however, be thought that elsewhere Savonarola's name was forgotten. The opposite is proved by the innumerable editions of his works which multiplied in and outside Italy. The many German editions and translations brought out by the Protestants, who presumed unjustifiably to use his great name to increase the reputation of their movement, form a group apart. Even in Catholic France and Spain his works were being printed, though these foreign editions are few in comparison with the countless ones which were made in Italian cities, and especially in that great emporium of books, Venice.

Not many editions of Savonarola had been printed in Venice in the fifteenth century. From 1503, however, as the fame of Fra Girolamo increased rather than diminished and the number of readers of his works also grew, the printer Lazzaro Soardi, who was first to perceive the fat profits to be made, began to publish, a volume at a time, an almost complete collection of the works and sermons of Savonarola then known, in octavo and in quarto; and each of the works he reprinted several times. He was soon followed by Arrivabene, who specialized, however, in editions of the sermons. The bitterness of his references, in the colophons of these editions, to the colleague who had got in before him, show the importance of the undertaking and the size of the profit. Both were followed by Bindoni, who succeeded in putting together an almost complete edition—in fact, the most complete collection of Savonarola's works—all in small format. Many other Venetian typographers printed a good number of the works: Scoto, Benalio, Zanni, Volpini, Nicolini da Sabio, the printing-houses 'all' insegna del Pozzo' and 'all 'insegna della Speranza', and others. But here we are more particularly concerned to show which printers were most active in publishing as complete an edition as possible of Savonarola's works. Briefly, in Venice the editions of the Friar's works and sermons number more than a hundred during the first half of the sixteenth century alone. And, as the printers put out what would sell, and what sold best was what was most read, one could not desire more certain proof of the vast diffusion throughout all Europe of the teachings and the fame of Savonarola. This is an aspect of his ever-increasing fortune, which is more important, though less striking, than any we have considered up to now.

The sermons were the most read. Fra Cristoforo Peraccini da Pistoia compiled and published in Siena in 1543 a most useful table of contents, or, rather, a kind of concordance. The inquisitors up to that time had placed no obstacle in the way of all these editions and re-editions, not even those of the sermons containing the strongest criticisms of the Court of Rome. On the contrary, the first edition of the sermons on the psalm 'Quam bonus', translated by Fra Girolamo Giannotti, was issued, as we read in the colophon, 'by the care and industry of the venerable father Fra Girolamo Armenino da Faenza, inquisitor in Lombardy against the heretics, diligently revised and sent to the printer for the satisfaction of many who desire to see it published'.

Encouraged by so much popularity, printers and Piagnoni alike set themselves to collect together even the fragments of Savonarola's writings; and finally they began to print also the Latin schemes of his sermons, either in the original text or after translating them and filling them out. These were then passed off as texts taken down verbatim. The collections of sermons were also much sought after by preachers as sermon books, which increased their sale. At the same time, the widespread sale also increased the diffusion of the Friar's teaching.

At this period, however, amid all the vast output of printed matter, apologies and refutations of the Friar's teaching are very few. Before the already mentioned Oracolo della rinnovazione della Chiesa

by Bettini, published posthumously by his brother, Francesco Caloro
had brought out, in 1513, his *Defensione*. At the same time, Giovan
Francesco Pico (first version before 1520, and second about 1530) and
the anonymous biographer (1528-9) both wrote their lives of Savonarola, but kept them jealously hidden, or circulated them in manuscript
to a few trustworthy readers. Pico's was not published until the seven-
teenth century, and the other not until the end of the eighteenth
century. San Filippo Neri himself had sought to have the latter published, but this had been opposed about 1580 by Alessandro de' Medici,
Archbishop of Florence. The Latin life, of which this is merely a
translation, also remained unpublished. And so Germany was to have
the honour of being the first to publish a biography of the Friar, in
1556, in a miserable little book by Spangenberg. In short, after Savonarola's execution, support and praise appear far to outweigh criticism
and vituperation.

Ambrogio Catarino Politi was a restless, vain, litigious Sienese
endowed with those virtues which Dante noted in the city of Sapìa.
Formerly a lawyer, he became at the age of thirty a monk in San Marco,
a Piagnone, and a theologian. Very soon he came into open conflict
with the brethren of his own Order, and eventually with the tradition
of Savonarola. Having achieved greater independence by becoming
Bishop of Minori, he published in 1548 a *Discorso contro la dottrina e la
profezia di Fra Girolamo Savonarola* (*Discourse on the Doctrine and Prophecy of Fra Girolamo Savonarola*), in which he undertook no less a task
than to convict the Friar of heresy. He was not new to tricks of this
kind, for shortly before, he had undertaken to show that the greatest
theologian of his time, Tommaso Gaetano, General of his own Order,
was tainted with Lutheranism! He saw heretics everywhere, and had
no difficulty in proving his suspicions, in his own way, as he was
one of those theologians who—not so much by employing sophisms
as by picking out certain isolated propositions divorced from their
context, noting in them any least apparent or contingent contradiction,
and hustling them into order like a policeman with his criminals—
succeed in proving anything they like. With such a method Catarino
could have convicted of heresy not just Savonarola, but St. Augustine
and St. Jerome, not to mention St. Thomas—for, though the Sienese
friar never in fact undertook to prove his heresy, I am inclined to
believe he would have been quite happy to do so.

It was also a clever move, because the sacrosanct Council was sitting at the time to establish the dogma and the purification of the Church, having been moved from Trent to Bologna. Catarino had no small part in this, for he had given the opening speech at the third session. Though the Synod was then suspended, it was inevitable that sooner or later it would resume its great mission. In the circumstances, Catarino's book might easily influence those of the prelates gathered together who knew only that little of the life of the Friar which was liable to be misinterpreted, and of his works only those passages which Catarino had skewered on the point of his pen. Truly, the ignorant were, are, and always will be the only enemies of Savonarola, the only slanderers of his doctrine.

This little work was almost universally disliked for its patent animosity and its not very well concealed fallacies; it also displeased the superiors of the Order, and even those who had no affection for the great Friar. The author acknowledged this himself in a letter of complaint on the matter, written to Bishop Pandolfini on the 16th of February, 1548: 'I was expecting some commotion of the waters, but not such a hailstorm as this. . . . Since that blessed *Discorso*, so many tongues are ready to tear me, it's a sorry business. . . . .' It was even said that Catarino had been summoned to Rome *ad se purgandum*, and that the *Discorso* had been bannned. Hence in the same letter to Pandolfini he offers a very ready obedience, in contrast to the 'true disobedience' of the Friar: 'I shall not flee, or do like Savonarola, who excused himself on the grounds of infirmity.' It does not seem impossible, although he denied it, that Catarino undertook this task to please Duke Cosimo, who had found no other means of avenging his recent discomfiture at the hands of the friars of San Marco and the hated memory of their prophet.

These follies of Catarino were dangerous on account of the circumstances already described, and because follies of this kind usually are dangerous. The first to refute him was Fra Benedetto, of whose early ardour nothing had been lost, in spite of his eighty years, in the long privations of imprisonment from which he had but lately been released. He composed an *Apologia,* which he sent to the '*Maestro del sacro palazzo*' [head of the Vatican censorship]; and the following year he also presented it to the fathers of the Council of Trent, as it was to them that Catarino had addressed his *Discorso* with evil intent. Sounder in its doctrine, and more effective because it appeared in

print, if a little late, was the *Apologia* written by Fra Tommaso Neri,
who point by point and with the greatest of ease refuted everything
in the *Discorso*. We find that even Lisa Deti, mother of Cardinal
Ippolito Aldobrandini, expressed her intention to reply to Catarino.
When the Pope heard of this, he said with a smile: 'If even women
take up their pens to defend Savonarola, what should learned men do?'

However, the bad seed cast by Catarino did give some bad fruits
at that time, though truth was to prevail in the end. What happened
was this: in 1557, while the *Index* bearing the name of its instigator,
Paul IV, was being compiled, Giacomo Laynez, later General of the
Company of Jesus, presented to the Pope a weighty act of accusation
against Savonarola. This, alas, was compiled, as usual at second-hand,
from the tendentious *excerpta* of Catarino; and Laynez thought he had
done something wonderful! He was confirmed in this belief when
some of these diligently extracted propositions were read out in the
Consistory and the Pope exclaimed: 'Yes, yes, indeed, this is another
Martin Luther! This man's doctrine is deadly! And what are you doing,
what are you thinking of, reverend cardinals, where are your eyes?
Do you not see that this mortal doctrine must be prohibited absolutely?' And, 'stamping his feet with indignation', he added 'that if
he had to die in the attempt, he would see Savonarola subordinated to
the Holy See, with all the other heretics, because Jesus Christ commanded that all should obey Him'. The Consistory agreed; but Cardinal
Ghislieri, a Dominican and the future Pope Pius V, replied with
dignity: 'Holy Father, we will do our duty, and give these criticisms
into the hands of learned men of our office, as we have done with the
other books.'

As a result, the cause seemed lost. Politi's little book had become
the bible of the Friar's enemies, and, using this source, they busily
presented the examiners with objectionable passages duly com-
mentated. But sometimes it happened that when they were asked what
came before or after, or for more details, they were lost in confusion,
as they knew no more than the bits they had prepared. On other
occasions, when the original text was referred to, it was found to have
been altered. On this account the cardinals took the accusers severely to
task: 'Why then do you condemn that which you do not know?' Many
also spoke up openly in defence of Savonarola. He had no advocate
more active and tenacious than Fra Paolino Bernardini da Lucca, who

possessed great knowledge of theology, courage and goodness of heart, and, what is more, a profound and first-hand acquaintance with Savonarola's works, which none of the accusers had. It was, therefore, easy for him to dismantle piece by piece the war machine constructed by Catarino and his successors. To take just one passage, already referred to in these pages: Laynez had commented indignantly on those words of the Lenten sermon *On Ezekiel,* 'the harlot of the Church'. Bernardini naturally took the opportunity to quote the preacher's subsequent justification of the phrase (omitted, of course, by Catarino), in which he cited the passage from the commentary of St. Jerome from which it was derived. For good measure, Bernardini also reminded the Jesuit that he had used very similar terms in one of his own sermons. At this, Laynez 'was struck dumb, and never dared to open his mouth again, or scarcely to raise his eyes'. In the subsequent debate on the question of 'disobedience', Bernardini quoted, among other arguments, a letter of St. Bernard, in which he says that one should not obey the Pope against charity. 'If St. Bernard says that,' cried Cardinal Alessandrino in a terrible voice, 'we must put him on the *Index* as well.'

This was on the eve of Christmas 1558, and these matters were more than ever hotly debated and canvassed. At that time 'it was a wonderful and astonishing thing to see the whole city of Rome agitated and in confusion on this account, and it was publicly discussed even in the banks and among the shopkeepers'. The Friar's works, too, were in great demand. So even the great reprobate of former days was at last conquered! While the cardinals of the Inquisition were meeting, the brothers of the convent of Santa Maria sopra Minerva, who had no less devotion for Savonarola than those of the Tuscan convents (especially since they had been joined by Fra Timoteo Bottonio, who compiled his own version of the *Life,* which was subsequently known under the name of Burlamacchi), gathered in prayer before the high altar. Likewise, the nuns of the Order in their convents and many laymen in other places in Rome offered the prayers of the forty-hour sacrament. Among those praying at the convent of the Minerva was Filippo Neri, who was deeply devoted to Savonarola and kept in his cell an image of him surrounded by rays of light, and all his works, which he constantly re-read and annotated with his own hand. On the morning on which the question of Savonarola was decided in the Congregation, and at the very hour, before news could have leaked out, suddenly Filippo arose joyfully from his prayers, and, *Deo revelante,* as the future Pope Benedict XIV wrote, he cried out: 'Oh, let us give thanks to the Highest! We have won! In vain have our adversaries attacked Girolamo and his doctrine: it remains unshaken, confirmed by the judgment of Our Lord and the Church.'

It had indeed emerged unshaken. However, so many prelates of high standing, including the Pope himself, had committed themselves to the opposite view that, to satisfy them (as it was openly suggested), some few sermons and the dialogue *De veritate prophetica* were suspended with the formula *donec emendata prodeant.* In these works, as the Cardinal of Trani observed, there were a few things which, 'though true, were ill understood by the common people'. In substance, the Congregation agreed to the proposals of Bernardini himself: that when the works of Fra Girolamo were published, the suspended passages should be accompanied by suitable glosses. San Filippo Neri might well cry victory. It is relevant to mention here that, like so many other followers of Savonarola, the courageous Bernardini, to whom miracles were attributed, died in the odour of sanctity.

After this victory, the cult and the fortunes of the Friar prospered for many years without being disturbed by further persecutions. We can hardly describe as such the barbarous snippings of the inquisitors' scissors in the sermons suspended in the *Index* of Paul IV, in every copy that fell into their hands. We can also discount the few discordant voices raised against him in some convents of the Orders traditionally hostile to Savonarola—as, for example, that of the Franciscan, Francesco Pulinari. In 1578 he was foolish enough, in his *Ricordi,* to deny the Friar not only saintliness and virtue but also those other qualities which men of quite different outlook recognized in him. He was not even ashamed to describe so great a man as 'a wretched friar of no importance'. Perhaps it never crossed his mind that later readers of his rubbish, of whatever faith or opinion they might be, would unanimously agree that the description fitted a Pulinari, but not a Savonarola.

Yet an attempt was made in 1583, though restricted to the Grand Duchy of Tuscany, to revive the war against Savonarola's memory. Alessandro de' Medici, Archbishop of Florence, was behind the move; and the Friar's adherents could hardly have expected anything more from this new joining of the spiritual and temporal power in the hands of the Medici family. How and with what energy the Archbishop attacked everything pertaining to the Friar, he himself relates with pride in his letter of the 26th of August, 1583, to the Grand Duke Francesco. The letter was written when, seeing that he was powerless to overcome the Friar's supporters by himself, he decided to ask the sovereign's help.

'The memory of Fra Girolamo,' wrote the worthy Archbishop, 'revives, multiplies, and is more flourishing than it has ever been . . .; they surreptitiously say the Office for him as though he were a martyr, they keep his relics as though he were a saint . . .; they make images of him in bronze, in gold, in cameos, and in prints, and, what is worse, they put on them inscriptions like Martyr, Prophet, Virgin, and Doctor. In the past I have done what my office required, to put an end to such things: I had the printing-blocks broken up, and had Fra Bernardo da Castiglione, who had designed them and had them made, removed from San Marco and sent to Viterbo, where he died. I prevented his likeness being painted in the cloisters of Santa Maria Novella among the saints of the Order. I prevented the summary of his life and miracles from being printed. I have put fear into the friars; I had them reprimanded, punished, and given penance by their superiors. . . .'

The better to influence the Grand Duke, the zealous Archbishop insinuated what was in any case perfectly true: that the friends of the Friar were the enemies of the Medici government, and that Pandolfo Pucci, who was hanged in 1560 for the conspiracy to murder Cosimo, was most devoted to the memory of Savonarola and used to read his works with his fellow-conspirators. Francesco I, who was extremely sensitive to such arguments, not only sent the Archbishop a letter of thanks, but expressed his indignation to the Pope. The Pope then complained to Fra Sisto Fabbri, General of the Dominican Order, and he came post-haste to Tuscany. There, in Chapter, he renewed the usual vetoes in general terms, and in private reinforced them with some more particular reproaches. But the friars of San Marco and the nuns of San Vincenzo seemed to be deaf when this kind of tune was played; it was so different from the 'sweet song' of the psalm 'Ecce quam bonum'. The friars of other Tuscan convents were evidently no less hard of hearing, for two years later the same General heard, possibly through the channels of the same zealous Archbishop, that his admonitions had had no effect, and he repeated them, this time more explicitly, in a letter of the 5th of April, 1585: 'No one shall venture to mention in

the presence of friars, nuns, or seculars the name of Fra Girolamo Savonarola, nor discuss his life and miracles, or anything regarding him or
his companions in any way whatever; neither shall they keep portraits,
images, or things of any kind that relate to the appraisal of his life.
It is decreed under the same penalties . . . and, furthermore, under pain
of perpetual banishment from the place, in which they shall have dis-
obeyed, that within twenty-four hours the friars must surrender all
such objects which they may have kept in honour of Fra Girolamo to
their superior; and he will be responsible, under pain of the same
punishments, for holding them in deposit and giving an immediate
account of them to us.'

Perhaps Fabbri believed that, if his spoken words had gone for
naught, his written orders would have more permanent effect. But the
only thing that remained permanent and unshakeable was the cult of
Savonarola, and his supporters continued their devotion as before. It
was, if anything, intensified, especially when, in 1592, Cardinal Ippolito
Aldobrandini became Pope, as Clement VIII; his mother had been a
Piagnone, and he himself was very favourable to Fra Girolamo's cause.
There was again talk of canonization, and this time the cause seemed
won before it was even prosecuted. It was perhaps for this reason that
the General of the Order, Father Beccaria, commissioned in 1597 and
1598 three different friars, each to compose an Office specially for the
cult of Savonarola—that is, a different Office from that which up to
that time was being said in many convents every 23rd of May. The Pope
had already said, when he was asked by someone in Ferrara, that when
the necessary testimonies were presented to him, he would be ready
to do his duty. The good Serafino Razzi had already collected many
such testimonies in his *Life of Savonarola,* which he sent to the Pope,
begging him to have it published and to republish the works and sermons of the Friar. Everything seemed propitious, and the Pope favourably disposed. On the other hand, the zealous Archbishop of Florence,
in whose hands the Pope had placed Razzi's *Life* and his hopes, was
irrevocably opposed to any such project. Razzi, in his infinite in-
genuousness, had at first believed Cosimo to be 'fond' of Savonarola;
now, full of hope, he declared that the Cardinal de' Medici was 'a
devotee of the Father'! Dvoted as he was, the Archbishop again raised
objections to everything, and he told Razzi that, although everything
in his book was all right, it was better not to publish it because of the

opposition that Fra Girolamo still aroused. He added that he had followed the same course with San Filippo Neri, who had also wanted to publish a *Life* of Savonarola. Thus, the Friars had to be content to recite in secret those Offices which their General had had composed with greater hopes.

Only after the decrees of Urban VIII (1625 and 1634), perfected after the studies of Clement VIII and Paul V (the constitutions of Urban V having fallen into disuse), did the Dominicans of the Tuscan convents, in obedience to a necessary general disciplinary order issued by the supreme authority of the Church, give up readily, after having practised it for more than a hundred years, a cult that they had been unwilling to abandon on account of a particular unjust persecution directed against the memory of the man who had been venerated as a saint by so many saints of their own and other Orders. They gave up the exterior forms of reverence towards him, but not the reverence in their hearts, as the Church had never censured the same cult in San Filippo Neri and Santa Caterina de' Ricci. The proceedings for the canonization of the latter was yet another occasion to revive the memory of Savonarola and do him justice once again. Begun in 1624, this cause had been brought to a standstill by the new decrees of Urban VIII. Its difficult course was again resumed in 1675, and during the papacy of Benedict XIII the virtues of the Saint were examined. The advocate of the Faith, Prospero Lambertini, objected *eam peccasse* on account of the cult she had rendered to Savonarola, although no exception had been taken to this in the case of San Filippo Neri. However, this rock was surmounted by a papal decree commanding the examiners to pass over it. The decree was later confirmed by Clement XII and by Lambertini himself when he became Pope in his turn.

If the Friar was honoured at the altars for more than a hundred years, for more than two hundred the charming custom survived of strewing with grasses and flowers the spot on which the martyr gave up his noble soul. This tradition has been revived in our own day. It is generally believed to have been begun by the descendants of the murdered Valori, and continued until the family died out in 1690, after which it was carried on by Giacinto Maria Marmi until his death in 1703. It was Marmi who gave to the convent of San Marco the habit of Fra Girolamo, the one over which the Friar had uttered such moving words when it was taken from him before his execution. The Prior of

San Marco, no longer preoccupied with the old prohibitions, received this relic joyfully.

The fortunes of Savonarola in the succeeding centuries are fortunes of editions and critical works, where previously they were concerned with a cult and with political and ecclesiastical passions. Here we do not intend to discuss these studies of Savonarola, since others have already done so admirably. Nor can I, within the limits of this summary account, examine in detail the judgments passed on Savonarola by scholars, annalists, and men of letters. I shall, therefore, say nothing of Bzovio, Spondano, Muratori, Buddeus, and Bayle (though the sharply sceptical attitude of the latter in his famous *Dictionary* certainly had some influence on more than one writer of the eighteenth century). We cannot, however, pass in silence over the defence of the Friar composed by the learned Magliabechi and, what is more important, his plan for an edition of all the works. We must mention the edition of Pico's *Life,* to which Quétif joined some valuable *Additiones* of Savonarolan opuscules and documents, illustrated with sound erudition. Important also are certain editions of works of the Friar, among them one of the *Triumphus Crucis* and the *Expositio in psalmum 'Miserere'*, made under the auspices of *Propaganda Fide* in fulfilment of the terms of the will of Cardinal Antonio Barberini, a Franciscan and brother of Urban VIII, who left a legacy of 500 gold scudi for this particular purpose. The Bolandists in the *Acta Sanctorum* (1685), though deferring to the decision of the Church, inserted under the 23rd of May, among the *prætermissi* an honourable mention of Savonarola, expressing their astonishment (ironical rather than innocent) that the Dominican Order appeared to show so little interest in their celebrated member, as Quétif, who was one of them, had been content to refer to the Friar as 'Reverend Father'.

Villari informs us that in the following century the fame of Savonarola fell 'into absolute oblivion, almost into contempt', with the general scepticism of the times. If this is partly true, yet that century already contained the germs of a revival. One of these may be found in an anonymous work of little value written by the Florentine Modesto Rastrelli, who was probably led astray by the brilliance of Bayle's writing. Not a year had passed before a reply came in the shape of the *Storia del Padre Girolamo Savonarola* of P. Vincenzo Barsanti, also published anonymously—the first attempt to construct a modern biography of the Friar. I believe that this book, which cannot be said to lack certain qualities of seriousness and objectivity, had, even more than the *Apologia* of Bartoli, a beneficent influence right down to the famous *Histoire* of Sismondi. We are now on the eve of the great revival of Savonarolan studies, on the verge of what Gentile calls 'the resurrection of Savonarola'.

The first signs of this revival seemed to come from Germany with the biographies written from the Protestant viewpoint by Rudelbach and Meier, of which Meier's work improved on everything that had gone before, by its breadth of information. In Florence, however, where the love of the memory of Savonarola had never failed, there began to appear the promise of that fine, learned school of the 'new Piagnoni'. Once again the impulse came from San Marco, where lived Padre Marchese, whose works have been so frequently drawn upon in these pages, and Padre Corsetto. These men had the idea of extending and implementing the fine plan of Magliabechi, and of republishing all the works of the Friar with the approval of the Congregation of the *Index,* which would have been quite satisfied if the suspended passages were accompanied by suitable notes. In 1844 the edition was announced as being the work of the two Dominicans and Bartolommeo Aquarone; and in 1845 the first volume was issued, containing the sermons on the First Epistle of St. John and those on the psalm '*Quam bonus*', edited by Aquarone. Also in that year, an announcement in the annual catalogue of the Tipografia Galileiana gave an idea of what the complete edition would be: 'ten volumes of about 30 folios.' Then the Grand Ducal censorship, in this case far more rigid and illiberal than that of the Church, successfully impeded publication by constantly demanding corrections of every passage that appeared in sympathy with the 'subversive spirit of the age'. Shortly afterwards Marchese and Aquarone had to go into exile; and there is no doubt that the cause of the banishment of the former was his particular Savonarolan fervour.

Then Cesare Guasti, who became the standard-bearer of the Tuscan Piagnoni after the exile of Padre Marchese, got his father, Ranieri Guasti, a printer in Prato, to buy the orphaned first volume, and he published it with a different frontispiece. He did not give up the idea of the edition of the Friar's completed works, for which he again did battle in 1877.

In the meantime Carlo Capponi, a gentle and timid scholar, was making a valuable collection of early editions of Savonarola and issuing limited editions of bibliographies and unpublished documents. Luigi Passerini, the genealogist, was another who was then transcribing documents of this kind with great enthusiasm. Tommaseo was also among the number of these new Piagnoni. His great friend Gino Capponi had at first been hostile to Savonarola, on whom in 1822 he had written, but not published, a few pages that were unworthy and untrue. Old and blind as he was, he now, under the influence of the new studies, wished to have re-read to him the sermons and the documents of the Friar's life, which, according to his own confession, he had never studied. After this he rewrote in splendid fashion the chapter on the Friar in his *Storia della Repubblica Fiorentina*.

This is what had happened. The peaceful Tuscan Piagnoni had been aroused by the arrival in Florence of Pasquale Villari, who, under the influence of Padre Marchese and perhaps even of the very soil and air of the city, put his hand to Savonarolan studies. As his enthusiasm grew, he unconsciously turned into a Piagnone himself, as far as a Neapolitan transplanted to the banks of the Arno could be. In fact, he kept a certain reserve, and was regarded with some suspicion by those who were Piagnoni by birth and tradition. Nevertheless, it was he, and not the Tuscans, tireless editors and subtle illustrators of documents, who finally produced that great *Storia di Girolamo Savonarola e dei suoi tempi* (1861). This work, with its breadth of original research and more accurate interpretation of Savonarolan doctrine, left far behind the monographs of the German Protestants, and that of Perrens, which had come out in the meantime (1853) and which, though not badly documented, was weak, uncertain, riddled with mistakes, greatly influenced by the books of Rudelbach and Meier, and generally badly constructed; not to mention the negligible and turgid biography compiled by Aquarone (1857).

This work of Villari's was, therefore, the third extensive *Life* of the Friar to be published in the space of barely nine years. Well written, 'eloquent' according to the taste of the author, it really directed Savonarolan studies into new paths. It has four principal defects: First, it was written too soon, at a time when study of and research on the Friar were barely beginning, and the author could not do alone what required the labour of several generations of scholars. Second, and most serious, he did not consider sufficiently the monk, the great man of God, which is the essential character of Savonarola; without doing so, it is impossible to understand him, let alone write adequately about him. Third, also a grave defect, he shows us not the Catholic prophet, but a civil prophet, or rather, 'the prophet of the new civilization', and not so much a reformer of Christian morality as a reformer of human thought, the forerunner of modern times—which is as false as the opposite opinion that he was a throwback to the Middle Ages. Fourth, Villari (in spite of his own disbelief in the Friar's prophetic powers, his lack of concern for his saintliness, his irreverence towards the religious cult devoted to him) believed in the credulous and miracle-hunting biography that goes under the name of Burlamacchi. This was the age of the humanism of the classicists and the romanticism of the Neo-Guelphs. Judgment of Savonarola was to suffer from both these influences; and it is not surprising if, taking the opposite view from those who wished to make him a reactionary against the Renaissance, Villari saw in him a great civil innovator and could not fully appreciate him as the great Catholic renovator.

Although Villari's work leaves something to be desired as far as the interpretation of Savonarola's thought and a historical judgment on him are concerned, it buried beneath an immense weight of new documents and studies all the previous Savonarolan literature and, with it, many false judgments and countless prejudices. Thus, when in 1868 a statue of Savonarola was placed at the foot of the monument to Luther inaugurated at Worms, what thirty years before, at the time of the works of Rudelbach and Meier, might have seemed an error attributable to the false inferences of these two Protestant scholars, now seemed and was, after Villari's work, a stupid and gratuitous outrage to the memory of Savonarola. I do not say 'outrage' out of any religious intolerance, but because it is manifestly an outrage to falsify the faith of a man who fought for it and died in it.

Where progress seemed particularly great in Villari's work was in the texture of the biography, when compared with the threadbare material available before. Successive editions kept up with difficulty (and sometimes failed to keep up) with the discoveries of new documents that the Tuscan Piagnoni, such as Gherardi and Del Lungo, and other Italian scholars were continually publishing. And, although Villari and his disciples were at pains to insist that such documents as these added nothing and changed nothing in the over-all judgment of

Savonarola, the truth was that they did add a great deal and did change some things in his biography.

Amid this extraordinary flourishing of studies and research came the year 1898 and the fourth centenary of Fra Girolamo's death. The portents were many and happy. Cardinal Bausa, a Dominican and Archbishop of Florence, accepted the honorary presidency of the celebrations, in which many cardinals, among them Capecelatro, and bishops took part. The proceedings of the centenary were published in a bi-monthly periodical, which contained, besides many absurd and valueless efforts, a few useful contributions. As was to be expected, this occasion not only gave an impetus to research and historical discussion, but also revived the religious disputes that for a long time had seemed dormant. They were inflamed particularly by the monumental *History of the Popes* of Pastor, when its third volume, containing the pontificate of Alexander VI, came out almost on the eve of the centenary. Unfortunately, the professor from Innsbruck had attacked this difficult subject without sufficient study of the life of the Friar, and without any first-hand knowledge of his works. This naturally made it difficult for a historian of the papacy to write with equanimity about Savonarola.

Savonarolan scholars found Pastor's book easy game, as it was generally biased and remarkably full of errors. Luotto particularly enjoyed himself when, as champion of the embattled Piagnone ranks, he skirmished with Pastor in a large and tedious book. The winner was Luotto, but he dragged out his victory at enormous length, and in a style at times too polemical and apologetic. The Austrian historian replied to these attacks, and thought that he had given good proof of his scholarship by quoting at second-hand such a great deal of Savonarolan literature; and at this, the battle flared up again. He was supported, out of traditional hostility and on principle, by some Jesuits who had collaborated a good deal in Pastor's work. He was opposed by scholars such as Schnitzer, the theologian Commer, and Grauert, the last two of whom challenged him on, among other things, the the theory of Alexander VI's illegitimacy. I much regret being unable in this brief account to pass in review the principal champions and the lances that were broken in this battle.

The echoes of this controversy may have helped the publicity of the centenary but not its nobler ends. But it did produce the greatest and most learned scholar that Savonarola has ever had, Josef Schnitzer.

He spent a good part of his life clearing the ground and preparing solid foundations with the publication of a fine series of unpublished documents and solid monographs, and finally built on them the splendid edifice of his *Savonarola,* to which he put the final touches in the Italian edition of 1931. If, quite objectively, I have had occasion in this book to note the general defects and some particular errors or omissions in Schnitzer's work, that is not intended to detract in any way from the great merits of this great scholar, to whom all other scholars interested in Savonarola must always feel grateful. For my part, I should think myself ungrateful if I did not say how much I owe to him, as much for what he taught me as for the kindness he showed me from the time of my first efforts in the field that he illuminated with so many honourable achievements. I cannot either forget the trusting words he wrote me when he received, towards the end of his days, one of my books on Savonarola: '*Nunc dimittis servum tuum in pace, Domine.*' Not without melancholy do I ask myself at this point whether I have been worthy of that heritage, whether I may have failed that trust.

Schnitzer's book ends with these words about the Friar, and I could not find better to close my own: 'He was a man dreadfully sinned against in his lifetime and after his death. He has not yet been canonized or beatified, but his time will come, as Joan of Arc's did. The time will come when Christianity will attain to moral heights where, far from regarding as a hateful rebellion his heroic resistance to an infamous Pope in exceptional times when the Church was at its lowest ebb, men will recognize and celebrate it for what it really was, as his greatest merit, and his most shining glory. It will not be that the altars will reflect glory on him, but that he will shed glory on them.'

In the Dominican Chapter General held in Rome in 1935, the postulator, Padre Benedetto Lenzetti, presented the customary report, in the course of which, having spoken of the cases of beatification in which the Order was concerned, some just put forward or already dealt with, others to be taken up again or to be promoted in the future, he discoursed at length and to much effect on the subject of Savonarola. Referring to the testimonies of Saints, and to the cultus, and to the many previous requests, he said: 'These testimonies in the course of time have by no means diminished; nay, rather they increase from day to day, and from various quarters requests are made to us that the cause of Savonarola should be taken up by our Order and presented to the Apostolic See, so that this great man of God, if he should be held duly worthy, should not be deprived, together with his companions, of the honour due, and so that the voices which attack him and them unjustly, nay, even wickedly, may be silenced.'

I have already said that this aspect of the subject is not my concern. But it is a matter of history that there has been this continued veneration, this religious cultus of the Friar over centuries, sometimes at the altar, sometimes in the secret of men's hearts, and sometimes in the solitary meditations of the scholar's study. Notwithstanding the shortsighted contempt of Villari, both that cultus and the studies, whose history I have here compressed into too small a space, are merely different forms of the mark left by Girolamo Savonarola on posterity, the complex aspects of a devotion, an admiration, and an interest which have lasted more than four hundred and fifty years and which will never be extinguished. They are stronger than any polemic, more eloquent than any apology.

On the eve of another Savonarola centenary, the fifth of his birth, may I, as a footnote to this book in which so much has been said about prophecies, risk one of my own and forecast that these imminent celebrations will be as fruitful as the last, and far more peaceful? I am convinced that they will be fruitful on account of the renewed interest in these studies. A bibliography of works on Savonarola which have appeared since 1800, and another of Savonarola's works, are in the hands of a veteran of these campaigns, Mario Ferrara. Above all, however, as I write, the hopes and noble efforts of so many generations of scholars, from Magliabechi to Guasti, are about to be fulfilled: all the works of the Friar are to appear in an edition to which will be given the dignity of a national enterprise.

For my prophecy that the celebrations will be peaceful, I am given good hopes by the quietening of passions and by the weight of new studies, which now make impossible certain accusations that only yesterday, if they were not true, were at least excusable. Finally, but above all these reasons, I place the reverence that now more than ever surrounds the name of Girolamo Savonarola. Either I am much deceived, or certain enmities due to traditional opposition or doctrinaire dissensions are becoming less acute. Hardly two decades ago, Schnitzer, not without a certain personal antagonism, was engaging in a polemic with the Jesuits. As they wrongly accused Savonarola of disobedience, he reminded them of their own record of disobedience. He spoke of an unbridgeable gulf between Savonarola and Loyola, perpetuated by their followers down to Pastor and beyond. But now there is no one who does not see that those two great spirits served the same ends under different conditions, at different times, and therefore in different ways; and that antagonism between them, which may once have been useful and necessary, today serves no purpose and has no meaning. The times and conditions of both are past, the means have changed; only the end remains the same. Present times demand a reverence for truth, and the respect of all for one who gave all for the attainment of that eternal end.

INDEX

INDEX

Blemmet, 127, 281

Bollandists, 312

Bonacossi:
  Borso, 23
  Elena (mother of Savonarola), 1, 7, 23, 27–8, 96–7

Bonsi, Domenico, 126, 214, 216, 220 ff., 228–9, 231 ff., 257

Borgia:
  Cesare, 121, 288
  Giovanni, *see* Gandia, Duke of
  Lucrezia, 54
  Rodrigo, *see* Alexander VI.

Boscoli, Pietro Paolo, 298

Botticelli, Sandro, 213, 293

Bottonio, Fra Timoteo, 307

Bracci, Ser Alessandro, 75, 185–6, 198, 204, 214, 220 ff.

Bracciolini, Giovanfrancesco Poggio, 294

Buonaccorsi, Francesco, 135

Buonarroti, Michelangelo, 79, 213, 235, 294

Buonvicini, *see* Domenico da Pescia

Burlamacchi (pseudo), ix, 29, 33, 50, 86, 209, 307

Busini, Fra Tommaso, 87, 123, 136, 207

Caiani, Fra Tommaso, 290

Caloro, Francesco, 304

Cambi, Giovanni, 209, 224, 232

Canacci, Giovanni, 238, 251

Canigiani, Carlo, 238, 251

Capaccio, Bishop of, 199

Capecelatro, Cardinal Alfonso, 316

Capponi:
  Agostino, 298
  Carlo, 313
  Gino, 282, 283, 285, 314
  Niccolò, 299, 300
  Piero, 82, 86, 89, 90, 93, 159

Caraffa:
  Giovanna, 209
  Oliviero, 62–5, 73–4, 148 ff., 160, 197, 199, 212, 214, 264

Carducci, Giosuè, 284

Carvaial, Cardinal, 295

Catarino, *see* Politi, Ambrogio Catarino.

Caterina:
  da Racconigi, the Blessed, 277
  de' Ricci, Saint, 277, 302, 311
  de' Vigri, the Blessed, 25

Ceccone, *see* Francesco di Ser Barone.

Charles VIII, 71 ff., 77 ff., 84 ff., 116, 119 ff., 161, 186, 287

Cherubino da Firenze, Fra, 292

Cinozzi, Fra Placido, 16, 33, 42, 50, 293

Cioni, Filippo, 201, 206, 214

Clement VII, Pope, *see* Medici, Giulio de'.

Clement VIII, Pope, *see* Aldobrandini, Ippolito

Clement XII, Pope, 311

Codiponte, Stefano da, *see* Stefano da Codiponte.

Collenuccio, Pandolfo, 146, 277

Colomba da Rieti, the Blessed, 277

Commines, Philippe de, 121, 124, 277

Corbizzi, Filippo, 106, 108–9, 164, 167

Corniole, Giovanni dalle, *see* Giovanni dalle Corniole

Corsetto, padre T., 313

Corsini, Luca, 222

Costa, Giorgio, *see* Lisbon, Cardinal of

Credi, Lorenzo di, 213

Crinito, Pietro, 98, 127

Cronaca, *see* Pollaiolo, Simone

Del Beccuto, Fra Paolo, 208

Del Benino, Carlo, 50

Del Caccia, Alessandro, 301

Del Fante, Alberto, x

Della Barba da Genazzano, *see* Genazzano, Fra Mariano

Della Bella, Giano, 282

Dell'Antella, Lamberto, 209

Della Palla, Battista, 298

Della Robbia:
  Ambrogio, 213 n
  Fra Luca, 213, 248

Della Rovere, Giuliano, 77, 264, 265, 295

Della Stufa, Enea, 234

Del Nero:
  Bernardo, 89, 90, 187, 210, 212
  Simone, 232

Deti, Lisa. *see* Aldobrandini, Lisa

Domenico:
  da Perpignano, 10
  da Pescia, Fra. 39, 40, 62–3–4, 74, 136, 149, 164, 175, 236–42, 249, 256, 265, 266 ff.

Drachisich, Giorgio Benigno, 188, 297

INDEX

INDEX

Maximilian, Emperor, 116, 174 ff.
Mazzinghi, Domenico, 232
Medici:
  Alessandro de', Duke of Florence, 301
  Alessandro de', Archbishop, 304, 308–10
  Contessina de', 183
  Cosimo de', 44, 47, 127
  Cosimo I de', Duke of Florence, 301, 305, 309
  Francesco de', Grand Duke of Tuscany, 309
  Giovanni de', Cardinal, 61, 296–7
  Giovanni di Pierfrancesco de', 193
  Giulio de', Cardinal, Archbishop of Florence, and later Clement VII, 296, 299, 300–1
  Leonardo de', 216
  Lorenzo de', il Magnifico, x, 13, 25, 29, 37 ff., 44 ff.
  Piero de', 51, 61, 64, 71 ff., 78 ff., 87, 88, 107, 123, 124, 139, 142, 148, 191 ff., 210
Mei, Francesco, 62, 117, 179, 189, 199, 295
Meier, F. K., ix, 313
Michelozzi, Michelozzo, 14
Morgiani, Lorenzo, 135
Muzii, Girolamo, 183

Naples, Cardinal of, see Caraffa, Oliviero
Nardi, Iacopo, 111, 152, 255
Neri:
  Filippo, San, 277, 304, 307–8, 311
  Fra Leonardo, da Sarzana, 184, 188, 200
  Fra Tommaso, 306
Nerli:
  Benedetto, 251
  Iacopo, 205, 244
  Tanai de', 197
Nesi, Giovanni, 99, 127
Niccolini:
  Agnolo, 37, 74, 266
  Iacopo, 267–8, 300
Niccolò da Pisa, Fra, 11
Nicolini da Sabio, 303

Orléans, Duke of, 173
Orsini, family, 71, 191

Paganotti, Fra Benedetto, 270
Pagnini, Sante, 127

Pandolfini:
  Niccolò, 151, 160, 305
  Pierfilippo, 37, 74, 90
Paolino del Signoraccio, Fra, 294
Paolo:
  da Fucecchio, Fra, 188
  da Soncino, Fra, 25
Parenti, Piero, 95, 113, 128, 141, 213, 266, 288, 295, 296
Parma, Bishop of, 228
Passerini, Luigi, 314
Pastor, L. F. A. von, 316
Paul III, Pope, 301
Paul IV, Pope, 306
Paul V, Pope, 311
Pazzi, Maria Maddalena, Saint, 277
Peraccini, Fra Cristoforo, 292, 303
Peraud, Raymond, Cardinal of Gurk, 122
Perrens, F. T., ix, 314
Perugia, Cardinal of, see Lopez, Giovanni
Piccolomini, Cardinal, 212
Pico, Galeotto, Lord of Mirandola, 162
Pico della Mirandola:
  Count Giovanni, 11, 29, 33, 39, 42, 43, 46, 78, 97–100, 107, 126, 277
  Giovan Francesco, ix, 50, 127, 203, 221, 234, 298, 304
Pierozzi, Antonino, see Antonino, Sant'
Pietro da Bergamo, Fra, 10, 11
Pietro da Padule, 201
Pietro Paolo da Urbino, Maestro, 127
Pitti:
  Carlo, 82
  Iacopo di Luca, 247
Pittorio, Lodovico, 209, 212
Pius III, Pope, 295
Pius V, Pope, see Ghislieri, Michele
Plato, 3, 98, 281
Poggio Bracciolini, Giovanfrancesco (the younger), see Bracciolini, Giovanfrancesco Poggio
Politi, Ambrogio Catarino, 304–7
Politian, Angelo, 41, 42, 50, 98, 126
Pollaiolo, Simone, 294
Popoleschi, Piero, 223, 256
Ponzo, Fra Domenico da, 47, 49, 108–9, 113, 116, 138, 189, 295
Pucci, Pandolfo, 309
Pulinari, Fra Francesco, 308

Quétif, J., 312

INDEX

325

INDEX